Becoming
Irish American

Becoming
Irish American

*The Making and Remaking of
a People from Roanoke to JFK*

Timothy J. Meagher

Yale

UNIVERSITY PRESS

NEW HAVEN AND LONDON

Published with assistance from the Mary Cady Tew Memorial Fund.

Yale University Press books may be purchased in quantity for educational, business, or promotional use. For information, please e-mail sales.press@yale.edu
(U.S. office) or sales@yaleup.co.uk (U.K. office).

Set in Fournier MT type by Integrated Publishing Solutions.
Printed in the United States of America.

Library of Congress Control Number: 2023935026
ISBN 978-0-300-12627-3 (hardcover: alk. paper)

A catalogue record for this book is available from the British Library.

This paper meets the requirements of ANSI/NISO Z39.48-1992
(Permanence of Paper).

10 9 8 7 6 5 4 3 2 1

To my brother John Henry "Sean" Meagher
1938–2022

Contents

Acknowledgments   ix

Introduction   1

1. Old Ireland: From Its Beginnings
to the Eighteenth Century   8

2. Irish Immigration in the Colonial
Era: 1585–1775   28

3. Irish America in the Age of
Revolution: 1775–1815   49

4. Irish America in Transition:
1815–1845   69

5. The Famine and Irish Immigrants
in America: 1845–1880   91

6. The Famine Irish American
Community in an America in Crisis:
1845–1880   110

7. A New Generation and New
Immigrants in Turn-of-the-Century
America: 1880–1928   133

8. Searching for Their Place at the
End of the Nineteenth Century:
The Irish American Community,
1880–1908   155

9. Finding Their Place: The Irish
American Community, 1900–1928   170

10. Rising Power: Irish Americans in
New Deal America, 1928–1939   193

11. The Old Order at High Tide:
Irish America in World War II and
Postwar America, 1940–1960   217

Epilogue and Conclusion   240

Notes   251

Index   309

Acknowledgments

This book has been a very long time in coming and so this list of thanks is long but should be longer. I would like to thank Chris Rogers and Adina Berk of Yale University Press for their patience; Michael Kazin, George O'Brien, and James O'Toole for reading much longer versions of this manuscript and offering encouragement; Catholic University, Boston College's Irish Studies Program, Notre Dame's Cushwa Center, and the Fulbright Program for supporting the research and writing of the book. There have, however, been a whole host of others, whose insights, encouragement, and friendship through this long process have been invaluable. They include my colleagues in the Catholic University Archives, W. John Shepherd, Maria Mazzenga, Shane MacDonald, and Jane Stoeffler; in the History Department, especially Leslie Tentler, Stephen West, and Julia Young; and from the rest of the University, especially William Dinges and James Youniss; as well as the faculties at Dublin City University's School of Humanities and Social Sciences and University College Dublin's School of History. They also include friends: some who share an interest in things Irish: Terence Patrick Winch, Kevin O'Neill, Michael O'Malley, Una Ni Bhroimeil, and Brian Mitchell; in things history, James Gilbert, Edward Abrahams, Colleen McDannell, and the late, but not forgotten, Lenard Berlanstein; and friends who have been a source of support throughout, Michael J. Smith, James Hudson, Anthony Gryzmala, Robert Dardano, Michael Walsh, Nirun Sakulmaka, Jacob Lenihan, Jian Zhang, Charles Goldfarb, and Coleman Baker; and my sister, Mary Meagher, and brothers, Sean, Dermot, Andrew, and Padric; and above all, my great man, Clement Ho.

Becoming
Irish American

Introduction

Yet a word ancient mother, . . .
. . . .

For know you the one you mourn is not in that grave,
It was an illusion, the son you love was not really dead,
The Lord is not dead, he is risen again young and strong in
another country, . . .
. . . .

What you wept for was translated, pass'd from the grave,
The winds favor'd and sea sail'd it,
And now with rosy and new blood,
Moves to-day in a new country.
　　　　　　　—Walt Whitman, "Old Ireland"

Walt Whitman had a special relationship with the Irish, both in Ireland and America. Irish professors and university students lauded him, and he became friends with an impressive mix of Irish and Irish American literati like John Boyle O'Reilly, poet and editor of the *Boston Pilot,* Oscar Wilde, Bram Stoker, and John O'Sullivan, leader of the Young America Movement and editor of the *Democratic Review.* Yet it was the Irish Americans on the streets of his beloved "Mannahatta" that made the most powerful impression on him.

　　Irish people had lived in New York long before Whitman, at age four, moved there with his family in 1823. As he grew up, became a poet, a newspaperman, a Democratic Party partisan, and aware of his longing for men, however, the Irish seemed to be everywhere in the city, arriving in a growing river and by the 1840s, and 1850s, a famine-provoked flood. They were among "the

1

manly race of drivers of horses," the firemen, policemen, and laborers he noticed while walking through New York. Yet he saw the women too, "just from Ireland," with their woolen capes and "well nailed" boots, crowding the Irish Emigrant Society, "waiting for some master or mistress to come along and give them a call" for a position as a domestic servant. They were a part, a huge and distinctive part, of "the common people," so critical, he believed, to the greatness of any community, but particularly to his New York. He acknowledged that they were "perhaps uncouth in manners," and "ignorant" of "booklore," but their rough simplicity seemed a virtue in the new democracy of the United States, for they came to America not only "pining and panting" for a new and better home, he believed, but also steadfastly opposed "to tyranny." His affection was not unqualified. He had little respect for the Catholic Church, and though honored as the poet of the common man, of democracy by a Trinity College scholar among others, he often brooded on its "weakness . . . corruption." Nevertheless, "in general, his remarks about the Irish are so generous" and threaded so frequently through his life and art, that his complaints seem like quarrels of the heart rather than a hidden animosity.[1]

On November 2, 1861, about ten years after the end of a famine that had devastated Ireland for five years, Walt Whitman published the poem "Old Ireland" in the *New York Leader*. Whitman contends in this poem that the Irish had not been broken by the catastrophe: "For know you the one you mourn is not in that grave . . . The Lord is not dead," Whitman reassures the mourning "Ancient Mother," but "is risen again . . . in another country." By the time "Old Ireland" was published, over three million Irish had already migrated to America since the first Irish landed there in the 1580s, part of Sir Walter Raleigh's ill-fated Roanoke colony on what is now the North Carolina coast. After Whitman's poem appeared, another three million or more Irish immigrants would follow in the next century and a half. In 2010, thirty-four million Americans claimed some form of Irish ancestry and another three and a half million described themselves as Scotch Irish in the U.S. census. Only those tracing foreign family origins to Germany or England were more numerous. Irish Americans, then, have been one of the largest ethnic groups in America for centuries.[2]

Yet their history does not just tell us about them, but also much about America. Historians studying a wide range of questions in American history keep bumping into them—for good or ill: in histories of the making of race; the making (or not making?) of class solidarity; social mobility and the American economy; the party politics of Democrats and Republicans; vaudeville; Catholics and Protestants; anti-immigrant nativism (as both the targets of nativists and as nativists); baseball; American anti-communism; women and work; democracy in America; Progressivism; the history of both the so-called American "frontier" and American cities, and much, much more.

Whitman sensed that something was at work here among the Irish immigrants that he saw on New York streets, something that he celebrated in moving verse, but he was not entirely sure what it was. The Lord's death, he wrote, was an "illusion": the Lord had not merely risen, but "was translated, pass'd from the grave" to a "new" country, "the winds favor'd and sea sail'd it." One critic argues that Whitman seems to suggest that the Lord's—the Irish—future is there, in the new country, the United States. Yet will the Irish be rescued from death by their new home only to be absorbed into its people, their Irishness disappearing? Whitman was immensely proud of America's promise, but his poem clearly delights in the survival of these distinctly Irish people in America— the "Lord is not dead, after all"—an Irishness enduring even three thousand miles away. Yet if the Lord endures in America, Whitman is not clear if this Lord was the same as the one buried and mourned, for the Lord in America is "young and strong," and not just resurrected and reinvigorated, but fundamentally new, "now with rosy and new blood." As he "moves to-day in a new country," he has been transformed—changed, even as he remains the Lord, remains Irish.

For Whitman, it was enough to marvel at this miraculous tale of immigration and delight in the mysterious experiences of the Irish in America that permitted them to be a distinct people in their new country but different than the people in their old home. For students of American immigration and ethnicity, however, there have been only questions.

For a long time, scholars studying European immigrants to America like the Irish (and, perhaps, most Americans even now) have thought of the immigrants' story and that of their American-born descendants in simple terms: those immigrants or their children or their children's children inevitably "assimilated," disappeared as a distinctive people and became "Americans." By the 1960s and 1970s, many Americans were not so sure assimilation was a good thing, as an ethnically diverse America seemed richer than a culturally uniform one. Indeed, the eagerness to become a proper "American" now seemed, to some, a denial of the authentic self, an abject capitulation to a dominant white Anglo-Saxon Protestant culture. Some scholars and ethnic group activists began to argue that even white ethnic peoples who seemed to be assimilating had really not been changing at all, either because the culture of their homeland was so deeply buried in their psyche or because they self-consciously resisted assimilation and preferred to maintain the culture of their ancestral home—or both. This swung the balance back the other way: if they had not really become American, then that was because they really were Italian, Polish, Greek, or Irish all along and would or should be so in the future. The problem left by this strict dichotomy is that all changes in ethnic or racial groups in America were seen as merely steps to assimilation or Americanization and all differences seen as the unconscious or self-conscious persistence of a more or less pure homeland culture.[3]

This book argues that there is an alternative to such a rigid binary in explaining what has happened to white ethnic groups in America. It is history: ethnic groups are made, "constructed," "invented" in history. They change, but not all the changes they make have to be steps on a linear path to assimilation. Yet they do change. As historians of American ethnicity have argued: "ethnic groups in modern settings are constantly recreating themselves and ethnicity is constantly being reinvented." Groups may, indeed, assimilate, disappear, but that can happen at any time in their history and that is only one of the possible range of adaptations they and their members might make over time. That immigrants or their descendants come to think of themselves as members of what we call ethnic groups at all—Irish, Italian, Polish Americans, for example—is a significant change many make in America, for immigrants often came to America thinking of themselves as people from specific places at home, provinces, counties, towns, or villages, not nations. Yet they can also create new groups in America, defined not by roots in a single nation but by broader identities like race, religion, or language, for example, that include people from a variety of nationalities who combine with others to invent larger pan-ethnic peoples. Thus Chinese, Japanese, and Vietnamese Americans and other people with roots in Asia became Asian Americans; or Puerto Ricans, Mexicans, Cubans, Dominicans and other Spanish speakers became Latino/a Americans. Members of ethnic groups make adaptations in their personal, everyday lives as well: Chinese immigrants carved out a niche for themselves in the United States as laundrymen, a trade that they never knew in China but, for a long time, became "their" work in America. More often, immigrants or their descendants reworked old world inheritances in the new world's environment of opportunities and constraints: Italians, for example, took advantage of America's abundance of meat to adapt an old world cuisine, creating spaghetti and meatballs, a dish "utterly invented in America." This theoretical frame looks not to some linear and predetermined march to an inevitable end in assimilation, then, nor to some static persistence of old world culture or identity, but to messy processes of continuous adaptation to historical contingencies in the invention and reinvention, the making and remaking of ethnic peoples.[4]

Such a frame is not new, and is, indeed, by now well accepted. Thus, it is not because of this book's theoretical assumptions but their application to the Irish American past—not because of the frame then, but because of the story—that it, hopefully, contributes to the understanding of Irish American history and to American ethnic history more generally. It builds on my own previous work, but with new insights and sources, and draws widely from the scholarly literature. It examines Irish American history on two levels. The first focuses on those adaptations made by individuals or families in their own everyday lives. That includes, for immigrants, the causes and processes of migration from Ireland itself, and for those immigrants and later American-born generations, as much as we can know about where they settled, how they made a living, entertained themselves, raised families, or practiced their religion. Yet Irish American people had to adapt as members of a group as well, determining collectively not only where their people fit into an ethnically and racially plural American politics and society, but also how they defined themselves, their people, their group: what were its boundaries, who was in the group and who was not; how did they understand their common destiny, their history and their future; what distinctive cultural values and customs marked them; what political and economic interests did they share, and what infrastructure, institutions, and associations would they create to mark those boundaries, define that sense of common destiny, cultivate that culture, and defend or advance those interests.

Even a cursory look at Irish American history suggests the limits of a simple dichotomy between assimilation and ethnic persistence and the relevance of a more flexible open conceptual frame in understanding their history. Irish definitions of their group in America, for example, hardly followed a linear path but, in fact, changed and changed again in unexpected, seemingly erratic ways over time. The first "Irish America" was only invented near the very end of the colonial era after more than half a century of heavy migration from Ireland. Intriguingly, it was a nonsectarian definition of Irish American community, including Catholics and Protestants. Yet by the middle of the nineteenth century, a more exclusively Catholic Irish America would replace it as Irish American Protestants did, in fact, begin to disappear as a self-consciously separate group, Irish or otherwise. At the turn of the twentieth century, Irish American Catholics would invent a new group, militant American Catholics, including other Catholic ethnics. Irish Americans then became the assimilators not the assimilated, remaining conscious of their own separate ethnic identity within this pan-ethnic people not simply because of the memories of their Irish past but because of their special position and power as leaders and models of this American Catholic people. If that seemed something of a sideways step from a linear path of assimilation, another vital, if less powerful movement emerged among Irish Americans about the same time, emphasizing a stricter, more narrow, exclusively Irish identity—seemingly a step backward on such a path. Over time, militant Catholic Americanism would triumph, reaching its apogee in the 1950s, when the Irish American–led Catholic Church flourished as it never had before.

A quick review reveals, as well, that Irish Americans not only shaped and reshaped their definitions of community over this time but also adapted and re-adapted the essentials of their personal, everyday lives. Again, as in the changing definition of their community, these adaptations were often surprising, following paths with unpredictable twists, turns, and outcomes. One of the best examples is the varying economic fortunes of Protestant and Catholic Irish in the United States. Irish Protestants seemed to have several advantages over Irish Catholics in their encounter with the American economy. The ancestors of most Irish Protestants in America, for example, arrived in America in the eighteenth and early nineteenth centuries at almost the very beginning of its development. They were, then, among the "founders" of American society. They were also more likely to be literate and have experience with a market economy than most others, including Catholics, in Ireland when they left it for America. Finally, they were Protestants settling in a Protestant-dominated America. The ancestors of most Irish Catholics left Ireland later, in the middle and late nineteenth and early twentieth centuries. Most came to an America already well established and thus were not among its founders but outsiders. Many were also desperately poor people with few craft skills and little experience with a modern economy. Finally, they arrived as Catholics in a largely Protestant country. Yet survey data from the turn of the twenty-first century reveals that Catholics claiming Irish ancestry had much higher incomes and were more likely to have gone to college than Protestants reporting Irish ancestry. The story of Irish Catholics' encounter with the American economy is even more complicated than that. By their own admission, through much of their history, American-born Irish Catholic men seemed to fare poorly in founding their own businesses— the seeming quintessential path to "making it" in America. Furthermore, again for much of their history, American-born Irish Catholic women would be more successful in finding professional work, largely as teachers, or white-collar work generally in America than their American-born Irish brothers. There are other examples of surprising twists and turns in the private lives of Irish American Catholics, such as in when they married or even whether they married at all, or variations over time in their commitment to Catholic religious practice. The contingencies in both the history of Irish Americans' private lives as well as in the evolution of their communities and group identities is clear.

If change in ethnic groups can now no longer be easily ascribed to an inevitable and linear process of assimilation, then finding out not just how they adapted, but why they did when they did and what shaped those changes becomes more crucial, and, if more challenging, also more interesting. The answers lie in those "changing realities" both within the group and in their new environment, which often combined in complex configurations to compel and shape their adaptations. That is their history, not a simple, linear narrative predetermined by their destination, where they are now, but a rich and complex story of the journey, where they have been.[5]

That journey begins in Ireland. Irish American adaptiveness and invention hardly meant that their Irish past was irrelevant to their American present—only that it was not the determinative influence upon them—so the book thus begins with a chapter on Ireland. It explains the powerful transformations of the island's economy and society over time that eventually prompted the first great wave of Irish emigration to America. Those transformations, however, also laid a seedbed for the causes of later migrations and helped shape Irish understandings of themselves and the world, which would endure through many later generations of Irish and Irish Americans. This opening chapter and later ones also reveal that even in Ireland the definition of who was Irish would change over time just as the definition of who was Irish American would in the United States. The book then proceeds chronologically, the Irish in colonial America, the early American republic, the era of famine in Ireland and civil war in America, the turn of the twentieth century, Irish Americans in a New Deal, and World War II and postwar United States. The book ends in 1960 with John F. Kennedy's election as president, one of a series of dramatic events that combined with long-term economic and other trends that began to revolutionize Irish Catholic America, and to a lesser extent, Irish Protestant America as well.

But a full treatment of that revolution is another long and complicated story.

1. Old Ireland

From Its Beginnings to the Eighteenth Century

There was a time when the Irish and Irish Americans talked and wrote proudly about themselves as a race, "the most genuine, unmixed and unchanged Celtic people that exist on the globe," as the Irish American priest and author Hugh Quigley insisted in 1865. Yet like Irish Americans, the people of Ireland were made in history and hardly remained "unmixed and unchanged." They evolved through a series of migrations to the island over several millennia. Processes of changing identity, like those which would take place among Irish immigrants and their descendants in America, also occurred in Ireland. Normans, for example, arrived in Ireland in the twelfth century as conquerors from England and quickly ran roughshod over the native Irish throughout much of the island. Over the centuries, however, the Normans evolved into a distinct people, who were different than the native Irish, but also the English in England. In the sixteenth century, confronting hostile Protestant new arrivals, called the New English, the Catholics among the Norman descendants would become the Old English. In the eighteenth century, religious boundaries triumphed over these ancestral distinctions and the Catholic Old English merged with the Catholic native Irish into what are recognized as simply Irish Catholics today, embodied in John Fitzgerald (a Norman name) Kennedy (an Irish one). On the other side of that Catholic-Protestant religious divide, however, the Protestant Irish victors in the wars with Catholics would remain divided after their final triumph at the end of the seventeenth century. That triumph confirmed the political and social dominance of members of the established church, the Protestant Church of Ireland. Yet they would not share that rule with their Protestant allies, dissenters, most notably the Presbyterians, who had begun migrating from Scotland to the Irish province of Ulster in the seventeenth century. These Ulster Scots were the largest and most powerful of the dissenters, and they would thus remain separate not only from Catholics but also from the "Anglicans" of the established Church of Ireland through the eighteenth century.

The Normans had been the first conquerors of Ireland to come from England, but there would be a second and much more thorough conquest led by the British Crown in the sixteenth century. It not only introduced a new religious boundary between Catholics and Protestants, but also made wrenching changes in the structures of the island's economy, politics, and social organization, plunging Ireland into two centuries of constant warfare. In the 1700s, as the turmoil of war finally ended, Ireland's economy tied into the emerging British empire's booming worldwide trade and grew enormously. The first significant wave of migrants to America took advantage of those new trade links to leave then, but the economic and population changes taking place in the eighteenth century also prepared the way for future migrations. Despite the island's new prosperity, Irish society's ethnic and religious fissures and resentments persisted, even worsened, in this new era of aggressive commercialization, leaving important legacies for those several generations of future immigrants to America as well.[1]

Ireland's first inhabitants slipped onto the island even as waters from melting glaciers were filling the seas around it. Only a few hundred came, and as hunter-gatherers, searching out game for their survival, they may not have grown to more than a few thousand people over the three or four millennia that they had the island to themselves. The next group, coming about 3,800 BCE from Britain and perhaps elsewhere in northern Europe, was part of a broad multicontinental diaspora originating in Mesopotamia. They brought farming and husbandry to Ireland, reflected most vividly today in their carefully laid out farms at the Céide fields in Mayo, as well as new levels of social organization manifested in the massive tombs they constructed at New Grange. Scholars argue that at some point between about 1,000 BCE and 100 CE (many estimate probably by 600 BCE), people in Ireland began to speak one of the recognizable versions of what are now called Celtic languages. It is not clear how that happened exactly. Very recent studies have discovered a massive migration from France to Britain a few centuries earlier and suggest that those migrants to that island might have brought the Celtic language with them, but to date, there is no evidence of a similar migration to Ireland. For now, the most likely explanation is that the Celtic language probably spread to Ireland through trade with Britain and the European continent because a common speech made that commerce easier.[2]

More abundant written and archaeological evidence allows us to get a clearer look at Ireland beginning about the sixth or seventh century CE. It was then an almost entirely rural society: it had no cities, nor even towns worthy of the name. Its economy was primarily pastoral, the herding of cows. Cow's milk products and beef were a major source of food; the size of a herd helped define the status of their owners; and their grazing range was the measure of land. Most of the population had begun to live in raths by that time, circular enclosures surrounded by dirt ramparts topped by a wooden palisade with houses and sheds at their center, and these, individually or in small clusters, were scattered around the landscape.[3]

Irish social organization was both communal and hierarchical. *Derbfine,* made up of all the people descended from the same great-grandfather, held land in common, parcelled it out among all adult male members and reallocated it occasionally to maintain some equity among them. Several derbfine gathered into a *tuatha* led by a *ri* or king, elected by all of the tuatha's male members. These ri were "kings without states," that is, without any real governing institutions or offices. Most tuatha were quite small and there were many of them, probably as many as one hundred fifty spread over the island in the sixth century. Despite elected kings and the communal ownership of land, Ireland was hardly a democratic idyll; indeed, it was "intensely aristocratic." In one Irish saga, a noble exclaimed: "it irks me that a serf's son should converse with me." Nobles were defined in part by birth, but also by their patron-client relations with those below them: they lent out cattle, land, or equipment to those commoners, who, in return, paid annual food rents and fought for them.[4]

There may have been Christians in Ireland as early as the late fourth century, but there were enough by 431 CE for the pope to send a bishop from France, Palladius, to minister to the Christians on the island; the more renowned Patrick came slightly later. The new religion soon thrived in Ireland, and the island became a vital center of Christian scholarship as well as a nursery for missionaries to Europe. Despite its international prominence and connections, however, the Church in Ireland evolved into a distinctive Irish Christianity that reflected the island's absence of cities and the native culture's heavy emphasis on familial inheritance and aristocratic privilege.[5]

Near the end of the eighth century, the Vikings began raiding Ireland. By the middle of the next century, they had established bases on the island, including Dublin, Wexford, Waterford, and Limerick. Those ports became important centers in the Vikings' worldwide trade network and would also become Ireland's first cities. For defense against Viking raiders and other reasons, smaller tuatha increasingly became tied to larger regional kingdoms covering roughly the same territories as modern Irish provinces—Leinster (East); Connaught (West); Ulster (North); and Munster (South). Yet even these regional kings as well as High Kings, who claimed the entire island as their kingdom, were themselves kings without states and thus ruled through rickety, temporary, informal networks of clients. The Vikings participated in Ireland's many small, local wars but did not conquer the Irish and were absorbed into the Irish population over time, as their names like Cotter, MacIvor, and Sugrue ultimately became Irish ones.[6]

The Normans, Viking descendants but long settled in France and later conquerors of much of Britain, were not so easily satisfied. They first arrived in Ireland in 1169, landing at a beach in southeastern Ireland, purportedly to help the Irish king of Leinster regain his throne. Their base would remain in the southeast, but they were among the best soldiers in Europe, and thus they found it easy to exploit the chronic rivalries among Ireland's competing kings and clans and overrun vast parts of Ireland within a few decades. Wary of the possible aspirations of ambitious Norman lords to build their own kingdom or kingdoms in Ireland, the king of England, Henry II, hastened there in 1171 to demand their fealty and that of the Irish kings as well, declaring himself Lord of Ireland.[7]

The Viking invaders had had a powerful impact on the island; the effect of the Norman conquest was revolutionary. They divided the land into estates or manors, owned by individual families, measured precisely, passed down from father to the firstborn son or oldest surviving heir, and rented to tenants not usually to herd cattle but to grow crops of wheat and other grains or cereals. The Vikings had founded many of Ireland's seaports; the Normans established many of its inland market towns: Kilkenny, Clonmel, Carlingford, Fethard, Athenry, and several more. They also created the forerunner of a parliament for Ireland in Dublin, introduced a new legal system in Ireland, and to administer it began "shiring" the island by carving out counties, including Meath, Louth, Dublin, Kildare, Kilkenny, and Tipperary. Norman lords and soldiers also brought over settlers from England and Wales and even the Lowlands in Europe to be tenants on their farms or artisans in their estate villages or towns. With their coming, scores of names became common in Ireland in the twelfth and thirteenth centuries, new and still strange then, unnoticed centuries later: Barrett, Barry, Roche, Fitzgerald, Prendergast, Redmond, Walsh, Dillon, and others. Meanwhile, the Normans dismissed the Irish as a "people that yet adheres to the most primitive way of pastoral living"; no "village life" or towns, no "civil society"; bearded and long haired, "barbarous . . . truly barbarous."[8]

The Norman conquest, seemingly so irresistible, ground to a halt by the middle of the thirteenth century. In part, this was because of the revival of Irish resistance, but it was also because England was now bogged down in wars with the Scots and the French, wracked with bloody dynastic struggles, and devastated by the Black Death and, therefore, could give the Normans little help. The Normans' own densely settled territories in southern and eastern Ireland also suffered severely from the plague, while sparse Irish settlements in the west escaped much of its ravages.[9]

The native Irish resented Normans taking Irish lands, but despite the Anglo Normans' new vulnerability, it was clear that the native Irish were neither capable of, nor really willing, to unite to push them off the island. Gaelic chieftains fixed their eyes not on a broadly shared goal of expelling the Anglo Normans but, as they had always done, on their own families' survival and advancement. With England distracted and thus no central state to impose order in Ireland for two or more centuries, Norman lords did the same, and late medieval Ireland descended into a chaotic melee of petty wars among Norman lords and Irish chieftains with no consistent alignment along ethnic lines.[10]

The very inability of either side, the Irish or the Anglo Normans, to conquer seemed to create a kind of "middle ground" in Ireland, which encouraged, even made necessary, cultural sharing between the Normans and native Irish. The Gaelic Irish had, indeed, grown stronger in this era, in part, because they adopted new technologies and even new modes of governing from the Normans. Many Norman lords, like the earl of Desmond in Munster, in turn, learned the Irish language, surrounded themselves with Irish poets, merged Irish and English law into a "March Law," and married their daughters off to Irish chieftains. A few even abandoned primogeniture and elected their lords as the Irish did. By contrast, almost all Anglo-Norman cities and towns in Ireland worked hard to maintain their Englishness, outlawing the Irish language, clothes, hairstyles, and even cuisine within their walls. The very defensiveness of such laws, however, testified to the extent of cultural interchange already taking place.[11]

Throughout this period, the bulk of Anglo Normans in Ireland were not becoming Irish nor even remaining English so much as evolving into a new kind of people. Some of them called themselves the English in Ireland, and both terms defined their distinctiveness. England's English treated them as different, even as foreigners, and the native Irish understood them not only as different from themselves but also from the English in England. In a letter to the pope in 1317, native Irish chief Domnhaill O'Neill described the Anglo Normans in Ireland simply as "a middle nation."[12]

In the early sixteenth century, England, free of its dynastic wars, broke the middle ground stalemate and began to remake Ireland in its image. The new English king, Henry VIII, declared himself King, not Lord, of Ireland in 1541. By that time, he had already begun efforts to forcibly transform Irish chieftains into English lords by pushing them to abolish communal landownership and the practice of electing their chiefs and eliminating both Norman and Irish private armies. When both Norman and Irish lords resisted these and other changes, Crown forces crushed them one after another throughout the sixteenth century. In some cases, they not only deposed the rebellious Norman or Irish lords and their families, but seized their property, created new "plantations," and tried to replace the old populations with settlers from Britain.[13]

By 1534, Henry VIII had also broken the English Church's ties to Rome. The reassertion of English power in Ireland thus became a kind of Protestant religious crusade. The Tudors had little success in converting the native Irish, however. Their episodic and inconsistent prosecution of those persisting in popery was too little to eliminate it, but just enough to tie Protestantism to the Tudors' broader effort to sweep away the old order in Ireland and, thus, reinforce resistance to both.

Protestant Englishmen hoping to find fortunes in a new, remade Ireland formed the vanguard of the Tudor conquest. They dismissed the native Gaelic, or "Old Irish," as obviously uncivilized, but they increasingly targeted the stubborn Catholic descendants of the old Anglo Normans, accusing them of cultural "degeneracy." Many, probably most, of the Anglo-Norman descendants themselves still looked down on the Irish Gaels as primitive and inferior, but they were frightened by the new aggressiveness of the Crown and the zealous Protestant English newcomers. The adaptations of Catholic descendants of the old Norman conquerors begun in the middle ground era thus continued. By 1580 they started calling themselves "Old English," as opposed to the brash Protestant "New English" fresh from the old country, and they became even more obstinate in their adherence to Catholicism. Most shied from open resistance, but Old English lords mounted most of the major rebellions against the Tudors in the sixteenth century, and many looked for help from Catholic Europe by proclaiming their rebellions Catholic crusades.[14]

The Gaelic "Old Irish" chieftain Hugh O'Neill, from the stronghold of "Irishry" in Ulster, led the last and most powerful uprising at the end of the sixteenth century, but, when he and his allies failed and fled to friendly Catholic nations on the Continent, they left vast parts of Ulster—as much as two and a half million acres—open to new settlement. The Crown moved to take advantage of these forfeited lands by carving out a new plantation for English and Scottish settlers in what is now parts of today's counties of Tyrone, Derry, and Armagh. By 1622, there were an estimated 6,400 British adult males living and working on the Ulster Plantation lands. Further east in Ulster, in the counties of Antrim and Down, there would be no plantation, but the destruction wrought by O'Neill's war had decimated the Old Irish lordships there and plunged the surviving ones deeply into debt. Younger sons of gentry in Scotland and parts of England, flush with capital, bought them out, and then lured Scottish tenant farmers to their new estates. By 1630, the two counties had nearly 10,000 British, mostly Scottish, settlers. In the mid-1610s and early 1620s fifteen ministers had also come from Scotland and England to East Ulster to serve the new settlers. At this point these clerics became, officially, ministers of the established, "Anglican," Church of Ireland, but theologically most were dissenters, and they would help lay the foundation for a Presbyterian Church in Ulster.[15]

While an older Gaelic world seemed to be dying in Ireland, an Irish Catholic diaspora was being born in continental Europe. Irish common soldiers and Gaelic Irish and old English Catholic clerics, as well as exiled lords, went there after the failures of the succession of rebellions in the latter half of the sixteenth century. By 1590, they were establishing their own colleges in continental seminaries and universities in Spain, France, and other nations, to train priests for the beleaguered Catholic Church in Ireland.[16]

These Irish colleges on the continent, however, also became intellectual nurseries of a redefined Irish Catholicism. Priests, bishops, and nuns trained there imbibed the new rigor of a Counter-Reformation Catholicism, producing devotional literature written in a colloquial Irish and laced with scathing attacks on Protestant leaders like Martin Luther ("Luther MacLucifer"—the Son of the Devil). As important, they also forged a new definition of what it meant to be Irish. The shared experience of Old Irish and Old English in exile, combined with the powerful Catholic Counter-Reformation's stark depiction of the common enemy of Protestantism, helped soften the rivalries between the two. In 1634, Geoffrey Keating, a Tipperary priest of Old English ancestry who had spent years in seminary in France, wrote a history of Ireland, *Foras Feasa ar Eirinn,* in the Irish language, which treated the Norman invasion as simply one of many migrations of newcomers into the island stretching back into the myths of antiquity. Keating thus created a seamless historical continuity for a new merger of Old Irish and Old English Catholics into a single people of Irish Catholics.[17]

In 1641, taking advantage of an England divided between king and parliament and hurtling toward civil war, Irish Catholics rose in rebellion, first in Ulster, then spreading west to Connaught and parts of Munster and Leinster. The leaders, Phelim O'Neill, Rory O'More, and Con Maguire, grumbled that they all had been "put out of their ancestors' estates"—dispossessed—but over 70,000 English and 30,000 Scottish tenant farmers and artisans had also flooded Ireland since the end of the sixteenth-century rebellions, pushing Irish peasants into marginal lands, who complained that "every *pedlar* ... that came out of England" prospered while they suffered.[18]

The rising in 1641 was only the opening battle in a bloody and very complicated twelve-year civil war, which engulfed both islands, Britain and Ireland. In Ireland, Old English and Old Irish would join together in an uneasy alliance, which drew inspiration for its cause and many officers and men for its armies from Irish exiles on the continent. It was not nearly enough. Oliver Cromwell and then his lieutenants snuffed out Irish resistance by the early 1650s. Between the war and the executions, famine, disease, and migrations—voluntary or forced—after it, perhaps 15 to 20 percent of Ireland's population disappeared. After Cromwell's confiscation of rebel estates, the Catholic proportion of landownership would plummet from 60 percent in 1641 to 9 percent by 1657. The restoration of the English monarchy in 1660 did most Irish Catholics little good. The new king, Charles II, though a Catholic sympathizer, left the Cromwellian land settlement basically intact.[19]

Meanwhile, continued migration to Ireland from Scotland during and after the war had made Scottish Presbyterians a majority of the British in Ulster and a fifth of the province's total population by the Restoration era. Even outside the plantation in County Armagh, a Catholic bishop complained: "one could travel twenty five miles without finding half a dozen Catholic or Protestant [Church of Ireland] families, but all are Presbyterians." The chaplains of a Scottish army sent to restore order in Ulster in 1642 had formally established the Presbyterian Church there, and by 1653 there were twenty-three Presbyterian ministers in the province. Despite their growing strength, or maybe because of it, the status of Presbyterians in Ireland was not much clearer than that of Catholics. King Charles thought them dangerous radicals and thus his government harassed their ministers and constantly sniffed for evidence of Presbyterian rebellious conspiracies in Ulster.[20]

When Charles II died after a quarter century of rule, his brother James ascended the throne, and the hopes of Irish Catholics began to soar again, for the new king had already pledged himself to Catholicism. Most Protestants in Britain and Ireland, established Church Anglicans and Presbyterian dissenters alike, however, rallied behind the claims to the throne of Mary, James's daughter, and her Protestant husband, William of Orange. In 1691, after two years of fighting, William's army forced the last of James's loyalists in Ireland to surrender at Limerick. The Catholics had lost—again.[21]

In 1729, Jonathan Swift wrote an acerbically satirical commentary on the Irish economy, "A Modest Proposal," suggesting that impoverished Irish people might well find the means to support themselves by fattening their children and selling them off for food. Swift wrote in the midst of a terrible agricultural failure that caused thousands to starve or flee to America. The foundations of Irish economic life had changed radically from the pastoral system of clans and cows that had existed before the Norman invasion or endured in some fashion and in some places through more recent wars and dispossessions. By the beginning of the eighteenth century, the economic revolution seemed well advanced: Ireland was now a world of landowners and tenants, individual property ownership plotted out precisely on plats, and market fairs and port cities enmeshed in global trade. Indeed, soon after Swift wrote in the 1720s, Ireland's exports rose, and the economy seemed to revive. In 1740–1741, however, a spell of extraordinarily cold weather—people played hurley on an iced-over Shannon River—destroyed crops and killed cattle, largely in Munster, but over much of Ireland. Now not thousands but hundreds of thousands, a fifth or more of Ireland's people, died in a famine that came to be called the "Great Slaughter." To many, then, Ireland seemed incorrigibly, inevitably doomed to economic failure and misery that even the selling of Irish children would not help.[22]

Yet over the next forty years or so after the Great Slaughter, Ireland's economy boomed. From 1730 to 1776, the island's national income and the value of its exports more than doubled from £15 million to £37.5 million and

Figure 1. *The Linen Industry.* This print, part of a set of twelve by William Hincks, published in 1791, shows women preparing flax fibers which they will later spin into linen yarn. Reproduced from the original held by the Department of Special Collections of the Hesburgh Libraries of the University of Notre Dame.

£1.3 million to £3 million, respectively. Cities prospered and grew enormously. Dublin's population rose from 62,000 to 182,000 between 1706 and 1800, as rows and rows of elegant red brick Georgian houses spread over the city's streets north and south of the Liffey River.[23]

The thriving economies of Britain and its empire prompted this revolution in Ireland's economy, for as they grew, their demand for a whole range of Irish products did too. The production of grains and cereals, most notably wheat, for example, started to rise in Ireland in the 1750s, first largely to meet the needs of a rapidly growing Dublin population but then for the British market. Similarly, after Britain began putting its resources into other kinds of manufactures, it opened its market to Irish linen: Irish linen exports thus rose from one and a half million yards in 1710 to six million in 1740 and twenty million by 1770. Finally, Irish butter, beef, and pork had long gone overseas as provisions for the West Indies islands, but as the island sugar economies now boomed, Irish food exports to the Caribbean skyrocketed.[24]

The economic boom touched off other revolutions in Irish life that were as much or more transformative—none, perhaps, more than the dramatic increase in the island's population. Often after a catastrophe like the Great Slaughter, a nation's population begins to grow again, before eventually swinging back like a pendulum as it reaches the limits of food and shelter that the nation's resources can provide. Ireland's population, however, did not swing back, but continued to grow: doubling from about two million people after the famine of 1741 to over four million in 1791. Irish peasants' housing hardly improved at the lowest levels, but they continued to enjoy rich, cheap sources of fuel for heat in the dried turf they could cut from the island's abundance of bogs. More important, more food was available to feed them now. The end of rebellions and wars with armies tramping across fields and slaughtering livestock helped increase the food supply, and transportation improvements meant easier access to grain supplies at home and overseas to stave off local famines.

More critical over the long run was the increasing reliance on the potato. Irish people in some parts of the country had cultivated the potato since the end of the sixteenth century. As the population's rapid rebound from the famine seemed to reach the limit of traditional sources of food, however, more tenant farmers and laborers seemed willing now to incorporate the potato into their regular diet. The potato offered several advantages to Irish farmers and laborers. It produced huge yields, often enough for a single acre to feed an entire family for a year. Through much of Ireland, potatoes also adapted well to the wet climate and soils. The yields were great enough, however, that Irish peasants would even create beds of soil—called "lazy beds"—for their potatoes on stone ledges, or on top of bogs or on rocky mountainsides. The potato's yields and nutrition thus combined with the cheap fuel of turf to create a uniquely rich bounty of life's necessities for Irish peasants. The results were astonishing. After traveling all over Ireland in 1776–1777, Arthur Young concluded that the Irish were "as athletic in their form, robust and as capable of enduring labor as any people on earth." Statistics bore out such observations. The Irish joining regiments of the East India Company in the 1770s, for example, averaged an inch taller, 5'5" to 5'4", than recruits from England.[25]

Yet it was not consumption of the potato alone that prompted Ireland's population growth but the expanding availability of the means to help them pay their rents for land. The spread of labor-intensive wheat, oats, and barley production—tillage—provided more work opportunities for tenant farmers and laborers and their children. Three laborers might find work on a thirty-acre wheat farm and support their families, but there was work for only one laborer on one hundred and sixty acres of pasture raising cattle. The southeast, the old Norman stronghold, had long been the center of the country's tillage, especially wheat farming, but now it spread west and north as wheat exports skyrocketed— "ceres triumphant"—helping to boost populations wherever it took hold.[26]

The links between economic change and population growth were complicated, however, as the radically different experiences of the two regions where population grew fastest, the west coast and Ulster, reveal. The Atlantic coast, including the westernmost regions of Connaught, Ulster, and Munster, had long been sparsely inhabited because there was no way to support more than a few families on its rocks and cliffs. Now, however, groups of families called *clachans*, taking advantage of the cheap rents for these stony and remote lands, their communal labor power, lazy beds, and high potato yields, managed to make them viable. Indeed, the populations on the western coast grew faster than anywhere else in Ireland in the eighteenth century. This region, nonetheless, remained Ireland's poorest, also with its lowest literacy rates and highest percentages of Irish language speakers. The population in the northeast, in Ulster, was growing about as fast as the western coasts in the eighteenth century even though the traditional oats, not potatoes, were the mainstays of the province's diet. Ulster, however, was the center of the new booming linen industry. Making and selling linen in the north so enhanced farmer/weaver families' income that they could pay their rents with it and live on smaller and smaller amounts of land devoted to growing food for themselves. The land in Ulster, therefore, could now sustain more families. Since linen created abundant work for children as well—older boys as linen weavers; girls as spinners of linen yarn—the linen boom also encouraged not just more families, but bigger ones.[27]

Ulster had been the poorest part of Ireland through much of the seventeenth century, but now, because of linen, it was rapidly becoming the richest. As early as the 1750s, Ulster seemed a striking contrast to the poverty of much of the rest of the island. John Wesley noted in his diary in 1756, "No sooner did we enter Ulster than we observed the difference. The ground was cultivated just as in England, and the cottages were not only neat, but with doors and chimneys and windows." It had also become orderly. By the 1750s, Ulster crime statistics suggest that it was a rougher, more violent place than English counties, but serious crimes were rare, only three murders per 100,000 people a year in

Armagh, for example. Finally, Ulster's people were also the best educated in Ireland by the late eighteenth century, with literacy rates of about 70 percent for men and 55 percent for women, as high or higher than England's rates or those of North American colonies.[28]

Economic development not only spurred population growth but changed how Irish people occupied the land and created new economic or occupational roles among them. As the economy took off over the course of the eighteenth century, some of the peasants, who would be called strong farmers, found opportunities in the new prosperity to build up their tenancies and carve out some independence for themselves. Others, however, fell into a class of laborers who held no land but worked for wages or to rent tiny plots to grow potatoes. The farmer/weavers and women spinners in Ulster were another new type in Ireland, whose families brought their products to market themselves, bargained there, and sold them for cash.[29]

The market forces of the new economy also seemed to force a new sexual discipline on Irish people. In an old Gaelic Ireland of communal land ownership, "illegitimate" children seemed of little concern, but peasants in the new economy were more careful. Illegitimacy rates were very low in Ireland compared to the rest of Europe in the eighteenth century, and communities often severely punished women who had children out of wedlock. The disappearance of the older communal land ownership and the progressive tightening of family ties—even of tenants—to specific parts of the land seemed to make them more conscious of family boundaries. The sacrifice of giving up illicit sex may have also been assuaged by the fact that the abundance of work meant that almost all could marry and marry relatively early.[30]

Over the twenty years or more after James II's forces surrendered at Limerick in 1691, Ireland's Protestant parliament passed the Penal Laws, which codified in detail the price of James's defeat for Catholics in Ireland: Catholics could not hold public office (and later vote); build churches; found schools; stage public religious processions; bear arms; own horses worth more than five pounds; or buy land or even take long leases on it. Current Catholic owners also had to divide their inheritances among all males, shattering their estates into progressively smaller and, thus, less economically competitive holdings. A complicated and often changing series of statutes also made Catholic priests, bishops, and women religious vulnerable to arrest, and even execution.[31]

The Penal Laws have figured significantly in the shaping of the public memory of Catholic persecution in Ireland among not only Ireland's Catholics but Irish American ones as well. Revisionist historians of Ireland, however, have questioned the decisiveness or significance of the Penal Laws in shaping Irish Catholic life in the eighteenth century or after. They point out that enforcement of the legislation, like draconian laws against priests and Catholic churches and schools, was haphazard at best. In 1731, well into the Penal Laws era, there were over 2,300 Catholic priests in Ireland, more per capita than there would be long after the repeal of most of the Penal Laws in the last three decades of the eighteenth century. Usually camouflaged by their plain architecture and hidden away on back lanes or roads to give no obvious hint of their purpose, there were also 900 Catholic "mass houses" and 549 Catholic schools in the same year. Furthermore, though the Penal Laws limited Catholic land ownership, many Irish Catholics carved out important economic niches for themselves as merchants in Ireland's new booming international trade in Cork and other southern ports while establishing or expanding family branches in the ports of Catholic Europe. Some Catholics also continued to draw substantial income from the land not as landowners, but as "middlemen" renting large tracts, often of their family's former holdings, and subletting them to tenants. The Catholic Church in Ireland drew on these middlemen and merchants to sustain itself, remaining vital in Leinster, large parts of Munster, and slices of eastern Connaught where such wealthy Catholics were most numerous. It also relied heavily on the Irish Catholic communities in Europe, and their seminaries, colleges, and houses of religious women in France, Spain, Spanish Flanders, and Italy for priests and nuns.[32]

The Penal Laws, however, did have some unintended but significant consequences. Notions of ethnic distinctions between the native or "Old Irish" and Anglo-Norman descendants, "Old English," had not entirely disappeared within Ireland's Catholic community, but by the time the Penal Laws were passed Protestants had already begun to lump them together. These laws confirmed that trend and "the obsolescence of a whole earlier vocabulary of identity." The only boundary the laws drew and enforced was the religious one, thus they essentially completed the centuries-long process, which fused Old English and Old Irish Catholics into what Irish Americans would come to recognize as simply Irish Catholics.[33]

Moreover, the effect of the Penal Laws or the broader intention they reflected of containing Catholic power should not be underestimated. If some Catholics managed to prosper, the laws clearly reinforced the long trend eliminating Catholic land ownership, still the most important source of wealth and status in the eighteenth century. By the 1770s, Catholics owned only 5 percent of the land, even less, 1.5 percent, of Ireland's total annual rental. Similarly, if the Church endured, the laws weakened clerical discipline and deprived it of a public presence. In a broader symbolic sense, the laws' subjugation of Catholics officially marked them as inferior and suspect. They were thus subject to periodic organized anti-Catholic attacks, like one on Edmund Burke's Catholic relatives in the 1760s, and hosts of public humiliations, like the storied assault on Art O'Leary, a former officer in the Austrian army.[34]

As Catholics in Ireland regained their footing and confidence in the mideighteenth century, some of the wealthy and well born among them mounted a cautious campaign for their inclusion in the island's political leadership, based on the rights guaranteed by the Glorious Revolution of 1688. They made no appeals to a broader Catholic population though even English observers, like Samuel Johnson, found Protestant rule in Ireland, "a minority prevailing over a majority," unsettling. Catholic leaders would not really recognize the power in the numbers of their majority until the nineteenth century. Thus, when a Jacobite rising on behalf of the exiled Stuart king set the Scottish Highlands afire in 1745, Catholics in Ireland could not be roused to rebel against their oppression.[35]

Nevertheless, a simmering discontent and frustration seemed to pervade Irish Catholic society in the eighteenth century, which would ultimately have important effects on how Irish Catholics in America came to understand themselves and their own politics. Irish Catholic peasants' conceptions of the ordering of society, particularly notions of the authority of aristocracy, became more confused as Anglo-Protestants, many of them of relatively recent residence in Ireland, took over the lands of the "rightful" lords, Old Irish or Old English Catholics. This dispossession was a powerful rupture for not only the Irish at home, but those exiled in Europe or even settled in America. Charles Carroll, who would become the only American Catholic to sign the Declaration of Independence, would not visit his remaining relatives in Ireland while studying in Europe in 1761: "How unavailing to remember what we cannot revenge! How melancholy to behold ancient, noble and flourishing families reduced to beggary." Yet as Arthur Young found in his tour of Ireland in the 1770s, "in most parts of the kingdom the descendants of the old landowners" did remember, and even "regularly transmit by testamentary deed the memorial of their right to those estates which once belonged to their families." Throughout the eighteenth century and after, Irish language poets, themselves suffering because of the dispossession of their former patrons, often excoriated the new Protestant aristocrats with barrages of insults and invective—"a new breed of upstart," "Cromwellian dogs," "churl," "treacherous boors," "black boors," "Saxon curs," "phony nobles"—underlining the new aristocrats' illegitimacy and looking forward to a broad reversal of Catholic fortunes that would raise up all the Irish, to be led by "the nobles to whom it is proper to be loyal."[36]

Irish Catholics on the European continent nourished this Catholic discontent back in Ireland but also helped strengthen its politically conservative character. As part of the settlement at the end of the Williamite War, thousands of James's defeated Irish soldiers were allowed to go into exile in France. Yet recruits from Ireland continued to flow into European armies, up to a thousand or more a year in the 1720s and 1730s, and an average of about five hundred a year for the first half of the eighteenth century. Catholics writing in Irish or English in Ireland thrilled to their exploits such as the charge of France's Irish Brigade against the English at the Battle of Fontenoy in 1745, an event that Irish American Catholics would continue to celebrate in the nineteenth century. If these "Wild Geese" exiles continued to sustain Irish hopes of resistance, however, they also continued to reinforce the conservative aims of such dreams: the return of the Stuart dynasty and Ireland's old aristocrats to their former stations and conformity to notions of monarchy and a rigidly ranked society that were gospel in the continental Catholic world.[37]

Yet it was not just romantic memories of true lords lost or hopes of their return that nourished Catholic peasant discontents. The potential profits of Ireland's booming economy tempted landlords there to squeeze as much as they could out of their estates. They ratcheted up tenant rents, but also overrode peasants' customary privileges by grabbing common lands. Historians have pointed out that landlords in Ireland were far more successful in exploiting their tenants than in Britain and more brutal in their treatment of them. To underline the severity of Irish peasants' poverty, some Irish Catholics in the 1760s would turn to comparing their plight to "Plantation Negroes in America," which would later become an increasingly exaggerated and recurrent trope in Irish American discussions of race.[38]

Peasant or worker resistance to such oppression seemed to rise to a whole new level in the 1760s. During the Seven Years' War, as British domestic and military demand for Irish cattle soared and prices took off, landlords, middlemen, and strong farmers in Munster, eager to take advantage of the cattle boom, began gobbling up whatever lands they could to pasture cattle. They also gained exemptions for their grazing lands from tithes mandated to support the established Church of Ireland, throwing the entire burden of tithes back on the small tillage farmers. Beginning in 1761 in County Tipperary and spreading to Counties Waterford and Cork, a peasant secret society, called the "Whiteboys" because they wore white shirts, sought to grab the land back for the tillage farmers and laborers dependent on their "potato patches." They leveled walls and fences around pasture lands, dug up that land to convert it back to tillage, houghed cattle (cutting their tendons), and gathered in the thousands to intimidate their enemies.

By 1765, authorities had broken the Whiteboys' rising, but they rose again in the late 1760s and rampaged through a broader area then, from County Carlow in the east to Cork in the west. Some of the grievances were the same, but the market now had swung back to favor tillage, and laborers in the wheat, oats, or barley fields made up the core of the Whiteboys. Their grievance was the competition of migrant laborers, *spalpini* in Irish, who had come from Kerry to find work, and so the Whiteboys attacked both them and the farmers who had hired them. These Whiteboys were more brutal and boldly violent than their predecessors, cutting out tongues or slicing off ears, and assassinating state officials. Once again, the government beat them down with a series of executions, but the new Whiteboys continued to stir up trouble until 1775.[39]

The meanings of the Whiteboy uprisings for Irish people then and in the longer term, for Irish Americans, were complicated. They did not attack only Protestant landlords, but also Catholic farmers and migrant laborers. They were not attempting a democratic revolution, which would eliminate aristocracy. They were trying to stop changes provoked by rapid shifts in international markets in an increasingly commercialized Irish agriculture. The encroachments on their older established privileges ruptured customary reciprocal obligations between them and their landlords and strained their local communal solidarity with their strong Catholic farmer employers. The divisions within the peasantry were real enough, but the seeming indifference of landlords or those in power to shield them from such changes nourished peasant ambivalence, not about the notion of an aristocracy, but about what made a proper or an improper lord. An improper one could be alien in ancestry and religion, but he was also greedy and calculating, lured by market profits to abandon traditional obligations. This kind of questioning of aristocracy would ultimately have a powerful impact on not only Irish but Irish American views of aristocracy and, more generally, of elites as well. Yet that was not all that Irish peasants learned from their secret society uprisings. They also learned that the power of ordinary people lay in numbers and an egalitarian, heavily masculine solidarity set not just against uncaring elites but even against poor outsiders from other places or backgrounds, and the uses of violence in resisting both.

Protestants of almost all sects had joined in the effort to dethrone James II and crush Catholic power once and for all. After that victory the migration of thousands of migrants from Britain to Ireland made the Protestant proportion of Ireland's population larger than at any time in the island's history before or since. Yet there were significant sectarian divisions among Irish Protestants. Church of Ireland members monopolized the island's politics, elite society, and land ownership and jealously guarded their privilege not just against Catholics but against dissenters like Presbyterians in Ulster. With Catholics finally broken, and Presbyterians relegated to second-class citizens, Irish Anglicans had become Ireland's political nation and, in the process, began rethinking their identity. Historians note that in the 1690s, most of Ireland's Anglicans called themselves the Protestants in Ireland or the Englishmen in Ireland, but by the early 1720s many of them began to call themselves Irish. Some began to collect Irish antiquities and even take interest in the Irish language, and many argued that they were the true Irish heirs of St. Patrick and Irish Christianity, not Catholics dominated by foreign Rome. Feeling secure enough now, they began protesting the British government's insistence that it could pass laws for Ireland or reject bills or attach amendments on bills passed by the Irish parliament and make Ireland a dumping ground for the British government's patronage favorites. These battles by Irish Anglican reformers with Britain both provoked and strengthened their new conception of themselves as Irish.[40]

After the victory over the Stuarts, Ulster's Presbyterians thought that their services in the fight against the dangerous James and his papist supporters would win them better treatment by Ireland's government. King William had been willing, but the Anglican Tories, always suspicious of Presbyterian radicalism, became more powerful under his successor, Queen Anne. In 1704, they attached an amendment to the Irish parliament's "Popery Bill" requiring all local public officials and militia officers to take communion in the established Church of Ireland or give up their office, thus effectively excluding Presbyterians from such positions. The Church of Ireland harassed Presbyterians in other ways as well: not permitting Presbyterian ministers to officiate at graveside ceremonies in cemeteries or even marriages, or sometimes blocking the building of Presbyterian chapels on Anglican-owned estates. Some of the restrictions on Presbyterians would be repealed, most notably in a Toleration Act of 1719, but, if the limits set on the Presbyterians were far less draconian than the ones imposed on Catholics, the Presbyterians nevertheless found them irksome and demeaning.[41]

This discrimination was hard for Presbyterians to bear, not just because of the sacrifices they had made in the Williamite War, but because they were growing both more numerous and richer and their expectations of political rights grew with their wealth, education, and sense of potential power. Soon after the end of the Williamite Wars in Ireland, about 50,000 Scots began to pour into Ulster, fleeing a Scottish agriculture suffering terribly then from bad weather and poor harvests but lured by Protestant landlords in Ireland desperate for Protestant tenants to become bulwarks against future Catholic rebellion. Presbyterians and other dissenters also dominated the linen trade, and by the second decade of the eighteenth century they were already prospering from its boom. Presbyterian commoners were thus becoming economically better off not only than Ulster's Catholics but even most ordinary Anglicans, and as a people of "the book" and increasingly engaged in trade, more of them were literate than any other group in Ulster, Ireland's most literate province.[42]

Their very success seemed to nourish tensions within the Presbyterians as they split between better off, more urban "New Lights" and poorer, rural "Old Lights" over creedal issues and ultimately about the extent of the Church's authority over the beliefs of its members. Both Old and New Lights as well as smaller Presbyterian sects, Seceders and Covenanters, however, shared frustrations with the established Church of Ireland. New Lights, influenced by Enlightenment ideals, were moving toward embrace of individual conscience; Old Lights, proud to be a covenanted people, despised the Anglicans' papist-like hierarchy.[43]

Like many Catholics, numerous Ulster Presbyterians also railed against Ireland's aristocrats. There were some Presbyterian gentry in Ulster, but they were few and almost none had significant land holdings. The vast majority of Ulster Presbyterians thus were tenant farmers—or increasingly over the course of the century, farmer/weavers—renting from religiously alien Anglican aristocrats. For them, as for Catholic peasants further south, economic change seemed to exacerbate tensions in their relations with their landlords. Ulster landlords kept ratcheting up rents to keep pace with the linen boom but also took advantage of their local political power to throw the burden of taxes on to their tenants or imposed a tax or labor burden on them for road improvements designed to improve the aristocrats' own estates. The linen industry grew spectacularly in the eighteenth century, but as Ulster families, mostly Presbyterian ones, became more dependent on it, they also became more vulnerable to its many busts during its long boom. The most severe came in the early 1770s with catastrophic falling prices and rising unemployment. Secret societies, the Hearts of Oak and the Hearts of Steel or Steelboys, emerged in Ulster in the 1760s and 1770s, respectively, carrying on the same kind of agrarian wars of intimidation and violence as Munster Whiteboys did in those years. Some of the Steelboys explicitly mixed religious grievances with economic ones in these uprisings: "Between landowners [rent] and rector [tithes for the established church] the very marrow is screwed out of our bones." Government forces in Ulster responded ruthlessly, as they had in Munster. In 1772, troops marched through the province, hanging suspected Steelboys on the way.[44]

By then, however, tens of thousands of Ulster Scot immigrants and their children had already fled across the ocean, and they and their American-born children were now involved in violent protests of their own in the American backcountry from Pennsylvania to the Carolinas.

2. Irish Immigration in the Colonial Era

1585–1775

In 1585, Sir Walter Raleigh established the first English colony in North America, Roanoke, on the coast of what has become the state of North Carolina. Raleigh had just picked up vast new estates in Ireland after English victories over Irish Catholic rebels there, and chose Colonel Ralph Lane, a veteran of the recent wars in Ireland and of late the new sheriff of County Kerry, to serve as Roanoke's governor. Several Irish-born men joined Lane on this expedition to America. Upon arrival, however, the colonists' venture quickly turned into a catastrophe of their own making as they provoked a disastrous war with local Native Americans. In the fighting, Lane's servant—Lane called him his "Irish boy"—shot the local chief, Wingina, and another Irishman chopped off the chief's head. Soon besieged by Native enemies, and starving, the surviving Irish and other colonists were rescued by a fleet commanded by Sir Francis Drake and left this "new" world.[1]

Despite such a disastrous beginning for them (and for Native Americans), more Irish would ultimately follow Raleigh's colonists to America, in a trickle in the seventeenth century but in a flood in the eighteenth. Ulster Scot Presbyterians would come to dominate this migration, far outnumbering the Catholic or Church of Ireland (Anglican) Irish who left for America. Making and selling linen had been central to the lives of these Ulster Scots in Ireland and the linen trade would play a crucial role in bringing them to America, but most of them came to America to be farmers and they would strike out into the far reaches of their new home looking for land. This movement would change them but so would events erupting in America, a great Protestant religious revival, war with the French and Natives, and growing political conflicts within the colonies. Their responses to these events would vary from colony to colony, but in all of them they would help shape how the Irish understood where they fit in America and whether and how they identified as a distinct people. At the very end of the colonial period, after tens of thousands had already emigrated from Ireland to America, an Irish America began to emerge, as some of them and their children in Pennsylvania would begin to identify as Irish, join with members of the province's tiny Catholic Irish community, and organize as religiously plural Irish Americans.

In the century or more after the Roanoke debacle only about 5,000 Irish would go to the emerging English colonies on the North American continent, a tiny number compared to the estimated 140,000 or more English and Welsh who settled there then. About 60 to 70 percent of the Irish (about the same proportion as among the English and Welsh) went as indentured servants. That meant that they paid for their passage by signing a contract to be a servant for up to seven years, which would then be sold to the highest bidder upon their arrival in the colonies. Perhaps three hundred or more of the Irish immigrants were prisoners, "transported" to the colonies in lieu of prison or execution, to be sold into service as well. Under Cromwell in the 1650s, some of these Irish prisoners were victims of a kind of licensed kidnapping, as local magistrates in Ireland simply declared them vagrants, arrested them, and sold them into service across the ocean. Initially, whether self-indentured or transported by the government, they went, or were taken, to Virginia or New England on the North American continent. Edward Howes, for example, sent four wild dogs and an "Irish boy," "a Roman Catholic" to tend them, to John Winthrop in Boston (then called Shawmut). Later, however, many Irish servants would wind up in Maryland or in the new Carolina colonies.[2]

Irish immigration to North America's British colonies would increase enormously in the next century. By one historian's recent calculation, Irish immigrants outnumbered every other white immigrant group then: three times the number of Scots, about a quarter more than the Germans and over 40 percent more than the English and Welsh (though the number of enslaved Africans shipped to America far exceeded the number of white immigrants). These are all estimates, because no one in Ireland or America kept consistent records of the people who left the former or landed in the latter. Some historians say the total number of Irish immigrants from the beginning of the eighteenth century to the Revolution may have been only a little over 100,000; others would more than double that figure to 200,000 or more.[3]

Historians agree, however, that at least half, probably more, of all the immigrants from Ireland to Britain's North American colonies between 1700 and the American Revolution were Ulster Scot Presbyterians. The best guesses of the other religious groups suggest that perhaps another fifth or more were native Irish of Old Irish or Old English stock, largely from the south of Ireland, and likely, but by no means certainly, born Catholics; another sixth, probably Church of Ireland members; and the rest from various of the Protestant dissenting groups, including some Irish Quakers.[4]

That so many Ulster Scots left Ireland, and so few of the island's Catholics did, has long been a puzzle, since Catholics outnumbered Presbyterians by about eight to one in the island as a whole in the eighteenth century and were probably more numerous even in Ulster. Ulster Presbyterians certainly had reasons to go to America: most notably, their continuing second-class citizenship and rapidly rising rents in Ireland. Irish Catholics' economic and political sufferings, however, were undoubtedly worse, but they did not migrate in nearly the same numbers, even in hard times. Most of the deaths from the famine of 1741, the Great Slaughter, occurred in Catholic Munster, for example, but few Irish left for America then, and most who did were from Ulster not Munster and more likely Presbyterians than Catholics. There had to be other reasons besides grievances and hard times why so many Presbyterians crossed the ocean and so few Catholics did.[5]

One was that the Ulster Scots were a people already in motion. The vast majority of the Ulster Presbyterians or their ancestors had settled in Ireland no later than the early seventeenth century, and some who would go to the American colonies in the eighteenth century, or their parents or grandparents, had left Scotland for Ulster as late as the 1690s. Ulster Presbyterians also did not understand leaving Ireland as an abandonment of their identity but as an expression of it, a heroic exodus, an opportunity to fulfill their destiny as a people like "Old Testament Israelites" finding deliverance "from their enemies" in flight to a new promised land.[6]

Most important, however, Presbyterians were more involved in the linen trade than any other group in Ireland. Very few Presbyterians migrated overseas from Ulster before the linen industry took hold there at the turn of the eighteenth century. The *Pennsylvania Gazette* noted in 1735 that the migrants "are Protestants and principally Dissenters and such as are remarkable for their knowledge in . . . all . . . branches of linen manufacture." Plummeting linen prices provoked dramatic spikes in Ulster Scot emigration, a large wave in the

late 1720s, but a vast flood, perhaps up to 40,000, in the early 1770s. Partici-
pating in the linen trade, however, also had less direct but perhaps more broadly
significant effects on their migration than the industry's boom and bust. Bar-
gaining in the market on their own may have made Ulster Scots accustomed
to risk, calculating, and confident in shaping their own fate. More clearly and
crucially, however, the linen industry in Ulster also created a chain of commercial relations and institutions, which made travel and migration to America far
easier for Ulster Scots than for others in Ireland. In just the twenty-five years
between 1750 and the Revolution, 442 ships sailed directly to America from
Ulster ports. Many had carried, among other things, American-grown flax, which
contained the fibers for linen yarn, to northern Ireland, and now took linen
cloth and thousands of immigrants, a most "advantageous returning freight," on
their trips back to America. This trade in flax and people was "all the more
systematic because it was managed by [Ulster Irish] families and commercial
interests that spanned the Atlantic." Ulster ports were not just well connected
to America, they had strong transportation and communication connections to
the dense network of local linen markets in their hinterlands. Ship owners thus
often sent agents or their captains to those towns to recruit immigrant passengers. Through all these linkages a "migration machine" developed in Ulster, which
grew only larger and more efficient as more and more migrants went overseas
and wrote home to relatives and friends. Those letters not only encouraged
others to follow but offered information and made connections in America that
reduced the risks and anxieties of the new emigrants' journey and adaptation
to America. As one prospective migrant in Ulster wrote to a "cusen" in Pennsylvania in 1758: "We depend on you for Derection."[7]

    Yet explaining why so many Ulster Presbyterians went to America solves
only half the puzzle: if so many of them went, why did not more from the much
larger and poorer Catholic population on the island go? It is not just historians
who have asked that question: contemporaries from the eighteenth century wondered why as well. In the 1770s, one observer claimed: "Catholics never went;
they seem not only tied to the country, but almost to the parish where their
ancestors were born." Most Catholics were clearly, in fact, *not* a people in motion but one deeply rooted in their Irish communities, and that was an important reason why they did not go to America. Moreover, to them America did *not*
seem a new Jerusalem as it did for Ulster Scots, but a lonely place "of dense
woods and deep glens," as an Irish-language poet wrote at midcentury, where one
could walk for miles and not see a "Christian." More concretely, most English

colonial governments, often at war with Catholic France's colony to their north or Catholic Spain's settlement to their south, treated Catholics as potential subversives, hounded their priests, and banned their religious services.[8]

Irish Catholics, nonetheless, did move to foreign lands, including the Americas, in the seventeenth century and continued to do so in the eighteenth. Some were forced into exile or shipped out as captives, to be sure, but others chose flight from an oppressive Ireland even to the steamy, disease-ridden islands of the Caribbean or to the raucous work camps of the Newfoundland fisheries. They went, in part, because they could, because merchants in southern Irish ports were already trading regularly with those destinations, like Cork with the Caribbean and Waterford with Newfoundland, and willing, indeed, often eager, to carry them there. The passenger trade to the thirteen colonies, however, was never as well "integrated into the broader commercial culture [of the southern ports] as it was in Ulster."[9]

Nevertheless, at a high estimate, maybe as many as 50,000 native Irish, likely born Catholics, and largely from southern Ireland did go to the thirteen colonies. They were overwhelmingly single and male: only about 5 percent were women. They had already "drifted" from the "mooring" of their families and rural townlands and wound up in Ireland's fast-growing cities. "With little to lose," they indentured themselves to ship out to America. Most of the 10,000 or more Irish prisoners, punished for their crimes by "transportation" from Irish or English jails to America, were also from southern Ireland and many thus likely to have been born Catholics as well. They too, however, had no links to home. Because they could not practice their faith throughout almost all the colonies, most of these Irish Catholic men probably remained unchurched or joined Protestant churches and married Protestant women in America. Unlike the largely Presbyterian emigrants from Ulster, then, the vast majority of native Irish were not links in an immigrant chain, following relatives and friends out to America. They were, however, not all that different from immigrants from southern England in the eighteenth century, also largely male, indentured, and single, though the English were Protestant and more likely to be skilled than the Irish.[10]

There were a tiny number of Irish Catholic immigrants who would, nonetheless, be an important exception. They were members of rich Irish Catholic merchant families, like the Meade family, living in Ireland or in France, Spain, or the Austrian Netherlands with trading connections throughout Europe and some with the West Indies. In the mid- and late eighteenth century those families now sent nephews and sons to establish branches of their firms in North America, more specifically in religiously tolerant and busily prosperous Philadelphia.[11]

Networks were important in this era of emigration because going to America was not easy. Eighteenth-century migrants bought their tickets from a variety of sources: ship owners, their captains, or agents, but also independent brokers, who sold fares for several different ships. Ships departed when they had filled up with cargo or people: in 1773–1774 they left on the average three and a half weeks later than their announced departure date. Sailing the Atlantic in the eighteenth century was a trial as well. Privateers and pirates were an almost constant danger through the century's many wars. The average length of the journey was a little over seven weeks, but beset by storms or lulls in the wind, journeys could drag on for weeks longer, while passengers starved.[12]

The settlement patterns of Anglican and Catholic Irish after they landed in America are hard to trace: the Anglican Irish were so at home throughout their empire that they easily dissolved into an American mainstream; Catholics remained largely hidden because of discrimination against them. Data gleaned from studies of their surnames in the first United States Census in 1790, however, suggests that aside from being overrepresented in Maryland, the Catholic pattern of settlement seemed roughly the same as that of the Ulster Scots between Pennsylvania and Georgia.[13]

The numbers and distinctive religion and culture of Ulster Scots make them much easier to track. Many in the first great wave of Ulster Scot immigrants in the late 1710s went to Boston, expecting to find friendly fellow Protestant dissenters there, but the Congregationalist descendants of the Puritans turned on them and harried them out of the city. Few Ulster Scots followed them to New England, in part because of that early hostility, but also because of the region's weak trade links with Ulster, its limited availability of land, and short growing season. New York City had much stronger trading connections with Ireland than New England ports, but land was not easy to purchase in rural New York either, and thus only a small proportion of the ships going from Ireland to New York seemed to carry immigrants there. In the 1790 census, Ulster Scots made up but 9 percent or less of the population of any state north of Pennsylvania.[14]

By contrast in the same census, Ulster Scots were 15 percent or more of the populations of five of the seven states from Pennsylvania south and 11 percent and 10 percent of the other two, Virginia and Maryland, respectively. Probably half of all Irish immigrants to America landed in Philadelphia or the other

Delaware River ports, Newcastle and Wilmington, which had extensive trading connections with Ireland and Ulster. Many stayed in Pennsylvania to take advantage of its booming economy—the "Best Poor Man's Country"—but others moved south along the "Great Wagon Road." They entered the Shenandoah Valley in Virginia as early as 1719, and western North Carolina by the 1730s, but continued to pour into both colonies thereafter and eventually by the 1760s into South Carolina and Georgia, either moving south from Philadelphia or west from southern ports.[15]

Some historians have long celebrated these Ulster Scots as quintessential Americans, the first "pioneers"; others depict them not as the forerunners of something new, but the bearers of something old, working to transplant Scottish or even ancient Celtic customs in colonial America.[16] More useful, as one historian has said, is to recognize that "from the start, what they [Ulster Scots in America] had was a mutating lifestyle, mediated through inherited patterns . . . that had not been fixed in Ulster either. Thus, the new way of life in America accentuated a preexistent adaptability." Their uniquely high participation in the new linen industry in Ulster had been proof of their adaptability in Ireland. They would not stop making linen in America, but it would not be as important to them there, as they could not sell it in an internationally connected market to make a living as they had in Ulster. Instead, they would keep it for their own use or, in an economy where money was scarce, barter it locally.[17]

They did not just adapt old practices or customs in America; new opportunities in this American environment bid them to change to take advantage of them. They learned much about tracking and hunting in American forests rich with game, for example, by copying Native American techniques like setting the woods afire to flush out the animals. Yet they also learned from fellow immigrant neighbors, adopting German wagon wheel styles or building homes as cabins of logs as the Swedes did, but adapting them to Ulster floor plans.[18]

More than America's terrain, animals, and new neighbors, it was its abundance of seeming open land that transformed their lives so dramatically. They could never own land in Ireland but seemed sure that they could in America, and that was the main reason why most of them went there. They wanted land not so much to get rich, but to gain freedom from the dependence of the tenant, to gain an "independency" or sometimes called a "competency," terms that connoted economic autonomy but something like self-respect as well. A British official claimed that even the "richer sort say if they stay in Ireland, their children will be slaves."[19]

Many of these "people in motion," therefore, stayed in motion after they landed in America, searching for land they could own and the independency or competency that it assured. Imperial or colonial officials in Virginia, South Carolina, Georgia, and Pennsylvania lured some of them to the edges of British settlement with offers of land so that they could act as defensive screens, protecting richer coastal settlements from Native American attacks. For most, however, it was the dynamism of the American economy that provoked their continued movement. As western settlements connected to eastern markets, the value and price of its land rose. If a family owned land where there was a market connection, they could hold on to it and prosper or sell it for a profit and move on to buy more, cheaper land further west; if they did not own it, rising prices where they were gave them few alternatives but to move.[20]

As they had moved through networks of kin and friends to America, so now they often moved in America not as individuals or single families but in larger groups of kin and neighbors. They settled in rural open "neighborhoods" of scattered farmsteads but most owned by kin or Ulster Scot friends: bartering in linen and other goods with them; depending on them for mutual support; and strengthening those bonds through older rituals and shared delight in the music that they had brought with them from Scotland and Ireland. More Ulster Scots would move to the farthest reaches of colonial settlement than members of any other ethnic group, but they would leave a long trail of Ulster Scot settlements between there and where most had first landed in eastern Pennsylvania. Ulster Scots settled in Opequon in the Shenandoah Valley in the 1730s, for example, but not only did the first settlers remain there but their children did too, marrying within a tight circle of the original families. By the third generation, however, many of the grandchildren had to leave to find cheaper land in Kentucky, but they also traveled in groups of kin and friends to their new home. Meanwhile, Ulster Scots could also be found among the artisans, shopkeepers, and professionals of the inland towns, such as Carlisle in Pennsylvania, Winchester in Virginia, or Camden in South Carolina, which began to sprout as settlement pushed further west after 1750. Nevertheless, by the beginning of the Revolution, even as Ulster was just beginning to evolve into an urban-industrial society, most Ulster Scots in America were a rural farming people, and a large proportion of their descendants would remain so as well and would like their ancestors make their homes in the rural South.[21]

However much Irish immigrants and their families maintained old world customs or adopted or created new ones in their everyday life in America, they also confronted questions about how they, as a people, fit into this very different and more diverse society. One historian has intriguingly argued that the Ulster Scots, the largest proportion of Irish newcomers in America, were "a people with no name" through most of the eighteenth century. They were British subjects of the same empire as in Ireland and Protestant dissenters who had landed now in a new world full of such dissenters. Yet a devastating war, a sweeping religious revival, and an emerging fractious democratic politics made America a tumultuous place in the middle and late eighteenth century. Ulster Scots became involved in public religious and political debates and conflicts that forced them to take sides and sort out where they fit in this new world. Importantly, however, though they confronted war, religious upheaval, and political conflicts wherever they settled in America, how they answered questions of fit and identity varied significantly from colony to colony, as Ulster Scot ethnic or religious identification faded in the South but flourished in Pennsylvania.[22]

Francis Makemie, from Ramelton in Donegal, founded the first Presbyterian Presbytery in America (a ruling body of elders and ministers for a number of congregations) as late as 1706, but the Presbyterian Church grew rapidly in the colonies thereafter. Presbyterians in the colonies included migrants and their descendants not just from Ulster but from England and Scotland as well, but the torrent of Ulster Scot immigrants in the eighteenth century gave the Presbyterian Church in America an enormous boost. By 1750 there were an estimated two hundred and fifty Presbyterian congregations in America.[23]

Yet as the American Presbyterian Church grew, so too did the divisions within it. The most significant sources of conflict lay at the heart of not only Presbyterianism but of a broader Protestant Christianity in the colonies. In 1734, Gilbert Tennent, a young minister born in Armagh in Ulster, rose at a meeting of the Synod in Philadelphia to suggest that the Church needed to judge its ministers not just by their educational qualifications and doctrinal orthodoxy but by their faith: whether they had or had not been saved and how their conversion to Christ had moved them. He and his friends would demand, as he had first broached, that the Church needed ministers capable of inspiring their flocks to truly accept Christ as their savior, not to debate finer points of doctrine or even to pledge their commitment to a list of dogmatic propositions.

Figure 2. *Portrait of Rev. Gilbert Tennent.* Tennent was the leader of the Great Awakening revival among Presbyterians in Pennsylvania. Engraving by John Sartain, 1855. Presbyterian Historical Society.

Such were "dry, sapless, unconverted men," in the opinion of Irish-born minister Samuel Blair and were hardly cut out to do Christ's work.[24]

"Ardent" preaching and emotional congregational responses had flourished in the early seventeenth century among Presbyterians in Ulster, but the revival tradition had faded there subsequently, kept alive largely by a Presbyterian splinter group called the Seceders. Moreover, Presbyterian revivals in Ulster had traditionally been more about the purification of the community, calling it back to its covenant; Tennent's and Blair's revivalism, in contrast, focused on individual salvation, like their fellow dissenters, the Congregationalists and Baptists. This emphasis on proof of individual conversion, not right thinking, "the life and power of godliness," not "the form," seemed to render dogma irrelevant and blast away distinctions between denominations.[25] Tennent himself invited George Whitefield, the famous Anglican evangelical preacher, to speak at his church. Whitefield had often dismissed sectarian doctrinal differences: "Don't tell me you are a Baptist, an Independent, a Presbyterian, a dissenter, tell me you are a Christian that is all I want." It was easy enough to trample sectarian boundaries at this time because it was the era of the First Great Awakening, an evangelical Protestant revival which spread throughout the colonies. It erupted in the late 1730s and early 1740s and continued into the 1760s and 1770s, transforming older churches like the Presbyterians and sparking the emergence of marginalized ones like the Baptists.[26]

The Presbyterian Awakening began in Pennsylvania and had an impact there, often splintering congregations along age and class lines, but, importantly, it did not provoke a significant exodus of the province's Presbyterians to other sects like the Baptists, as it would in other colonies. An educated clergy had long been essential to Presbyterianism in Ireland and Scotland, and where Presbyterianism suffered in America, it would be because its churches could not find trained ministers. Conservatives resisting the revival were called the "Old Side," and they worked hard to establish new Presbyterian schools in Pennsylvania to train ministers. Though Tennent and his New Side allies may have demanded that ministers show evidence of their conversion to Christ, even he also ultimately insisted that Presbyterian clerics must be educated as well. Thus, Pennsylvania had easier access than other colonies to educated clergy, whether from overseas, the New Ark Academy in Philadelphia, or the nearby Presbyterian College of New Jersey (later called Princeton). Perhaps as important to Presbyterianism's success in Pennsylvania, however, was the rising sectarian conflict in the province's politics, which would eventually help unite Presbyterians of both Old and New Sides against Quaker enemies and reinforce Ulster Scot loyalties to their old church.[27]

Further south in Virginia, the alignments were not so clear. In the 1750s, war with Native Americans seemed to strengthen Old Side ministers in the Shenandoah Valley, like John Craig, who took the lead in organizing resistance against Native American raids and stiffened it by invoking Old Side traditions of a covenanted people besieged by their enemies. New Side churches multiplied quickly in the Virginia backcountry, however, and a New Side Presbytery was created there in 1755. The Presbyterian clergy in many places in Virginia were also still stretched thin among several congregations.[28] Nevertheless, Ulster Scot Presbyterians did not appear to be especially susceptible to defection to the Baptists in Virginia, who flourished in the colony but largely in regions east of Ulster Scot settlements.

In the Carolinas, however, Ulster Scots abandoned Presbyterianism in droves to join the Baptists or gave up on organized religion entirely. By the early 1770s, there were six Presbyterian ministers in North Carolina, but they served thirty congregations spread throughout the backcountry. In western parts of North Carolina, Ulster Scots and others often met for religious services in rough, nondescript, wooden, nonsectarian meeting houses, where "adherents of different denominations spoke one right after another to much the same audience." The Baptists, who cared little about the education of their ministers but much about evidence of their ministers' faith, flourished in this environment. As early as 1765, the anti-Presbyterian Anglican minister Charles Wood-mason cackled that the Separate Baptists in North Carolina "have Worn'd the Presbyterians out att these ther Stron Hold and drew them away." By the early 1770s, perhaps, one-eighth of all the people in the Piedmont were Separate Baptists and many of them were Ulster Scots. The situation was similarly gloomy for Presbyterians in South Carolina. They had established three congregations there by 1755 and twenty-one by 1768 but had only two resident Presbyterian ministers. By then Baptists already outnumbered the Presbyterians in the colony's backcountry,[29] while many other Presbyterians simply drifted into indifference to organized religion. By snapping a critical link between Ulster Scots and their Irish past and erasing a religious boundary that had long marked them as a distinct people, the withering of Presbyterianism in the South dealt a serious blow to Ulster Scot group identity there.[30]

Since many moved to the edges of white settlement, it seemed inevitable that Ulster Scots and the native Irish, who often settled among them, would become embroiled in battles with Native Americans. Initially, however, that would not be true for the Irish in Pennsylvania or the Virginia backcountry. The Province of Pennsylvania had slyly convinced the Iroquois from northern New York—the most powerful Native people in eastern North America—to assert their dominion over Natives like the Delaware in eastern Pennsylvania and force those people to move west. In return, the Iroquois gained "leverage" from Pennsylvania's support for them in their relations with the colony of New York. For their own purposes, the Iroquois also helped clear Virginia's Shenandoah Valley of other Natives as well. For years then, Irish and other white settlers moved west

in Pennsylvania or turned into the Shenandoah Valley in Virginia without confronting serious Native resistance. Yet by the 1740s and 1750s, all that was
about to change.[31]

In 1744, the Iroquois signed a treaty at Lancaster that they believed
merely gave the Shenandoah Valley to the English, but that whites claimed actually ceded all Native lands west to the Pacific Ocean to them. Pennsylvania
traders, like Dublin-born George Croghan, began to move into the Ohio River
country, and, in 1754, a Virginia expedition led by George Washington lunged
at the strategically critical river forks where the Monongahela and Allegheny
Rivers flowed into the Ohio—the site of modern-day Pittsburgh. The French
moved to the forks as well and tangled with Washington's Virginia troops, igniting a tinderbox of multiple conflicting international interests into a world war
(called the French and Indian War in America and the Seven Years' War in England) fought among the British, French, and Spanish empires and their allies,
in Europe, Asia, and the Caribbean as well as North America.[32]

If the war was worldwide, however, it would have an especially powerful
impact on the Irish on the Pennsylvania and Virginia frontiers. Indeed, in the
beginning it was an unmitigated disaster for them and other frontier settlers.
The Delaware and Shawnee, who had been shoved to western Pennsylvania by
the Iroquois, were intent now on standing their ground in their new home and
joined the French. In the early summer of 1755, that alliance routed Edward
Braddock's British army (including two regiments from Ireland) in the woods
south of the forks of the three rivers and left virtually the entire Virginia and
Pennsylvania frontiers exposed to raids by France's Native American allies.
Deaths, capture, and flight cut the heavily Ulster Scot and native Irish population of Augusta County in Virginia by over a half between 1754 and 1758, and
"at times" Cumberland County in Pennsylvania "where 5,000 people, the vast
majority Ulster Scots, had lived, was all but deserted."[33]

Virginia had a militia, even if it melted before the French and Native
American onslaught, but Pennsylvania had none. Quaker leaders had long been
successful working through the Iroquois to keep the peace, but it soon became
evident that the Iroquois could not stop the attacks. Some Quakers left the
Pennsylvania Provincial Assembly rather than make war on Native Americans.
Even without them, however, the legislators fell into a wrangle over taxes and
offered little help to the Ulster Scots and native Irish and other families bearing
the brunt of the attacks. Ulster Scot settlers thus organized on their own to
fight the Native American raiders. Such forces were largely blundering and inef-

fective, but through them Ulster Scot backcountry settlers did mobilize as they never had before. They focused on two enemies: not just Native Americans, but also the Province's leaders, the Quakers in particular, for exposing them to the attacks. Western Pennsylvania's Ulster Scots largely forgot about the assembly's bickering over taxes and "reduced the Assembly to Quakerism and Quakerism to pacifism," which, they believed, had crippled the province's response to their plight. Eventually, both Virginia and Pennsylvania decided to organize their own regular army regiments to stiffen militia or local volunteer resistance. A substantial proportion of both colonies' regiments were Irish born, either Ulster Scots or native Irish: in Virginia about one sixth (16 percent) and in Pennsylvania two-fifths (40 percent) were Irish immigrants.[34]

Finally, in 1758, British forces, including the heavily Irish Pennsylvania regiment, made a powerful and carefully planned advance on the French at the forks. As the British army approached, negotiations by Pennsylvania leaders helped lure away France's Native allies. French soldiers then blew up their new fort at the meeting at the rivers, Fort Duquesne, and retreated north. Their threat to the Irish in Pennsylvania and Virginia was over.[35]

Ulster Scots and the Irish in the South Carolina backcountry, however, now faced their own battles with Native peoples. Over several years the Cherokees had worked out an accommodation with South Carolina's colonists, and thus seven hundred Cherokee warriors had even traveled north to join the British expedition against the French in Pennsylvania. By that time, however, years of war had convinced the Irish and other whites in Virginia's Shenandoah Valley that any Native people they encountered were their enemies. They thus attacked those Cherokee allies as they were returning home to South Carolina. Virginia and South Carolina militia also attacked Cherokee homelands. The Cherokees retaliated in the winter of 1760, and the largely Ulster Scot Long Canes settlement bore "the brunt of the assault." Ulster Scots and other whites fought back savagely, gloating about the Cherokee scalps adorning the walls of their forts. White invasions of Cherokee territory, a harsh winter, and the exhaustion of Native Americans' supplies of arms and gunpowder all forced the Cherokees to sue for peace in the summer of 1761.[36]

In 1763, the worldwide war begun in the Pennsylvania woods ended, but Irish settlers' bloody encounters with Native peoples would continue. As the war was nearing its end, white colonists, including Ulster Scots and native Irish, quickly moved over the mountains into the western Pennsylvania territories that the Province of Pennsylvania had promised to preserve for Native American peoples in its negotiations to end the conflict. Provoked by this new white invasion, a Native American coalition rose up in a new rebellion, led by Pontiac, an Ottawa chief. Natives killed or captured trespassing traders with Irish names like Farrell, Linehehan, Neal, Dunn, and McCann and threw the western Pennsylvania frontier into chaos once again, before their rising petered out in 1766.[37]

By this time, a broad consensus seemed to have emerged among most Irish and other ordinary people settling in the colonial west that all Natives were irredeemably inferior and hostile and best dispatched quickly to make way for white conquest in America. As important, however, Irish settlers in the Pennsylvania backcountry were also angry at their own provincial government for taking the part of the Natives during the wars, allegedly coddling them and permitting Native American attacks on the Irish and other men and women on the frontier. The settlers thus mixed a growing racist hatred of Native peoples with an angry, populist anti-elitism.[38]

The most famous, dramatic, and consequential expression of that sentiment came in the Paxton Boys massacre. On December 14, 1763, while the Pontiac Rebellion still threatened the Pennsylvania frontier, a group of Irish Rangers, raised by the Presbyterian minister Rev. John Elder in Paxton Township to suppress that insurrection, slaughtered a settlement of peaceful Christian Indians at Conestoga. After being roundly condemned for the massacre by Pennsylvania's leaders, an even larger band of "Paxton Boys" and their allies marched on Philadelphia to confront their critics. They made it to Germantown, near Philadelphia, where a delegation headed by Benjamin Franklin dissuaded them from going further.[39]

A hot controversy ensued. The Paxton Boys and their defenders insisted that the Conestoga Indians had secretly aided the attacks by the Pontiac conspiracy on their settlements. They had no proof, but argued that none was necessary. No real distinction, they contended, could be drawn between hostile and friendly Indians: "Who will make War with a part of a nation, and not with the whole?" Yet the Paxton Boys and their partisans were also furious with the way the Quaker-led government had supposedly "openly caressed" Native Americans, while "hundreds of poor distressed families of his majesty's subjects . . . obliged to abandon their possessions and flee for their lives . . . [were] neglected." In turn, not just the Quakers, but most people in the eastern parts of Pennsylvania were outraged by the Paxton Boys. Many condemned them as radical, anarchic Presbyterians, naturally given to rebellion and violence. Some critics of the Paxton Boys, however, thought the trouble with the Paxton Boys was not that they were Presbyterians but that they were Irish. William Logan, a member of Pennsylvania's provincial council, called them "Irish Rebels" moved by the Bible to "extirpate" all Indians. Others derided them as "a parcel of ragged arse tatterdemalion fellows" with names like "O'Haro" and "O'Regan."[40]

In some ways, the Paxton Boys were but the most notorious manifestation of the War's broad impact on the stability and order of the backcountry in many colonies. The crotchety Irish Anglican minister on the Carolina frontier, Charles Woodmason, suggested that the end of the War had unleashed "loose fellows . . . who for seven years had been accustomed to Murder and Pillage" and "chusing A life of Idleness form'd ymseves into Gangs and rang'd over . . . y whole continent." The Paxton Boys were unique, however, and especially important, because their heinous attack helped prompt an Ulster Scot political movement, one defined by their enemies, but that they ultimately embraced, as a religious and even an ethnic one.[41]

For much of their history in America, Ulster Scots and other backcountry people hardly participated in colonial politics and government. That was, in part, because Ulster Scots kept outrunning both, moving beyond government's effective reach or easy access to political institutions. Yet it was also because coastal merchant and planter elites were usually reluctant to include them by extending political representation or courts to where Ulster Scots lived in the west. Imperial officials often backed up such eastern elites because they feared that new counties or parishes meant more representatives in the colonial assemblies and thus simply more troublemakers who would be hard to control. After the French and Indian War, Ulster Scots would become more involved in politics, but here, as in the evolution of religion, there would be important differences in their experiences among the many colonies.

In Virginia, the integration of backcountry areas, including such Ulster Scot strongholds as Augusta and Rockbridge counties, was easier and, indeed, smoother than in any other colony with significant Ulster Scot settlement. Between 1728 and 1763 Virginia created twenty-four new counties and by 1770 nearly doubled the size of the legislature, the House of Burgesses, to represent them. Eastern elites in Virginia were open to extending government to the west because many speculated in land there to hedge against an increasingly unreliable transatlantic tobacco market. Ulster Scots, however, took advantage of the political opportunities in the new regions. Archibald Alexander from County Down became sheriff of heavily Irish Rockbridge County, for example, and Irish-born William McKee would represent the county in the House of Burgesses in the colonial era. Furthermore, though the Anglican Church was established in Virginia, agreements negotiated with royal governors permitted Ulster Scot Presbyterians in the west to practice their religion freely.[42]

In North Carolina, by contrast, the coastal counties dominated the colony and were hostile or indifferent to the extension of government to the west. Furthermore, Ulster Scots and other settlers, pouring into what seemed the open spaces of the North Carolina Piedmont, had found that most of the land there was tied up by large grants to British grandees and speculators. Purchase of that land was also a hopelessly corrupt business orchestrated from Britain and the eastern parts of the colony and abetted by colonial officials.[43]

In 1768, the bitter frustration in the North Carolina backcountry eventually blew up in a broad uprising, called the Regulation (its participants called the Regulators), a term for popular extralegal assertions of local control, which had been used in England and the colonies since the seventeenth century. After contesting elections in 1768, Regulators met in town meetings and hammered out their reform goals: secret ballots, abolition of poll taxes, and land rights for squatters. One historian has claimed that "no other ... vision of agrarian reform has come down to us from the Pre-Revolution period" as "wide ranging, radical and concrete." Meanwhile, farmers refused to pay taxes and attacked the courts and their officers. The agitation went on for nearly three years, before Governor Tryon raised an army in eastern North Carolina, marched inland, routed a disorganized Regulator force at Alamance, killed about fifteen to twenty Regulators during the battle, and executed twelve more after it. Six thousand eventually took an oath of allegiance to the colonial government.[44]

Presbyterian and other Ulster Scots and native Irish or their descendants were noticeably active in the Regulation, as their troubles with the landowners and colonial officials must have resonated with their experiences with landlords and the government in Ireland. North Carolina's rulers even sent Presbyterian ministers to the west to try to convince the Regulators from their church to stand down, though with little apparent success. Several prominent Irish Presbyterians and Baptists were among the Regulation's leaders, and Presbyterian congregations such as ones at Buffalo and Alamance Creeks were active in it. Yet the movement also attracted people of English and German ancestry and a variety of religious sects; the battle lines between the Regulators and their enemies were not religious or ethnic but regional, west versus east, or economic, poor farmers versus rich elites.[45]

Before Governor Tryon crushed the Regulation in North Carolina, a movement also called the Regulation had emerged, fought, and already faded away in neighboring South Carolina. Because the Regulations in the two colonies were both extralegal movements, bore the same name, and happened about the same time, they are often lumped together. Yet the Regulation in South Carolina was very different than the one in North Carolina. In South Carolina, angered by the chaos which had erupted among gangs in the backcountry after the Cherokee War, over 1,000 men organized in 1767 "to execute the laws against all villains and harborers of villains" and "assumed the title of Regulators." Though coastal Carolina's indifference to the west, principally its failure to create new parishes (South Carolina's version of counties) and courts, was responsible for much of the backcountry's turmoil, the South Carolina Regulators had not wanted to fight the eastern elite so much as to join it. The Regulation leaders were owners of middling sorts of farms but on their way to becoming respectable big planters and slave owners. By 1768, they had broken the back of criminal activities in the South Carolina backcountry, and when the colony managed to pass a circuit court bill and then gain approval from the British government to create new parishes the next year, the Regulator movement disappeared.[46]

It is hard to say where the native Irish and Ulster Scots fit into the Regulation fight in South Carolina. They were probably on both sides, though there are certainly names—Morris Murphy or David, Edward, Enoch and William McCraven and Patrick Calhoun (father of future vice president and pro-slavery spokesman John C. Calhoun)—that suggest they were well represented among the Regulators.[47]

Finally, in Pennsylvania, Quaker settlers, their descendants, and their allies dominated politics for much of the colonial era. They elected most of the eastern representatives to the legislature and used that stronghold to stifle opposition from the west and control the province. Into the 1760s, Pennsylvania had only eight counties and the five in the west, collectively, had only ten representatives while the three eastern counties and the city of Philadelphia had twenty-six. Marginalized by the eastern elite's lock on the province's politics, Ulster Scots occasionally elected one of their own to the legislature, but they had little political power and not much sense of a group political identity.[48]

That had begun to change during the French and Indian War and gained momentum after it. From the early days of the colony, Quaker settlers in Pennsylvania had chafed at the privileges and orders of the Penn family proprietors, and organized as an Anti-Proprietary faction or party, which became the instrument of their rule in the legislature. In the early 1760s, however, the Anti-

Proprietary party, led by Benjamin Franklin, overreached, as it sought to dump the proprietor, the Penn family, and convince the British parliament to make Pennsylvania a royal colony. Coming on the heels of the Paxton Boys' controversy and fought out amid a new suspicion of the empire's effort to assert control over the colonies, the legislative election of 1764 was the most hotly contested in the history of the province. The two sides produced over forty pamphlets and broadsides, some patient and reasoning, others vituperative and slanderous (Ulster Scots and other members of the opposition Proprietary Party singled out Franklin, the "lecher," for most of their barbs). The Proprietary Party also enlisted ministers from several denominations as spokesmen and created ethnically balanced slates including Germans and Ulster Scots. In the end, the bitterly fought campaign produced an enormous voter turnout. The Quakers' Anti-Proprietary party suffered heavy losses—even Franklin, its leader, lost his seat—though it would quickly regain its footing and manage to hold on to its dominance until the Revolution.[49]

Nevertheless, the Ulster Scots were now emerging as critical players in a rapidly changing Pennsylvania politics. The French and Indian War and the controversy that followed the Paxton Boys massacre, with its torrent of anti-Irish, anti-Presbyterian obloquy, seemed to provoke a new and acutely self-conscious political identity among them. Franklin, who detested the Paxton Boys, made no secret of his disgust for the Ulster Scots—"the Piss-Brut-arians" he called them—but also his fear of them, his party's most "bitter enemies," the "Irish Presbyterians," "a bigoted, cruel and revengeful sect." The "people with no name" who had disappeared into the wilderness had a name now, Presbyterian: anathema to their enemies, but a source of pride to them. In the 1764 elections they had worked hard to repair the differences between New Light and Old Light and stand as a "united front" against the Anti-Proprietary party. More remarkably, however, Ulster Scot Presbyterians had a new sense of their future as a people in Pennsylvania's politics. Meeting in Lancaster to back the Proprietary Party and oppose a royal charter, they had issued a manifesto: "Presbyterians have as good a right to Pennsylvania as the children of Israel had formerly to the land of Canaan.... It is right and lawful for Presbyterians to make use of the same means in extirpating Quakers, Indians or any other foreign or domestic enemies that the Israelites did to extirpate" the Canaanites.[50]

During the Paxton Boys controversy, Hugh Williamson, a Presbyterian pastor and professor of mathematics at the University of Pennsylvania, had moaned: "For God's sake are we always to be slaves, must we groan forever beneath the yoke of three Quaker counties?" He thus proposed an alliance be-tween Presbyterians in the city of Philadelphia with their fellow Presbyterians in the west to battle the Friends. Williamson's Presbyterian Party did in fact emerge in 1766, and, though it would not be strong enough to defeat the Quak-ers before the Revolution, it did replace the Proprietary Party as the colony's chief opposition party. Though the Presbyterian Party would be broadly based and enlist strong support from German evangelicals, Ulster Scot Presbyterians were critical to it and their power rose with the party's in the fight against Brit-ain just before the Revolution. In 1756 only two Ulster Scots held seats in the Pennsylvania legislature, 8 percent of its members. On the eve of the Revolution in 1775, seven Ulster Scots did and they made up 21 percent of that body.[51]

In December 1774, James Caldwell wrote home to relatives in Ulster, breath-lessly recounting the colonies' march to revolution. Caldwell talked of support for the Patriots' cause in terms of ethnic groups: the English divided; the Scottish-leaning Tory: "but among the Irish nine tenths espouse the American cause." Caldwell overestimated Irish unanimity, but what was most important was that he talked of an Irish people in America. For a long time Ulster Scots like Cald-well had "no name" in America and vehemently denied association with the southern or Catholic Irish. Yet Caldwell proudly defined the Irish as a combina-tion of "our countrymen of the north," descendants of "the Scottish Lowlander," and "the native[s] of the Emerald isle."[52]

Four years before Caldwell wrote his letter, an organization had appeared in Philadelphia called the Friendly Sons of St. Patrick, which already embodied that new Irish identity. Surprisingly, there had been a formal Irish organization, the Charitable Irish Society in Boston, since 1737. It was, however, more a prod-uct of the city's lack of diversity and Irish isolation there—a tiny minority in a sea of suspicious Yankees—than the Boston Irish capitalizing on any emerging, local, ethnic pluralism. The Sons in Philadelphia would be different. Their or-ganization was made up of elite merchants of all faiths, publicly recognizing—as the Boston Charitable Society could not—the new prominence of Catholic Irish merchants drawn to Philadelphia by its expanding trade network and religious toleration. The Catholic Stephen Moylan, who had migrated to Phil-adelphia only in 1768, would be the Friendly Sons' first president. Philadelphia already had other ethnic societies, dating back to the Welsh Saint David's Soci-ety founded in 1729 and the first German society in 1764, but the timing of the Friendly Sons' organization was significant. By the early 1770s, "a new . . . economic and social elite" had formed in Philadelphia, developing "largely out-side of, and increasingly . . . in opposition to the provincial establishment." The Friendly Sons thus drew on the momentum of the Presbyterian assault on Quaker economic and political power, expanding now to include the Catholic Irish, to stake their claim to being part of that new elite, as Philadelphia and America began to hurtle toward revolution. Still emerging in Philadelphia as Caldwell wrote excitedly to his family back in Ulster in 1774, this freshly minted nonsectarian Irish American group identity would flourish during the Revolution and its aftermath throughout much of the new United States.[53]

3. Irish America in the Age of Revolution

1775–1815

In the midsummer of 1775, about a half year after James Caldwell had written to his brother, John, describing the American colonies' challenge to the British empire, Jane Orr, nurse of John's six-year-old son, Johnny, took her young charge to the top of a mountain in County Antrim in Ulster. "On the news of Bunker Hill . . . the young and aged were assembled [there] before a blazing bonfire," Johnny later recalled, "to celebrate what they considered the triumph of America over British despotism, when my nurse cried out—'Look Johnny dear, look yonder to the west. There is the land of liberty and there will be your country.'"[1]

Irish American participation in the American Revolution, which Johnny and his friends cheered so lustily, would actually be quite complicated, varying from state to state in the new republic. That revolt, however, would be but the beginning of an Age of Revolution, spreading across Europe and the Americas, which would spark a bloody rebellion in Ireland. Johnny would be involved in that rebellion, but it would fail, and as his nurse predicted he and thousands more would leave for the new United States. Some sought a haven to escape punishment for their rebellion; many went there to taste the new republic's economic and political promise. They would find it a nation still in the making, riven by continuing political conflict even after the Revolution. Many of them would join in those fights, allying with the Ulster Scots and other Irish who had already settled in America during the colonial era. Through those nationwide political battles, the new nonsectarian Irish American identity, born in Pennsylvania before the Revolution, would spread throughout the entire new United States.

Infuriated observers and officers in the British army or even among their Hessian mercenary allies often blamed the American Revolution on Presbyterian troublemakers or more broadly on the Irish: "Call it not an American rebellion, it is nothing more nor less than an Irish-Scotch Presbyterian rebellion." The list of revolutionary military heroes of Irish birth or descent is, indeed, a long one but, perhaps even more tellingly, no less than a quarter of the American regular army, the Continental soldiers, were Irish born. Nevertheless, Irish Protestants and Catholics in America were hardly unanimous in their opinions about the Revolution as their responses to it varied significantly from colony to colony.[2]

Nowhere in the colonies was Irish support for the Revolution stronger or more radical than in Pennsylvania. There were Irish Loyalists, often called Tories, in the new state who resisted breaking with the Crown. About 150 Irish Catholics in Pennsylvania, for example joined a Tory regiment. Yet almost double that number of Irish Catholics became soldiers in the new nation's Continental army, and Irish Catholics were prominent officers in both the revolutionary army and navy. John Barry, a native of Wexford, for example, proved a brave and savvy naval commander whether on the high seas or as head of a flotilla of small craft on the Delaware, and would always be known to later Irish American Catholics as the "Father of the American Navy." It was Irish Presbyterians, mostly Ulster Scots, however, who made up the bulk of Pennsylvania's huge contingent in the Continental army, led Pennsylvania into revolution and dominated the new state government thereafter. In 1776, Pennsylvania's assembly, still dominated by Quakers and other conservatives, remained reluctant to consider American independence. Yet, after Ulster Scot revolutionaries scored important victories in the countryside, Dublin-born Presbyterian George Bryan and Thomas McKean, American-born of Ulster Scot immigrant parents, decided to ignore the colonial assembly and called for a public meeting in Philadelphia on May 26, 1776, to "determine the public will" on revolution. In the pouring rain, that gathering demanded a convention to establish a new government and set Pennsylvania on the path to breaking its ties to the British empire. Bryan, once a successful businessman but now a fiery radical, was committed not just to independence but to the rule of "the people . . . in opposition to those termed the well born" and openly denounced "the wellborn few" who "lord it over their fellow creatures." He and others thus helped to recast long-brewing Ulster Scot anti-aristocrat and recent anti-Quaker elite sentiments in

Figure 3. *Thomas McKean*. An active leader in the independence movement in Delaware and Pennsylvania in 1776, McKean would later be elected governor of Pennsylvania as a Democratic-Republican in 1799. Painted by Charles Willson Peale after 1787. National Portrait Gallery, Smithsonian Institution, transferred from the Smithsonian Museum of American Art, gift of the collection of George Buchanan Coale, 1926.

the light of newly popular radical republican, even democratic, ideology. When the convention met in July, two-fifths of the delegates were Ulster Scot Presbyterians. The constitution that the convention proposed for the new state, ratified in September, would be the most radical of any state in the new American nation. It had a unicameral legislature—no senate smacking of aristocracy to frustrate the people's aspirations—and a rotating and weak executive—no kings or their imitations.[3]

Having helped create the new government in Pennsylvania, the Irish quickly made it theirs. In 1775 Presbyterians had made up a fifth (21 percent) of the old colonial assemblymen; by 1777–1778, almost 70 percent of the new state's legislators were Presbyterians. As Benjamin Franklin acknowledged: "It is a fact that the Irish emigrants and their children are now in possession of the government of Pennsylvania." To secure their power, the new legislators instituted loyalty oaths, which excluded most Quakers and many members of some other religious groups from voting, but they liberalized voting requirements for immigrants and vastly expanded representation of the western counties in the state legislature. By 1779 western representatives held more seats in the new unicameral legislature than eastern ones.[4]

While the Irish in Pennsylvania, led by Ulster Scots, had to pull down an old elite and smash an old order to accomplish their revolution, the Irish in Virginia joined with the colony's planter aristocrats to break the colony's bonds with Britain. Committees of Correspondence spread quickly and easily across Virginia after 1774, eventually sprouting in every county. During the war, the House of Burgesses also solidified backcountry support by commuting taxes there during trying economic times.[5]

There was no such broad backing for the revolutionary cause in the Carolinas. Indeed, the two new states were so consumed with fratricidal violence during the Revolution that historians have called the war in the Carolinas an "uncivil War." Most of the leaders of the Revolution in North Carolina were from the coast, and westerners had little love for them. North Carolina's Moravians noted in their annals that many former Regulator rebels were reluctant to join this new rebellion, "afraid of hurting themselves again, for the burned child dreads the fire." When a British army invaded the state late in the war, however, its heavy-handed attempts to crush the rebel cause enraged many people in the backcountry. Ulster Scots thus made up a substantial part of the American forces at the battle of Hanging Rock and probably most of the American troops in the later American victory at Kings Mountain. Loyalties in South Carolina, too, were murky and even more complex than in its northern neighbor. The province seemed a "patchwork" of conflicting and often changing loyalties. Presbyterians and Baptists were divided. The British thought the backcountry was Loyalist, but most leaders of South Carolina's very different Regulation, including Irish immigrants like Patrick Calhoun, backed the Revolution. Many recent Irish immigrants in the colony, however, were reluctant to take the risk of disloyalty, and joined the Tories.[6]

In Ireland, most Ulster Presbyterians shared the enthusiasm of John Caldwell, his nurse, and his neighbors for the American Revolution, but the responses of the island's other religious groups were more varied. Like young Caldwell, many Ulster Presbyterians had kin among the revolutionaries, but long nursing their own grievances against an established church and their exclusion from politics and power, they were also inspired by the Americans' ideals. Perhaps surprisingly, however, many members of Ireland's small Catholic elite backed the king. They believed that Catholic loyalty during this crisis would convince the British government to force Ireland's parliament to repeal its Penal Laws. (It may have also been their influence that convinced some Irish Catholics in Pennsylvania to join the Tories.) The empire desperately needed soldiers now, even Catholic ones, as well as good diplomatic relations with potential Catholic allies, like Austria. In 1778, the British government did, in fact, compel a reluctant Irish parliament to revoke the Penal Law ban on Catholics buying land or taking long leases. Some poorer Irish Catholics, however, cheered the Revolution in America, but mostly because they hoped that it would prompt the Catholic monarchs of France and Spain, America's allies in this war, to bring the Jacobite Catholic king and old Catholic lords back to Ireland.[7]

Ireland would have its own revolutionary movement, committed like the one in America to the creation of an independent republic and nonsectarian in its aims, though tragically not always in its execution. Political reform flourished in Ireland during the American Revolution, but it petered out after the Revolutionary War ended as Britain became less vulnerable to Irish protests. The eruption of revolution in France helped revive it, however, and in the fall of 1791, the partisans of this reborn reform movement created a new organization, the United Irishmen. The combination of France's example and repression by a British government soon at war with the new French Republic quickly pushed the United Irishmen beyond reform to revolution.[8]

Made up largely of a sprinkling of liberal gentry with urban merchants, professionals, and artisans, the United Irishmen had to broaden and deepen their support to fulfill their new revolutionary ambitions. They thus built a "remarkable propaganda machine" of newspapers, pamphlets, broadsides, and chapbooks and mounted mass demonstrations, proclaiming the "poor man" is

Figure 4. *Chromolithograph of Wolfe Tone.* Tone was a leader of the United Irishmen and a powerful voice for a nonsectarian, independent Ireland. Chromolithograph produced by the Irish Store, n.d., The Catholic University of America Special Collections (ACUA), Washington, D.C.

as "useful" as "the rich" and aiming "to persuade the people of the irresistible force of numbers." They were, however, also a Protestant organization in an overwhelmingly Catholic country. They recognized that the reform efforts of the early 1780s had suffered from a failure to include Catholics. They realized as well that if they excluded them now, Britain might offer Catholics enough concessions—like the ones it had made in 1778—to tie Ireland's Catholics to the empire and doom any Irish uprising. Protestant United Irishmen were also convinced (or convinced themselves) that the French Revolution had proved Catholicism's weakness and that further prejudice against the Catholic Church in Ireland would only help keep it alive. Thus, as Wolfe Tone, who actively fought for Catholic inclusion in the organization, proclaimed: the United Irishmen must "abolish the memory of all past dissension, and . . . substitute the common name Irishmen, in place of the denominations of Protestant, Catholic, dissenter."[9]

The United Irishmen originated in the eastern provinces of Ulster and Leinster and would remain strongest there. In East Ulster, their principal stronghold, many of them were members of the prosperous Presbyterian middle classes, who were inspired by New Light ideas of free conscience and frustrated by a corrupt aristocratic political system that denied them participation. The American Revolution, the fall of the French king, and prophecies of a new world being born, however, had roused the more middling and rural Presbyterian Old Lights, too. They were the people of the covenant, who now called themselves "the people," the United Irishmen's "true democrats." Since there were few Catholics in East Ulster, Presbyterians there did not compete with Catholics for land or in the linen markets, as they and other Protestants did in other parts of Ulster or in the rest of Ireland. The United Irishmen there were, therefore, more open—for the moment at least—to allying with Catholics than Protestants were elsewhere. They even found allies in a Catholic secret society, called the Defenders, which had emerged out of ferociously bloody sectarian rivalries in County Armagh but was heavily influenced by the French Revolution's egalitarianism. Over time, however, the United Irishmen would become popular in parts of western and southern Ulster as well as the eastern part of the province. The movement also flourished in Leinster, particularly in Dublin, but in County Wexford to the south as well. In Leinster as in Ulster most of its members were Protestants, but Catholics played an important role in Wexford's United Irishmen. Most of them were English speakers, many were literate, and thousands of them had been involved in a bitter local battle for Catholic rights in the early 1790s. The United Irishmen had trouble, however, gaining any traction in the poorer, illiterate, heavily Catholic western provinces of Connaught and Munster, where they confronted the Catholic Church's adamant opposition to their radical movement.[10]

Nevertheless, by early 1797, the United Irishmen were riding high throughout eastern Ireland and poised for rebellion. Government forces beat them to the punch, rampaging through Ulster and smothering the United Irish in Dublin, leaving the organizations in both places in tatters. The United Irish rose, nonetheless, in Ulster and Wexford in the spring and summer of 1798 only to be crushed. It was a brutal war, as the government committed atrocities against Catholics in the north and Catholics and Protestants committed them against each other in Wexford. Munster would remain quiet. In Connaught, some rebels joined an unexpected French invasion at the end of the summer, but that forlorn venture was run down and broken by a British army. The rebellion was over at a cost of at least 10,000 dead, probably more.[11]

In 1803, twenty-five-year-old Robert Emmet led an uprising in Dublin aimed at seizing Dublin Castle. His rebellion was a fiasco, but young Emmet's eloquence at his trial would make him a hero beloved in Ireland and as much or more in Irish America. By the time Emmet was executed, however, an Act of Union in 1800 had already made Ireland part of a United Kingdom ruled not only by one king but by only one parliament sitting in London.[12]

While Ireland noisily rattled and thundered with debate and bloodshed as it tilted toward rebellion, the silent demographic and economic revolutions begun there earlier in the eighteenth century were gaining momentum. Ireland's population continued to grow from about four million people in 1791 to approximately six and a half million by 1815. Prices for Irish agricultural products doubled, forced up by wartime Britain's need for Irish grains and other foodstuffs to feed its own and allies' armed forces in its two decades of war with revolutionary and later Napoleonic France. As before the wars, the resulting expansion of labor-intensive tillage created new opportunities for work that helped power the sustained population growth. The rise of the textile industry had been critical to Ireland's mid-eighteenth-century economic surge, and during the war, linen spinning and even weaving had begun to spread into southern parts of Ulster, as well as bordering counties in Connaught and Leinster and even further south into Kerry and Cork. Wives and daughters of farmers or even farm laborers outside of Ulster now found that they too could earn precious cash by spinning and selling linen yarn, which also contributed to population growth. The area where population grew fastest in Ireland during the wars, however, remained the rocky coasts or rugged hills of the west. There tenants of communal farms continued to mix intense potato cultivation for food while employing various means, from raising young livestock to selling illegal liquor, to pay their rents.[13]

Ireland prospered then and its population grew, but many, probably most,

Irish people did not profit much from this "golden age." Laborers and small and middling farmers on short leases often suffered from war-inflated prices and rising rents and taxes. Thus, like the Whiteboys or Hearts of Steel before them, rural secret societies, like the shotgun-wielding Shanavests in Tipperary, emerged in the early 1800s and fought increasingly bloody battles to maintain local control of labor markets and gain some leverage in the changing economy.[14]

Bloodied and battered, but unevenly prosperous, revolutionary Ireland would send thousands of immigrants, including a stellar roster of republican heroes, to the United States. This migration began with a rush at the end of the American Revolution in 1783, remained strong through the 1780s, fell off after Britain's war with France erupted in 1792 and declined even more after 1802, when war between France and Britain resumed with new intensity until Napoleon's fall in 1815. In all, perhaps about 150,000 Irish men and women went to the United States between 1783 and 1815, and they constituted about three-fifths of all immigrants to America in those years.[15]

Most of the immigrants came, as they always had, from Ulster, as that province's migration machine kicked back into gear almost immediately after the end of Britain's war with its colonies. Between the end of the American Revolution and 1812, 90 percent of the Irish arriving in America came on ships leaving from Ulster ports and, by one estimate, up to 1798, half left from the port of Londonderry alone. Immigrant chains of relatives first forged before the Revolution were now revived and new ones created after it ended. As before, the emigrant trade remained "undernetworked" and much more "casual" in southern Ireland.[16]

If the immigrants were from the same part of Ireland as before, they were on the whole better off than the colonial-era Irish immigrants. Britain had tried to continue to dump convicts in the new nation immediately after the Revolution, but Americans warned them off. More significantly, for economic and ideological reasons indentured servitude had begun to disappear in America, and thus indentured servants among the immigrants did as well: they made up less than 10 percent of the Irish arriving between 1776 and 1809. Most immigrants came as parts of families. The fathers in such families had usually been farmers or skilled workers, most often weavers, in Ireland—hardly rich but not desperately poor, as they were fleeing a robust economy not an economic disaster. Nevertheless, many were frustrated by the high taxes and rents of the wartime economy. For this generation of Irish immigrants as much as any before or after, however, it was America's pull as much as Ireland's push that seemed to compel them to emigrate. John Chambers wrote home to his family in County Antrim in Ulster from America in 1796: "Here we have peace and plenty . . . Dear Mother and Brothers come . . . Wait for nobody." Even many ordinary immigrants were also attracted by the political promise of America as well as its abundance. In 1810, immigrants sending letters back to Ulster marveled that "they could speak as man to man [and were] not obliged to uncover the head or bend the knee to any stern Lord." Since most were from Ulster, it seems likely that many had participated in the United Irish movement, even if only as foot soldiers, or knew people that did, but a host of radical Irish leaders also went to the United States in this period, including Mathew Carey, Thomas Addis Emmet, and William James MacNeven, as well as some Irish-born like John Binns, who had participated in Britain's radical politics.[17]

Many of the newcomers flocked to the growing metropolises of New York, booming after the Revolution, and Philadelphia, itself flourishing, if now a step behind its northern rival. By the 1790s, Irish immigrants, combined with the American-born of Irish ancestry, made up as much as one-quarter to one-third of the populations of both big eastern cities. Their numbers included most of the exiled Irish political leaders and the immigrant merchants on the make, but also substantial numbers of artisans and the poor. In Philadelphia in this period an estimated 10 to 15 percent of the city's white population was both poor and Irish.[18]

America's big seaport cities were growing faster than the nation at large, but the United States was still an overwhelmingly rural nation at the turn of the nineteenth century and most Ulster Scots and other Irish would continue to seek their fortunes in the country. As before the Revolution, they went west to find land—the best means, they still believed, to gain some autonomy and independence in a market economy. An estimated three-quarters of the Irish immigrants who landed in Philadelphia between 1805 and 1808 moved on to farmlands, some to nearby tenancies, but many more further west. Perhaps as many as one-third of Pennsylvania's western counties and about a quarter of the populations in the new states of Kentucky and Tennessee were Ulster Scot or native Irish in the 1790s, and by the early nineteenth century they were already spilling over into the even newer state of Ohio.[19]

If the war with Britain ended in 1783, political battles among Americans about the meaning of their Revolution did not. Irish Americans would participate enthusiastically in these battles, but importantly they also became the subjects of some of these disputes. Their fitness to participate in the politics of the new republic and their loyalties to it and even Ireland and the righteousness of its rebellion became hotly contested issues in American partisan political wrangles in the first few decades after the Revolution. Significantly, too, neither their friends nor their enemies—usually—made religious distinctions in their praise or abuse of them in these controversies but called both Irish Catholics and Protestants simply Irish or Irish Americans, thus reinforcing the nonsectarian Irish American identity born just before and during the Revolution. The fact that both Catholic and Protestant Irish eventually landed in the same political party strengthened that identity as well.

The first big postwar political fight would be over remaking the national government through a new federal constitution in 1787. Wealthy international merchants in big cities were nearly unanimous in support of the new constitution, but urban artisans also backed it, hoping that a strong central government would protect American manufactures from British competitors. Most back-country settlers, Irish and otherwise, remained suspicious of both a strong federal government and their eastern fellow citizens, however. Since Ulster Scots were overrepresented in the west, they were notably numerous among the opponents of the new constitution, but even in eastern Pennsylvania many Ulster Scots also voted against its ratification.[20]

The struggle over the meaning of the Revolution, however, had only just begun. Americans began this political era with a real fear of the dangers of political parties and factions in a republic, but political parties, if loosely organized by later standards, did emerge in the 1790s: the Federalists and their opponents, the Democratic-Republicans. Irish and other voters in these parties divided over many issues, but at its heart, the battle between Federalists and Democratic-Republicans was a fight over the roles of elites and "the people" in the new republic. The Federalists wanted to be "recognized as the rightful rulers of society," because their wealth, social standing, and especially their education gave them the knowledge, authority, and above all the broad disinterested perspective necessary to govern. The Democratic-Republicans, in contrast, believed that they—not only poor farmers or workers, but also shopkeepers, middling merchants, and manufacturers—had fought the revolution to earn the right to govern themselves. They constantly derided the Federalists as would-be aristocrats, puffed-up phonies "whose claims of disinterested superiority had no basis in reality." For many Irish people, but especially Presbyterians and Catholics, this partisan contest was another battle in an old war over the legitimacy of elites that both of them had already been waging in Ireland.[21]

In the west, specifically in western Pennsylvania, the political battle erupted in a rebellion over what might now seem a trivial issue: the federal government's imposition of a tax on whiskey. Westerners consumed whiskey in great quantities, but it was also an essential means of barter: it "assumed the place of money." In western Pennsylvania, bands of men, the friends of "Tom the Tinker," faces blackened or hidden by kerchiefs, attacked the excise men who tried to collect the tax and those who helped them. Opponents of the tax even established local Committees of Correspondence, imitating Revolutionary bodies of the same name. After President George Washington and his Secretary of the Treasury, Alexander Hamilton, began mobilizing an army of 13,000 men to subdue them, many of the protesters gave up, but Washington sent troops into the Pennsylvania backcountry anyway and the rebellion dissolved.[22]

There is no way to know for sure how "Irish" this protest was, but newspaper reports and other commentary suggest that the Irish, mostly Ulster Scots and their descendants but Irish Catholics as well, played an important role in it. Illicit distilling, of course, was also common in Ireland, particularly in western Ulster, and a judge in Pennsylvania observed: "many now in the country talk of their having seen the riots against the excise in Ireland . . . this country in great measure settled from Ireland." The *Pennsylvania Gazetteer* later mocked the movement, invoking old stereotypes of the drunken Irish fighting "in defense of their beloved bottle."[23]

The failure of the Whiskey Rebellion did not end the resistance of the Ulster Scots and other Irish to the Federalists in western Pennsylvania or throughout much of the rest of the backcountry. Democratic-Republican societies, enlisting many Irish, had already appeared before the Whiskey Rebellion from Kentucky and South Carolina to western Pennsylvania, where one, inspired by the United Irishmen, called itself the United Freemen. Support for the Democratic-Republicans was not universal in the west, however. The Federalist Party flourished, for example, in the Shenandoah Valley among Ulster Scot farmers, who profited from a thriving international export trade in wheat.[24]

Nevertheless, to friends and foes alike, the backcountry already seemed the nursery of democracy and Irish immigrants the iconic democrats. In 1792, Hugh Henry Brackenridge, nominally a moderate Democratic-Republican but a graduate of the College of New Jersey with a Federalist sensibility, began publishing a series of fictional political satires mocking the rapid democratization of American politics. The satires were later republished as the novel *Modern Chivalry*. The hero of the tale was a Captain Farrago, but the central character was Teague O'Regan, his servant, a takeoff on "stage Irish" stereotypes long popular in English theaters by then. Brackenridge wrote that O'Regan's very name "imports what he was," but, as in most political stereotyping of the Irish in this era, he did not identify him as Catholic. In Brackenridge's version of the topsy-turvy world of the new republic's backwoods, the blundering, ignorant O'Regan was wildly successful, even invited by adoring backcountry residents to run for Congress. His supporters (which included many of his Irish countrymen, Brackenridge noted) contended that "This young man may be [a] servant; but it is better to trust a plain man like him than one of your highflyers that will make laws to serve their own purpose."[25]

There would be bitter political battles in the cities as well. Immediately after the passage of the constitution, Federalists ruled in Philadelphia and New York, and wealthy international merchants, including Irish Catholics like Don Juan Stoughton and Dominick Lynch in New York and Thomas Fitzsimons in Philadelphia, were among their leaders. Indeed, Fitzsimons, born in Ireland, would become the head of the Federalist junto which dominated Philadelphia's politics as well as the city's congressman. As it became clear to urban artisans and small traders that there was little in the Federalist economic program to help them, however, the Democratic-Republicans began to emerge as potent rivals. Democratic-Republican clubs began to appear in Philadelphia by 1793, and even Thomas Jefferson took notice of how many of their members were Irish. A year later, Irish and other voters in Philadelphia's working-class districts voted against Fitzsimons, ousting him from his congressional seat. By now, Great Britain was at war with the new republic in France, and the battles between Federalists and Democratic-Republicans took on an international dimension: the Federalists backed Britain while the Democratic-Republicans supported France. At one of many Democratic-Republican rallies in Philadelphia protesting Jay's treaty, a conciliatory Federalist agreement with the British, Derry-born Blair McClenachan threw a copy of the treaty from the stage into the crowd, shouting, "Kick this damned treaty to hell."[26]

In the mid-1790s, as the British began to crack down on the United Irishmen as well as republicans in England, those Irish and other radicals began pouring into the United States. Many were experienced political operatives, pamphleteers, or journalists and were quickly hired by the Democratic-Republicans, who hoped the exiles' aggressive "rabble rousing" would convince the voters "to throw off their traditional passivity and deference" to social betters like the Federalists. Irish and other radical exiles thus wound up editing no less than seventeen newspapers in the United States during this era. William Duane, the American-born son of Irish immigrant parents, had run radical newspapers in Britain and India before becoming editor and eventually publisher of Philadelphia's *Aurora,* one of the most important Democratic-Republican papers in America. Duane was an uncompromising democrat—"Experience proves that there is no check—there can be none, but the people"—and even took on the revered Federalist George Washington, whom he denounced as an "ardent" defender of the "privileged orders."[27]

As Irish and other radicals began to enter the United States, however, American relations with France were deteriorating rapidly, drifting into a quasi-war of harassment on the seas and raising the specter of real war between the two republics. When the United Irishmen rose in rebellion in Ireland with French help, Federalists jumped to link Irish republicans in America to the United Irish rebels and to their French revolutionary allies and heaped a torrent of abuse on the Irish exiles. Federalist Senator Uriah Tracy of Connecticut condemned them as "the most God-provoking democrats on this side of hell." His Federalist colleague from Massachusetts, Senator Harrison Gray Otis, complained of "hordes of wild Irish" flooding America, and the acerbic Federalist newspaper editor John Ward Fenno wrote darkly of the "vagabonds and renegades of Ireland . . . outlaws, assassins, traitors" infesting Philadelphia. Importantly, as noted earlier, they only rarely hinted at distinctions between Protestants and Catholics, and most often did not distinguish between the two: all Irish were dangerous radicals. Democratic-Republican papers edited by Irish immigrants responded to these critics by attacking the British empire as the real root of Ireland's and indeed much of the world's troubles. John Adams and his Federalists, playing on the war scare with France, managed to push legislation through the Congress aimed at immigrants but especially Irish ones, making it easy for the federal government to deport aliens, and extending the residency period required for citizenship from five to fourteen years.[28]

When Adams later backed down from war with France, however, his party split into hostile factions, tensions with France eased, and the Democratic-Republicans rebounded stronger than ever. America's Bishop John Carroll and Catholic clerics were incensed by the French Revolution's assault on the Church in France, and some priests worked hard to try and hold the laity to the Federalists. Meanwhile some pro-Federalist Irish Presbyterian ministers condemned the Democratic-Republican party as a nest of papists and sought to pry Ulster Presbyterians out of it as well, insisting that they distinguish themselves from Irish Catholics by calling themselves not Irish, but Scotch-Irish. Both these Catholic and conservative Presbyterian clerical efforts failed. In Philadelphia, a stunning 870 Irish immigrants were naturalized in 1798 and 1799 alone. That was six times the number of Irish who had been naturalized between 1789 and 1797 and equivalent to over half of Philadelphia's vote for Jefferson in the presidential election of 1796. In these registration drives, the Democratic-Republicans often relied on the help of networks of Irish immigrant workingmen, such as the soap boiler Neil McGinnis, who sponsored thirteen of the new Irish citizens. Meanwhile, by 1800, New York City Democratic-Republican leaders were boasting that they had registered more than 2,000 Irish, including both Presbyterians and Catholics. In 1799, the Democratic-Republicans elected Thomas McKean, second-generation Irish, a leader of the independence movement in 1776, and former president of Philadelphia's Hibernian Society, governor of Pennsylvania. A year later Jefferson carried both New York and Philadelphia in his election as president, and George Clinton, the son of Presbyterian immigrants from Longford and nicknamed the "Old Irishman," was elected governor of New York.[29]

After the Democratic triumph in 1800, however, Irish American politics in the two cities became more complicated. Democratic-Republicans in both Philadelphia and New York broke into factions, with Irish Americans taking different sides. The Irish in New York City would find new leaders in famous United Irish exiles Thomas Addis Emmet, William James MacNeven, and William Sampson, who landed in the city in successive years, 1804, 1805, and 1806. The instant success of these United Irish heroes, like that of so many United Irish journalists, reflected the importance of transnational republican influences on Irish American politics in the early republic. As Emmet later claimed, it was his international reputation as a republican hero that "procured for me the effective friendship of the leading characters of this state [New York] and the union at large."[30]

Nevertheless, Irish American politics was already pointing to its future, when it would not be the international prestige of its leaders but its embodiment of democratic egalitarianism that would be the key to its success. Just as Brackenridge made the fictional Teague O'Regan the fearful specter of the new democratic politics in the country, so Irish American workers became real-life emblematic heroes of Democratic-Republicans' egalitarianism in the city. In November 1795, two recent Irish immigrants Thomas Burk and Timothy Crady, working the ferry connecting Brooklyn to Manhattan, refused the demand of an impatient Federalist alderman, Gabriel Furman, to leave early for Manhattan. Furman bullied the ferry's owner into forcing the ferrymen to depart immediately, but he was still furious with the two Irish men. Crady, smarting from Furman's insults, retorted that he and Burk "were as good as any buggers," and he would use his boat hook on anyone who tried to arrest him. When they reached Manhattan, however, Furman had the two ferrymen arrested and whipped them with his cane. His Federalist colleague, Mayor Richard Varick, then sentenced both to two months' hard labor. Their case went unnoticed until a young Democratic-Republican lawyer named William Keteltas wrote about them in the press, recognizing the power of the image of two Irish American workingmen abused by a Federalist aristocrat and making them iconic victims of aristocratic oppression. When Keteltas himself was sent to jail for insulting the legislature, thousands of Democratic-Republicans protested, some carrying a "large picture of a man being whipped, above which was an inscription, 'what you rascal, insult your superiors?'"[31]

Yet Irish Americans' participation in the Democratic-Republican triumph and their emerging symbolic importance as iconic images of the white workingman had some disturbing consequences for their relations with African Americans. Most obviously, they had committed to a party that would be dominated by southern slaveholders. It was an alliance that Irish Americans would convince themselves they needed to fend off Federalist and later Whig and Republican enemies. Because many Federalists were also more critical of slavery, however, and more sympathetic to Black rights, Democratic-Republican papers spun scenarios that suggested that Irish Americans, now the very embodiment of the white common man, were locked in a zero-sum battle with African Americans over rights. Such depictions implied that Irish Americans would lose their rights if Blacks gained theirs, and the agents of that reversal of status would be Federalist aristocratic elites. In the 1810s, for example, Democratic-Republican newspapers in New York complained that Federalist judges were letting African Americans vote without checking their manumission papers, while meticulously scrutinizing and rejecting Irishmen's naturalization records.[32]

Changes in American religion in the revolutionary aftermath were also important to Irish Americans, both Catholics and Protestants. The reconciliation of Catholic and Protestant in Ireland had ultimately foundered in brutal sectarian violence during and after the '98 rebellion. Many of the United Irish exiles who came to America, like Emmet, MacNeven and Sampson, however, were determined that such religious fratricide would not divide the Irish here. Catholic-Protestant reconciliation among Irishmen in America had begun well before the arrival of United Irish exiles in the United States. It started in Pennsylvania, but it became part of a much broader movement for religious freedom in America, stoked by the First Great Awakening but blossoming during the Revolution and its aftermath.[33]

In this atmosphere of soft religious loyalties and growing tolerance, Irish American Catholics began to tentatively emerge from the shadows throughout the new nation. After being so long suppressed, however, they could only count about 25,000 adherents in 1790, many, but by no means all, Irish born or of Irish ancestry. Catholic numbers would quadruple to about 100,000 by 1815, though, even then, they remained a tiny sliver of the American population. Some of those new Irish Catholics were recent arrivals in America, but others were pre-Revolutionary immigrants, who had been born Catholic in Ireland but remained unchurched or worshiped in Protestant churches in America for years, before returning to the newly open Catholic Church.[34]

The revival of Catholicism among the Irish in Lincoln County along the coast of Maine illustrates how this could happen. Irish migrants of Catholic background to the county in the eighteenth century had been largely men, drifting down from Newfoundland or up from Boston. Most had married Protestant women before the Revolution, when Catholicism was proscribed. Even after it they had usually worshiped in Protestant churches (if they worshiped at all) because of the lack of Catholic churches or priests. In 1798, however, two Irish Catholic immigrants, James Kavanagh and Matthew Cottrill, who had established themselves as successful merchants and manufacturers in the county, drew on their employees to form a Roman Catholic society. They convinced a priest, Jean Cheverus, to come up from Boston occasionally to serve it; and later built a church, St. Patrick's. This congregation of Irish Catholic men and their Protestant wives, rebaptized as Catholics, flourished under lay leadership until 1821, when its first resident pastor was appointed. Indeed, by that year, it boasted over five hundred parishioners, or one-seventh of the known Catholics in all of New England.[35]

American Catholic leaders understood very well their vulnerability should toleration of them in a fundamentally Protestant country suddenly disappear. Anti-Catholicism was more muted and less political in the Revolutionary era than it would become later, but it had hardly disappeared then. Because of this strategic necessity, but also taking advantage of a weakened papacy in a revolutionary age and drawing on enlightenment-inspired trends in Catholic theology, the first Catholic bishop in America, John Carroll, cultivated a special kind of Catholicism in the new republic. As bishop, he served on the boards of several nonsectarian institutions in Baltimore, shrugged at mixed marriages between Catholics and Protestants, dismissed the "pomp and shew" of elaborate liturgies and processions, and, deviating from Catholic doctrine, praised the separation of church and state that prevailed in the United States.[36]

Irish American Presbyterians would be affected by the changes of the Revolutionary era too, but it would have an entirely different impact on them. They had lost many Ulster Scot adherents to other sects in the South during the First Great Awakening before the Revolution; now, in the Second Awakening, which began in the late 1790s, they continued to hemorrhage members. Even more than the First Awakening, the revivals of the second seemed to emphasize individual conversion over doctrinal orthodoxy and an inspired clergy over an educated one, chronic problems for Presbyterians in America. Thus, while the number of Presbyterian church members in the South grew two and a half times from 16,000 in 1776 to 40,000 in 1803, white Methodist numbers rose over twenty-five-fold to 107,000 and Baptists nearly sixfold to nearly 91,000 whites in the same period.[37]

There would be a revolution in Irish American social life as well. The organization of the Friendly Sons of St. Patrick in Philadelphia before the Revolution proved to be the precedent for an explosion of Irish societies and clubs after it. Wealthy Irish Americans in New York founded their own Friendly Sons after the Revolution, and successful Irish Americans would create similar clubs in other cities thereafter: New York, Baltimore, Charleston, Savannah, Albany, Pittsburgh, and St. Louis. These Irish elites were exploiting new opportunities for recognition emerging out of the Revolution's turmoil, as the dominance of older elite groups collapsed, was contested, or, in newer cities, had not yet been firmly established in the first place.[38]

Yet Irish Americans of the "middling sort," shopkeepers and artisans, had learned from their participation in the Revolution and the subsequent democratization of politics that they too could organize and join with like-minded people to address important community needs or goals. New Irish societies, like the Hibernian Society for the Relief of Immigrants in Philadelphia, thus emerged to offer aid to recent Irish newcomers flooding America after the Revolution. By 1797, Irish Americans had even founded an American Society of the United Irishmen, an organization devoted to "the emancipation of Ireland from the tyranny" of the British government and the republican cause around the world.[39]

As historians have pointed out, however, even the banquets and dinners put on by almost all of these societies and clubs on St. Patrick's Day were not just simple occasions for male fellowship, but public acts too. If nothing else, the toasts and speeches at such events—often published in pamphlets or newspapers—publicly affirmed the members' Irish roots and allegiances. Over time, as many of the organizations became more political their toasts did too. In 1802, for example, St. Patrick's Day toasts by the Hibernian Provident Society of New York mourned the 1798 martyrs to "British tyranny," lambasted the "venal . . . Irish Parliament" for passing the Act of Union, praised the United States as an "asylum from oppression," and denounced the threat of "designing aristocrats" to America's Constitution.[40]

There were reasons, however, why Irish Americans in particular produced so many societies at this time. By the end of the eighteenth century, their numbers had grown enormously and included many more wealthy merchants, prosperous shopkeepers, and successful artisans than ever before. The new significance of ethnicity in a changing American political environment, however, was important too. The vituperative controversies in national American political discourse over rebellious Ireland and Irish American loyalties publicly defined them as an ethnic people. Radical Irish exiles were not only critical contributors to those debates but themselves the subjects of them, and they would also play important roles in the new societies in several cities.

The emergence of these clubs marked a critical moment in Irish American history. They were the first tangible, public embodiments of an Irish American identity. Importantly, however, they differed from later Irish American organizations because almost all of them, like Philadelphia's Friendly Sons, were nonsectarian manifestations of the common identity of a people of a distinctive national origin but of different faiths.

In 1812, the United States would engage in a second war with Britain, electrifying Irish Americans and, momentarily, overriding most of their internal political squabbles. Thomas O'Connor, direct descendant of Ireland's last high king, former United Irishman, and editor of the *Shamrock* newspaper in New York, saw this war as a chance to gain revenge against the British. For most Irish Americans, however, the war also offered a chance to demonstrate their allegiance to their new republic. Indeed, it raised that question directly for Irish immigrant soldiers. The British government insisted that they were still subjects of the king, even if they had become naturalized citizens of the United States. British forces, therefore, shipped twenty-three Irish-born American prisoners back to England and threatened to execute them for "treason." Despite that danger, Irish immigrants made up most of America's foreign-born soldiers.[41]

On January 8, 1815, just outside New Orleans, Louisiana, American forces under Andrew Jackson, the American-born son of Ulster immigrants, slaughtered a British expeditionary force, led by Sir Edward Pakenham, a member of the County Roscommon gentry and brother-in-law of the duke of Wellington. The Battle of New Orleans was a postscript to a war that was already over (the peace treaty ending the War of 1812 had been signed in Belgium on Christmas Eve, 1814), but a glorious end to an Irish American–backed conflict that had been a muddle for nearly three years. About six months later Wellington would defeat Napoleon Bonaparte at Waterloo. Jackson's victory over the British at New Orleans would help make him the iconic figure of American politics over the next few decades and a hero to most Irish Americans. Waterloo would close a quarter of a century of European wars but in the process end Ireland's long eighteenth century of prosperity as well, provoking a mass migration to America, which would dwarf any previous Irish flight there.[42]

4. Irish America in Transition

1815–1845

In early April 1834, a mob of Irish American Democrats gathered outside the home of William James MacNeven bombarding it with boos, hisses, and catcalls. MacNeven, a distinguished doctor and scientist, and his Protestant friends William Sampson and Thomas Addis Emmet, United Irish heroes all, had ruled over New York City's Irish community for decades, a living triptych of the nonsectarian, passionately republican Irish America of the revolutionary era. In 1834, however, both MacNeven and Sampson had condemned President Andrew Jackson's assault on the Bank of the United States. Most of the crowd outside MacNeven's house were Irish and Catholics like him but were recent immigrants to America. The bulk of them had been farmers with small tenancies in Ireland or their sons or daughters, but they also included laborers, servants, and a few artisans. All had left an Ireland now troubled by economic stagnation and divided by an increasingly sectarian politics. To them Jackson was the new tribune of the common man, a warrior in the "contest between the aristocracy and the people," and the bank a nest of aristocratic and foreign corruption. They were at MacNeven's door to denounce him as a traitor—some even claimed he had been bribed by English gold. They would soon take out their vengeance on Sampson as well and, as Emmet had already died, the old United Irish troika's rule in New York was over. Indeed, across the country, not just its leaders but the older revolutionary, nonsectarian Irish America was fading fast.[1]

Yet if the nonsectarian Irish America was disappearing, it was not just because of these Catholic newcomers. Most Irish Protestants in America seemed at best ambivalent about an Irish identity now; indeed, in some cities growing numbers of them were becoming increasingly hostile to Catholics. Irish Protestant estrangement from their Irish Catholic ethnic fellows would be a slow and complicated process: Jackson was a hero to most of them as well as to those recent Catholic immigrants. Nevertheless, by 1815, perhaps even sooner, few Protestants in Ireland, even Presbyterians, seemed as enamored of Irish nationalism as many had once been in the 1790s. Protestant Irish immigrants to the United States by then were also no longer denounced as dangerous threats to the republic as they had been earlier. Thus as Protestant Irish, heavily Presbyterians as before, migrated to the United States in the tens of thousands from 1815 through the 1830s, they seemed to slip into the country unnoticed and, indeed, have remained largely ignored by historians to this day.

Meanwhile, a new, Catholic Irish America began to emerge as the old nonsectarian one dissolved. The new Catholic Irish immigrants found their own leaders, none more important and visible than the steely bishop of New York, John Hughes, who boldly defended and advanced the interests of the Catholic Church in New York and America. Yet they also confronted new, daunting challenges, like the increasing significance of race, rising class conflict, and a resurgence of anti-Catholic nativism in America. Even with Hughes' swagger and the growing waves of Catholic immigrants from Ireland, their community remained weak and fragile: their numbers were still too small, their people too new to America, too poor, too restlessly moving about the country searching for work, and their communities too wracked by old country regional rivalries or class conflicts to command much respect or build sturdy institutions and thriving organizations.

They could not know then the cruel irony that a famine in Ireland would ultimately bring enormous numbers of Irish Catholics to America, creating significant problems for their community but also new strength. Until that time this new Catholic Irish America would be a community in transition.[2]

In the 1830s a close observer of Ireland's economy looked back on the island's last half century of boom and bust and sighed: "It would [have been] better for the Irish farmer if Buonaparte had never lived . . . or died." If Napoleon never lived, there would have been no French wars with Britain pumping up Ireland's prosperity and population; if he never died (or as it happened was defeated and imprisoned), the wars and Irish prosperity might have never ended.[3]

Yet in 1815, he was, for all intents and purposes, "dead," and Ireland's wartime boom fell with a resounding crash. Between 1812 and 1816, the average prices of wheat at the Dublin market fell by nearly 40 percent, shakily rebounded for a few years, and then crashed again. Beef, pork, and mutton prices fell too. Paradoxically, however, the *value* of Irish agricultural exports to Britain would begin to rise, even as those *prices* remained low, because the volume of the exports would grow over the next few decades. Yet Ireland's huge numbers of poor farmers and agricultural laborers, as we shall see, did not benefit much from this increasing trade. Meanwhile Irish manufacturing staggered as well. The island's fledgling cotton industry died after the war. Linen survived, but by the 1820s it was suffering from the competition of Britain's booming cotton industry. More important, it was going through a wrenching restructuring. By the 1820s, factories spinning linen began to emerge in East Ulster, which had a devastating effect on women hand spinners, reducing the profits on their yarn to a pittance and cutting deep into peasant family incomes in the north and other parts of the island. In the 1830s, between 50,000 and 150,000 women gave up spinning linen yarn.[4]

In 1833, the government created a commission to investigate imposing a new "Poor Law" on Ireland. The new commission asked local notables from parishes all over Ireland whether "the general condition of the poorer classes in your parish [the government subdivision] has improved or deteriorated or [remained] stationary since the peace in the year 1815?" Of 1,394 of those witnesses answering only 324 thought the lives of the poor had improved and 318 believed they had stayed the same, but 752 testified that the condition of the poor in their parishes had deteriorated, with comments like "considerably worse," or "poverty increasing." These witnesses pointed to the fall in the price of grains and cereals, declining wages, and other causes, but more blamed the "decline," "end," or "extinction" of linen spinning—women's work—in their local parishes.[5]

These economic troubles after Napoleon's death fell on an already huge population—the curse left by his life of war and the prosperity those wars had bred in Ireland for two decades. Population growth did slow after 1815, but it did not stop, in part, because the Irish still had access to abundant food in the potato and cheap heat from turf. Their life expectancy was as high as the British and higher yet than almost all the peoples on the European continent. Military and prison records suggest that they were also taller than the English and the Scots. Nevertheless, historians estimate that about 40 percent, maybe even 50 percent of Ireland's more than eight million people were "poor" in 1840, and their share of national income, about 10 to 15 percent then, had probably shrunk over the pre-famine era. Ireland's poverty became notorious. Visiting writers and tourists marveled at the island's landscape but seemed fascinated by the exoticism of the country's desperately impoverished. Some compared them to African slaves in the Americas, though the visitors caught themselves before suggesting that any white people could possibly be inevitably condemned to such degradation as Blacks.[6]

Confronting difficult economic times, Irish peasants, as before, turned to violence to try to prevent them from getting worse. Such violence erupted often from the late 1810s to the early or mid-1830s, ranging from big movements, county- even province-wide, bearing a cacophony of names, the Rockites or Captain Rock, Whitefeet, or the Terry Alts (a deliberately complicated ironic joke), to ad hoc forays by a few peasants that flashed for an evening or two and then snuffed out. This "nightly" or "smothered" war raged worst in Munster, with its huge number of laborers and chronic fights over the conversion of tillage to pasture. Local instances of unrest, however, could and did break out elsewhere.[7]

Now as in the past, the strength of Irish secret societies lay in communal solidarity. For the big secret societies like the Rockites or even the smaller Terry Alts, such solidarity meant they could recruit up to thousands for demonstrations or even for attacks on the police. Yet even the smallest acts of violence depended on broad communal acquiescence to shield their participants from the law. Sectarian sentiments, often stoked by millenarian fantasies, occasionally threaded through secret society violence. Pastorini's Prophecy (drawn from a biblical commentary by an English Catholic bishop, Charles Walmesley, first published in England in his *The General History of the Christian Church* in 1771), for example, predicted that by 1825 the "hereticks" would be overthrown and Catholics would be restored to their rightful lands, power, and status. Catholic communities, however, were often divided: laborers' grievances might be with the local Catholic strong farmer who employed them or migrant laborers from another county who competed with them for work—not the distant Protestant landlord. Tenant farmers and laborers did have some interests in common as well, however, most notably the resentment of tithes charged to support the Church of Ireland. More generally, however, the vast majority of poor Irish shared a common desperation born of the chronically depressed economy and an absence of alternatives to address it. Breaking solidarity might unleash a competition in their scarce economy, which a few might win in the short run, but in the long run would ruin them all. Thus, taking up another man's job after he was let go or a fellow tenant's land after he was evicted was the worst offense a peasant could commit in his community.[8]

As before, the secret societies had no real ambition to overthrow the structure of the existing order, no program or plan to replace it; they were simply banding together, to fix the market, freeze the status quo, and slow down change. In that they may have been marginally successful in holding down rents or slowing the conversion of tillage land to pasture. They did, however, reinforce legacies for Irish and Irish Americans inherited from the earlier Whiteboys, nourishing egalitarian values and teaching lessons about the importance of numbers, community solidarity, and the uses of violence in economic and political competition.[9]

As secret societies' violent responses to the depressed economy raged in the 1820s, Daniel O'Connell, a superb lawyer and member of the west County Kerry Catholic gentry, took over the effort to repeal the last penal law, the ban on Catholics serving in parliament. In the process, his Catholic emancipation movement ignited a revolution in Irish political organization that would make Irish Catholics the most politicized peasantry in Europe. O'Connell realized that what he needed to do to break the impasse over emancipation was what the secret societies had already been doing: take full advantage of Irish Catholics' greatest political resources, numbers, and solidarity. He thus encouraged thousands of Irish peasants to give their pennies to a "Catholic rent," which not only helped fund the movement's national and local expenses but offered concrete proof of its mass support. Some Irish Catholics, whose rentals met certain criteria, had had the right to vote since 1793, but their landlords had controlled their votes with threats of eviction since then. In operations that would have made the later Tammany Hall proud, the local parish committees of O'Connell's Catholic Association identified potential voters for their side, tracked them closely to keep them in line, arranged work and support for those likely to be evicted, transported them to the polls, placed priests in the voting tents to ensure their loyalty, and provided "muscle" to protect them. After the Association managed to elect liberal Protestant candidates pledged to Catholic emancipation in five counties in 1826, and a smashing victory by O'Connell himself two years later in 1828 (in an election for a seat that he, as a Catholic, legally could not take if victorious), the government gave in and passed emancipation.[10]

The Irish Catholic conquering hero, O'Connell soon launched another crusade, a quest to repeal the Act of Union and restore the Irish parliament. In 1843, one and half million people—again numbers—turned out for his giant Repeal rallies, dubbed "Monster meetings," at towns and historical sites across southern Ireland, many marching to the meeting in parades with bands and elaborate floats. In creating a self-consciously Catholic mass politics, tied to the Catholic clergy and built on Catholic solidarity, O'Connell may have mobilized the Irish peasantry as never before, but he also helped to encourage the revitalization of the kind of sectarianism many United Irishmen had hoped to erase.[11]

He was not the only one to do so, however. A Church of Ireland evangelical revival, called the "Second Reformation," emerged just after the '98 rebellion and, with landlord assistance, engaged in aggressive evangelization among Catholics, especially in the Ulster borderlands. In many places in Ulster, Presbyterians, once the heart of the United Irish movement, had stood aside from the battles between members of the Church of Ireland and Catholics. As the rapidly changing economy was transforming Ulster from farmer/weavers into factory hands, however, many Presbyterian workers adjusted to a new industrial order by turning to a new kind of Presbyterian evangelicalism, which encouraged not political and social reform but strict personal discipline and self-improvement. This new evangelicalism, combined with the sobering effects of their '98 defeat, fear of awakening Catholic power, and a new appreciation for the benefits of the Union, seemed to draw more and more Presbyterians into Ireland's militantly Protestant coalition.[12]

Meanwhile, Catholics in Ireland were changing too. The Church suffered from a lack of priests well into the nineteenth century, and those it did have lacked discipline and were often obsessed with plots and intrigues against each other and their bishops. It may be no surprise, then, that only about 40 percent of the laity attended mass every Sunday, though the proportions were much smaller in the north and on the west coast. A "popular" religion of devotions rooted in Ireland's rural landscape of "holy well" shrines and "pattern days" (saints' days) festivals flourished outside the formal church's reach. Yet O'Connell's emancipation movement and the threat of the Protestant Second Reformation reinforced Catholic group loyalty, strengthened clerical authority, and stiffened a Catholic counterattack against Protestant evangelicals in a "Bible war," which erupted in debates, lectures, pamphlets, and newspaper articles in Ireland in the 1810s and 1820s. Irish Catholic culture, however, was also in flux. By the 1830s and 1840s, as publicly funded national schools emerged, literacy and numeracy (being able to understand and work with numbers) was rising among women as well as men, and the Irish language was continuing to decline. In 1838, Father Theobald Mathew also launched a temperance crusade, gaining pledges to refrain from alcohol from two and a half million Irish people over two years, most of them in Catholic Leinster and Munster.[13]

ꙅᕁᕜ

About 800,000 to one million people left Ireland for North America between
1815 and 1845. It is not hard to understand why so many Irish would want to
leave, given the island's hardships. Indeed, as many as left, historians have wondered why so many more stayed.[14]

The migration began with a rush in 1816 after the Irish economy plunged
and sea lanes opened to ocean traffic following the war. It slowed considerably
in the early 1820s, but between 1827 and 1836 over 341,000 Irish left for North
America. The depression of 1837 in the United States would bring it down
again, but only temporarily. By 1840, over 50,000 men and women were leaving
Ireland for North America, and by 1842, over 90,000.[15]

In the beginning most came from the north, though not from eastern
Ulster so much now, but from western and southern parts of the province, as
well as northern Leinster and Connaught, where the linen industry was in crisis,
but the migration machines that linen networks had helped build still endured.
Catholics numerous in such areas and involved in the linen industry joined
the emigrant flood. Beginning in 1825 and over the next half century or so, for
example, at least 148 people, the vast majority—but not all—Catholics, made
their way from Clogher and two adjoining parishes in Tyrone through migration
chains of friends and families to Providence, Rhode Island. Most were going to
textile jobs there, many in a single factory, Allen's mill, on the northwest side of
the city.[16]

The business of Irish immigration to America would change radically
over this era, however, with dramatic effects on the origins, numbers, transatlantic journeying experience, and destinations of Irish immigrants. Beginning in
the 1820s, Liverpool's share of the Irish immigration trade grew steadily until
the English city came to dominate it by the time of the famine. It did so because it had become the principal destination in Britain for the new booming
cotton trade with the American port of New York. As that trade grew, Liverpool's traders looked to Irish immigrants as profitable return cargo for the fleets
of New York cotton ships arriving in their harbor. To gain control of that immigrant trade and enhance it they hired hundreds of agents in Ireland to drum up
migration business. They also took advantage of the new steamship lines, which
now connected their port with Ireland to ferry the immigrants to Liverpool
quickly and cheaply. The Ulster ports' competitive advantage in the Irish immigrant trade, forged in the eighteenth century on the basis of linen connections

with America, thus now declined. Through preferential shipping regulations, however, the British empire kept it alive, by making passage from the Irish and other British ports to Canada cheap enough to attract about as many passengers to Canadian ports as to American ones for much of the period. By the 1840s, however, the volume of trade from Liverpool to New York had driven fares for passage to the United States so low that it eventually wiped out even those artificial Canadian advantages. The result of all this was that more and more people were coming from southern Ireland, meaning not only that Catholics would dominate Irish immigration to America by the 1830s but a higher proportion of immigrant men would be laborers, rising from about a quarter in the 1820s to three-fifths in the mid-1830s. Since young women in northern and southern Ireland were now without linen spinning work, increasingly likely to be literate and numerate, and confident that they could find service jobs in America, they left in greater numbers too.[17]

If the empire's manipulation of shipping laws succeeded in landing hundreds of thousands of Irish immigrants in Canada, over half, maybe more, did not stay there, but kept on going south to the United States. Canada's economy was growing modestly, while America's was exploding. Construction of turnpikes boomed in the United States, reaching a peak in the mid-1820s, and canal building reached its high point about the same time, expanding markets—a market revolution some historians have called it—and prompting enormous increases in agricultural and industrial production. Settlers rapidly filled up the rich farmlands in new western states like Ohio, Indiana, Illinois, and Alabama. Populations also shot up in the big coastal *entrepots* like New York, Philadelphia, and now New Orleans, as well as older, small cities like Providence, Rhode Island, once sleepy villages like Worcester, Massachusetts, and instant industrial towns like Lowell, Massachusetts.[18]

Changes in American politics, more specifically the emergence of a new kind of white democratic politics, once called Jacksonian democracy, would also be important to the new Irish immigrants. By 1840, the American republic was "unrivaled" by any contemporary or past government in the "breadth and intensity of its electoral process": White male suffrage had been expanding for decades, voter turnout was skyrocketing, and the trend to convert appointed offices to elected ones and shorten terms for all offices meant that "elections were going on all the time." Political parties were transformed, as the work of politics became labor intensive, requiring regiments of workers to canvass voters, bring

them to the polls, distribute ballots, monitor elections, and, because a masculine, martial "rough politics" became pervasive, battle partisan opponents in
the streets.[19]

This electoral revolution commenced about the same time as urbaniza-
tion took off in America and the two trends combined to lay the foundation for
a new kind of political organization in American cities, eventually called the
political machine. City growth helped build machines by expanding the resources of jobs, licenses, contracts, franchises, and other favors, great and small,
that urban politicians could use to reward cadres of loyal voters and those necessary party workers, fund the operations of their organizations, and, of course,
enrich themselves. These were divisible benefits offered by politicians to individuals in exchange for votes and services, as opposed to the universal benefits
that they made available to all through legislation. The leaders of these machines
would soon be called bosses. If the term suggested their power, it underlined
their lack of pretense, for *boss* was a corruption of a Dutch word used by white
workers in the antebellum era, which became a kind of slang for employer or
foreman, that had no socially hierarchical connotations. Tammany Hall, which
had roots in the New York City politics of the 1790s, would ultimately become
the iconic Irish-run political machine in America by tapping the patronage and
other political resources of the nation's rapidly growing, largest city to staff its
organization and reward its loyal voters.[20]

Recent research has revealed that even Irish immigrant canal workers as
early as the 1830s were extraordinarily savvy players in American democratic
politics. Many were veterans of O'Connell's emancipation and repeal campaigns,
but also former participants in rural secret societies, who thus not only knew
well the techniques of electoral politics, but recognized the usefulness of male
solidarity, the importance of numbers, and the employment of group violence
in efforts to gain power. In the 1820s and 1830s, even in the early 1840s, however, Irish Catholics in most towns or cities, especially in the East, would be
too few, too transient, and/or too suspect in the eyes of native-stock Americans
to take full advantage of their political acumen. Nevertheless, the "business" of
politics in America had been born, and as Irish Catholic numbers grew and new
American-born generations matured, it would become their business.[21]

It is important not to forget, however, that Protestants, largely Ulster Scots,
not Catholics, dominated Irish immigration from the end of the wars in 1815
through much of Jackson's presidency in the early 1830s. This was a huge mi-

gration, probably larger than the Protestant Irish ones in either the colonial era or in the first three decades of the early republic. Yet, despite their great numbers, people then (and historians since) hardly noticed these Protestant Irish newcomers. The broad rancorous stigmatization of them from the 1790s had weakened considerably. Meanwhile, American-born generations had come to dominate the Ulster Scot population, and the stunning political success of second-generation Ulster Scots—Presidents Jackson and James Buchanan, Vice President John C. Calhoun, and other Ulster Scot descendants—suggests how much the Protestant Irish had come to be accepted as quintessential Americans.[22]

Unlike earlier waves of Presbyterian immigrants from Ulster, evidence suggests that these Ulster Scot immigrants settled largely in the North not the South. This was in part because they landed further north in New York or even in Canadian ports, but it was also because of the South's limited economic opportunities. The dominance of big slaveholders pinched opportunities to start a small farm in the region's lowlands, while farmers in the South's uplands suffered from the new competition of booming farms in the Midwest. Those southern mountain areas were beginning to descend into an impoverished economic backwater, and, by the middle of the nineteenth century, they would be filled with many landless and illiterate laborers and tenants and be notorious for squalor and violence. The new Ulster Presbyterian Irish immigrants thus stayed in the North. Some, particularly artisans or merchants, settled in eastern big cities or new mill villages. Many others struck out for the new midwestern states of Ohio, Indiana, and Illinois, where farms were smaller and cheaper and transportation links to market better than in the South. The Presbyterian Church would not only survive in Pennsylvania and these midwestern states but flourish there in a way that it never had in the South.[23]

Orange-Green battles, reminiscent of Ireland, erupted on the Erie Canal and even aboard ships bound for Philadelphia, but a consistent pattern of antagonism between Irish American Protestants and Irish American Catholics was slow to emerge in America during the pre-famine era. Most Irish Protestants and Catholics in America were Democrats through this period. They shared not only the same hero, Andrew Jackson, but also the same enemies: both Ulster Scots and Irish Catholics had long "actively" hated New England Yankee Congregationalists, their fierce Federalist tormentors in the 1790s and now the backbone of the anti-Jackson Whigs. Nevertheless, as new Protestant immigrants came from an increasingly religiously divided Ireland, and as Irish Catholic numbers soared in American cities in the late 1830s and 1840s, many Protestant Irish there began to leak out of the Democratic Party to join the Whigs or even nativist parties.[24]

As the huge Protestant Irish immigration seemed to disappear into thin air in this period, Irish Catholics, long a small minority hidden in the shadows, were growing rapidly and becoming more noticeable. Historians estimate that the number of all Catholics in the United States may have grown from about 200,000 in 1820 to over 660,000 by 1840. Not all of them were Irish, of course, but by the early 1840s the Irish dominated the Catholic clergy and hierarchy in many of America's major cities. By the early 1830s, the "stage Irishman," a mocking stereotype of the Catholic Irish peasant, had also displaced the Yankee, "Jonathan," as the principal comic character in American theaters.[25]

With their emigration running now at flood tide and Irish construction workers ranging widely throughout the nation pursuing work, Irish Catholics began showing up in places in America where they had hardly been known before. In the Midwest, canal workers were the first Irish Catholics in Cleveland, Akron, Chicago, and other emerging towns and cities. Taking advantage of cheap tickets to nearby Canada and the region's need for cheap labor, they also began to appear in New England in significant numbers for the first time, as canal workers in Worcester, Massachusetts, for example, and construction workers in Lowell. Boston attracted male laborers, too, but also Irish women to take jobs as domestics in the homes of the city's rapidly prospering middle classes. By 1825, Boston would have 5,000 Catholics, and by the early 1840s, a high estimate suggests as many as 30,000—the vast majority Irish of all generations.[26]

Irish Catholics flooded some of their older haunts as well, like the big cities of Philadelphia and New York, in the mid-Atlantic states. Irish Catholic weavers, largely from Ulster or the Ulster borderlands, settled in large numbers in Philadelphia and even New York. Both cities also attracted Irish laborers, and, as early as 1826, 60 percent of New York's servant girls were Irish immigrants. Irish immigrant populations would grow to about 30,000 in the Philadelphia area before the famine, and in New York from an estimated 30,000 to 40,000 in 1834 to 68,000 in 1845.[27]

In all of these places and others, Irish Catholics would have to figure out how and where they fit, a complicated problem not just because of their sudden great numbers but because America was changing. Race and slavery were becoming more contested issues than ever before; the new economy emerging out of the market revolution provoked class conflict; and sectarian suspicion was spreading throughout the country.

The Irish American Catholic encounter with African Americans and their white allies began in earnest in the 1830s as the abolitionist movement grew rapidly and slavery began to become an important issue in American politics. In Ireland, Daniel O'Connell had fiercely opposed slavery, but Richard Lalor Sheil, a key figure in the emancipation movement before a later falling out with O'Connell, would echo an old comparison between Irish and Blacks that became commonplace in Irish American talk about slavery: "The common Negro enjoys more practical liberty than the wretched Irish peasant. . . . The philanthropists of England pity the state of the African and yet were insensible to the conditions of the Irish peasant." It is more difficult, however, to determine what the peasants in Ireland, who might soon be in America, thought about Africans or race in the pre-famine era. There are bits of evidence in Irish-authored fiction from the period that suggest that even in Ireland poor peasants had some vague ideas about Blacks. In William Carleton's "Poor Scholar," published in 1845, for example, Irish peasants badger the "poor scholar" Pether to give some of his money to the priest: "give his reverence the money, you nager . . . you dirty spalpeen you—hand it out, you misert." The writer Charles Lever also had Irish peasants speaking of "naygurs" in his 1839 novel, *Harry Lorrequer.* If this limited evidence does capture Irish peasant racial attitudes, it suggests that "nager" or "naygur" was a pejorative, not necessarily denoting someone who was thought of as an inferior, but one outside the community, "you dirty spalpeen" (a migrant laborer), or who refuses to be bound by its mutual obligations, a "misert."[28]

Such attitudes hint that Irish people coming to America did not come with a blank slate about how they would deal with Blacks. That would have been true regardless of whether they came with any ideas about Africans at all, however, for they brought with them all sorts of ways of thinking about how groups related to each other, which would influence how they understood race in America. They were, for example, acutely aware of boundaries (though these had been religious in Ireland, not racial); valued group solidarity; were conscious, as a dispossessed people, of the fragility of group status; understood group economic and political competition as inevitable; and were accustomed to employing violence in that competition. Sensitive to status lost in Ireland, they often bridled at efforts by African Americans to act above their alleged proper station in the United States. Similarly, used to battling with migrant laborers from different counties at home, it was easy for Irish Catholic immigrants to also see Blacks as economic competitors in the United States. Irish immigrants fought with all sorts of groups over work in America—most often actually, with other Irishmen from another Irish county or province—but they understood Black workers' unique vulnerability to their aggressiveness. Ferocious attacks by Irish draymen, for example, eventually drove Blacks out of that trade in New Orleans in the 1820s and 1830s.[29]

Irish Catholics, however, were coming to see not just African Americans but also the African Americans' white allies, the abolitionists as enemies. Irish Catholics opposed abolitionists, most obviously, because they were whites who took up the African Americans' cause. Racist opposition to abolition and Blacks also helped Irish Catholics strengthen their ties to their Democratic allies, in places as diverse as Worcester, Massachusetts, and St. Louis, Missouri. Yet Irish Catholics also differed sharply from abolitionists in their conceptions of politics: Irish American Catholics were workingmen seeking material rewards through the "rough politics" of male solidarity, mobilizing masses to vote or fight; abolitionists were self-conscious reformers, women as well as men, provoked by slavery's manifest immorality and corruption to protest it through petitions and exhortation in blizzards of tracts, novels, and speeches. Irish American Catholics, however, also insisted that most abolitionists were *their* enemies, Protestants, usually evangelicals, who were out to get *them,* or as the *Boston Pilot* proclaimed, "These anti-slavery societies are thronged with bigoted and persecuting religionists, with men, who, in their private capacity desire the extermination of Catholics by fire and sword."[30]

The pairing of Irish Catholics and African Americans in a competition for rights, which had emerged in the revolutionary era, persisted in this one. In 1842, Rhode Island's Whigs put down a Democratic Party rebellion that sought to expand the state's suffrage to include all adult white males but at the same time prevent Blacks from voting. Irish Americans came from New York to back this rebellion, but the Catholic Church in Rhode Island squashed local Irish participation in it. The victorious Yankee Whigs nonetheless imposed a property requirement on immigrant voters—most of them Irish—in their new constitution while they also restored Black suffrage. A contemporary observer suggested that most Rhode Island native-stock voters "would rather have the Negroes vote than the damn Irish." Rhode Island, however, was an anomaly: states all across the country in this era were expanding the suffrage to include Irish and other poor whites while simultaneously denying or even eliminating African American voting rights.[31]

In an America, especially an urban America, where manufacturing was rapidly growing and changing, racial divisions were not the only lines being drawn through society. To serve new, broader markets created by transportation improvements, some industries, like textiles, mechanized, provoking Protestant and Catholic Irish American hand loom weavers to join together to strike in protest in Paterson, New Jersey, in the 1820s and 1830s, for example. Most industries did not mechanize, but as their markets expanded, masters in those trades began to gather hand workers, journeymen, together in shops to mass produce goods. For most such journeymen, wages and standards of living declined after 1820, and as important, their chances of becoming masters themselves declined.[32]

By the mid-1830s, facing fundamental changes in their work and prospects for improvement, these artisans and other workers, including many Irish, both Catholics and Protestant, began to form unions. In 1835, a federation called the General Trade Union in Philadelphia counted fifty-one unions with about 10,000 members, and in May of that year a walkout by the Irish-dominated Coal Heavers ignited a citywide general strike. In 1836, in New York City, as many as two-thirds of the city's workers had joined unions, including many from heavily Irish occupations like weavers, women tailors, and laborers.[33]

The unions in both cities would collapse almost as quickly as they had arisen. A depression beginning in 1837 combined with an influx of new immigrant workers swept most of them away within a few years. By then, many discouraged Protestant workers in both cities had also begun to look not to class solidarity but, like the Presbyterian workers in Ulster, to the self-improvement promised by evangelical Protestantism to survive in the new economy.[34]

Not just race and class, but as noted, religion was becoming a critical source of division in America. Anti-Catholicism had never really gone away in the revolutionary era, but it drew new energy from America's Second Great Awakening. Many of the most popular revival leaders preached a hopeful message about the perfectibility of men, women, and society that inspired reform movements like abolition and temperance. Those evangelicals, however, also worried that Catholicism's conservatism not only discouraged Irish Catholics from seeking their own self-improvement but made them enemies of broad social reform.[35]

Nevertheless, relations between Irish Catholics and native-stock Protestants in this period would not be uniformly antagonistic. They varied, for example, from region to region. Southern New England Protestants with long traditions of suspecting outsiders, and awash in evangelicalism, seemed the most hostile to the new Irish Catholic immigrants. Not only did Rhode Island insist on a property requirement for Irish immigrant voters, but Massachusetts passed an Alien Passenger Act in 1837, preventing alleged potential paupers from landing in the state and deporting suspected ones. Between 1837 and 1845, the state expelled 4,706 paupers from Boston alone, including 706 sent back to Ireland. Places like St. Louis, New Orleans, Detroit, and Texas in the West, in contrast, were ethnically complex borderland communities where French or Mexican Catholics had often been the founding people, and white Protestants had no advantages of prior settlement as they did in the East. Irish Catholics had thus settled comfortably into French Catholic St. Louis society in the revolutionary era and mingled easily thereafter not only with French Catholics but Irish and even Anglo-American Protestants.[36]

Irish Catholic relations with native-stock Protestants in this era also seemed to vary as much by the sizes of places as by the regions where they settled. Because of the transportation revolution and incipient industrialization, some small towns, even in New England, had only recently sprung up out of nothing, like Lowell, or grown from tiny villages, like Worcester. Local Protestant elites were thus emerging even as Irish Catholic immigrants arrived, and the relationships between the two were, therefore, fresh experiments. Irish Catholic populations were often so small, as in Worcester, or so transient, as in Lowell, that they did not constitute much of a political threat, and local Irish labor bosses served as useful intermediaries between Irish immigrants and local elites. In Lowell and Worcester, Yankee Protestants helped the Irish build their own Catholic churches and later in both towns negotiate public funding for Catholic schools. The Gunpowder Mills owned by the Dupont family in Delaware offered another example. The manufacturing process was so exceptionally dangerous there that it required especially reliable workers. The Duponts, therefore, helped their Irish workers bring relatives over from Ireland—eastern Donegal specifically—to work in the mills and build a tightly knit, dependable work force. The family also sold the Irish land for their Catholic church.[37]

Irish American Catholics would encounter much stiffer nativist resistance in the nation's big cities in this period. There, Irish Catholic numbers were increasing rapidly, and they were, therefore, a more threatening presence than in the small towns. If Irish immigrants seemed too numerous in large cities to go unnoticed, however, they were not numerous enough, too recent in their arrival, or too mobile in most places to be politically powerful and demand help from native-stock leaders. There were only two hundred Irish Catholic voters in Boston in 1834 and but five hundred five years later, for example. Even in New York, where Irish Catholic numbers were greater and a second-generation Catholic Irish leadership had already begun to emerge, the local Democratic Party initially ignored them on education issues in the early 1840s. Though soon after that incident, the Democrats protected Irish immigrant suffrage rights and rewarded them with city patronage, the "First Hurrah [for the Irish] was a long time in coming" in New York.[38]

Organized anti-Catholic nativism had begun to take root in Boston, New York, and Philadelphia as early as the late 1820s and early 1830s with newspaper wars, rival lecture series, and bitter public debates much like the Bible war in Ireland. In all three, however, it soon escalated into mob actions and street battles and, as Irish Catholic immigration reached mass levels in the early 1840s, to powerful, overtly nativist local political parties and massive anti-Catholic riots. Small towns like Worcester and Lowell had worked out compromises on the public funding of Catholic schools, but in New York the issue provoked disgruntled Whigs and angry Democrats to form a separate nativist American Republican Party, which won the mayoralty and control of the city's common council in 1844. In the same year, in Philadelphia, nativist protests over the reading of the Catholic Bible in the public schools touched off two major riots, which included the torching of Catholic churches, cannon fire, and even a cavalry charge, and left thirty people dead.[39]

The new Irish Catholic immigrants had problems not only with enemy outsiders but with fellow Irishmen, including the long-established Protestant and Catholic republican leaders of the revolutionary era's nonsectarian Irish community. In New York City, as noted, they attacked the old United Irish heroes, MacNeven and Sampson. The *Shamrock* newspaper, edited by the United Irishmen veteran Thomas O'Connor, went under, replaced by the aggressively Catholic and pro-Jackson *Truthteller*. Nonsectarian associations from the revolutionary era suffered, pushed aside by militantly Catholic ones like the Hibernian Universal Benevolent Society, which began to proudly parade on St. Patrick's Day.[40]

The new Catholic Irish not only turned on the old republican leaders, but in many places, they also rebelled against the lay leaders, the lay trustees, of their churches. Lay trustees had significant power in Catholic churches then,

RIOT IN PHILADELPHIA
JUNE 7ᵗʰ 1844.

Figure 5. *Riot in Philadelphia, June 7, 1844.* A stylized depiction of the anti-Catholic nativist riot. Print by H. Bucholzer, 1844. Library of Congress: LC-DIG-pga-05259 DLC.

usually controlling parish finances and sometimes seeking a voice in the appointment of priests. By the early nineteenth century, the American church, pushed by a rejuvenated Vatican, was becoming more conservative, and the American hierarchy, including John Carroll before his death in 1815, increasingly bridled at the trustees' presumption and began to move against them.

The conflicts over trustees, however, were not merely between bishops and laymen but among the laity itself, tearing apart many of America's oldest and most important congregations, like St. Mary's in Philadelphia and St. Peter's in New York. In those battles, new Catholic immigrants seemed to align with the bishops against the trustees. Historians have sometimes depicted this as a conflict between old world traditions of authoritarianism and deference and new world revolutionary legacies of lay initiative and representation. Such an interpretation is true to an extent, though it seems to underestimate peasant skepticism of the clergy in Ireland, and the weakness of the island's institutional church in the 1810s and 1820s, especially in the Ulster borderlands where many of the immigrants came from. Importantly, however, it was also true that the tribal identity of "Catholic" and the boundary between Catholics and Protestants was quite important to the new Catholic immigrants especially—again— to the many from the north of Ireland where the Second Reformation flourished. Religious boundaries mattered as much or more to the new immigrants as obeisance to clerical authority, and they were, therefore, easily susceptible to charges that the lay trustees were too willing to smudge the differences between Catholics and their Protestant enemies.

As important, these battles often appeared to be as much about class and politics as religion. Trustees were usually wealthy and politically conservative, and they often formed self-perpetuating oligarchies in local churches. As the fights erupted, they castigated their opponents as "the scum of the earth," and the "canaille Irelandaise," while proudly proclaiming themselves as the "wealthier Catholics," and "most respectable persons," who had been cast aside in favor of the "lower orders." In contrast, new Irish immigrants attacked the trustees as self-satisfied aristocrats, hostile to Irish nationalism. In New York, they hired as their lawyer William Sampson, the prominent United Irish exile, who mocked the trustees of St. Peter's Church as "grandees." In 1831, Alexis de Tocqueville noted the paradox of Catholic hierarchy and equality in America: "among Catholics, religious society is composed of only two elements: the priest and the people. The priest alone is raised above the faithful: everything is equal below him. . . . Catholicism is like an absolute monarchy. Remove the prince and conditions are more equal in it than in republics."[41]

By 1839, the bishops had all but won their war on trusteeism. In one of the last battles that year, Bishop John Hughes routed the trustees of St. Patrick's Cathedral, by appealing not to Church authority, but to the congregation's identity as Irishmen and the historic and hallowed boundary separating Catholic and Protestant: the "sainted spirits" of their ancestors, he said, were looking down on them from heaven, ready to "disavow and disown them if . . . they allowed pygmies among themselves to filch away the rights of the Church which their glorious ancestors would not yield but with their lives to the persecuting giant of the British Empire." Many in the congregation wept, Hughes remembered, slyly adding, "I was not far from it myself."[42]

If the trustees were often wealthy elitists, however, most had, nonetheless, also been heirs to the American Revolution and its notions of rights of representation and constitutional guarantees. The new Catholic Irish immigrants may have won equality with their lay peers in De Tocqueville's terms, but they

had not removed the "prince," and had gotten an even stronger "absolute monarchy" in the bargain.

Having seen old leaders fade away or having overthrown some of them
themselves, it was hard for poor and politically weak recent Catholic immigrants
in most cities and towns to produce new lay leaders of their own. There were
more successful new Irish Catholic immigrants and impressive young second-
generation Irish Catholics in New York City, for example, but there and in
Philadelphia, it was the two bishops, John Hughes and Francis Kenrick, respectively, who had the most impact on their communities. Hughes, for example, led
a political fight for funding Catholic schools in New York in 1841 and was, by
far, the most prominent opponent of nativism throughout the period. Nevertheless, for all of his bravado, Hughes' church in New York was a tattered, rickety,
patchwork institution chronically teetering on financial collapse in the late
1830s and early 1840s. Even St. Peter's, founded in 1785 as the original Catholic church in New York City, suffered under a $140,000 debt, and was actually
sold at auction (though bought back by Catholics).[43]

Moreover, internal conflicts did not cease in the new Irish Catholic America after the old revolutionary generation had been deposed and the trustee
issue settled. Post-1815 Irish Catholic immigrants also fought with each other.
Squabbles among the clergy, endemic in parts of Ireland, erupted in Irish America too, as Irish priests cultivated rival followings among the laity for control of
parishes. In Boston, members of one divided Irish Catholic parish even hooted
the local bishop, Benedict Fenwick, off the altar, when he came to resolve one
such conflict: "we won't have you? Pull him down. Down with the Tyrant." Temperance also became a source of internal conflict in Irish Catholic churches as
well, most notably in Philadelphia. There Irish Catholic shopkeepers and skilled
workers embraced temperance, seeing it as a way to mark off their own respectability from rowdy, poor Irish workers. By the late 1830s and early 1840s, Catholic temperance societies in Philadelphia had grown to over 5,000 members.
After the 1844 riot, many Irish Catholic temperance men blamed the Irish poor,
not the nativists, for provoking the violence and abandoned their own Catholic
temperance societies. Some even joined Protestant ones.[44]

Conflicts rooted in old country county and provincial rivalries, however,
were especially numerous, divisive, and violent in Irish communities. Though
common throughout the 1830s, they seemed to become more pervasive near
the end of the pre-famine period as more immigrants came from southern Ireland and the Irish regional origins of immigrants became more diverse. They

also seemed particularly prevalent in the new Irish Catholic settlements of New England, where they fractured Irish Catholic communities in Worcester, Lowell, Providence, Boston, and other cities and towns.[45]

The most numerous and bloodiest old country rivalry fights among the Catholic Irish, however, were on canal and railroad construction sites scattered around the country. Contractors were responsible for putting together their own work crews to build a canal or road or at least sections of it, and those work gangs would often be made up of people from the same parts of Ireland—from counties, Cork or Longford, for example, or provinces, Ulster or Connaught. Workers were competing for work with other gangs and did so by scaring competitors from other Irish regions away, just as Whiteboys in the eighteenth century or Rockites more recently had rousted Kerry migrant workers out of laboring jobs in Tipperary or other counties back in Ireland. Andrew Leary O'Brien, a young seminarian who worked briefly on a canal, remembered, "one of an opposite party dare not seek employment on a contract where the other party were in employ." In what one historian has called the "great riot year" of 1834 in America, no less than seven of the nation's twenty-four major riots (and three more major riots the next year) involved Irishmen working on canals and railroads. They included one on the Chesapeake and Ohio canal in January 1834, when hundreds of Corkonians battled Longford men in the woods near Williamsport, Maryland, leading to the death of at least five of the Corkonians.[46]

Their new American communities were not Irish Americans' only concern in this era; they were also passionately interested in Ireland's fate. In 1826, they and their allies began meeting in cities and towns across the country to form pro-Catholic emancipation organizations, and by 1829, perhaps, as many as thirty such local groups had formed. There were hints of the new Irish America emerging in this—canal workers in Pennsylvania sent some of their hard-earned money for "suffering Ireland"—but in New York, the old '98 rebels, MacNeven and Sampson, ruled the local associations. The commitment to a nonsectarian Irishness thus continued in this movement despite emancipation's seemingly sectarian object and increasing religious tension in Ireland.[47]

Irish American nationalism remained largely dormant thereafter, until O'Connell began to reenergize his repeal campaign in 1840. In 1843, as O'Connell was staging his monster meetings across Ireland, backers of repeal in America held their own gatherings of support in Buffalo, St. Louis, New Orleans,

Figure 6. *O'Connell's Call and Pat's Reply.* Irish American immigrant "Pat" praises America and thus rejects O'Connell's demand that he leave the United States because of America's commitment to slavery. Drawing by William Edwards Clay, 1843. Library of Congress: LC-USZ62-28072.

Baltimore, Mobile, and elsewhere. In New York, 20,000 to 30,000 people came out every night for seven nights to back repeal in June of that year.[48]

Irish American repealers, however, soon became embroiled in a controversy with O'Connell over American slavery. In late 1841, O'Connell lent his name to an address signed by over 60,000 Irishmen to the Irish in America, urging them to take up the antislavery cause: "Treat the colored people as your equals . . . cling to the abolitionists." Hostile responses from the American repeal societies caused O'Connell to temporarily back off, but by May 1843, exasperated by Irish American excuses for opposing abolition, he exclaimed: "Come out of such a land you Irishmen; or if you remain and dare to countenance the system of slavery that is supported there, we will recognize you as Irishmen no longer."[49]

The repeal agitation in America, however, revealed more about Irish Americans than what they thought about slavery and race. It reflected well their status as a group in transition. Though Irish repeal leaders were often middle class and respectable, such men were few in most of their communities, and they stood on small and weak local organizational bases often divided by factionalism and burdened by debts. Indeed, they still had to trot out '98 exiles like the now ancient MacNeven or native-stock American notables at meetings or even to lead branches. Robert Tyler, son of the U.S. president John Tyler, for example, was president of the national repeal association.[50]

The repeal agitation had largely collapsed by 1845 when a fungus which fed off and destroyed potatoes crossed the Atlantic, crept into Europe, and eventually reached Ireland, beginning a catastrophe there so great that a million and half Irish would flee to America. They would not spurn or "come out from such a land" because they had no better place to go. They would create a much more powerful Irish America, but neither their new nation, nor therefore they, would be able to dodge the evil of African American slavery any longer, nor the suffering of the bloody civil war that it would provoke.

5. The Famine and Irish Immigrants in America

1845–1880

On a pretty July day at the beginning of the twenty-first century, you could look almost all the way down to the water, Lake Kilglass, and see nothing but broad, bright green fields, occasionally broken by lanes or lines of hedges or trees. There is a stone cottage and a few ruins, but only one house is really noticeable here, a Victorian relic of the nineteenth century, the slates falling off its roof now. The rest is open country, seemingly fresh as the day of creation. A cloud blows in, darkens the day, spills a quick torrent of rain in large drops, but passes almost as quickly, and the fields are lit up again. This could be many places in rural Ireland, all suggesting something pristine, natural, as if it has always been thus.[1]

Yet it had not always been thus. These empty fields of about six hundred acres, in a townland called Ballykilcline, teemed with life in the early 1840s. And this was true all over Ireland. In 1845 over eight and a half million people lived on the island. That meant it was almost half as large as the population of the United States in 1840 (a little over seventeen million) and was over half the population of neighboring England (about fifteen million). This was not an urban population, packed into city alleys and overflowing tenements, but one scattered over the rural landscape, as one historian has suggested, "a vast rural congested slum." And then it was gone—or much of it. By that July afternoon in 2003, the only marks left by Ballykilcline's own five hundred residents in the famine era were below ground, not above it: in pits dug by archaeologists where two stone houses of the Nary family had been in 1847.[2]

The late 1840s were the beginning of drastic depopulation all over Ireland. In Ballykilcline, the cause of the people's going was serendipitous and their story unique. The United Kingdom, the Crown, owned Ballykilcline and neighboring lands, but in the confusion of the local lord's descent into madness the tenants managed to avoid paying rents. In 1846, the government, however, won a suit against the tenants, sent them away to America and leveled their houses the next year. That year, "Black 1847," was one of the worst in the many millennia of human inhabitation of the island of Ireland. The potato blight had crossed the Atlantic, reached Ireland by the summer of 1845, and began to eat away at the island's vast fields of potatoes. It would linger until 1851, ultimately killing over a million Irish people by the time the catastrophe ended. Those that could leave did. By 1847 about 250,000 to 300,000 had arrived in America; by 1855 one and a half million had. Irish Americans in the twentieth century as diverse as the Kennedys; Margaret Higgins Sanger; Joseph, "Joe," and Eugene McCarthy; Georgia O'Keeffe; Ronald Reagan; Flannery O'Connor; Eugene O'Neill; and Fulton Sheen would trace their ancestry to famine immigrant ancestors.[3]

A really close look at the period might raise questions not just about whether it was the origin of the Irish in America, but whether it was even a decisive moment in their history at all. Some of the critical trends remaking Irish America—mass migration, or the balance between Protestants and Catholics among migrants, for example—had started by the early 1840s or even the 1830s. And yet the famine migration's significance is not entirely a facile fairy tale. More Irish came to America in the fifteen years between 1845 and 1860 than in the nearly three centuries since Roanoke. Trends in who left Ireland, which had begun before the famine, now accelerated during it or, intriguingly, in the years immediately following it, thus, for example, significantly shifting the balance of Irish regional origins and genders among Irish immigrants. The famine migration also helped to reshape the geography of Irish emigration. It established the United States, for example, as far and away the principal destination within the broader Irish diaspora for the next seventy-five years. Within the United States, it also lent powerful momentum to a process already in motion of Irish American concentration in eastern cities and mill towns, a redrawing of the map of Irish American settlement that has endured into our own time.

The blight, the fungus that destroyed the potatoes, was called *Phytopthora infestans.* It quite literally choked potato plants to death and then fed off their remains. Microscopic spores, which kept reproducing themselves as they devoured the plants, spread the blight through the air, blowing over fields, alighting on new plants and beginning the process over and over again. People would later recall skies darkening and thick fog rolling in, and the "next morning when they woke and went out . . . their lovely potato plants were all covered with black spots." The fungus came to Ireland in 1845 and about one-third of the potato harvest was lost, but in the next year, 90 percent was destroyed, and at least a third to a half over the next few years. Deaths thus rose in 1846 and then doubled to 250,000 in 1847, the famine's nadir, fell in 1848, and then jumped again to near 1847 levels in 1849. When the blight had largely disappeared in all parts of the island by 1851, it was not because anyone had determined exactly how it worked and why, much less figured out how to stop it. The famine had a geography as well as a chronology. Because the poor died, that meant more people in the South and West did, but it is difficult to determine because no one counted deaths. By one estimate of "excess death" rates from 1846 to 1851, Counties Cork, Clare, Galway, Mayo, Sligo, Leitrim, Roscommon, and Cavan suffered the most.[4]

When the blight first struck in 1845, Sir Robert Peel and his Tory United Kingdom government bought £100,000 worth of what the British called Indian corn meal from American markets and sold it through government depots. In the meantime, the government began a public works program hiring the destitute to work on roads, bridges, and sometimes piers and wharfs so that they would be able to purchase the food. Governments had faced such food shortfalls in Ireland before and had followed much the same policy. The expectation was that this would tide the poor over without seriously disrupting private markets and allegedly corrupting the peasants by merely giving them food. Private markets unaided, however, simply could not provide enough food to fill the gap in calories caused by the destruction of the potatoes. Furthermore, sending many of the poor, clothed in rags, out on "relief" jobs during an abnormally cold, wet, and raw winter, now proved lethal. A new Whig government replaced the Tories and in March 1847 began phasing out the public works program, feeding the poor directly but temporarily through soup kitchens, serving over three million people that summer, "by far the most effective of all the methods adopted by the government to deal with [the famine's] starvation and disease." The new government, however, only kept the soup kitchens open until the new harvest in the fall of 1847 and then threw the burden of relief on to locally financed Poor Law Unions in Ireland, expecting them to relieve the able-bodied but offer relief *only* in the workhouses to discourage loafers. William Gregory, a member of Parliament (also the husband of the famous Lady Gregory of the late nineteenth-century literary revival), proposed and won an addition to the Poor Law amendment which required that any tenant holding more than a quarter acre had to give up his or her lease or be denied food. The new Poor Law thus set off a massive round of evictions, and at least 42,000 families, maybe 200,000 people, were forced off their lands for good between 1849 and 1852.[5]

Some Irish poor fought to save themselves by individual pilfering or collective protest, but over time the famine wore them down and riotous disturbances petered out. O'Connell's Repeal Association would not agree to violence, and O'Connell himself died in Genoa on a pilgrimage to Rome in May 1847. Frustrated young nationalists, calling themselves Young Ireland, inspired by the outbreak of revolutions on the continent, tried to incite famine-stricken Ireland to do the same. The result was a debacle: their "rising" in 1848 ended with a minor skirmish in the Widow McCormack's cabbage patch in Ballingarry, Tipperary. Though their little rebellion became a joke, Young Ireland exiles would play crucial roles in building a new Irish nationalism throughout the diaspora.[6]

Not relief, nor resistance, but flight to America offered the best hope of survival for most Irish. In American currency, a steerage berth from Liverpool to the United States cost about $15 by the late 1840s. Some, convinced that Ireland was doomed, were wealthy enough to pay their own way. Landlords occasionally stepped up and paid their tenants' passage, but the number of emigrants financed by them was tiny, only 50,000 to 100,000 of the famine flood to all destinations. Many more had family in America already and relied on remittances or prepaid tickets from them: between 1850 and 1855, Irish Americans sent an annual average of £1.2 million back to Ireland, "largely in an effort to reunite with their relatives in the New World." Pleas from Ireland to American relatives were often plaintive and frantic. Maurice Prendergast of Milltown in west Kerry, for example, had two brothers, Jeffrey and Thomas, and a sister, Julia, in Boston. In June 1848, he wrote them that "our gaols filled, people only doing crime to get something to eat or to be transported" and pleaded that they "take James [Maurice] [his son] out as I see no prospect of his being able to do any good here." With help from his relatives, James Maurice left for Boston soon after and many others in the family followed.[7]

Nevertheless, if such chains suggest continuity between pre-famine and famine immigration, there were significant changes in the makeup of Irish immigration over the course of the famine era. The poorest of the poor and largely

Irish speakers who lived along the west coast had long seemed immune to emigration, but now people there began to go. Some left in dribbles, establishing a foundation for a larger, later migration, as from Louisburg in Mayo to Clinton in Massachusetts, but others fled en masse as the disaster forced them out. A new landlord's evictions in 1848, for example, pushed hundreds of Irish speakers off the island of Aranmore in Donegal to America, where they eventually settled on Beaver Island in Lake Michigan.[8]

Yet the more important change was the shift of the center of migration from the north to the south. More specifically, the province of Munster replaced Ulster as the principal source of Irish immigration to the United States. As noted in previous chapters, this process had begun in earnest by the 1830s and picked up momentum in the early 1840s. Nevertheless, in the first few years of the famine, 1846 to 1848, Munster's share of immigrants landing in New York was less than 20 percent. That rose to over a quarter by 1850, but in the years immediately after the famine, from 1851 to 1854, when immigration from all of Ireland to America peaked, Munster's percentage grew to one third of all Irish immigrants landing in New York. The number of immigrants arriving in the city from Cork, Tipperary, and Limerick in the early 1850s was twice as high as the number from those counties earlier, at the famine's climax between 1846 and 1849.[9]

It is not entirely clear why so many more people were leaving Munster at that time. Historians have pointed out that "there was an enormous increase in the proportion of landless [laborers} among the emigrants" between 1851 and 1854. Most had been too poor to escape the famine as it raged, and huge numbers of them died, but as the famine ended and Ireland's economy began to recover, the wages of the laborers who had survived shot up, permitting them to pay their or a family member's passage to the United States. Munster had had an enormous number of agricultural laborers before the famine—Cork, in particular, had over 150,000, more than any other county in Ireland. Irish tenant farmers in several of the Munster counties also suffered severely from famine deaths and evictions in the last few years of the famine.[10]

It appears that a large proportion of Irish emigrants continued to come from Munster through the next two decades after the famine, though the absence of reliable statistics makes it hard to track. Some sources suggest immigration from Munster, as well as Galway and Mayo in Connaught, peaked again in the early and mid-1860s. Successive bad harvests and declining agricultural prices combined then with the Lincoln administration's encouragement of immigration to America to prompt over 400,000 Irish immigrants to leave for the

United States. More reliable United Kingdom statistics indicate that about 40 percent of Irish immigrants to America in the late 1870s came from Munster.[11]

Yet why did it matter to Irish American history that so many more of the immigrants came from Munster? They were poorer than people from most of Ulster and its borderlands, a poverty cruel enough that it registered in their bodies, making them noticeably shorter in stature than those from Leinster and Ulster. Yet, if in its western reaches Munster poor often lived in relative isolation like those in Connaught, much of Munster was laced with roads and dotted with market towns, and even the impoverished there were more familiar with a market economy than the poor farmers in Connaught, though they suffered as much or more. Munster also reflected well some of the cultural diversity of an Ireland in transition. A much higher proportion of Munster's residents were Irish speakers than those in Ulster or most of Leinster. Combining emigrants from Munster and Connaught, where the proportion of Irish speakers was even higher, one historian estimates that "perhaps a fourth to a third" of all famine immigrants spoke Irish. In contrast, aside from western Kerry and Clare, mass attendance rates were higher in Munster than Ulster and Connaught, and especially high in eastern parts of the province, suggesting the strength of institutional Catholicism there. Importantly, O'Connellite nationalism, both the Emancipation and Repeal movements, thrived in Munster much more than in most parts of the north and much of the west. The province had also been the heartland of another kind of politics, secret society resistance, since the Whiteboys of the eighteenth century. One historian has suggested that east Munster and south Leinster made up the most politicized region in the country.[12]

The rise of Munster migration was not the only important trend in the famine's remaking of Irish immigration; there was also a growing shift in the gender balance of young adult male and female Irish immigrants to America. Most scholarly attention has focused on Irish women's emigration to America in the late nineteenth century, when women's predominance has long been clear. Yet growth in the numbers of young adult women among Irish emigrants was noticeable even before the famine, as work spinning linen yarn disappeared for them and they became aware of employment opportunities in domestic service in America. This trend then accelerated during the famine, and like the growing number of Munster immigrants, it became stronger in the last years of the catastrophe and the few years after it ended. Statistics from the 1860 U.S. Census revealed that Irish-born women in their late twenties and early thirties significantly outnumbered men in those age categories—thus including women who had left Ireland in their late teens and early twenties in the early 1850s. Passenger lists confirm that women dominated among the fifteen- to twenty-year-old migrants from Ireland landing in New York in 1853. Literacy and numeracy had continued to rise among women, but they may have also profited from the multiplying and strengthening immigration chains and the huge increase in remittances sent back to Ireland by the end of the famine, which made it easier to go. Continuing explosive growth in women's job opportunities in American domestic service, clothing, and textile industries no doubt must have also made it seem worth the risks.[13]

As might be expected, the famine only enhanced the dominance of Liverpool and its large brokerage houses in the Irish immigrant trade. Only in 1847, when the full horrors of the catastrophe became clear, setting off a huge panicky flight of desperate peasants, did Irish ports seriously challenge Liverpool's preeminence. Cheating had already plagued the trade since the big brokerage houses took over in the 1830s, and as not just the number of immigrants but the proportion of poor among them rose, the chicanery got worse. Fraudulent immigration agents multiplied in Ireland, and Liverpool itself became rife with "gangs of runners, touts and mancatchers," preying on prospective passengers. The flood of immigrants and the lack of enough ships to carry them also caused widespread delays in ship sailings, especially in the early years of the famine, forcing emigrants with scarce resources and little or no knowledge of the port to somehow find lodgings there.[14]

The Great Famine migration took place at the very end of the age of sail, and so the journey was still long for some and difficult for most. The average time for most sailing ships to cross the Atlantic remained about six weeks, though with great deviations because of the quality of the ships and variable winds or storms. The voyage was still uncomfortable for many, then, and far worse for some, fifty-nine Irish immigrant ships sank, burned, or foundered between 1847 and 1853. In 1849, Henry David Thoreau visited the wreck of the brig *St. John* from Galway, which had been driven onto the rocks in Cohasset, Massachusetts, killing scores of Irish passengers, including "a drowned girl,— who probably had intended to go out to service in some American family . . . a human hulk, . . . with wide-open and staring eyes, like the cabin windows of a stranded vessel." The percentage dying in shipwrecks was tiny, however; the diseases Irish emigrants carried with them on board ship were the greatest killers on the passage to North America. Illnesses were devastating, in particular, on the ships to Canada in 1847, "Black 47," when, by a recent estimate, about

11 percent of the nearly 100,000 Irish passengers died en route or in quarantine. Some Irish immigrants to America did travel on "coffin ships" as they came to be called, but such death rates were rare on ships carrying Irish immigrants to the United States in the famine years. In only one year during the period from 1847 to 1851 did death rates on Irish immigrant ships from Liverpool to New York exceed 3 percent.[15]

Not all the people leaving Ireland during the famine, or in the ten or fifteen years after it, were heading for the United States, but the vast majority of Irish emigrants were, and, as noted earlier, would continue to do so until well into the next century. The Irish-born population in Britain began to level off and even drop by the 1870s, and the falloff of Irish settlement in Canada was even quicker and more drastic. The catastrophe of "Black 47" prompted Canadian ports to impose expensive new taxes on arriving passengers, and thereafter Irish migration to Canada fell to a trickle. Canada's limited economy, however, also had trouble even holding its own people; in the 1850s, 150,000 Canadians migrated south. The United Kingdom and Australia's provinces subsidized the migration of thousands of Irish to that southern continent in the famine years. Even so, only 177,000 Irish-born individuals lived in Australia by 1861, about one tenth of the 1,611,000 who had settled in the United States by then.[16]

The advantages of the United States were not hard to see. In 1845, when the famine began, America had 4,463 miles of railroad track; fifteen years later it had 30,626. Between 1839 and 1859 U.S. production of cotton bales grew 172 percent, from 1,976,000 to 5,387,000, and bushels of wheat 103 percent, from 85 million to 173 million. Yet if the nation's agriculture prospered, its future was in manufacturing. Between 1840 and 1860 the number of men and women working in manufacturing rose 200 percent and went from 9 percent of the labor force to 14 percent. The number of construction workers, an industry which would also become important to the Irish, rose by nearly 80 percent in the same period. In 1850, the United States had the third largest gross national product (GNP) in the western world behind the United Kingdom and France; by 1870, it had outstripped both. The GNPs of Australia and Canada lagged far, far behind.[17]

It was to America they meant to go, then, but where? Irish people going to America traveled to many American ports, but three-quarters of them landed in New York. Of the hundreds of thousands of Irish who stepped ashore there in the 1840s, before and during the famine, about one-sixth still lived there by

1850 and about one-eighth by 1860. Most of those who left, however, did not go very far. Over 60 percent had not moved beyond two hundred fifty miles of the city by the end of the 1850s. 24 percent had taken the Fall River line boats or trains up into New England, and 38.1 percent went to Pennsylvania, New Jersey, or other parts of New York state; only 12.7 percent went to the midwestern states. By contrast, over 60 percent of the German immigrants who landed in New York in the same decade had moved more than two hundred and fifty miles from the city at the decade's end, over 43 percent to the Midwest. German immigrants would continue to flood the Midwest thereafter, and the number of Irish immigrants settling in the region would tail off during the Civil War and virtually stop after 1870 (except to Chicago). The high costs of traveling further west, about 60 to 100 percent as much as the price of the trip across the Atlantic, were a greater hindrance for the Irish than for the wealthier Germans. Irish settlers often moved to the Midwest in more painstaking fashion, making several stops or settlements in cities or towns for months or even years along the way. Not just travel costs, but the happenstance of travel routes and shipping lines had an effect on where Irish people settled as well. The large number of Irish going to the United States through Canada until 1847 undoubtedly accounted for some of the continued heavy Irish presence in New England.[18]

Nevertheless, Irish immigrants in the mid-nineteenth century, as poor as they were, were not simply victims of being dumped in certain ports or trapped in place by high railroad fares. Remember that 24 percent of the Irish immigrants who landed in New York in the 1840s went east into New England, not west to the Midwest, paying as much as five dollars for tickets on steamships or trains, about the equivalent of a fare to Buffalo.[19]

Prospects of economic opportunity were important to Irish immigrants in deciding where to go in the United States, but opportunities for women may have mattered as much or more as those for men in shaping Irish settlement. The thousands of young women emigrating to America immediately after the famine were looking for jobs in service, in textile mills, or in making clothing. In 1860, 76 percent of Irish immigrant women working as domestic servants, 98 percent of the Irish cotton textile operatives, and 72 percent of the Irish seamstresses and milliners lived in New England or the mid-Atlantic states. These jobs had been growing rapidly in the 1840s and 1850s in the East, especially the number of service jobs, which skyrocketed in big cities in those decades. Women thus made up over 56 percent of the Irish populations in the largest eastern cities like New York, Philadelphia, Baltimore, and Boston in 1860.[20]

Yet as for the Irish immigrants who had come before them, emigration chains or networks of friends and relatives were crucial in determining where they settled. The Ballykilcline exiles, for example, landed in New York but many wound up in Rutland, Vermont, where people from their own part of Roscommon had already settled. An eclectic mix of parish records, census schedules, Civil War military rosters, and lists of bank depositors, which have survived in places spread around the country, reveal that no mix of the counties of origin for Irish immigrants was quite the same in every parish, city ward, or regiment. According to census manuscript schedules, for example, Tipperary men and women were more numerous than immigrants from any other Irish county in the largely German Second Ward in St. Louis, and Wexford people the largest proportion in the city of Savannah. Catholic parish records reveal the same kinds of distinctive mixes of county clusters: immigrants from County Kerry and County Sligo among Irish Catholics in Transfiguration parish in the Five Points on New York City's Lower East Side in the 1850s and 1860s; Kerry and Cork immigrants in St. Peter's parish in Cambridge, Massachusetts, in the early 1870s; and Corkonians alone nearly half of the Irish in Newburyport's Immaculate Conception parish (44.4 percent, the next highest being Kerry at 15.8 percent) at the same time. In Pittsburgh's St. Mary's parish located at the city's historic "Point," where the French had built Fort Duquesne, over three-fifths of the Irish immigrants were from Galway in the 1870s, while St. Malachy's in another Pittsburgh neighborhood had high proportions of both Galway and Mayo people. Such patterns thus suggest the importance of chains or networks of family and friends to Irish immigrants in easing the migration process.[21]

Data about married couples, boarders, and baptismal godparents also reflected the importance of community and family ties. Again in New York's Five Points, two-thirds of the men from Sligo and Kerry marrying in the neighborhood's Catholic Transfiguration church in the 1850s (1853 to 1860) married women from their own counties in Ireland. In some cases Irish-born marriage partners in the Church were not just from the same county but from the same rural parish: ten of fifteen male natives of Tuosit parish in the hills of the Beara peninsula in County Kerry, for example, married women from Tuosit. Boarders also appeared to seek out people from the same county. In Boston's North End in 1860, five laborers from Donegal lived with James Campbell's and John Guild's families, both from Donegal, while Frank McLaughlin from Fermanagh and his Fermanagh-born wife hosted four Fermanagh boarders. Finally, in the

1870s at least half (probably more since the records are incomplete) of the parents seeking baptism for their babies at St. Peter's in Cambridge could call on relatives (people with the same surname as the father's or mother's maiden name) to act as godparents.[22]

If chains influenced where famine Irish immigrants settled, the absence of chains influenced where they did not. Fewer Irish immigrants to the United States moved to the country to start a farm or a ranch than Irish immigrants to Australia. This was not simply because the Irish immigrants to Australia were wealthier or responding to better opportunities there but also because they were taking advantage of networks that led them to rural areas. Earlier Irish immigrants transported to Australia as prisoners often completed their penal terms working in the countryside, settled there, and in turn brought family and friends there through sponsorships subsidized by the imperial or local governments.[23]

There is some suggestive evidence that the circumstances of migration and life in America loosened old country bonds. Though most of the Irish parents in the baptismal registers from St. Peter's and Immaculate Conception parishes had spouses from the same county in Ireland, for example, a sizable minority married across county boundaries. Many of them were from counties with few members in the parish, and they therefore had to look outside their American neighborhood or native Irish county boundaries for partners.[24] Further movement west across the country might have also worn down old world ties. No one or two Irish counties seemed to dominate in the Irish populations of Milwaukee's Fourth Ward, Belle Plaine in rural Minnesota, or the ranks of depositors in San Francisco's St. Patrick's parish bank, for example, as they did in communities further east.[25]

In 1859, two Irish prospectors, Peter O'Riley and Patrick McLaughlin, stumbled upon a vein of silver in Nevada of breathtaking size: the Comstock Lode, the "largest and most valuable single pocket of silver ever discovered in the world." O'Riley and McLaughlin would not profit from it. They sold their leases for almost nothing; O'Riley worked as a kind of handyman for the rest of his days, and McLaughlin died in an insane asylum. By the early 1870s, three Irish immigrants, James Gordon Fair, John William Mackey, and William S. O'Brien, and an American-born Irishman, John C. Flood, the "Irish Big Four," gained control of the heart of the lode and became rich beyond all imagining. Mackey had been born penniless in Dublin in 1831 but parlayed his Comstock discoveries into becoming one of the richest men in America, perhaps the world. The story of the Comstock Lode in exaggeration reflected the American economy's paradox of seemingly unlimited promise and all too often cruel realities for famine Irish immigrants. For many Irish, surely just escaping to America in the famine years was a triumph, even if that meant only survival, since remaining in Ireland for them meant a very real chance of starvation and death. Beyond that, however, the success or failure of famine Irish immigrants is harder to measure, and more important, the nature of their experience in the American economy is difficult to easily summarize. If almost none matched the success of the Big Four, for most, life in America was a complicated mix of survival, small victories, and hardship.[26]

The national occupational distribution of Irish American immigrants in the federal census of 1860 reveals a grim picture of Irish immigrant economic adjustment. In 1860, only 7 percent of Irish-born men in the work force were white-collar workers and about another 17 percent were skilled craftsmen. Nearly half were laborers. The proportion of white-collar workers would grow and the percentage of laborers fall over the next two decades: white-collar workers to 8.1 percent in 1870 and 10.5 percent in 1880; laborers falling to 41 percent and then 36 percent in 1880, while the percentage of Irish-born skilled workers or artisans also fell, as manufacturing production moved increasingly from craftsmen working in shops to operatives tending machines in factories. Throughout all three censuses, the Irish had far fewer skilled workers, white-collar workers, and farm owners, and far higher proportions of laborers than their immigrant rivals, the Germans and the English. They measured up even worse against native-born Americans, at least in most parts of the North.[27]

Tracing the career tracks of individual Irish immigrants offers a different perspective on Irish economic success in America than static snapshots of census data. Such studies do show some substantial Irish immigrant upward occupational mobility, but they also reveal significant downward mobility as well, and again they seem to confirm that the Irish did worse than other immigrants in the 1840s and 1850s. A study including Irish, Germans, and English landing at New York City in the 1840s found that no less than 62 percent of the Irish arriving as white-collar workers in the 1840s fell into the unskilled ranks by 1860, compared to 23 percent of British immigrants and 22 percent of Germans who began at the same high status. The study also found that 41 percent of the unskilled or farming Irish who landed in New York City in the 1840s moved up to skilled or white-collar work by 1860, but 81 percent of the Germans and 76.8 percent of the British did. As the author notes, "the Irish clearly had the worst outcomes: the highest percentage moving down and the lowest percentage moving up."[28]

One reason for the Irish failure to find better jobs than other groups was the prejudice against them. Some historians have questioned the extent of anti-Irish discrimination in the famine era and have dismissed the infamous phrase "No Irish Need Apply" as an Irish American invention to encourage group solidarity. Recent, careful research by a perceptive and indefatigable young scholar, however, has found substantial use of that phrase during the famine era in the classified employment advertisements of many newspapers, including the *New York Sun, New York Tribune,* and *Boston Herald,* as well as papers in St. Louis and Cincinnati. Furthermore, another recent researcher studying the *New York Times* in this period noted "hundreds" of classified advertisements that restricted jobs to "Protestants" or "Americans only," "effectively excluding Irish Catholic immigrants." Most such advertisements, it appears, were aimed at Irish women applying for jobs in service, but at least some were aimed at Irish men seeking jobs ranging from laborer to tailor, as well as agents and clerks and jobs "in light and genteel" and "honorable business."[29]

What hurt famine Irish immigrants most, however, was the simple lack of money, craft skills, or even familiarity with a modern commercial economy. A study of Irish immigrants nationwide in 1850 suggests that Munster immigrant men earned about a quarter more income annually than Connaught men. That may have been because, as noted earlier, Munster immigrants—even laborers— came from a more commercial world of towns and markets than men from underdeveloped Connaught. Yet all Irish peasants seemed at a disadvantage in the American economy when compared with other immigrants or native-stock Americans.[30]

As had been true in the past and would be in the future, however, where Irish immigrants settled in America had an important effect on how well they would manage the adjustment to the new world. Irish Americans were least successful in New England, which had the smallest proportion of Irish immigrant men who became white-collar workers and highest percentage of Irish laborers north of the Mason-Dixon line in 1860. Evangelical Protestantism was more powerful there, elites more entrenched and resistant to outsiders than anywhere else in America, and the economy, despite the region's accelerating shift into factory production, offered famine Irish immigrants few positions in manufacturing beyond the entry level.[31]

For Irish immigrants, the Pacific region and its capital, San Francisco, was nearly the polar opposite of New England and Boston. There, they arrived just when almost all other whites did, so there were no established elites to block their way, the economy had just begun to take off and thus was rich with abundant opportunities, and the Irish were not "the other," the focus of community antagonism: the Chinese were. Thus, the Irish were able to work their way into local social and economic elites quickly, and more Irish immigrants became white-collar workers in that region than anywhere else.[32]

In other regions, Irish achievements were more mixed. In the Middle Atlantic states, substantial proportions of Irish men in economically vibrant New York City and Philadelphia worked as skilled artisans or craftsmen or semi-skilled factory operatives than almost anywhere else. In Troy, New York, Irish Catholics gained a foothold in the iron-working industry, but the Irish in Pittsburgh had a harder time breaking into the same trade. Meanwhile large proportions of Irish immigrants in Jersey City and in the new coal mining regions of Schuylkill County in northeastern Pennsylvania remained laborers. The Midwest had the most Irish farmers: one-quarter of working Irish-born men in the midwestern states east of the Mississippi River were farmers, and one-third in the states just west of it, but surprisingly, Irish immigrant occupational success in many growing midwestern cities was limited at this point. Regional differences in Irish economic performance in the famine era would become more important over time, but, in the end, what is more striking— aside from San Francisco—are the similarities in Irish immigrant men's occupational success, especially before the Civil War: the large proportions of unskilled, and, conversely, small percentage of white-collar workers in most places.[33]

As famine Irish refugees poured into American cities, they encountered a whole new world. These were still walking cities, where public transportation remained limited and prohibitively expensive. These cities were thus densely packed—most New Yorkers lived below Fourteenth Street in this era—and most areas were jumbles of commercial, industrial, and residential land uses as well as mixes of ethnic and racial groups with few large, discrete ethnic or racial neighborhoods. Aside from Boston, then, the Irish were rarely segregated in large ghettoes in most of these cities but scattered throughout them. In Philadelphia, for example, the Irish made up majorities in just two of the city's twenty-four

Figure 7. *View from School House in 42nd Street between 2nd and 3rd Avenues, Looking North.* A "shanty" village of Irish and German immigrants on the East Side of New York City in the 1860s. W. C. Rogers and Company, 1863. Lithograph, PR020, New-York Historical Society, 74193.

wards and those wards were home to but 9 percent of the Irish adult population (over age sixteen). In New York City (then still only Manhattan), there was a notable Irish immigrant concentration in the southern part of the city, but the Irish-born were majorities in only four of the city's twenty-two wards, which contained but 15 percent of the adult Irish. This did not mean that the Irish escaped the consequences of their poverty in New York. They were not only packed into overcrowded tenements amid leaking outdoor privies and streets piled with garbage on the Lower East Side, but stuck in makeshift shanties in undeveloped uptown, in what is now Hell's Kitchen or 42nd Street near Second Avenue on the East Side or even living in mud hovels in what would become Central Park. If not segregated in big cities, however, in big cities and small ones, as well as mill villages, Irish immigrants did often cluster in multiple streets or blocks with fellow Irish, often, as previous evidence suggests, people who were part of their networks from counties back home.[34]

In such environments, simple survival was often a struggle. Family budget data from Irish working-class families in Massachusetts in 1875 suggests that even laborers ate meat daily, as well as gingerbread, pies, pudding, pickles, and cakes, and coffee, tea, and milk regularly, so Irish Civil War soldiers would be taller than even Irish men in Ireland. Nevertheless, Irish-born men and women seemed especially vulnerable to a variety of infectious diseases. Tuberculosis "fattened" on famine Irish immigrants in Boston and ravaged the Irish in New York City so much so that Archbishop John Hughes called it "the natural death of the Irish emigrant." In a small sample, but a telling one, taken from the Irish Transfiguration and German Holy Redeemer parish baptismal records, over one-fifth of the Irish fathers of babies baptized in 1850 had died within the next ten years, but none of the Germans had. There were local differences in this Irish physical vulnerability. The Irish suffered terribly in the near tropical climate of New Orleans with its plague of diseases like yellow fever. Boston also had far higher Irish mortality rates (37.2 per thousand) than its sister big cities, New York (21.2) or Philadelphia (12.2). Irish-born women, who were economically vulnerable outside service, were also especially susceptible to sufferings of the heart and the mind. Native stock or other better-off immigrants could treat emotional distress at home and avoid asylums. Doctors' stereotypes of Irish emotional instability probably also increased medical professionals' propensity to send Irish immigrants to institutions. Nevertheless, the statistics are sobering. The 1860 census revealed that 60 percent of all the foreign-born women in insane asylums in the United States were Irish immigrants; 44 percent of all the foreign-born men in such asylums were. Jails all along the East Coast were filled with Irish men. In Boston in 1859 and New York in 1858, about half of the people sent to prison were Irish-born, as were 60 percent jailed in a small city like Worcester, Massachusetts, in 1850, where the Irish were about one-fifth of the city's population. Irish-born women made up 68 percent of all women incarcerated in New York, as well as substantial proportions of the women arrested for prostitution not just in East Coast cities, but even in St. Paul, Minnesota. That they were more likely to work as domestics made Irish women more vulnerable to the sexual harassment, and rape by masters, which often led to prostitution (about half of New York's prostitutes had been domestics).[35]

Nevertheless, for all their hardships and troubles in America, most Irish immigrants were not merely the passive victims of Ireland's catastrophe and the hardships of urban industrial America, the "scattered debris" of the Irish nation as their own archbishop, Hughes, called them. In 1860, about 29 percent of Irish-born household heads told census takers that they owned real estate; over 58 percent reported that they owned "personal property," largely savings, and over one-quarter claimed such property valued at two hundred dollars or more. Again, they lagged behind the native stock in the North (85 percent personal property; 61 percent real property) and other immigrant groups, English (73 percent personal; 44 percent real) and Germans (74 percent personal; 44 percent real), in the accumulation of wealth (and barely edged out free Blacks in the North with 55 percent personal; 28 percent real). Yet the percentages do testify to the active resilience of many Irish famine immigrants in the face of the many hardships and calamities in their lives.[36]

Evidence from bank records in Philadelphia and in New York confirm that many famine Irish, even laborers and servants, were avid savers. Thousands of Irish immigrants in New York deposited savings in the Emigrant Savings Bank, founded in 1850 by Irish American Catholics. One-third of the male famine Irish immigrants with an account at the bank managed to save $325, and 80 percent did so within eight years of their arrival in America. Day laborers' average peak balance was $280, and domestic servants' was $196.[37]

How did they accumulate so much money so fast?—$325 was the equivalent of a year's wages for laborers. As important, how did they maintain those balances over time amid the difficulties that afflicted so many of them in the new world? About 40 percent of the male depositors were unskilled workers, such as laborers, and over half the women were domestic servants. We are accustomed, perhaps especially in America, to think of economic success as individual, the product of the efforts, ingenuity, or self-discipline of self-made men or women. Yet, given famine Irish immigrants' limited upward occupational mobility and significant downward mobility, most did not accrue such savings simply because they found a better job. A recent study has found that what seemed more important to these New York famine Irish savers was the strength of their networks of friends and relatives—probably the same networks that brought them to America and settled them in New York. "Those who lived in [neighborhood] enclaves with others from the same parish [in Ireland]" and those "who created occupational niches with natives of the same parish" accumulated "substantially more savings than those who did not." These included economic niches of charcoal burners from County Tyrone parishes and peddlers from Donegal ones as well as construction day laborers from parishes near Kenmare in Kerry living together in Five Points. Networks even provided opportunities for some Irish immigrants to move out of manual labor and establish their own small businesses like neighborhood groceries, but especially saloons. Saloons were often the hearths of Irish American networks, celebrating the reciprocity of friendships every day in communal rituals of treating, but also providing meeting places for Irish American societies or gatherings of local politicians (often the saloonkeepers themselves) and their followings. It is important not to dismiss either the effort or the adaptability of these immigrants either in saving money or creating businesses. Nonetheless, it appears that the communal solidarity bred in the scarce economy and peasant resistance of Ireland had a powerful effect in helping them find and keep jobs in a new world, survive its hard times, and for some make economic progress. Interestingly, this reliance on networks was most often a rural inheritance. Immigrants from cities or even large market towns in Ireland did not save as much as rural peasants in such enclaves did, perhaps because they were accustomed to city or town life and felt enough at home with it to find places to live and work on their own.[38]

Networks and the fierce values of communal solidarity that held them together, however, could hinder economic success as well as help it. They could limit members' knowledge of opportunities outside the niche, and ambition for individual success could conflict with ties to community, provoking resentment among those left behind and confused feelings of guilt among those leaving their longtime fellows. To some, Irish men and women seeking bourgeois status might seem to be deserting their friends, their community and, indeed, not being "authentically" Irish. Middle-class, American-born Irish James Mulligan of Chicago joined an Irish militia unit in 1854, for example, because some Irish Catholics "had grave doubts whether I was 'true blue.'" These problems would emerge more clearly later as the children of the famine immigrants grew to maturity, were savvier about American opportunities, and had better access to education, skills, and capital. For now, however, networks were critical to the survival and even modest prosperity of an immigrant people with few such resources.[39]

Famine Irish immigrants also looked to their children to sustain them. Some of course had been married before coming to America, but Irish immigrants who had arrived in America unmarried were slower to marry than members of most other immigrant groups though the vast majority did marry (men 90 percent; women 93 percent in 1880) and married earlier than the rural Irish back home. Once an Irish immigrant woman married, she gave birth to about seven children over her lifetime on average, again not in the same high numbers as in Ireland, but more than most other immigrants (German women had slightly more children over the course of their marriages) and many more than native-born American women. While the children were still toddlers, Irish immigrant couples routinely took in boarders to tide the family over in the lean times, but as soon as children could work, they were hurried into any occupation that might make money. In an 1875 survey by the Massachusetts Bureau of Labor, Irish fathers earned only about two-thirds of their family's income; children supplied the rest. Nearly one-third, or 103 of the 133 Irish families in the study, had working children under fifteen, and their wages made up almost 20 percent of their families' income. Nevertheless, there was more to the big Irish family than crass exploitation of its children; in Philadelphia and Detroit, not just the poorest Irish but skilled Irish workers also had many children. Moreover, as poor as many were, Irish immigrant parents were not insensitive to the fates of their offspring. In cities like Detroit and Milwaukee, for example, Irish-born parents were more likely to keep their children in school than German immigrants of the same economic level. Marriage and building their own family, however, could be a gamble, especially for women, for the Irish men whom they married were especially vulnerable to illness and accidents (43 percent of Irish immigrant women over age fifty were widows in 1880, significantly higher than the proportion of native-born or other immigrant women) and, many observers suggested, Irish men were more likely to desert their wives than husbands from other groups.[40]

If most famine Irish immigrants had survived in their new country, and some did much better than that, many still ached for Ireland, even if they got no closer than sitting in stuffy, American city theaters and the "Ireland" they found there was no more than mountains and castles painted on stage backdrops and "stage Irish" characters, who were cartoonish stereotypes of the rural peasants that they had once been. In 1874, an Irish-born playwright, Dion Boucicault, premiered a new play, *The Shaughran,* in New York. The lead, which Boucicault insisted was not a stage Irish "mindless buffoon," but "a comic hero" who manages to rescue his lord, the true scion of an old aristocratic family, from the schemes of an evil parvenu villain. For the moment immigrants in the audience could dream of a different Ireland than the famine nightmare they had left, but they would not, could not, return to it, for there was no future there for them. Like the new personal and family lives they were making in America, they would thus have to make a community for themselves in the new country as well.[41]

6. The Famine Irish American Community in an America in Crisis

1845–1880

In March 1862 during the Civil War, five African American women approached the defense works of the Union Army, more specifically the entrenchments of the Ninth Massachusetts Infantry, an Irish regiment, commanded by Patrick Guiney, an immigrant from Tipperary. Guiney was a former mechanic but had attended Holy Cross College in Worcester and had become a lawyer in Boston before the war. During the war he embraced the abolition of slavery and after it, he would become a Radical Republican. Yet he was also a fierce Irish nationalist, a Fenian, devoted to the liberation of Ireland, and a strong advocate of workers, eventually running for Congress on the Workingmen's Party ticket. The women walking toward him now were fleeing slavery. As they entered the Ninth's lines, a jubilant Guiney could not help himself and, though by escaping their plantation the African American women had actually freed themselves, he shouted: "In the name of Old Ireland and Massachusetts, I set you free."[1]

As a million and a half Irish immigrants fleeing famine entered the United States, they found not just new and unfamiliar worlds of work and life in industrial urban America, but a country descending into political chaos and ultimately into civil war. By the 1850s, provoked by the alleged threat of such great numbers of Irish flooding the country and frustrated by a national political stalemate over the future of slavery, anti-Catholic nativism became a mass movement and spread throughout the nation. Catholic Irish America, though weak before the famine and burdened with absorbing so many impoverished newcomers during it, nevertheless seemed to emerge a more united and stronger community after the nativist onslaught. As the distraction of nativism dissolved, however, a new political party, the Republicans, emerged, eager for a showdown on the question of slavery. Most Irish American Catholics, increasingly dependent on a weakening northern Democratic Party, shrilly resisted the abolition of slavery. When the war came, however, thousands of them, like Patrick Guiney, joined the Union army, though unlike him the vast majority did so to save the Union, not free the slaves.

The war had an important impact on northern Irish American Catholics, nonetheless. It changed, though did not revolutionize, their relations with African Americans, but it also prompted them to define their own position in America, trying to make sense of their loyalties to both "Old Ireland and Massachusetts." That process continued after the war as they worked both to shape the memory of their role in the conflict and to rally an Irish American Fenian army to fight for Ireland's freedom. Catholic Irish America seemed to flourish in a post–Civil War America, building more and increasingly massive churches and enjoying new success in local politics and the labor movement. Yet when the country's economy collapsed in the 1870s, it exposed the continuing ambiguity of Irish American Catholics' place, where they fit, in their new home of the United States.

A year after the blight crept into Ireland, the United States bullied Mexico into war and invaded it. Some Irish Catholic soldiers deserted the invasion force, complaining of poor treatment by anti-Catholic officers. Many more Irish Catholics, however, fought for the American cause. Though the war was easily won, conflict over what to do with the spoils—territory stretching from Texas to California—would plunge the United States into a political crisis that would end in civil war. Would the new states carved out of the lands won in the war with Mexico be slave or free and upset the delicate political balance of power between the free North and the slave South? And thus would they be preserved as potential small farms for white workingmen or open to big slave plantations? Through the early 1850s, American leaders struggled to find some compromise over the future of the newly conquered territory to hold the country together. The nation's politics blew up, however, after Congress passed the Kansas-Nebraska Act in 1854, for the new law seemed to concede that slavery could now be extended to new territories anywhere in the country, North or South. The act tore the Whigs apart and they disappeared entirely: the Democrats survived but were soon dangerously leaking voters in the North.[2]

In the chaos of this crisis, anti-immigrant, anti-Catholic nativism finally emerged as a national movement centered on a mysterious organization nick-named the "Know-Nothings," (officially, the Order of the Star Spangled Banner, OSSB). The Know-Nothings drew on boiling fears and resentments: most obvi-ously, the tripling of the proportion of immigrants in the population after 1840, and the enormous power these Irish and many German newcomers now gave the Catholic Church in America. Yet Know-Nothing anger also fed on native-stock American frustration with an American politics infested, they believed, with behind-the-scenes "wire pullers" and toadies to Catholic power, and thus rendering the government incapable of addressing the crisis over slavery and the increasing regional division it caused. In just the few months after the Kansas-Nebraska Act, OSSB membership rose from 50,000 to over one million. The Know-Nothings, however, would become more than just a single organization; they would be a national political movement, in many places calling themselves "the American Party." In many parts of the North, the nativists opposed slavery as well as immigrants and Catholics; in the South they often stood for the union. Nowhere were they more powerful than in New England, where they thoroughly dominated the local and state politics of Massachusetts, Rhode Is-land, Connecticut, and New Hampshire, but they were strong, if not so domi-nant, throughout much of the country. In Massachusetts, the Know-Nothing government stepped up its deportations of immigrants, mainly Irish, and there and in other states, nativists pushed laws to restrict immigrant voting. Know-Nothing mobs also attacked Catholics and their churches in places like Man-chester, New Hampshire, and Lawrence and Dorchester, Massachusetts; Brook-lyn, New York, and Newark, New Jersey. This combination of political assertion and street violence swept away for good the fragile, friendly relations that Irish Catholics had once enjoyed with Protestants in places like Worcester and Lowell or even St. Louis, Missouri, where ten people died in a riot in 1854. A St. Louis merchant claimed, "there will be a lot of blood spilt before the Irish find out which stall they belong in."[3]

The Know-Nothing attacks fell upon weak, divided Irish American Cath-olic communities, which hardly seemed capable of standing up to the assaults. As noted earlier, in 1845, when the famine began, many Irish parishes in America were in debt, with their congregations fighting among themselves over rivalries rooted in old country county origins or disputes over new issues like temper-ance. Then the famine dumped over a million and half largely poor, Catholic immigrants on them in less than ten years. The new immigrants' huge numbers, their poverty, the weak ties many had had to the institutional Church in Ireland, and the fact that, like many poor in nineteenth-century America, they moved often in cities, combined to pose enormous problems for Irish Catholic communities in America. In 1850, in New York's Five Points neighborhood, where up to 40 percent of the Irish residents were unskilled, only 21 percent of the children baptized in the local Transfiguration parish were the children of unskilled fathers. Furthermore, only 41 percent of the parents of children baptized at the church in 1850 were still in the city by 1859 and only 17 percent by 1869. The continued dramatic shift in the Irish origins of the immigrants from the north to the south and west of Ireland meant that conflicts between natives of different Irish counties continued into the famine era, even seemed to escalate, in places like Lowell, Jersey City, Pittsburgh, and Chicago. Finally, even the old country's suffering did not provide a rallying point for Irish American communities, as squabbles over famine relief donations and support for Young Ireland seemed to worsen community divisions in some places rather than heal them.[4]

Irish American Catholic communities, however, did not fold under the nativist pressure but, rather, grew stronger. The number of Catholic churches (not all of them were Irish but a substantial number of them were) doubled or more than doubled in Massachusetts, Rhode Island, and Pennsylvania, and nearly tripled in Illinois in the 1850s. Older Catholic parishes, like long-troubled St. Patrick's in Lowell and St. John's in Worcester, built new churches. The Ballykilcline refugees and other Irish in Rutland, Vermont, built a new St. Bridget's Church and a school; Transfiguration parish in New York's Five Points cleared its debts, moved to a new church, and opened a school; St. Patrick's in Chicago built a grand new church; and Irish railroad workers in Jacksonville, Illinois, built a small church and then a grander one.[5]

Irish American Catholics did not shy from celebrating these achievements or demonstrating their confidence. They marked almost every stage in the building of the new churches with parades. At the cornerstone ceremony for a new Immaculate Conception Church in Newburyport, the *Boston Pilot* crowed: "It appeared to some of the worthy descendants of the Pilgrims that the Pope had taken solemn possession of the town." St. Patrick's Day parades had begun to emerge in some cities in the 1830s and 1840s, but they took place only haphazardly then and were usually small sideshows on back streets. By the 1850s, boasting greater numbers, and drawing on experiences with Catholic Emancipation and Repeal processions, the parades now grew to throngs of thousands, stepping out on major thoroughfares. Ten thousand men were in the line of march for the parade in New York in 1860, for example.[6]

As much as the famine flood of immigrants may have seemed a burden to them, there were also significant resources for Irish American Catholic churches in the new immigration. Though some of the famine Irish immigrants came from the west of Ireland, where the institutional Church was weak, many were also coming now from Munster and from Leinster, parts of the Catholic heartland, where mass attendance rates exceeded Ireland's average. The high proportion of women among the Irish immigrants, especially in the cities, helped the Church as well. Historians agree that Irish immigrant women were more involved in parish devotional life and attentive to their religious duties than men in this era, and though their wages were meager, the "disposable income" of the vast number of live-in female domestic servants was a rich source of funds for Catholic churches. Women also began to run parish fairs or bazaars, major sources of church financing, by the late 1850s. Priests were moving to America from Ireland in increasing numbers too. Some were from the new All Hallows Seminary, recently founded for the overseas missions, but others came from diocesan seminaries like Carlow as well. The number of Irish women religious also grew. The first Irish Sisters of Mercy arrived in Pittsburgh in 1843, and Presentation Sisters from Ireland arrived in San Francisco in 1854. It would be largely religious women's initiative and hard work that built the infant Catholic charitable network of orphanages, hospitals, and refuges for single women in this period.[7]

The long-brewing transformation of the western world's Catholic religious practice called the Catholic Revival also peaked in America just as the famine immigrants settled and the Know-Nothing assault began, and this too strengthened the Church. Directed by the Vatican and taking advantage of new technologies for cheap printing and image reproduction as well as Irish immigrant literacy (according to the 1860 U.S. Census, 79 percent of Irish-born men and 70 percent of women in America over age sixteen were literate), the Revival gave new life to old Catholic devotions like the Blessed Sacrament or the Sacred Heart of Jesus and popularized new ones like the cult of the contemporary apparition of Mary at Lourdes in France. Yet it also drove home its fundamental tenets: the model of a suffering Christ, the Church as a refuge in a hostile world, and the ultimate authority of the pope and the bishops. More new Catholic prayer books and titles appeared in the United States in the 1850s than in any other decade between 1800 and 1880 and more than had appeared in all the years between 1800 and 1840. The number of new devotional confraternities and sodalities per parish also more than doubled in America in the mid-nineteenth century.[8]

Of all the new "tools" of the devotional revolution, however, none perhaps was as useful or powerful as the parish mission. The mission was a kind of Catholic revival meeting, of one, two, or more rarely, up to four weeks long, conducted in parish churches but led by mission bands from religious orders like the Jesuits and Redemptorists, who included priests from many ethnic backgrounds. The missions were often exceptionally well attended and sometimes extraordinarily emotional. At the first mission at St. Joseph's Church in Greenwich Village run by the Redemptorists in the 1850s, over 6,000 people went to confession, and on the last night the preacher could not be heard because of the "weeping of the congregation." The Redemptorists preached 188 missions in that decade, five times more than they had in the 1840s. In Philadelphia, Catholic parish missions became so frequent in the 1850s that one historian has suggested that the decade seemed like "a perpetual revival." Many who attended the missions drifted away from the Church after the religious fervor subsided. Still, the revivals had lasting effects. As historians have pointed out, they helped bolster Irish American Catholics' religious identity by setting Catholics and non-Catholics apart "in a clear and distinctive way . . . emphasizing devotions to doctrines which Protestants rejected such as . . . devotions to Mary."[9]

Yet the hostility of the Know-Nothing enemy outside the group drew that distinction as neatly and powerfully as any changes within the Church, and in the process, ironically, also helped strengthen Irish American Catholic communities. In places like Lowell and Worcester in Massachusetts, Know-Nothing pressure pushed Irish county factions to abandon their rivalries to meet the common threat, lest they seem like traitors. As Archbishop John Hughes suggested in a letter to the president of the University of Notre Dame in 1858, "In some respects . . . their [Know-Nothings'] violence was very serviceable to the Catholic cause."[10]

If Irish American Catholicism survived the 1850s, indeed, even seemed to thrive, the Know-Nothing battles left some disturbing legacies for the Catholic Church in America. Irish Catholic writers made clear that the religious war between Catholics and Protestants was unrelenting and ongoing and efforts to try to bridge the sectarian divide would no longer be acceptable. As Father John Roddan, editor of the *Boston Pilot,* emphatically stated: there was no room for "LIBERAL Catholics" in the Church anymore. Emboldened by the Know-Nothing battles' reinforcement of their authority, Irish American Catholic bishops and priests also attacked radicalism and reform in the Irish American community outside the Church. They cracked down heavily on any hint of Irish nationalist "red republicanism" in Irish American newspapers; counseled the resignation of a suffering Christ, not reform or resistance, to the impoverished; and opposed the abolition of slavery. They treated enslavement as just another rank in a natural social hierarchy, but they also despised the abolitionists as evangelical Protestant troublemakers. Even Father Sherwood Healy, rector of Boston's cathedral and son of a Black slave and an Irish-born father, complained that the abolitionists' interest in the slave was "only a pretext" for their attack on their real enemy, the Catholic Church.[11]

Issues of slavery and race had never really gone away as nativism thrived, but as the Know-Nothings disappeared in 1856, a new Republican Party emerged which confronted the threat of slavery's expansion head on, and those issues so long evaded could no longer be ignored. In the small, densely packed "walking cities" of mid-nineteenth-century America, Irish Americans and African Americans in the North often lived in the same neighborhoods, like Five Points in New York, even on the same streets, frequented the same saloons, shared the same urban slang, "flash talk," and songs and dances. African American men were also more likely to marry Irish women or find lovers among them than other white women. Nevertheless, Irish Americans often fought ferociously with their Black neighbors and became among the fiercest defenders of slavery in the North. Irish American racism was not new in the 1850s, but circumstances in that decade, like the arrival of thousands of immigrants fresh from the famine disaster, the eruption of nativism, and increasing open sectional and partisan division over slavery, helped make it more intense than ever before.[12]

Comparisons of the Irish and African Americans had long been common in both Ireland and America, but they seemed to have a special edge in the America of the 1850s. Southern defenders of slavery in that decade ratcheted up old fantasies that Black slaves might have been better off than either peasants in Ireland or poor Irish workers in America because they had masters to take care of them. Irish American Catholics, who had often made that argument in the past too, also cranked it up now, making special note of its corollary that northern or British abolitionists "who weep and howl over the negroes [they] never saw" were indifferent to "the white slavery of the wretched Irish poor." Such comparisons, combined with their attacks on greedy and uncaring Yankee

industrialists, seemed in part a reworking of older Irish Catholic contrasts between the true, dispossessed Catholic lords of Ireland and the phony Protestant
ones who replaced them. With little direct evidence of Irish immigrants' feelings, it is impossible to know for sure, but such contentions may have had a
special resonance for the newest Irish immigrants, only recently abandoned by
their landlords to the horrors of the famine and now suffering the insecurities
and hardships of industrial life in America. Minstrel shows, popular among the
Irish, may have also reinforced the budding racism of the new Irish immigrants.
Such shows celebrated slavery's paternalism, which could have stoked hidden
Irish envy and resentment of the African American slave's supposed economic
security, but the shows also mocked Black inferiority, reminding Irish newcomers that no white man in America should choose such abased dependence.[13]

Some historians of antebellum Irish Catholics' racism and support for
slavery argue that Irish immigrants were not certain that they were white and
became fiercely anti-Black to distance themselves from African Americans and
prove they belonged among whites, not nonwhites. Hostility to Blacks was, then,
a means of gaining acceptance from the white mainstream, a strategy of assimilation. In the South and perhaps the West (where the Chinese were the racial
other), racial boundaries might have fully overridden religious or ethnic ones
and helped Irish Catholics gain easy acceptance. By the 1850s, however, relations among white groups and the interconnections of those relations with race
and slavery were more complicated in the Northeast and parts of the Midwest. In
New England by then, Irish American Catholics recognized clearly Yankee Protestants' growing abolitionist sympathies and that their own attacks on Blacks
would hurt, not help, them gain Yankee acceptance. In 1854, for example, they
knew of the enthusiastic and broad Yankee commitment in Massachusetts to
prevent an escaped slave, Anthony Burns, from being sent back into slavery, but
deliberately chose the other side, helping federal officials to ship him South and
back into bondage.[14]

Most evidence suggests that Irish Catholic immigrants in the North already believed that they were white, but in the heat of this nativist decade, they
seemed more uncertain than ever about whether they would be allowed to retain
the privileges of whiteness. They often described nativist attacks as efforts to reduce them to the status of Blacks. They also specifically identified abolitionists
as the principal group trying to so reduce them, continuing to describe them
not just as opponents in a fight over slavery, but *their* enemies targeting *them.*
In 1857, the *Boston Pilot* charged that "The persecutors of the foreign-born

citizen and the negro party in the free states are one and the same thing." In defining abolitionists thus, Irish Catholics also returned to the notion that Irish and African Americans were locked in a zero-sum fight for rights: if Blacks gained their rights, they would lose theirs. In 1855, the *Pittsburgh Catholic,* for example, claimed that nativist antislavery men proposed "to take off from the Negro his manacles and put them on the hands and feet of Catholics."[15] Some Yankee abolitionists, most notably the famous Unitarian minister Theodore Parker, did invoke the same comparisons of African and Irish Americans to laud the former and disparage the latter as inherently lazy or given over to thievery. Irish Americans and their Democratic allies, in turn, appeared to pound attacks on Yankee abolitionists' prejudice to undermine the reformers' claims to a higher morality or egalitarianism and try to transform their own opposition to abolition into a democratic crusade against elites. As Irish Catholic opponents of anti-slavery continued to harp on the zero-sum game between Irish and African American rights, they also asserted not just their outrage at abolitionists, but an inevitable and immutable logic of mutual hostility between themselves and Blacks.[16]

With the destruction of the Whigs and the Know-Nothings, the Republicans stepped up quickly to become the principal competition for Democrats in the North. As early as the 1856 election for president, just two years after the new party's birth, they won eleven of sixteen free states. While the Republicans rose in the North, the Democrats began to decline there, and now came to depend more and more on Irish Catholics as a critical element in their northern base. During the explosion of Know-Nothings' popularity in the mid-1850s, even the Democratic hero of the New York Irish, Fernando Wood, had briefly joined the nativist chorus. Wood, however, quickly scampered back to the Democrats and the Irish as the Know-Nothings collapsed. Foreign-born voters, the bulk of them Irish Catholics, had become over half of New York's electorate by then and could no longer be kept at arm's length. The Irish also became vital to the Democratic Party in Chicago, and in smaller cities like Lawrence, Massachusetts, where Irish immigrant Terrence Brady ran the local Democratic Party caucus by 1859 "because [Irish immigrants] were so essential" to the party.[17]

If the Democrats were more dependent on Irish American Catholics in the 1850s, however, the Irish were increasingly dependent on the Democrats. Though they had survived the Know-Nothing onslaught and their numbers had grown, the nativist upsurge had, nonetheless, revealed their continuing political vulnerability. The principal focus of the new Republican Party was on stopping the expansion of slavery, but the new party's base was made up of Yankee evangelicals, Congregationalists, Baptists, and increasingly even Ulster Scot Presbyterians in the North, who suspected Rome and were strong backers of temperance as well as opponents of slavery. Republican Free Soil ideology also saw Catholicism as similar to "the Slave Power," a benighted aristocratic conspiracy that blocked all prospects for common people's education and self-improvement. In attacking congressmen who tried to lengthen the waiting period for naturalization in the nation's naturalization law, the *Boston Pilot* noted that of the sixty-eight congressmen who did so, "sixty-three were firm supporters of [the Republican, John C.] Fremont [in the presidential election of 1856]. Not a Democrat has disgraced himself by placing his name in the list." Much was at stake for Irish Catholics then in this new conflict between Republicans and Democrats, intensifying their commitment to the Democratic Party, but also tying them to the party's pro-slavery racism that had seemingly become its sole cause by the 1850s. Irish Catholic David Broderick, born into "Dickensian" poverty but now a U.S. Senator from California, was a Free Soil Democrat and scourge of southern slaveholder pretension, but he was killed in a duel by a southern sympathizer in 1859, and few Irish Catholics took up his cause. Indeed, in that same year, American-born Irish Charles O'Conor, distinguished lawyer, direct descendant of the last High King of Ireland, son of a United Irish exile, felt compelled to publicly insist that "slavery is not unjust," for "the negro is decreed by nature to a state of pupilage under the dominion of the wiser white man."[18]

As soon as the next year, however, the reckoning with slavery finally arrived.

As fierce Democrats, Irish Catholics almost everywhere in the North (except Illinois) voted nearly unanimously against Lincoln. If unhappy with Lincoln's victory, however, the southern secession that followed gave them pause. In an intriguing editorial the *Irish American* implored the South not to secede and abandon the northern "working class . . . who are as much the victims of abolition misrule. . . . as the Southerners are . . . just at the moment. . . . of a common danger [Republican victory]." Nevertheless, the paper insisted that "we cannot be induced to foreswear the allegiance we have pledged to our adopted country to gratify the secessionists."[19]

About 140,000 or more Irish-born fought for the Union during the Civil War, about one- sixth as members of Irish regiments or companies, like the 69th New York, 9th Massachusetts, and 23rd Illinois. Contemporaries and historians since have sometimes depicted these Irish Civil War soldiers as shiftless, unskilled workers, many of them recent newcomers, scarcely tethered to their new country or their new communities. Military records reveal that Irish-born soldiers were, indeed, far less likely to be farmers and far *more* likely to be non-farm "manual workers" than native-born American or Scandinavian or German immigrant enlistees. Some of them undoubtedly looked to service in the war as an economic opportunity. It was a job, the pay and work were "regular," and room and board, such as they were, were free. Recent studies of Irish American soldiers in several Irish and non-Irish regiments and of enlistments in Concord, Massachusetts, however, have found that skilled Irish immigrant manual workers were more likely to join the army than unskilled ones. The study of the Irish regiments also discovered that the Irish soldiers were also significantly older, on average, than most Civil War soldiers and a substantial proportion of them were married.[20]

So why did so many older, modestly successful family men, likely of long residence in America, join this fight?

Peter Welsh of the Irish Brigade's 28th Massachusetts regiment bridled when his wife wrote to him at the front that her relatives in Ireland thought he should let the Americans, "them," fight their war; who are "they," he wrote back, "this is my country as much as men born of this soil." In what became a very popular theme in Irish American soldiers' rhetoric about the war, Welsh insisted that the United States, the Union, must be saved for the sake of oppressed emigrants: what would have been the fate "of hundreds of thousands of the sons and daughters of poor old oppressed erin," he asked, "if they had not had a free land like this to emigrate to [with] famine and hunger staring them in the face." Some historians argue that many may have joined more to learn the arts of war to help free the old country rather than to serve the new. As we shall see, however, most soldiers did not commit to Irish independence by joining the new Fenian Brotherhood—founded in 1858 to fight that war of Irish liberation—until near the end of their service, or after they had grown confident in their martial skills and become eager to apply them to rebellion in Ireland.[21]

Moreover, they did not see a contradiction in their dual loyalties, or the need to choose between the two. Observers noted that support for the Union was particularly strong in the Irish regiments and among Fenians in the North. Furthermore, if Irish Catholic soldiers believed fighting in the war proved their loyalty to the United States, it was not because of a need for acceptance so much as a demand for recognition. As Thomas Francis Meagher, a Young Ireland leader and now commander of the Irish Brigade, said, by serving in the war they could stand before the native-born soldier, "look him straight and sternly in the face and tell him that he has been equal to him in allegiance to the Constitution."[22]

Yet they sought not just recognition of their American patriotism, as individuals, but as members of an Irish American people. They looked to history to help make that case, transforming their shady notoriety for toughness as streetwise thugs into a reputation for military valor by setting it in a long tradition of Irish martial heroism. Doing so also helped them define who they were, the Irish, a people, some of them would say a race, not limited to a place, Ireland. Thus, though they often cited old heroes in Ireland as proof of their people's courage on the battlefield, they looked, in particular, to the history of Irish soldiers on the European continent, who won glory fighting in French and other armies, to create this martial tradition. The battle of Fontenoy, where a bayonet charge by Irish soldiers serving France turned the tide against a British army in 1745, became their mantra. John Mitchel, a Young Irelander now a fierce southern sympathizer, complained that "Fontenoyism" seemed to have become a mania among the Irish in the North, as it appeared in countless speeches, recruiting broadsides and posters, the names of regimental barracks, rallying cries on the battlefield, and even the diary entries of women supporters.[23]

Yet the cost in blood for this effort was enormous among the "Irish" regiments from Massachusetts, Pennsylvania, and New York: the percentage killed was about 12 percent or one in eight, or over twice as high as the proportion for Union armies as a whole. The Irish Brigade alone suffered over 4,000 casualties, "more than ever belonged to the brigade at any one time." Data from a few New York and Illinois regiments suggest that Irish casualties in non-Irish units were higher than the Union average too but not as high as in some of the Irish regiments.[24]

Irish American Catholics seemed to find such costs less bearable as Abraham Lincoln's Emancipation Proclamation appeared to shift the principal purpose of the war from saving the Union to freeing the slaves. Infuriated by the new policy, Irish American newspapers laid into Lincoln: even New York's staunchly pro-war *Irish American* condemned Lincoln's "negrophilism" and lamented the "malignity of the abolitionist hatred of the Irish race." Peter Welsh and probably most Irish soldiers had little sympathy for the slaves and seemed to simply want to wish them away. Not long after the Emancipation Proclamation took effect, the federal government introduced a national draft to reinforce the army, and riots broke out to protest the draft in Boston and many Irish American commu-

Figure 8. *Group of Irish Brigade as they lay on the battlefield of Antietam, 19ᵗʰ Sept., 1862*. These dead soldiers were but some of the 113 members of the Brigade killed in the battle September 17, 1862. 422 were wounded. Statistics from the Irish Brigade Monument: Antietam National Battlefield, Maryland: National Park Service. Photo by Alexander Gardner. Library of Congress: LC DIG-ds-05164.

nities, but most notably in New York. There the largely Irish American rioters wreaked havoc in the city for four days, cheering Jefferson Davis, attacking Republicans, Chinese immigrants, Irish women in relationships with African Americans, and, most often, Blacks of all ages, torturing, lynching, and even mutilating their dead corpses with a furious cruelty. Whites could avoid rioters' assaults by claiming: "I am a Democratic Catholic." In the 1864 presidential election, the Irish in Massachusetts voted an estimated nine to one for General George McClellan, Lincoln's opponent.[25]

Nevertheless, the war had begun to open some cracks in Irish opposition to abolition and African Americans. Some Irish American soldiers like Guiney became sympathetic to abolition, and a few like Felix Brannigan and the later Fenian leader John O'Neill served as officers in Black regiments. "The War has been a great educator," an Irish immigrant from Cincinnati wrote in 1864.[26]

After the Civil War, Irish American Catholics in the North initially seemed not to learn its lessons, joining enthusiastically in efforts to hold back the tide of Black rights, but the outcome of the war would force them to change, if reluctantly. By the early 1870s, Democrats across the North, Irish and non-Irish, had begun talking about a change in their approach to racial politics, a "New Departure." American-born Irish Peter Sweeny, a key figure in New York City's Democratic Party, told the *New York Herald* frankly in 1870: "We ought to get rid of the [anti-Black] agitation. . . . It hurts [us] more than the Negro vote could injure us." It "introduces a moral issue—a sentiment of justice," Sweeny sniffed dismissively, which nonetheless, he acknowledged, "carries away many voters, especially among Germans." Sweeny still believed African Americans were inferior to whites, but as one historian has suggested, Sweeny's comments meant that "politically, race no longer made sense" for the Democrats in New York. Moreover, Sweeny and the Democrats did not mean to ignore African Americans; they were, after all, the party of poor people: "Our boys understand how to get them," he boasted. Irish American Catholic Democrats also cautiously connected with African Americans in Connecticut and Philadelphia in the 1870s, and Boston in the 1880s. Much of the "New Departure" was tokenism, but it was a change. More striking evidence of new Irish attitudes about race appeared in the Irish American press, particularly the two most prestigious and popular Irish newspapers in America, the *Boston Pilot* and the *Irish World.* Only recently viciously racist, the *Pilot,* under new editor, immigrant and former Fenian John Boyle O'Reilly, celebrated Black pride, hailing "The Negro" as "a new man, a free man, a spiritual man, a heart man, and he can be a great man, if he can avoid modeling himself on whites." Meanwhile Patrick Ford, who had worked for William Lloyd Garrison's abolitionist newspaper, the *Liberator,* as a teenager and had been a soldier in Guiney's Ninth Massachusetts, became editor of the *Irish World,* where he made "tireless efforts," as one historian has pointed out, "to connect Irish nationalism with the African American struggle for equality." There were limits to both men's support for federal enforcement of such equality in the South, however, and Irish American Catholics continued to violently resist Black integration of their neighborhoods and workplaces. Irish American attitudes about African Americans in this era were thus beginning to settle into a paradox that would persist for a long time: a cautious public and political acceptance of African American rights, if initially only in the North, combined with recurring, sometimes violent opposition to them in city neighborhoods or on job sites.[27]

An important part of Irish American Catholics' adjustment to post–Civil War America was to shape the memory of their part in the war. This effort began soon after the war, but it grew stronger after the end of Reconstruction. It would not be easy, given their wartime opposition to abolition and Lincoln, but over time, most people in the North began to focus increasingly on battle-field heroism and soldierly valor in remembering the war and not on the past issue of African American slavery and the persisting one of Black inequality. Irish American veterans, like St. Clair Mulholland, who won the Congressional Medal of Honor in the war, capitalized on that trend as well as the popular image of the fighting Irish to celebrate the battlefield valor of Irish soldiers in the war through the erection of monuments, St. Patrick's Day speeches, books, and articles. It was a memory not made up out of whole cloth—there were he-roes and sacrifices at Antietam, Fredericksburg, Gettysburg, and other battles—but it left out much—no draft riots, desertions, or opposition to Lincoln and emancipation. Nevertheless, this Irish American Catholic memory-making per-mitted an anti-abolitionist, pro-South, often racist, antebellum Irish American people to become a better fit for a new postwar, post-slavery North.[28]

In the South both old and new Irish rallied to the Confederate cause. There were fewer Irish immigrants there than in the North, but perhaps as many as 20,000 Irish-born men fought for the South, nearly one quarter of the region's Irish immigrant population. In the North, Irish Catholics would have to go to war as allies of one enemy, Yankee Protestant Republicans, for the lib-eration of another, African Americans. In the South, there were no such compli-cations. Harder to estimate, historians have suggested that untold thousands, perhaps, hundreds of thousands of descendants of the Ulster Scots and other Irish immigrants of the seventeenth and eighteenth centuries fought for the South as well. As ardent for the Confederacy as the new and old Irish might have been, however, many became disgruntled with the war or simply tired of it as casualties mounted and sacrifices grew. Irish-born men deserted from the rebel army at an extraordinarily high rate. Some areas of the South, which had long been strongholds of that early Ulster Scot settlement—parts of Tennessee, Kentucky, and Virginia—had even flirted with abolition in the 1830s, and some there remained either skeptical participants in the Confederate war effort or even openly opposed to it.[29]

Yet as the war ended and the North began its reconstruction of the de-feated Confederacy, few Irish, old or new, in the South were willing to accommo-date either the Yankee victor or their newly freed Black neighbors. In 1866, Irish immigrants played a prominent role in vicious race riots in Memphis and New Orleans. An Irish American Catholic priest named Abram Ryan also became the poet laureate of the South's "Lost Cause" after the war. That was hardly a coincidence, for southern white Americans and the Irish were, as one author has suggested, "strange kin," both understanding themselves as victims of powerful, modernizing, soulless conquerors and mourning the demise of an allegedly more genteel, lost world.[30]

Making war had not ended for Irish Americans in April 1865. As the Union triumphed and the United States was saved, they turned in earnest to plotting a new war to liberate Ireland: a war led by the Fenian Brotherhood. To many at the time and since, the Fenians seemed laughable. They were riddled with English spies, but as Mark Twain asked, who needed spies? "All the air is filled with stage whispers. . . . in the dead of night they [the Fenian leaders] secretly plan a Canada raid and publish it in the *World* in the morning." Such raids as well as attempted guerrilla risings in Ireland failed, sometimes ludicrously, but the Fenians were no joke. Their image as violent revolutionaries was so powerful and widespread that it filled the obsessive nightmares haunting madmen as diverse as W. C. Minor, a contributor to the *Oxford English Dictionary,* and Quimbo Appo, a Chinese immigrant and convicted murderer imprisoned in Sing Sing. More important, the Fenians were stunningly popular among the Irish in America. By the end of the Civil War, the Fenians had 45,000 members, and an estimated 250,000 supporters, who went to their speeches, parades, rallies, and picnics and gave them money. They thrived among the Irish in places as diverse as New York City, Chicago, San Francisco, Worcester, Lowell, and Troy, as well as small communities like Atchison, Kansas; Gilbertville, Massachusetts; Whitewater, Wisconsin; and among the Ballykilcline immigrants in Rutland, Vermont.[31]

The Fenians were popular in part because they offered a new opportunity for ethnic fellowship for Irish Americans. Fenian picnics, replete with parades, speeches, athletic contests, dancing, and "sham" battles, attracted tens of thousands in cities like Buffalo, New York, and San Francisco, but also hundreds regularly in places like Peoria, Illinois; New Haven, Connecticut; Framingham, Massachusetts; and Hoboken, New Jersey. Irish American men had few alternatives for such fellowship then: women dominated most parish societies, and infant Irish fraternal societies, like the Ancient Order of Hibernians, could not yet match the Fenians' national reach or their martial glamor.[32]

There were, however, other reasons why Irish Americans embraced Fenianism at this moment of the mid-1860s, and they can, perhaps, best be understood by looking at who the Fenians were. Sometime in 1865, Fenian leaders compiled a roster of soldiers in an "Irish American Army," whom they expected to fight in some manner for Ireland. The roster listed the birthplace, age, information on wartime service, and Fenian induction dates of the "army's" members. Almost all were Irish born, a disproportionately large proportion, 53 percent, from Munster, where secret societies and O'Connellite nationalism had once ruled. Over 70 percent of them had been born in the ten years before the famine, likely emigrating to America during or after it and personally aware of its hardships.[33]

The memories of the famine's horrors had seemed suppressed from the shock of emigration and then buried under a succession of crises in the Irish American community, but the Fenians and others reawakened them in the late 1860s. If these Fenians and their sympathizers were seeking revenge for the famine then, however, they did so because they now thought they could. Their core members were battle-tested veterans, convinced of their own fighting ability, backed by an Irish American public convinced as well by their wartime heroics. In William O'Brien's novel *When We Were Boys,* Mick McCarthy, a veteran of the Civil War and now a Fenian who had returned to Ireland, recalls: "I never slept the night before a battle that I did not dream of [my]" family's eviction during the famine "and wish we had the Ninth Massachusetts coming up the glen at the double that morning . . . we soon may."[34]

Scores of Irish American Civil War veterans in recognizably American-style, square-toed boots would travel to Ireland to provoke rebellions there in 1865 and 1867, but it would have been hard to send many more and it proved impossible to keep many of those who went there from getting caught by the British. To give the bulk of the Irish American army an opportunity to fight, the real war would have to be fought in North America. The notion of an attack on Canada to somehow bargain an exchange for Ireland had been bruited about in Irish American nationalist circles since the 1840s. Whether such a strategy could somehow actually free Ireland or not, however, may not have been as important as the desire of thousands of Irish American veterans to take on their British enemy in Canada *à la Fontenoy* and have a chance to redeem Irish American pride and erase the famine's humiliation. They were the "Irish American Army" as a popular Fenian song rang:

> Who in a flood of Irish blood [the southern] Rebellion's flame extinguished . . .
> And soon you'll see Ould Erin free
> By the Irish American Army

The members of this army themselves at the time, and their admirers after, seemed to imagine that their fight would mimic formal conventional warfare:

Figure 9. *The Battle of Ridgeway. C.W. June 2, 1866.* This depiction of the battle of Ridgeway, Ontario, fought during the Fenian invasion of Canada, reflects well Irish Americans' imagining of it as a formal conventional war. Print by Thomas Kelly, 1870. Library of Congress: LC DIG-pga-01485.

neatly uniformed soldiers would be arrayed in long lines in open fields with "bayonets . . . banners and sashes," as James Stephens derisively complained. Stephens was head of the Irish Republican Brotherhood (IRB), founded at the same time in Ireland as the Fenians in America and their revolutionary collaborator, but he looked to the American Fenians to send money to fund the IRB's guerrilla war in Ireland, not invade Canada. Later prints and even picnic re-enactments would depict the principal fight of the 1866 invasion of Canada, the Battle of Ridgeway, as that romantic, conventional conflict, even though many of the Irish who fought there wore their own clothes or pieces of uniforms and it was actually a confused tangle of skirmishes in the Ontario woods.

If there had been no Civil War, the Fenians may have still emerged in America, but probably more slowly and not as a grand crusade fought by a conventional Irish American army but more likely as a smaller secret society, and as Stephens hoped, supporting the IRB's war in Ireland. Indeed, in 1867, shortly after the first Fenian invasion of Canada failed, IRB men and some American Fenians met in New York City to launch just such a new, clandestine, and tightly disciplined organization that took the name Clan na Gael (clan of the Gaels). The Clan soon embraced new tactics of dynamite terrorism to overthrow British rule in Ireland.[35]

Despite their failures, the Fenians were critical to the history of Irish America. They helped make Irish American nationalism, like the Democratic Party and the Catholic Church, more or less permanently central to the experience of Irish Americans. Nationalism, and physical force revolutionary nationalism in particular, would emerge much more easily and become more popular in the United States than in Canada, Australia, and Britain, where preaching violent overthrow of the empire was treason. Fenianism also helped make Irish American nationalism vital to nationalists in Ireland. For Daniel O'Connell, Irish American support had been potentially helpful to his Repeal movement but not necessary for its success. Now, Irish nationalists had to come to America and to Irish Americans for money, possible influence on the powerful United States government, and in the Fenian case, even the soldiers to fight a war for independence.

The Fenians were also important to Irish Americans, however, because they continued the reinvention of Irish American identity and the crusade for group self-respect that Irish American soldiers had begun during the Civil War. The Fenians' American patriotism, ardent republicanism, and exploitation of northern hostility to Britain over its wartime dalliance with the Confederacy made them crucial actors in harmonizing Irish aspirations with American republican ideals and interests. A broad spectrum of Americans backed them, including Henry Wilson, a former Know-Nothing governor, later Radical Republican senator of Massachusetts and vice president of the United States, who roared at a Fenian picnic: "I am a Fenian." Ironically, the Fenians arrested by the United Kingdom government in Ireland probably contributed the most to this process of ethnic reinvention. They mounted a broad media campaign, demanding that the United States defend them, its "adopted [naturalized] citizens," as fully as any native-born ones against highhanded United Kingdom courts. In doing so these Irish revolutionaries extolled American greatness, insisted on their American patriotism, and pointed to the wounds that they had suffered in service to the Union during the Civil War.[36]

Drawing on Fenian energy, unburdened by the politics of slavery, and enjoying a new acceptance—if wary and fragile—from native-stock Americans, Irish American Catholics enjoyed great success after the war. By 1870, Irish-dominated American Catholicism was flourishing: the number of Catholic churches across the United States had tripled since 1850 and the value of Catholic property had increased sixfold. A five-hour procession opening a huge new St. Patrick's Cathedral in New York City in 1879 marked the triumph. Irish American Catholics also became key figures in a revived wartime and postwar American labor movement, making up a substantial proportion of the members of the Knights of St. Crispin, the huge shoe and bootmakers' union in Massachusetts, as well as members and leaders of the Workingmen's Benevolent Association (WBA), the miners' union in the Pennsylvania coal fields, and powerful local unions in Chicago and New York. In politics, they provided William Marcy "Boss" Tweed's Democratic Tammany Hall political machine with an enormous and loyal mass base, crucial to its rule over New York City from 1869 to 1871, but they also gained important representation in his "ring's" inner circle. Meanwhile they became potent forces in the city governments of Chicago, Jersey City, New Jersey, and Troy, New York, among other cities.[37]

With growing Irish Catholic numbers, institutions, and public presence, "Irish" more clearly than ever meant "Irish Catholic." Protestant Irishmen had been abandoning their Catholic fellow Irish for several decades by now. A particularly bloody Catholic assault on an Orange parade in New York City in 1871 seemed to seal that break for all but the most stalwart Protestant Irish American nationalists. Elsewhere in the diaspora, in Canada and Australia in particular, Protestant Irish found homes in the Orange Order, but that organization seemed too tainted by allegiance to the British empire for Irish Protestants in the American republic, who simply continued to melt into a Protestant American mainstream. Meanwhile, the Catholic Church's aggressive conservatism made reconciliation with any Protestants, Irish or not, unlikely. As the First Vatican Council in 1869–1870 voted to assert the infallibility of the pope in all matters of faith and morals, the American-born Irish bishop Bernard McQuaid warned, "we can look out for hard times in all countries in which Catholics and Protestants are . . . to live together. In fact we furnish them with good reasons to drive us out of the country."[38]

On the morning of September 18, 1873, the investment house of Jay Cooke and Company closed its doors, and the American economy began a steep descent into a long depression. By 1875, three million workers were unemployed, and two-fifths of the work force was working only six or seven months a year. The value of railroad stock fell by half by 1877, and the laying of new rails virtually stopped during the same time. For many Irish immigrants who had fled the famine, this sudden economic collapse revived memories of the icy terror of that earlier catastrophe.[39]

Workers tried to fight back against wage cuts and layoffs but found it difficult. Many of the new unions like the Crispins or the miners' WBA collapsed. In July 1877, 80,000 railroad workers across the continent struck to overturn company wage cuts, and their uprising in turn ignited strikes by 500,000 other workers who walked out in cities and towns along the rail lines from Pittsburgh to San Francisco. Federal troops and state militias broke the railroad strike within a few weeks, however, and most of the others collapsed. An estimated one-third of the railroad strikers were Irish.[40]

Meanwhile, Irish American Catholic experiences during the depression in two cities on opposite coasts, San Francisco and New York, threw into bold relief the continuing ambiguity of their status in post–Civil War America.

In San Francisco, Irish American Catholics responded to the depression by turning on Chinese immigrants, who had been drifting into industrial work in the city since the gold mines had played out and the transcontinental railway neared completion in the late 1860s. As San Francisco plunged into economic depression, Chinese immigrants proved the perfect scapegoat, an "indispensable enemy" for whites frightened and frustrated by the economy's crash. Irish immigrants led this attack. Dennis Kearny, a Cork immigrant, became notorious as its public voice, delivering incendiary anti-Chinese speeches with a "brogue you could cut" to workingmen on the city's sandlots. Yet it was the very proper Irish-born Philip Augustine Roach, merchant, newspaper editor, mayor of Monterey, praised for his "gentlemen like instincts," who carried the cause of Chinese exclusion to Washington and helped make it a national law. Few questioned Irish Americans' right to lead this white supremacy crusade in San Francisco, where they had been members of the business elite, among the city's most prominent elected officials, and leaders of the labor movement since California became part of the United States in 1850.[41]

New York City started to feel the effects of depression almost immediately after the economic collapse began in the fall of 1873. Within a year one-quarter of the city's work force had lost their jobs and many, probably most of the others had seen their wages slashed. In 1871, the *New York Times* had begun to reveal that Boss Tweed and his Irish American supporters had engaged in an

Figure 10. *The Ignorant Vote: Honors Are Easy*. This cartoon reflects both Thomas Nast's persistent depiction of the Irish as apes and the long tradition in American racial discourse of pairing them with African Americans. Drawing by Thomas Nast, published on the cover of *Harper's Weekly* on December 9, 1876. Library of Congress: USZ62-57340.

orgy of corruption while dominating New York, and Tweed was sent to jail just as the depression hit the city. Josephine Shaw Lowell, head of the State Board of Charities, now complained of the "vicious and idle" poor, "worthless men and women," and led an effort to eliminate outdoor relief and force people to the workhouse. With Tweed gone, city spending on relief began to fall from $2.23 per capita in 1871 to ninety-three cents in 1875.[42]

By the 1860s and 1870s, a new ideology, Social Darwinism, had become popular among wealthy elites in New York and elsewhere. Allegedly applying Darwinian principles to human society, it explained human progress as the product of an inevitable competition, weeding out the inferior and rewarding the fittest. Such a notion obviously justified the depression-era relief cuts, but it also lent seemingly scientific sophistication to racist attacks not merely on Blacks but also on whites like Irish Catholics, who were not Anglo-Saxon Protestants. In the 1860s and 1870s, cartoonists like the Radical Republican Thomas Nast popularized such Darwinian anti-Irish, racist ideas through images of Irishmen as apes. Meanwhile, by the 1870s, many wealthy Republican merchants and manufacturers had joined in Democratic attacks on Reconstruction governments in the South, which they saw as wallowing in the same kind of expensive corruption as the Tweed regime in New York City. The cause of the corruption, they believed, was the same in both cases: racially inferior voters, poor Blacks in the South and poor Irish in the North—or in the words of the patrician George Templeton Strong, "a brute n[——] constituency" and "New York City's Celtocracy." In 1876, Nast published a now famous cartoon equating the two in *Harper's Weekly*. Provoked by Tweed's excesses and emboldened by the depression's seeming fiscal necessity, these rich reformers now sought to eliminate universal manhood suffrage, and probably bar most Irish Catholics from voting, by imposing a high property tax qualification on voter eligibility in New York City. Racialization of the Irish, defining them as naturally inferior, had been going on in America since the famine, but now, over two decades later, such anti-Irish racism had reached a new level of grotesque popular imagery and public ridicule, challenged Irish "whiteness," and threatened to cripple their political power in Irish America's capital.[43]

American-born Irish Catholic John Kelly had taken over Tammany Hall after Tweed's fall, but he went along with the budget cuts, at least in part because the city's economic elite were too powerful to resist. He did manage to defeat the imposition of a property qualification for voters because that would have destroyed Tammany. Unlike the Chinese in San Francisco, the Irish in New York still had the vote and turned out to keep from losing it. After Kelly saved their right to vote and assured Tammany's survival, however, he would go back to help the squeezing of the poor. He did offer a sop to the Irish and other workers—he joined the anti-Chinese chorus.[44]

7. A New Generation and New Immigrants in Turn-of-the-Century America

1880–1928

"We all Fellows Bran' New," they sang, "All born on Manhattan Isle," confident that they were the epitome of turn of the twentieth-century "cool," knew what to wear, where to go, how to play, and "every twist in manufactured slang." They were American-born Irish men, characters in a show called *The Mulligan Guard Ball,* opening in New York in 1879 just five years after Boucicault's *Shaughran* had debuted there in 1874. It was one of scores of popular musical plays and sketches about Irish Americans on New York's Lower East Side created by the American-born Irish Ned Harrigan and starring his partner, second-generation Irish Tony Hart (born Anthony Cannon). The lead roles in the *Ball* and the series of Mulligan Guard plays were immigrants: Dan and Cordelia Mulligan. As late as 1900, over 367,000 famine Irish immigrants were still alive in the United States, and over 1.7 million new Irish immigrants would arrive in America in the half-century after 1880. Yet the second-generation Irish, "the fellows bran' new" and their sisters, would eventually overshadow them both. When the *Mulligan Guard Ball* opened, there were already more second-generation Irish than immigrants in America, though two-thirds of the American-born were still under eighteen years old. By 1900, however, they would outnumber immigrants among adults by three to two and ten years later, when the second generation's numbers peaked, by three to one.[1]

Thus, though old and new Irish immigrants would have their say in Irish American communities at the turn of the twentieth century, the second-generation Irish would ultimately dominate them. It was not just their numbers that made them dominant. Surviving famine immigrants were getting old by the twentieth century and most of the immigrants pouring into America from Ireland after 1880 would struggle in adapting to American life. These American-born Irish, both men and women, on the other hand, felt at home in their native United States. They would, indeed, be "bran' new," not replicas of their parents. They would not, however, be mere imitations of native-stock Yankee Americans either. They would invent a new version of Irish American, as they adapted to the challenges and opportunities of the era in vital dimensions of their everyday lives: their work; whom they married and at what age; how many children they would have; the meaning and practice of their religion; and the games they played and the songs they sang. Some say that even their "manufactured slang," so new, so seemingly quintessentially American, was nonetheless another such adaptation with many of its words rooted in the Gaelic language.[2]

It was no surprise that the phrase "lace-curtain Irish," denoting a new Irish American middle class, emerged in the 1890s just as the second-generation Irish began to reach maturity. Nothing distinguished the experience of the new generation in the turn-of-the-century era more clearly from that of the famine immigrants in the 1850s and 1860s than their occupational success. By 1900, nearly one-quarter of second-generation Irish men (24.2 percent) were working at white-collar jobs. That was about three times the white-collar proportion of famine Irish immigrant men in 1860, and twice that of recent Irish immigrants (migrating to America after 1880) in 1900. It was also higher than the percentage of American-born German men, whose fathers' economic performance had so easily outstripped their own fathers at mid-century. Second-generation Irish women, however, were even more successful. Over 30 percent of second-generation Irish women in the work force were white-collar workers in 1900, a proportion about fifteen times that of working immigrant Irish women in 1860. Even more impressive, a stunning one-third of those white-collar women, or about 9 percent of all American-born Irish women workers, were schoolteachers.[3]

Occupational progress continued for both second-generation men and women in the twentieth century: by 1930, close to two-fifths (39.8 percent) of the men were white-collar workers and over three-fifths of the women (60 percent) were. Both continued to surpass the proportions of American-born white-collar German men and women, but the white-collar percentage of second-generation Irish women now also matched that of American-born English women. Finally, there is no census data to prove it, but survey research data from later in the twentieth century suggests that Irish American Catholics' occupational status had also surpassed that of Irish American Protestants by the 1920s.[4]

Both second-generation Irish men and women profited from living in the right places at the right time. When famine Irish immigrants came to the United States in the mid-nineteenth century, most settled in cities in the Northeast, Midwest, or Pacific Coast. They had neither the network connections nor the capital to take up farming, nor did they have the skills to compete for most artisan or craft jobs with native stock or German and English immigrants in the cities. As pointed out earlier, by relying on communal networks, most survived and some prospered, but many suffered from their handicaps. Yet over the course of the turn of the century the number of farmers in America hardly grew at all (23 percent, 1880 to 1900, and 6 percent between 1900 and 1930), and, though the number of skilled blue-collar jobs did increase (87 percent between 1880 and 1900 and 105 percent between 1900 and 1930), white-collar occupations grew much faster: for men fivefold between 1880 and 1930; and for women a stunning seventeenfold over the same fifty years. Most of that growth was in cities (over 25,000 people) where a majority of the second-generation Irish lived.[5]

Yet, if they were in the right place at the right time, education, especially for younger members of the second generation, had prepared them to take advantage of these new opportunities. In 1880, the percentages of second-generation Irish American men and women remaining in school to the end of high school (21.7 and 18.6 percent at age seventeen and 6.3 and 4.1 percent at ages eighteen to twenty-two) lagged behind the American-born English (31.5 and 30.3 percent at age seventeen in school, 10.8 and 7.8 percent at ages eighteen to twenty-two in school), and to a lesser extent American-born Germans (19.3 and 18.9 percent at age seventeen and 12.8 and 5.5 percent at ages eighteen to twenty-two). Yet the proportions of second-generation Irish men and women remaining in school into their late teens and early twenties increased significantly in the next two censuses with available data, 1900 and 1910. By the latter year, about one-third of American-born Irish men remained in school until the end of high school (age seventeen) and one-eighth through the college years (eighteen to twenty-two), surpassing second-generation German men in both age categories. Some Irish American Catholic men went to state or even Ivy League universities, but they dominated Catholic colleges, which were beginning to transform from muddled hybrids of colleges and prep schools into strictly colleges and were expanding rapidly. The number of students at Holy Cross College in Worcester, for example—the vast majority of them Irish Americans—more than doubled between 1902 and 1910. Again, however, women's educational achievements were more impressive: in 1910, nearly half stayed in school until age seventeen and a sixth into their late teens and early twenties, presumably attending college. Some American-born Irish women went to the new Catholic colleges for women appearing in the 1890s, like Trinity College in Washington, but substantial numbers had already been attending state teachers' colleges, normal schools, for decades.[6]

It is not clear why the proportions of second-generation Irish staying in school grew so much by the early twentieth century. Rates rose for members of other groups too, as states raised mandated school ages, secondary schools multiplied, and colleges expanded. Many may have stayed in school because they were more likely to have been the younger children in their Irish families. Their parents allowed them to stay in school longer than their older siblings, who had been forced into work at early ages because of family economic needs. About half of the male second-generation professionals, owners, and managers, and two-fifths of the women teachers, in the 1910s, for example, had been born between 1865 and 1880, long enough after the famine migration to suggest that many of them were probably near the bottom of their families' birth order.[7]

Irish American women, however, had special advantages. The Irish American community clearly gave special encouragement to young women to stay in school, as they significantly outnumbered second-generation Irish men in secondary schools in 1900 or even earlier and by far more than the American-born in any other ethnic group. The Irish American Catholic community also supported working women, as the proportion of second-generation Irish women in the labor force substantially exceeded those from other groups. The example of immigrant mothers, who had been educated in Ireland and had come to America to work, was undoubtedly important to their daughters' commitment to school and work, and the devotion of Irish women religious to women's education probably also helped encourage many to stay in school as well. Irish political breakthroughs at the turn of the century also eased women's access to teaching and other public white-collar jobs. In addition, as we shall see, second-generation Irish women were more willing to postpone marriage than American-born women from other ethnic groups, which meant that they could keep white-collar careers alive longer and garner a greater return on their educational investment than other ethnics. Finally, popular culture often depicted American-born Irish women as simply more ambitious than their brothers as well, such aspirations perhaps, in part, another legacy of mothers who had gone into service in America and had seen the rewards of success firsthand.[8]

Better educated, more successful, and as the fellows "born on the Manhattan Isle" suggested, simply more at ease in their native America, the second-generation Irish were more willing than the immigrants to marry outside the group. Indeed, the plot of *The Mulligan Guard Ball* turned on the intention of Dan Mulligan's son, Timothy, to marry his American-born German sweetheart, Katy Lochmuller, the daughter of Dan's chief political rival. In almost every local study of Irish intermarriage at the turn of the century, second-generation Irish like Timothy Mulligan were more likely to marry outside the group than Irish immigrants. Like Mulligan, however, they also usually found their non-Irish partners among fellow old immigrants, the British or Germans, or their children, and only rarely among Italian and Polish newcomers.[9]

The emergence of the second generation coincided with a transportation revolution that drastically transformed American cities. The invention of the electric streetcar in 1887 permitted settlement in cities to expand enormously: Chicago extended into the broad expanse of the prairie to its south, for example, while Boston gobbled up the rural villages of Dorchester and West Roxbury beyond its southern border. As the new streetcar lines stretched cities out, however, they also reorganized them, dividing them into large, discrete, commercial or industrial districts and ethnically or racially homogenous neighborhoods. While this process increasingly trapped African Americans in giant ghettoes and even segregated new immigrant groups like Italians, Irish Americans moved on from old mid-nineteenth-century neighborhoods and seemed able to roam free. By 1910, the Irish foreign stock, first and second generation together, were less isolated, more broadly spread throughout cities like New York, Chicago, Philadelphia, and Boston than the Scandinavians, Germans, Poles, and Italians; only the British foreign stock were less segregated. For the second-generation Irish specifically, statistical indices measuring their segregation from native-stock Americans were already low in 1900 and continued to fall by 1930, both in big cities like New York and Philadelphia as well as small ones like Providence, Jersey City, and St. Paul.[10]

The most visible evidence of how much the second generation had changed from their immigrant parents, however, may have been their embrace of a newly emerging American urban popular culture. Irish Americans were prominent in every dimension of it: the boxing ring, the baseball diamond, and the vaudeville

Figure 11. *Maggie Cline "On Broadway."* Cline was born in Haverhill, Massachusetts, to Irish immigrants in 1857 and was a vaudeville star from the 1880s to 1917. 42041 U.S. Copyright Office Created by The H.C. Miner Litho. Co., N.Y. Management, Harry Williams. No. 4563. Library of Congress (Theatrical poster collection).

and popular theater stages. In the 1890s, for example, eight of the fourteen American-born world prize-fighting champions were of Irish ancestry. One historian has also dubbed the turn of the century the "Emerald Age of Baseball," when, by a cautious count, about one-fifth of American baseball players were second-generation Irish Americans. In entertainment, Harrigan and Hart, early on, and George M. Cohan, the "Yankee Doodle Dandy," later, as well as a slew of vaudevillians, including Marie Cahill, the Savage sisters (performing as the Elsinore sisters), and Maggie Cline, "the great big . . . darling of the gallery boys," were all extraordinarily popular in this period. Yet it was not just the visibility of American-born Irish stars that suggested the second generation's widespread passion for American popular culture in this period, but also the hundreds of baseball and football teams, vaudeville shows, and popular theater plays sponsored by Irish American parishes, Catholic colleges, high schools, and clubs and fraternal societies.[11]

The second-generation Irish seemed, simply, a new people to observers, boys and girls "bran' new," distinctly different from their immigrant parents or recent Irish immigrant "cousins" in almost every aspect. In 1905 St. Paul's *Irish Standard* moaned that this seemed deliberate: "Too many young men of immigrant [parents] think that the acme of success is to be as different as possible from their parents."[12]

Nevertheless, they were still very different from WASP or Yankee Americans. Indeed, they were distinct even in ways that they could not self-consciously will, nor, perhaps, even suspect. A study done in New York City in 1906 found that second-generation Irish death rates not only exceeded those of the native stock but were twice as high as those of second-generation Germans and even higher than Italian and Russian (largely Jewish) and Polish immigrants. Like their immigrant parents, they were especially vulnerable to tuberculosis.[13]

Furthermore, as impressive as second-generation men's economic achievements seemed, they varied by region and there were significant limits to their success. In New England, for example, Yankee dominance and the weakness of the region's maturing economy still hindered Irish Americans' ascent. Meanwhile, Irish newspapers in cities as diverse as St. Paul and Worcester shared complaints about Irish American men's failure in business. That complaint exaggerated, but, in 1900, second-generation Irish men were less likely to be retailers, bankers, and manufacturers than the second-generation English or Germans, and less likely to be retailers than American-born Italians. Moreover, few Irish Catholics had broken into the ranks of the national business elite and few even into local economic elites. In New York City, Irish Americans owned only 2 percent of the city's biggest companies in 1885 and but 1 percent in 1910, compared to 27 percent and 25 percent for German Americans in those years.[14]

Enduring, pervasive cultural values may have contributed to second-generation Irish American men's economic shortcomings. Catholic priests, for example, worried that social and economic ambitions might carry men out of the faith. As one Irish Catholic priest lamented: "Because Protestants as a body were rich, they [young Catholics] believed simply to be one was to receive uplifting." Yet many felt that it was actually Irish American men's communal loyalties to old friends and communities that undermined their ambitions. Observers in the turn-of-the-century era noted that though communalism seemed strong among almost all ethnic peoples, Irish American Catholic communalism was "distinctive." Political patronage dependent on connections, after all, would be a hallmark of Irish American politics in this era, as we shall discuss in more detail later, and helped Irish Americans carve out niches in an array of government jobs such as policemen and firemen. From Finley Peter Dunne's Mr. Dooley newspaper columns to the comic strips of George McManus, to Harrigan and Hart, and a host of vaudevillians, a pervasive joke began to run through Irish American popular culture in this period about the conflicts between Irish American women, eager to move "uptown" to enhanced social status, and Irish American men, who steadfastly resisted, clinging to ties with their friends in the old neighborhood and saloon. There was also, however, a more insidious desire at the center of that male world that affected men's mobility: addiction to alcohol. Arrests for drunkenness remained higher among the second-generation Irish as well as the first than other groups at least through the 1920s.[15]

Irish Americans themselves often blamed second-generation Irish men's "failures" in business on the competing attraction of respectable professions like law or medicine or the allure of politics and government employment. Second-generation Irish men were overrepresented among university students studying law as early as 1910, and among native-born lawyers in every region of the country in 1930. In 1910, they were also underrepresented among engineering students in universities. Some Irish American Catholics debated whether Catholic colleges stifled pursuits of scientific and other vocationally practical studies in favor of a classical education. Preference for jobs in government, however, was probably more significant in diverting Irish American Catholics from business than the appeal of professions like the law and medicine. In 1910 and 1930 the proportion of second-generation Irish who were in public administration was far higher than the percentages of lawyers and doctors, and about double the proportions of other ethnic groups.[16]

Irish American Catholics, however, did not choose their occupations in a free field. The "No Irish Need Apply" advertisements seemed to have faded away by the 1880s, as discrimination at the lower levels of the economy had, if not gone, at least, become more covert. At the top, however, exclusion of Catholics seemed to harden in the late nineteenth century. A Protestant establishment, made up of social clubs and preparatory schools, defined perhaps as much now by Anglo-Saxon or Nordic racial distinctions as religious ones, emerged, depriving Irish American Catholics of access to useful networks and connections. As one American-born Irish man trained in the law lamented in 1898: "Where if I am a lawyer must I get my clientage?. . . The young American has friends and connections to look after him." The extent of the institutional thickening of an exclusive Protestant establishment obviously varied across the country: Irish American Catholics had long been part of San Francisco's economic and social elite, but the Irish were still excluded and would be for decades in Boston. Irish American Catholics had significant advantages over other groups, being white and Christian, of course, but the Protestant establishment did set an upper limit to the Irish rise that would frustrate the most ambitious among them through much of the twentieth century.[17]

Furthermore, if the second-generation Irish were "spatially integrated," finding homes in almost all parts of most cities that they lived in, they were often "socially segregated" in those spaces, creating their own ethnic worlds amid seas of strangers. Sometime in the mid-twentieth century, Father James Aloysius Geary, a professor at Catholic University, drew a map of the neighborhood where he grew up in Worcester, Massachusetts, in the 1890s. In his mental map of what was actually an ethnically and racially mixed neighborhood, he identified all the houses where Irish families lived by name but left other house plots blank or labeled them simply "Protestants!" or "Black." Often Irish churches with their parochial schools and panoply of societies and clubs for all ages and genders anchored these Irish communities amid ethnically diverse populations. Three-quarters of the Irish parishes established in Chicago between 1843 and 1878 were in the center of the city, but "the vast majority" of Irish parishes founded after that were located in the "outlying districts" and almost all of them soon had schools. Moreover, even though Irish American Catholics were "spatially integrated," paradoxically, they were fiercely "territorial." Observers noted that they often claimed whole neighborhoods (or parts of

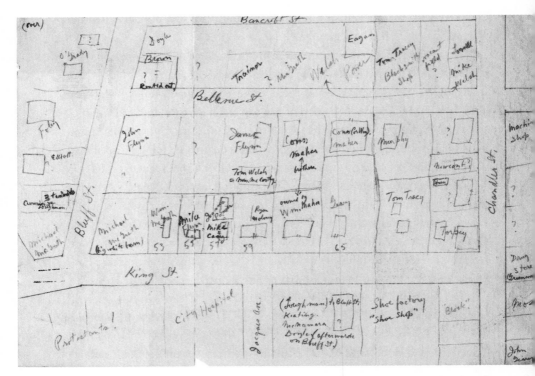

Figure 12. Father Geary's childhood neighborhood in Worcester, Massachusetts. Note that the only residents named are Irish—Walsh, Trainor, Flynn, Power, Maher, McGrath, for example—though Geary acknowledges the presence of "Protestants!" (lower left corner) and "Blacks" (lower right corner). Drawn by Father James Aloysius Geary. The Catholic University of America Special Collections (ACUA), Washington, D.C.

them) as their turf, even where they were minorities, and backed up such claims with violence by American-born Irish youth gangs like Chicago's Ragen Colts. Finally, though the second-generation Irish were more likely to marry outside the group than the immigrants, in cities as diverse as Lowell, Worcester, New York, and Butte, Montana, and even the plains of South Dakota, two-thirds to three-quarters of the American-born Irish married second-generation or immigrant Irish at the turn of the century.[18]

Yet it was not just whom they married but also when they did and how many children they had after marriage which distinguished them from their native-stock and other neighbors. Both second-generation Irish men and women married later than not only their famine immigrant parents but also recent Irish immigrants, and both were more likely to forego marriage altogether—remain "celibate"—than old or new Irish immigrants as well. Indeed, second-generation Irish marriage behavior at the turn of the twentieth century more closely approximated Ireland's, with its late marriage ages and high celibacy rates, than those of their immigrant parents or recent Irish immigrants in America. They married late, in part, because their parents wanted their income and support in old age, but also because they, themselves, believed children must inevitably follow marriage and the costs of raising them might hinder their own ambitions. Almost all children of immigrants of any ethnic background married later than their immigrant parents, but for no other second-generation ethnics was marriage so late or celibacy so pervasive as the second-generation Irish. Strict Catholic notions of sexuality in America, as in Ireland, undoubtedly helped reinforce efforts by the second-generation Irish to delay or avoid marriage. Second-generation Irish American wives also had fewer children than Irish immigrants because they married later, but once they did marry, they had children at about the same rate as the immigrant Irish, and at a much higher rate than native-stock Yankees. Catholic norms, of course, were important here too. Indeed, the contrast between Irish Catholic families with children and so many native-stock Protestant ones without them became a publicly proclaimed point of pride in some Irish American Catholic communities at the turn of the twentieth century.[19]

Historians of American Catholicism have often called the nineteenth and early twentieth centuries the era of the "immigrant Church," but doing so, perhaps, obscures how important Catholicism was to second-generation people and how they adapted it to meet their own needs. Second-generation Irish Americans' Catholicism at the turn of the century is a good example. The breadth and pervasiveness of the new Irish generation's commitment to the Church, or at least their submission to its institutional discipline, was probably greater than among their immigrant parents. By the turn of the century, American-born Irish bishops outnumbered Irish-born ones, and American-born Irish priests had begun to dominate eastern and many midwestern dioceses. Meanwhile American-born Irish women were filling the ranks of even non-Irish major religious orders, like the Sisters of Notre Dame and the Sisters of St. Joseph. Indeed, by 1920, second-generation Irish women "comprised by far the biggest proportion" of the 90,000 Catholic women religious staffing the Catholic Church's infrastructure of schools, hospitals, and charitable organizations in America.[20]

Yet the commitment to Catholicism was strong among second-generation laymen and laywomen as well. The Catholic revival which had emerged in the middle of the century did not slacken, but, indeed, gained momentum as they grew to maturity at the century's end. Aided by the appearance of a new magazine, *Saint Anthony's Messenger,* in 1893, for example, shrines to St. Anthony of Padua popped up all over the country in the turn-of-the-century era. Parish missions also flourished at the end of the nineteenth century and were notably popular among the younger generation. Priests at Sacred Heart and St. John's parishes in Worcester gleefully remarked on the high attendance of "young" people, men and women, at parish missions in 1891 and 1892—"few" missing them and those attending "among the most fervent."[21]

A turn-of-the-century boom in Catholic organizations also reflected the laity's Catholic commitment. A slew of new Catholic men's clubs and societies, among them the Knights of St. John, the Catholic Benevolent Legion, and Catholic Foresters, emerged between 1877 and 1883, just as the American-born generation began to grow to maturity, and most of these organizations thrived throughout the rest of the turn-of-the-century era. Membership data for the Knights of Columbus, the most successful of these groups, reveals that second-generation Irish began to predominate among the Knights shortly after the organization was founded in 1882, and they remained a powerful element in it thereafter. Catholic temperance societies boomed in the 1880s and 1890s and were especially attractive to the American-born Irish. Membership in Holy Name societies, a devotional organization popular in Irish and other Catholic parishes, more than doubled to 1.6 million men just between 1910 and 1917. Second-generation women joined national societies too, like the Catholic Daughters of America, founded in 1903, but women were also the mainstays of local parish clubs and sodalities, which multiplied rapidly as Catholic churches increasingly became centers of "organizational networks" after 1880.[22]

There were several reasons for this second-generation Irish enthusiasm for Catholicism. Its grandeur, huge buildings, elaborate processions, and music, which often rivaled opera, had a special allure for young men and women, who grew up in rough, sooty urban neighborhoods. Boston's second-generation Irish John F. Fitzgerald, grandfather of John F. Kennedy, remembered that the spectacle of special feast days celebrated at his St. Stephen's parish "was so beautiful I thought I would faint." Yet many of the reasons for the second generation's commitment to Catholicism were more "practical." For the young men and women who became priests and nuns, for example, the Catholic Church offered a chance to gain an education, secure a professional job, and enjoy status or prestige in their community. For laymen and laywomen, if it was a grand religion, it was a stern one too. If Catholicism's strict sexual discipline helped them delay marriage, the relation between the two was mutually reinforcing: the more that Irish American Catholics wished to avoid marriage, the more useful the Church became to them. Yet as a historian studying the poor Irish in turn-of-the-century Hell's Kitchen in New York contends, Catholicism offered more than simply support in avoiding early marriage. It provided a broad strategy of discipline to achieve respectability, a behavioral guide that became "a basis for pride in a situation of suffering and humiliation."[23]

There were, however, certainly limits to the Church's power over this generation, particularly over men, that distinguished Catholic norms from evangelical Protestants' notions of respectability. The Church led a Catholic temperance movement, a "Hibernian Crusade," which was very successful in the turn-of-the-century era, but only a few zealots in it endorsed prohibition. Even had there been more, it would hardly have mattered, given, as previously noted, high second-generation arrest rates for drunkenness as well as their overrepresentation among saloonkeepers. Participation in or enthusiasm for sports by Catholic clubs, fraternal societies, schools, and even devotional societies, like the Holy Name societies; the Catholic Church's opposition to "Blue Laws" preventing the playing of sports on Sunday; and Irish clerics hobnobbing with hardnosed, street-tough if brilliant baseball players like John McGraw also marked their differences from evangelical Protestants. There was a gendered looseness then in Irish American Catholicism's forgiveness for the rowdy male and openness to his amusements, even as it strictly condemned the fallen woman.[24]

Even the second-generation Irish embrace of American popular culture at the turn of the century was not a clear sign of assimilation but a complex adaptation that distinguished them from Yankee Protestants as well as their parents. In their enthusiasm for baseball or vaudeville, the American-born Irish were not desperately trying to grab on to something already made by "Americans." Rather they were joining immigrants and the second generations of many groups, as well as native-stock "Americans," to forge a new urban world of popular culture and leisure at the turn of the century. In making this new popular culture, not taking on one made by someone else, most Irish Americans thus saw little need to disown their ethnicity, but, indeed, made it part of what they were creating. As the vaudeville song praising the boxing champion John L. Sullivan "Our True American" went: "His colors are the stars and stripes, he also wears the Green." Many baseball players, managers, and fans in this period thought there was a distinctly Irish American way to play that game: like McGraw, rough, even mean, but also tactically clever. Meanwhile, Maggie Cline became the "swaggering, bragging, good hearted. . . . Irish Queen" of the Bowery, belting out Irish American songs such as "When Hogan Pays the Rent" (he never does). Even the "Yankee Doodle Boy," George M. Cohan, produced more and more Irish ethnic material as he aged, cranking out several Irish American themed shows, like *Little Nelly Kelly* in the 1920s. Perhaps most interesting in the first two decades of the twentieth century, American-born Irish songwriters like Chauncey Olcott and non-Irish ones like his partner, Ernest Ball, wrote many of what would become the twentieth century's Irish American musical staples: "A Little Bit of Ireland," "My Wild Irish Rose," "Mother Machree," and "When Irish Eyes Are Smiling."[25]

Through much of this, Irish Americans and others were also burnishing an older image of the Irish American as the urban American common man. Harrigan sang of it, but even George M. Cohan celebrated Irish Americans with a phrase that soon became attached to them, the "regular guy." The image also quickly became apparent in the new medium of the movies in the 1910s, as in director Raoul Walsh's film *Regeneration* in 1915. It persisted because as Irish American Catholics became more prominent and powerful in the theater industry, they had found it easier to "invert the terms" of the stereotypes that mocked them rather than try to uproot or erase them, making virtues of what had been portrayed as defects. Even drinking might no longer be a sign of Irish debauchery, but a sacrament of fellowship, as in Harrigan and Hart's song "Pitcher of Beer." An alleged Irish penchant for violence also became mere manly toughness in Maggie Cline's signature song, "Throw Him Down Again McCluskey." The "lace-curtain satire" of Dunne, McManus, and a host of vaudevillians' comic depictions of Irish American Catholics' doomed attempts to break into society by crashing the elite ball or dinner party were as hilarious at the turn of the twentieth century as they had been for Teague O'Regan at the turn of the nineteenth. While having a good laugh at Irish American men's social embarrassments, however, these Irish writers and performers—unlike Brackenridge a century earlier—were not condemning them. Indeed, they were suggesting that these Irish "common" men may have been right in preferring the company of friends and the good cheer of the saloon to the pompous fakery and presumption of America's new crop of tycoon would-be aristocrats.[26]

Sometime in the spring of 1902, Paddy and Anne Brennan of the townland of Carrownaddy in County Roscommon, Ireland, received an "American letter" from cousins living in Boston. The letter included an offer to "bring out" one of the Brennans' children to America, and that or a subsequent letter may have also included passage money for the one chosen. At the time, the Brennans were raising seven children on only thirteen acres of land, but only one child, Margaret, age nineteen, was both old enough to emigrate and without prospects in Ireland. Paddy thus bought her a ticket on the Cunard steamship line, perhaps, from a grocer in nearby Athlone, who also served as an agent for the steamship company. A week or so before she left, she probably went "round on all the neighbors to say a goodbye," and there would be an "American wake," or a "spree," the night before she departed. She walked five miles the next day with her family to pick up the first of three trains that took her to Queenstown (now Cobh in County Cork), where she stayed overnight. The S.S. *Campania* sailed out of Liverpool in the morning of the next day, already filled with over 400 passengers from England, Sweden and Norway before it arrived in Queenstown that afternoon and picked up Margaret Brennan and eighty-three others. The trip to New York took five days and twenty-one hours. Margaret slept on a bunk in a third-class compartment for single women and ate regular meals of fish, meat, soup, and eggs in a giant dining hall, seating 350 people. Arriving in New York City at Ellis Island, she eventually found her mother's New York cousins who would send her on to Boston, where her father's brother and wife met her train at that city's South Station. She soon found a position as a domestic servant for a rich Yankee lawyer, John Ford Tyler, at 16 Chestnut Street on the city's Beacon Hill. In 1903, Margaret "brought out" to America her sister Nora, who, in turn, in 1925 brought out their brother Patrick, who brought out their brother John in 1927.[27]

Every immigrant story is unique, full of twists and turns of fate and decision. Nevertheless, Maggie Brennan's story was about as typical of important trends in Irish emigration to America in the turn-of-the-century era as any other: a young adult, single, unskilled woman, from a farm in the West; part of a chain of immigrants who came before her and others who would come after; leaving not in a panicked flight, but as part of a routine, seemingly preordained, process of departure; traveling without her parents or a husband on a steamship from a port in Ireland—not Liverpool; though heading for Boston, landing first in New York; and finding work as a domestic servant.

By the late nineteenth and early twentieth centuries, Ireland's economy had evolved in a way that virtually demanded a steady exodus of its young out of the country. The balance between tillage and pasture had shifted dramatically back to pasture during and after the famine. With the repeal of the Corn Laws protecting the grain market and without the cheap laborers decimated by the famine or gone to America, tillage farms had few advantages now. To raise cows and sheep, tenants needed much more space than to grow crops. Thus between 1841 and 1880, the number of small farms, one to five acres, plummeted from 310,436 to 64,292. Still the number of farms between fifteen to thirty acres grew by 72 percent to become about a quarter of all Irish farms in the same period. Only marginally successful in the new pastoral economy, these farms would be fertile fields for the new Irish migration.[28]

Ostensibly the new post-famine Irish economy worked well. Irish per-capita income increased significantly; the old mud hovels virtually disappeared; life expectancy rose to fifty years by the early 1870s and fifty-eight by 1920; national schools became nearly universal and thus literacy nearly universal as well—90 percent by the early 1900s.[29]

There was a darker side to the Irish economic revival, however. Ireland's new agriculture was not very efficient and produced fewer calories of food in the 1910 to 1914 period than it had between 1850 and 1854. Meanwhile, Irish industry south of east Ulster continued to wither away. Ireland's wages and standard of living improved, then, not so much because of its modest economic growth, but because of its falling population. More people were avoiding marriage in turn-of-the-century Ireland, but because the people who did marry continued to have large families, there were still too many young people, men and women, who could not find work in the pastoral economy. Only a single son could inherit the necessarily larger farm now and only one daughter receive the dowry she needed to marry an heir to some other family's farm: most of the other children had to leave. Ireland and their families profited, however, not only from sending them away, but from the remittances these emigrating children sent back to parents in the old country. In the early twentieth century, an observer claimed that families "all the way from Glengarriff to Castletownbere" in northwestern Cork "live for the most part by American contributions" from their children.[30]

The proportion of women among Irish immigrants to America had been rising since before the famine, but it peaked now in the late nineteenth century with the departure of so many more like Margaret Brennan. By 1900 over 54 percent of the recent Irish immigrants living in the United States were women (recent meaning Irish-born who had arrived in America after 1880) and that margin held steady, more or less, through 1930. Only among the Scandinavians would the numbers of unmarried migrant women be nearly as high as the Irish. There was less need for working women on farms raising cattle than there had been on ones growing crops, and few opportunities for work as servants or shop-keepers' assistants in rural Ireland. Younger daughters also understood well that without dowries they had limited chances of marrying in Ireland. Because they had fewer opportunities for work than their brothers, however, girls were more likely to stay in school longer than boys, and that education made them both more knowledgeable about America, and more confident about surviving or even prospering there.[31]

Again, like Margaret Brennan, more and more of the Irish going to the United States in this period came from the west, her native Connaught or the coastal regions of Munster, particularly County Kerry, or the western reaches of Ulster, especially Donegal. Almost all Connaught and other western Irish emigrants were going to the United States and not to Australia or Canada, making the Irish regional background of America's Irish immigrant population increasingly distinctive in the Irish diaspora. In 1884, marginal farms of under thirty acres made up over 70 percent of holdings in Connaught. Meanwhile, the province's marriage and marital fertility rates were the highest in Ireland after the famine. In the late 1870s and early 1880s, the fragile western economy crashed, as falling farm prices combined with terrible weather to wreak havoc on the region's agriculture. In some places, it seemed like 1847 all over again. Even after that catastrophe subsided, western tenants suffered from increased international agricultural competition and shrinking opportunities to supplement their income as migrant laborers on British farms. Such changes provoked a massive migration from the west in the early 1880s, but it was not temporary; even more now for the west than anywhere else in Ireland, emigration would continue as a routine necessity.[32]

By the 1880s, the entire journey from leaving home to arrival in New York was nothing like the agony of 1847 or the hardships of the famine years. As the *Campania* did for Maggie Brennan, steamships now came to Ireland, leaving Liverpool and stopping over at an Irish port: at Queenstown in Cork in the south or Moville in Donegal in the north. In the 1880s, they took about ten days or two weeks to cross the Atlantic, but by the time Brennan left in the early twentieth century, trips like hers were usually a week or even less. Ships had dormitories or even separate small sleeping compartments, provided food on a regular basis, and had doctors on board. As early as the 1880s, less than a tenth of 1 percent of passengers from all of northwestern Europe's ports died en route to America.[33]

Ireland's well-developed "migration machine" of immigration chains or networks was as important as the steamship companies in protecting the vulnerable and making this emigration routine. An estimated 75 percent of the Irish came to America on tickets prepaid by friends or relatives in America, but well-developed networks also helped the immigrants find a place to stay in America and often a job, while providing ongoing advice, as well as the company of friends and relatives. Networks, many of them women, sisters, aunts, or cousins helping women, were thus critical to the single Irish women who left, especially since a higher proportion of them than the emigrating men were teenagers and thus they were more vulnerable than their male counterparts. A group of young women in Ireland confronted by the choice of migrating to New York or moving in with relatives thirty miles away chose New York; "it is nearer," they said. The migration machine was also useful to Irish speakers, who, in 1910, made up close to a fifth (19.4 percent) of the immigrants who had arrived in America since 1880. Chains thus brought people from Irish-speaking western places to several cities or towns in Massachusetts: from Louisburg at the far western edge of Mayo to Clinton; from Galway to North Newton; and the Blasket Islands off the Kerry coast to Springfield.[34]

With notable exceptions like Chicago in the Midwest and Butte, Montana, in the mountain states, Irish immigrants concentrated even more in the cities of the Northeast than they had in the famine era. By 1900, about 49 percent of the Irish immigrants arriving in America after 1880 had settled in the mid-Atlantic states and close to 27 percent in New England. As before, Irish immigrant women substantially outnumbered Irish immigrant men (58 to 42 percent) in both eastern regions that year. Again, as in the famine era, these women stayed in the East because they were looking for the kinds of jobs best suited for them, most often in service but also in the needle trades of New York or the textile mills of cities like Lowell, Fall River, or Pawtucket in New England.[35]

Turn-of-the-century Irish immigrants to America seemed to have many advantages over their famine Irish predecessors, but for most of them, life in the United States was still hard. In Manhattan in 1906 and Chicago in 1920, Irish immigrant mortality rates were more than double those of native-stock American Yankees, but they were also higher than any other immigrant group, including new immigrant Italians, Poles, and Bohemians, and only slightly lower than those of African Americans. Their tuberculosis rates were also double the rates in Ireland and among the native stock in the United States, and again higher than almost every immigrant group in the United States. Furthermore, in a study of early twentieth-century child mortality among fourteen immigrant groups, the children of Irish immigrant mothers had higher death rates than the offspring of all but Italian and Mexican women. Only five of the eleven children born to the fabled Irish immigrant Annie Moore, said to be the first immigrant to step ashore at the new Ellis Island immigration station in 1892, would survive to adulthood.[36]

Though there has been less study of the occupational mobility and saving habits of the turn-of-the-century Irish immigrants than their famine era predecessors, the available data suggests that their economic success was limited. Across the nation, less than one-third of recent Irish immigrant men were white-collar or skilled blue-collar workers by 1900, and nearly 40 percent were unskilled workers. They stood much closer to recent Italian or Polish immigrants in the national economic hierarchy than German or English ones then. In 1901, a national study found that the Irish-born proportion of inmates in jails or charitable institutions was higher than any other ethnic group in the country. Though literate and English speaking, Irish immigrants were still a rural people, without any industrial skills or urban experience, and as the sons and daughters of small farmers, many seemed wary of individual ambition and risk. Even Italian and Jewish immigrants seemed more "enterprising": reports of the Immigration Commission in 1911 found that 45 percent of Russian Jews in Boston owned their own businesses and 22 percent of Italians, some no more than pushcarts, but only 5 percent of Irish immigrants did. Irish-born men who arrived after 1900 fared somewhat better than those who had come in the last two decades of the nineteenth century. By 1930, about a fifth (19.8 percent) of the men were white-collar workers, but 54 percent were semiskilled or unskilled workers—not much less than the percentages of Italian or Polish immigrants and far more than German or Swedish ones. The economic achievements of Irish-born women were similarly limited in the turn-of-the-century era, though their story was different. In 1900, 56 percent of all single working Irish immigrant women who had arrived in America since 1880 were domestic servants, falling in 1930 to 51 percent of those who came after 1900. As with immigrant men, about a fifth of the immigrant women were white-collar workers by then.[37]

Almost all new Irish immigrants married other Irish in America, and coming from an Ireland where late marriage and high celibacy rates were becoming almost universal, they married later and more of them never married than native-stock Americans and immigrants from other groups. Nevertheless, they married earlier than the Irish in Ireland and were much more likely to marry than the people back home. Women usually found domestic service a respectable shelter after migration, but they almost never thought of service as a career. Most men, it appears, boarded initially in households of Irish immigrant friends or relatives upon arrival. Some evidence suggests, however, that if they remained single into their thirties, they eventually wound up in large, commercial, impersonal, multiethnic boardinghouses, a bleak alternative to marriage. Without great prospects for upward mobility on their own, immigrant Irish men and women at the turn of the century, like the earlier famine Irish, looked probably to networks of friends and relatives, though we know little about such connections for this era. We do have evidence that they depended on their children's wages to help them throughout their lifetimes. Pointing to her "little pug-nosed boy," Mrs. Murphy, an Irish immigrant mother, told a Boston settlement worker in 1905: "'More insurance for my old age you see.'"[38]

Despite poor economic circumstances that limited Irish immigrants to seek cheap lodgings, they did not live in segregated ghettoes as African Americans or even many new immigrants did in most cities. In 1900, for example, nineteen of Boston's twenty-five wards were home to one to three thousand Irish born, and only one ward had over five thousand. Similarly in Chicago in the same year, there were about one to three thousand Irish living in twenty-one of the city's thirty-five wards; as many as three to six thousand in only seven. Statistical indices from the 1910 census make clear, however, that Irish immigrants clustered on a smaller scale even in midwestern cities like Chicago and Cleveland. Some of those clusters were not just Irish immigrants, but immigrants from specific parts of Ireland. In the 1880s, for example, immigrants from Roscommon dominated the Irish population in Boston's Mission Hill neighborhood, and of immigrants arriving in New York City, a higher proportion of immigrants from Donegal, Longford, and Westmeath were heading to Brooklyn than of newcomers from any other county in Ireland.[39]

Because of Ireland's ongoing nineteenth-century "devotional revolution," Irish immigrants at the turn of the century were notably more institutionally disciplined Catholics than their famine predecessors. They thus displayed little interest in contesting clerical rule in America, as some of their predecessors had in the 1830s and 1840s and adhered to a more rigid sexual code than the famine immigrants—reflected, for example, in the smaller proportions of prostitutes among them. Meanwhile, finding their career paths at home blocked by an overstocked "market" for clerics and women religious, Irish Catholic priests and nuns flooded the United States in this period. Priests became particularly numerous and sometimes predominant in western and southern American dioceses, where, as in Australia, there were fewer homegrown, diaspora-born Irish priests and nuns.[40]

Catholicism's new power and puritanism, combined with the famine's devastation of the western Gaelic-speaking lower classes and the heavy post-famine emigration, had drained traditional amusements in Ireland of much of their vitality by the end of the nineteenth century, but they did not disappear. Though the Church had revived Ireland's temperance movement, the Irish were actually imbibing more alcohol per capita than the rest of the United Kingdom or even Europe by the turn of the twentieth century, and more than they had earlier in the nineteenth. In America, they found communal bonds in city saloons as they had in Ireland's rural pubs, but as in the famine era they were also far more likely than members of other groups to be arrested for drunkenness. Traditional music, too, had endured in Ireland and in some respects flourished in a more successful economy because of the availability of cheaper and more affordable manufactured instruments, tin whistles, fiddles, and concertinas. It thrived in America as well, in family kitchens, in barrooms, and at picnics sponsored by Irish American parishes or the Ancient Order of Hibernians' divisions. In the 1910s, the newly emerging American recording industry discovered the potentially rich market niche for Irish music in America, and in the 1920s newly invented radio did as well. Accomplished Irish musicians like the fiddler Michael Coleman thus joined the exodus from Ireland to the United States and ushered in an American golden age of traditional Irish music. Intriguingly, those American recordings were also sent to Ireland and played on the radio of the new Irish Free State in the 1920s, helping to define canonical playing styles of traditional music in the homeland.[41]

Though troubled by illness and largely stuck in the lower ranks of the American occupational hierarchy, Irish immigrants would still matter in Irish American communities at the turn of the twentieth century. After an initial spurt in the early 1880s due to the agricultural crisis in western Ireland, they arrived in America not in a dramatic rush like the famine migrants but in a steady river of tens of thousands nearly every year through the 1920s, but by then their numbers about equaled the famine flood of the 1840s and 1850s. Fewer in number, less successful, and less savvy about America than the second-generation Irish, they would not dominate Irish America, but their numbers were still huge and they would find opportunities in the changing circumstances of the American environment to have their own say in shaping its evolution.

8. Searching for Their Place at the End of the Nineteenth Century

The Irish American Community, 1880–1908

In 1881, Leonora Barry, an immigrant from Cork, lost her husband and daughter to disease, forcing her into factory work—seventy hours a week tending a machine for a pittance in wages—to support her two surviving sons. Five years later she was a national officer in the Knights of Labor, a union formed in 1869, but which now boasted over half a million members. Many of its leaders and rank and file were Irish American Catholics. As general investigator for women's work, Barry was constantly on the road, crisscrossing the continent, reporting on working conditions for women and organizing them into local Knights' assemblies. A striking, "tall commanding figure" with a "warm voice," she was also one of the organization's most popular lecturers. She was not the only woman engaged in this struggle. By 1887, Barry estimated that one-tenth of the Knights, about 60,000 members, were women. They included other Irish Americans of note—Mary Harris "Mother" Jones, the legendary radical labor advocate, and Mary Elizabeth Lease, a key figure in the Populist Party—but in the Knights' heyday, Barry was the most prominent female national figure in the organization.[1]

By the end of the 1870s the cruel depression was over, fostering new hopes of economic promise, and Reconstruction ended, prompting celebrations of a reunited nation (though not among African Americans, whose last chance for achieving equality disappeared for generations with the end of Reconstruction). Two very different, though not mutually exclusive, important movements emerged in Irish American communities in the decade that followed: a labor upheaval

155

Figure 13. *Portrait of Leonora Barry.* Leonora Barry was born Leonora Kearney in 1849 and married William Barry in 1871. Photo by G. H. Norton, n.d., Terrence Vincent Powderly Papers, The Catholic University of America Special Collections (ACUA), Washington, D.C.

and a new liberal Catholicism. The new labor uprising, embodied for most of the 1880s by Barry's Knights of Labor, attempted to preserve or regain the power and dignity of workers, like Barry herself, from the oppression of spreading factory labor and to defend the American republic from the rising threat of corporate power. At the same time, many Irish American liberal Catholic bishops, priests, and laymen saw an opportunity in the nation's new national unity and other changes within and outside the group to reconcile the differences between American Catholics and Protestants and shed the American Catholic Church's immigrant "foreignness." Both movements were fresh and optimistic responses to a post–Civil War, postdepression America very much in flux. Yet they also drew inspiration from a revival of Irish nationalism in Ireland and America, which helped inspire Irish American and other participants in the labor upheaval, while encouraging a new cooperation between Irish American Catholics and native-stock Protestants. Irish American Catholic politicians, consumed with the practical realities of winning elections, had no such grand visions, but had new success in pursuing their own efforts to win offices in the eighties and early nineties, both locally in cities and nationally in the Congress, and had an impact on both labor's struggle and Catholic liberal hopes.

The Knights of Labor would collapse in the late 1880s to be replaced by the more conservative American Federation of Labor (AFL). While heavily Irish unions in Australia were creating a labor party there in the early 1890s, in 1894 the AFL rejected a proposal to do the same in America. A revival of anti-Catholic nativism and Vatican condemnation would bring down Catholic liberalism too by the end of the nineteenth century, and there would be no Catholic rapprochement with Protestants in America until the Second Vatican Council in the 1960s. In what had seemed to be a possible watershed in Irish American Catholic history, potential turning points, like the labor uprising or Catholic liberalism, did not turn, leaving the questions of where Irish American Catholics fit in America and how they defined themselves still unanswered. The Irish and Irish American nationalist movements of the 1880s would also crash by the early 1890s.

Provoked by increasing ethnic and religious conflict in the nineties, emboldened by growing Irish American Catholic political power in that decade, and drawing on a cultural revival erupting in Ireland at the same time, recent Irish Catholic immigrants stepped into this vacuum to fashion a new Irish Catholic ethnic revival in the United States. It would be a retreat of sorts into ethnic isolation and an aggressive reassertion of an Irish identity, a seeming deliberate rejection of Americanization. This Irish ethnic revival would thrive through the 1890s and into the first decade of the twentieth century. Yet by then, it was not clear even to its leaders that the revival was the answer to Irish American Catholics' search for their place and a definition of who they were in turn-of-the-century America.

In June 1879, Charles Stewart Parnell, leader of the Irish Home Rule Party in the United Kingdom's parliament, John Devoy of the Clan na Gael, and Michael Davitt of the Irish Republican Brotherhood stitched together a new strategy for nationalism in Ireland called the New Departure. The New Departure brought together all the various strains of Irish nationalism. They included Parnell's party in parliament working for Irish self-government or home rule within the United Kingdom, Devoy's physical force nationalists seeking an independent republic through a national revolution, and Davitt's social and economic radicals fighting for land reform. These nationalist movements had various and eventually conflicting goals, but for the moment they worked through a common instrument, a Land League, enlisting thousands of peasants as voters for home rule and participants in a mass agitation for land reform.[2]

There was no greater potential source of funds in the diaspora, nor one better positioned to garner the pressure of a powerful government on Ireland's behalf, than Irish America. There would be, then, a Land League in America, which would grow to an estimated 1,000 to 1,500 branches with up to 300,000 members, dwarfing any previous Irish nationalist organization in America. Yet it, too, like the Land League in Ireland, would be divided into factions not just over tactics or goals for Ireland, but even more about hopes for Irish people in America.[3]

The conservatives, one of those factions, would be dominated by middle-class Irish immigrants and the young American-born who were eager to make it in America. They were led by John Boyle O'Reilly of the *Pilot,* once a Fenian but now a poet celebrated by the Yankee literati in Boston, and they included almost all the priests involved in this nationalist revival. They were attracted to Parnell, the gentleman, admired his soberly limited goals and cautious methods, and delighted in the support that middle-class and wealthy Protestant Americans offered to his version of home rule. Ironically, Davitt, the radical so unlike them, may have articulated their nationalist hopes best: "You want to be honored among the elements that constitute this nation [America] . . . regarded with the respect due you . . . then aid us in Ireland to remove the stain of degradation from your birth and [you] will get the respect you deserve."[4]

Opposing the conservatives were the radicals, led by Patrick Ford of the *Irish World* in alliance with Davitt in Ireland. The radicals wanted autonomy, indeed independence, for Ireland, but, as Ford suggested, national independence did not matter so much to Irish peasants if they could not control the means of their survival: the land. Conservatives thought of that as a simple transfer of ownership from the parasitic landlords to their tenants, but Ford and Davitt wanted to nationalize the land: the democratic government of an independent Ireland administering all of the island's land for the good of all of its people. In America, the radicals' support came largely from Irish American Catholic workers, who were now caught in a convulsive transformation of the American economy. It was a "second industrial revolution," creating giant corporations and employing new technologies and management techniques that workers, like Leonora Barry, believed were trampling their rights and reducing them to "factory slaves." Workers also worried that the rich owners of these mammoth corporations were so powerful that they could destroy the American republic and set themselves up as a new aristocracy. As Davitt told Irish miners in Leadville, Colorado: "You have no aristocracy yet . . . [but] rich Americans may want to perpetuate their families . . . on American soil." These workers saw in the fight for Irish land reform, then, a situation much like their own.[5]

John Devoy's physical force nationalists of the Clan na Gael were less numerous than either of the other factions. Their primary goal was an independent Irish republic created by force of arms. They egged on the land reform and home rule causes, hoping they would rouse the Irish people to such a fever pitch, that, when Britain rejected both of them—as the Clan men believed it inevitably would—Ireland would be ripe for their revolution. Probably most of the physical force men were blue-collar workers, but their ranks were sprinkled with political worthies or men of ambition like Alexander Sullivan of Chicago and passionate idealists like Devoy himself.[6]

There was another group in the Irish American nationalist fight, not envisioned in the New Departure: women. In October 1880, Parnell's sister Fanny had published a letter in the *Irish World* calling on Irish American women "to put their shoulders to the wheel" of the nationalist movement and followed that up with a meeting at Cooper Union in New York City to found the first branch of the Ladies' Land League. Women textile factory workers in places like Woonsocket, Rhode Island, who joined the Ladies' Land League shared the class resentments of their working-class brothers and found a natural home among the radicals in Ford's faction. Some white-collar women like second-generation teachers in Worcester, Massachusetts, however, also joined the Ladies' Land League because it gave them an opportunity for a public role that even their own church denied them, despite their education and accomplishments. Hectored by some

Irish men, even excommunicated in Cleveland by the local bishop, members of the Ladies' League nonetheless traded on conceptions of women's superior moral purity to make themselves players in the new American crusade for Ireland.[7]

Over time, Patrick Ford's radical faction became the largest of the three factions in the American Land League, sent the most money overseas, and as peasant protests escalated into a land war in 1882 seemed to dominate the movement in America. When Parnell made peace with the United Kingdom government and ended the land war, however, the radicals collapsed on both continents. The Clan tried to replace the old Land League with a new Irish National League, but that failed too, and by the mid-1880s, Parnell and his Home Rule Party dominated not only in Ireland, but with rich donations from conservative Irish Americans, in the United States as well.[8]

The Land League had critical consequences for Irish Catholic America, but especially for its workers. Ford's Land League faction radicalized thousands of them, and following its demise they flocked to unions, especially Barry's Knights of Labor, an older union just emerging from the 1873 depression's devastation of its membership. Indeed, radical branches of the Land League often simply turned themselves into Knights of Labor councils. In 1881, half of the Knights were first- or second-generation Irish Catholics. The proportion no doubt declined as the Knights grew, but they were still both vastly overrepresented among the Knights' rank and file, and importantly, prominent among its leaders, including the Grand Master Workman through much of its history, second-generation Irish Terence Powderly. Irish American Catholics had now moved into the leadership of the American labor movement, where they would remain, more or less, through the end of the twentieth century.[9]

Knights' thinking resonated deeply with long-held Irish values of anti-elitism and communal solidarity. Knights leaders did not talk of classes or class conflict but, like secret society members in Ireland, did speak of the masses and numbers set against the few, in this case, the new industrial aristocracy. Powderly made that point directly: "The landlord drove the Irish men to America, where a new aristocracy barred him from the land [and] drove him into servile pay and an eight-story tenement." Yet Irish Americans also appreciated the Knights' emphasis on communal solidarity. The Knights, for example, adapted not just the tactic of the boycott being used by the Land League in Ireland but invoked the same kind of values of solidarity that made the tactic so successful in Irish villages to make them work in Irish American city neighborhoods like Olneyville in Providence and the South Side of Chicago. Knights' notions of community were broadly inclusive, however. They welcomed white unskilled workers and factory operatives, African Americans, and, of course, inspired by the Ladies Land League, women, like Leonora Barry, into their organization.

The Knights grew amazingly fast in the 1880s from a little over 50,000 members in 1883 to over 700,000 in 1886, but after a bomb exploded at a labor rally in Haymarket Square in Chicago in May of that year killing seven policemen and touching off an early "red scare," they began to fall apart. Historians disagree over whether the Knights' "working-class republicanism" ideology was too vague, too nostalgic for a pre-factory economy, or insufficiently conscious of the realities of class conflict for it to succeed in their time. A more concrete reason for their failure was that their challenge to business provoked the rise of powerful anti-labor industrial associations in turn: the Knights of Labor fell to the stronger "Knights of Capital."[10]

That was not the end of the revived labor movement, however. In 1886, union representatives, largely from craft unions, plumbers, carpenters, machinists, and the like, established the American Federation of Labor. Second-generation Irish were well represented by now in many of the craft unions like the building trades, and some of them, like Peter McGuire of the carpenters, played critical roles in forming the new federation. There were clear echoes of Irish experience in the craftsmen's emphasis on masculine solidarity and their efforts to prevent outsiders from breaking their monopoly over the skilled work that they performed. That combination of solidarity and monopoly of vital skills gave them the power to bargain for their own wages and interests. Unlike the Knights, however, that meant that they had little concern about the plight of working women or unskilled workers or factory operatives, who, after 1890, were more likely to be southern and eastern, not northern, Europeans and thus, to many AFL men, racially inferior. Powered by their craft unions, the AFL rose as the Knights fell apart, reaching 250,000 members by 1892.[11]

Conservative Irish nationalists left no such similar clear organizational legacy in Irish American communities as the nationalist radicals did, but they did seem to have much in common with members of another important movement in the Irish American community during the 1880s: Catholic liberalism. Many liberal leaders had little sympathy for Irish nationalism, but they did share John Boyle O'Reilly's and the conservative nationalists' optimism about

America, the potential for Irish American Catholics to collaborate with native-stock Americans, and, as O'Reilly said, to "build themselves into the republican walls of this country."[12]

In 1889, Archbishop John Ireland of St. Paul, Minnesota, one of the two principal liberal leaders, wrote to the other, Cardinal James Gibbons of Baltimore, that in "Abp. [Archbishop John] Carroll's time the Church was truly American . . . [but then] the flood of Catholic foreign immigrants overpowered us and made the Church foreign in heart and act." Ironically, Ireland and an approving Gibbons were both refugees from the famine, but they believed that if the Irish and other Catholics did their best to shed their "foreignness" and build bridges to their Protestant neighbors, the Church could now return to that pre-immigrant "Carroll's time." They thus began to question the necessity of Catholic schools, the foundation stones of Catholic separatism and for many Catholics the essential means of preserving "foreign" languages and cultures. Some liberals, like Ireland, openly praised public education, though most, even Ireland, sought a kind of compromise solution to education by providing "released time" opportunities for religious teaching within the daily instruction of public schools. Many liberals also criticized Catholics for voting in ethnic blocs, notably the Irish for the Democrats, and opposed Catholic conservative efforts to win Vatican condemnation of the Knights of Labor, not so much because of great sympathy for the Knights' economic aims, but because to condemn them would segregate Catholic workers.[13]

The 1880s and 1890s seemed a propitious time for such changes in the American Church. In 1878, Leo XIII replaced the reactionary Pius IX as pope and was intent on improving the Church's relations with republics like France and the United States. By the 1880s, the nativist Know-Nothings seemed long past and easily forgettable, as memories celebrating the shared sacrifice and common valor of Americans of all faiths and nationalities in the Civil War became increasingly popular. Significant numbers of the American-born Irish children of the famine immigrants were also just reaching maturity by the 1880s, with fresh yet unbroken dreams of their acceptance as simply Americans. Many of them, as noted earlier, were thus now seeking a new respectability by joining the revitalized Irish American Catholic temperance movement.[14]

Most of the liberal leaders, like Gibbons and Ireland, seemed to come from the periphery of Irish settlement in America, west and south of the Irish core in New England and the mid-Atlantic states. Irish immigration into the Midwest and South (except for Chicago) had slowed considerably after the Civil War and

thus Irish Americans were much smaller minorities in those regions than in
the East, where combining numbers and solidarity was a much more plausible
strategy for group success. Because of the decline in Irish immigrant numbers
in the periphery, the proportions of American-born Irish were also much larger
in those Irish American communities as well. American-born Irish Humphrey
Desmond from Wisconsin, the owner of several Catholic newspapers in the
Midwest, was, perhaps, the principal Catholic liberal lay voice in the region. He
derided efforts to preserve old world cultures and languages as a waste of time.
"We are Americans," he argued, and "it is our duty to assert the fact." "We cannot
segregate ourselves . . . Protestants are our fellow citizens in every sense of the
word."[15]

The liberals encountered stiff opposition. Some Irish Catholics still feared
proselytization in the public schools or worried about creeping secularization
in American life. Yet it was French Canadian and German Catholics who most
adamantly opposed the liberals. Both groups relied on parochial schools to
preserve not just the faith but the culture and language of their people. They
thus complained vigorously to the Vatican about Irish liberals' Americanization
efforts and even demanded a formal division of the American Church along
ethnic lines.[16]

These battles suggested how fears as well as new hopes inspired the new
Irish American Catholic liberalism. German immigration grew enormously in
the 1880s and the increasing number of German Catholics posed a serious challenge to Irish American control of the Church, especially in the Midwest. Irish
American liberal leaders also worried about the consequences of not reaching
an accommodation with American Protestants. In an interview with the pope,
John Ireland pointed out: "We [Catholics] are only one to eight in the United
States without wealth or influence, and a larger proportion than that of wealth
and population did not prevent a Kulturkampf in Germany." By positioning
themselves as the *American* not Irish leaders of Catholicism in America and
building an *American* Church, Irish American liberals believed that they could
more easily fend off both challenges to their leadership within the Church and
to the Church itself from outside.[17]

While new dreams and movements emerged in Irish American nationalism, Irish-led labor, and the Church in the late 1870s and 1880s, Irish American
Catholics were beginning to reach new heights of political power in America.
From 1875 to 1890, Irish American Catholics were elected mayors for the first
time in New York City and Boston, and in smaller cities like Lawrence, Lowell,

Holyoke, and Fall River, Massachusetts; Hoboken, New Jersey; and Scranton, Pennsylvania. In the late 1880s and early 1890s, Irish American Catholics even rode a Democratic resurgence led by Grover Cleveland to national prominence, electing New York's first Irish American Catholic senator and sixteen members of the House of Representatives. Yet as important, Irish American Catholics also emerged as "bosses" of powerful Democratic Party city organizations, many tagged as "political machines," a term becoming popular in the late 1870s and 1880s. These bosses included John Kelly, who remained the head of Tammany; Robert "Little Bob" Davis in Jersey City; Patrick J. Maguire and Patrick Collins in Boston; Michael McDonald in Chicago; and Christopher Buckley, the "Blind Boss," in San Francisco, as well as bosses in smaller cities like Lawrence, Massachusetts, and Troy, New York. Irish numbers accounted for much of this success. In five of the cities which elected their first Irish mayors in this period, first- and second-generation Irish made up over 33 percent of the males of voting age in 1880, and in three other cities they were more than 30 percent. That so many of the Irish breakthroughs occurred in New England then is no surprise, as the Irish made up such a large proportion of the region's population and, along with New York and other mid-Atlantic states, were the principal destinations for Irish immigrants throughout the 1880s.[18]

Yet as impressive as it seemed, Irish political success in this period was still limited. The Irish American foreign-stock population in Philadelphia was second in numbers only to New York, but Irish American Catholic Democrats would not rule the city until well into the twentieth century. The Republican-leaning native-stock population was especially big in Philadelphia (including a large number of African Americans), but Pennsylvania's powerful and patronage-rich state Republican Party also helped maintain the city's GOP machine.[19] Yet even where Irish Catholic Democrats won high office or headed party organizations depicted by their enemies as fearsome machines, their power was usually hedged about and qualified. As large as their potential vote was in cities like Boston or New York, their own numbers were never enough to assure them a majority. The American-born generation was still young and their full political impact would not come until later, and though the Irish immigrant population grew in the urban Northeast in the 1880s, those immigrant additions would come too late and still be too small to create majorities. German Americans were the only other powerful ethnic bloc in most cities, including New York, where they were almost as numerous among potential voters as the Irish (30 percent and 33 percent, respectively). Irish American Catholics and most Germans shared a virulent antipathy to restrictions on the sale of liquor, but the religious, class, and ideological diversity of German Americans in places like New York made them conditional allies at best.[20]

Many of the new city machines led by Irish American Catholics thus had trouble fending off competing Democratic Party factions and were dependent on winning some support from middle- and upper-class native-stock Americans. In New York, for example, a faction of rich businessmen in the Democratic Party called the Swallowtails continued to force John Kelly, head of Tammany, to nominate wealthy candidates for mayor and agree to stingy budgets and low taxes as he had during the depression of 1873. Thus, even the first Irish Catholic elected mayor, immigrant William R. Grace, was a successful shipping magnate and a tight fiscal conservative. In Boston, Maguire and Collins, like Kelly, never fully dominated the city's Democratic Party, but did manage to control the party's nominations for mayor, and they looked to put "blood"—prominent Yankee elite Democrats—at the head of their tickets. That arrangement, dubbed an alliance between "Harvard College and the slums" by one Yankee Republican, helped them attract Yankee reform Republican and Democratic voters but, intriguingly, also avoid faction fights among Irish ward leaders over mayoral nominations. When Maguire and Collins did nominate an Irish Catholic for mayor in 1884, he was, as in New York, a successful immigrant businessman, Hugh O'Brien, who slashed the city's budget and lowered taxes. O'Brien lost his bid for reelection in 1888, knifed by some of those disgruntled Irish ward bosses, and thus Maguire and Collins went back to nominating members of the Yankee gentry—less likely to divide the Irish vote than an Irish American—for the top spot in city politics.[21]

Though Boston, as well as nearby Worcester, were far outside Catholic liberalism's strongholds on the periphery of Irish American settlement, political accommodation in the two Massachusetts cities seemed to encourage religious accommodation as well, as Irish American Catholics in both cities quietly avoided building parochial schools. The Yankee-Irish political alliance seemed to have a powerful effect on Boston's Irish nationalist movement, too, as Collins and John Boyle O'Reilly, eager to attract Yankee support for the Irish cause, made it the center of a conservative Irish nationalism in America.[22]

Terence Powderly had long steered the Knights of Labor away from participation in politics, but successful corporate attacks on the Knights and other unions in the mid-1880s provoked workers to create their own local labor parties in 189 cities and towns across the United States. In Rutland, Vermont, for example, the second-generation children of the refugees from Ballykilcline, as well as the town's other famine immigrants, wrested control of the town government from the local Yankee elite in 1886. Once in office they committed town funds to provide work for the unemployed, a public library, and adult education and declared St. Patrick's Day a public holiday. In big cities like San Francisco and New York, Christopher Buckley's and John Kelly's submission to elite insistence on low taxes and budget cuts had seriously weakened the Irish bosses' support among workers. In San Francisco, a revived local labor movement in the mid-1880s joined a successful effort to dump Buckley later in the decade.[23]

The great labor political battle with the bosses, however, would take place in New York in 1886. That fight was as much an internal Irish American Catholic conflict as a class war, as it seemed to become a cockpit for battles among all the contesting movements and interests roiling Irish American Catholic communities in the 1880s. The Central Labor Union, formed at a meeting of radical Land League advocates in 1882, recruited Henry George, an ally of Patrick Ford and Michael Davitt, to run for mayor as the candidate of a United Labor Party (ULP), opposing yet another Tammany-backed Swallowtail businessman, Abram Hewitt. The Catholic Church was drawn into the fight as well, as liberal Catholics and Catholic conservatives joined opposing sides in the mayoral contest, and radical and conservative Irish nationalists pitched in, too, reviving their mutual enmity from Land League days. Generational as well as class conflicts also emerged as the second-generation Irish rallied to the ULP's George, while Irish immigrants largely remained loyal to Tammany. George would lose the election and the ULP and almost all the other recently formed labor parties would disappear over the next few years.[24]

The Irish American movements, which thrived in the 1880s, unraveled quickly in the next decade. Parnell's Home Rule Party had been riding high as late as 1889 but fell apart after the exposure of his involvement in an extramarital affair. After some of his successors failed to pass a home rule bill in 1893, home rule became a dead issue in Ireland for the rest of the decade. The Clan na Gael had its own scandal, the murder of one of its leaders, Dr. Patrick Henry Cronin, by an opposing faction, and declined rapidly after that. Left-wing Irish nationalism had already disappeared when Patrick Ford backed off his radicalism during the divisive battle between Irish American labor and the Church in the

New York 1886 mayoral election. Liberal Catholicism waxed strong until the middle of the 1890s, when the pope began to crack down on it, and finally condemned "Americanism" in his encyclical *Testem Benevolentiae* in 1899. The AFL endured, but at its national convention in 1894, it refused by a narrow margin to take the bold step of forming a labor party. In Australia, where existing political parties were weak, Irish Catholic union men led the creation of a labor party in the early 1890s, and it would be their political stronghold for generations. In the United States, where existing parties were strong and tied to fierce ethnic loyalties, however, most Irish American AFL delegates argued against the formation of a labor party at the convention.[25]

While the Irish American nationalist movements of the eighties foundered, liberal Catholicism collapsed and the labor movement backed down from a historic turn, ethnic and religious tensions were beginning to revive in America. In 1889, prompted by Unionism's rise in Ireland, a small group of largely Ulster Presbyterian immigrants sought to give some substance to a Scotch Irish identity in the United States and emphatically distinguish it from an Irish and Catholic one by founding the Scotch Irish Society of America. It failed to attract much support—little or none in the South—and soon folded. The Republican Party, however, had already been ratcheting up ethnic and religious tensions with crusades for prohibition and against Catholic schools by then, and a small anti-Catholic organization, the American Protective Association (APA), had appeared in 1887. When the American economy crashed yet again into a major depression in 1893, the APA reached over two million members by some estimates.[26]

Irish American political power continued to grow in American cities, however, as more and more of the famine immigrants' children grew to maturity. In New York, after defeating Henry George, Abram Hewitt refused to continue the two-decades-long tradition of flying the Irish flag on St. Patrick's Day, pointedly noting that the Irish were overrepresented in the city's jails and almshouses and proclaiming that the city must be ruled by "American" not "foreign" ideas. Hewitt lost the next election and the Swallowtail businessmen's faction in the Democratic Party soon disintegrated. Riding Irish and other ethnics' reaction to an emerging new reform nativism in the city and building a network of political clubs, Tammany finally shrugged off elite control in the 1890s. Their pitch to the electorate was, as one historian neatly summed up: "Common people don't need the better element to run the city for them."[27] In Boston, meanwhile, it would take a little longer to break Irish dependence on the Yankee elite, but a new generation of Irish American politicians began to emerge by the mid-1890s, who would smash that old alliance by the next decade. Though their national presence in Congress all but disappeared after a Republican landslide in 1894, Irish American Catholics not only built on the local political break-throughs they had achieved in the 1870s and 1880s in several cities, but also made new ones between 1890 and 1910, electing mayors for the first time in Chicago; New Orleans (the first since 1820); Cambridge and Worcester in Massachusetts; Providence, Pawtucket, Newport, Central Falls, and Cranston in Rhode Island; New Haven, Hartford, and Waterbury in Connecticut; Burlington, Vermont; and Bayonne, New Jersey. As early as 1894, a young Virginian of elite, old family background, John Paul Bocock, was sounding the alarm in the *Forum* magazine about "The Irish Conquest of Our Cities."[28]

In this environment of revived nativism and growing Irish political power, a new Irish American Catholic ethnocentrism, combining militant assertion of Irish ethnic interests with self-conscious efforts to preserve or revive Irish culture, began to emerge—a seemingly surprising step backward in any classic model of linear ethnic assimilation. It was surprising, too, that it took place at this time because though the number of second-generation adults was increasing rapidly, this was a movement principally of recent Irish immigrants. They worked largely through the Ancient Order of Hibernians (AOH), but also Irish county clubs, the American Gaelic League, Gaelic Athletic clubs, and the Irish nationalist newspapers the *Gaelic American* and the *Irish World.*

AOH membership took off in the 1890s and early 1900s, rising from 53,000 in 1888 to over 107,000 men in 1901 and to nearly 200,000 men and women by 1908. The Hibernians' membership increased only where the post-1880 immigrants settled in great numbers in America: New England and the mid-Atlantic states and some places in the mountain states like Butte, Montana, but not in the Midwest or South. It was not just the number of new immigrants that was important to this ethnic revival, but also their activist experience in the Ireland of the Land League, home rule campaigns, and for the most recent newcomers, the Gaelic cultural revival: a Gaelic Athletic Association, founded in 1884, to revitalize Gaelic sports like hurling; and a Gaelic League, established in 1893, to foster a rebirth of the Irish language.[29]

It was the new American environment of rising ethnic tension, however, that sparked and sustained this new Irish American ethnic assertion. The Hibernians and their allies locked in on the APA, attacking it relentlessly as it emerged in the 1890s, and later launched a campaign to rid theaters of the "stage Irish" stereotype. Yet their style of attack was as important as their targets, a pugnacious, chip-on-the-shoulder Irish aggressiveness: invading theaters, for example, to shout down stage Irish performers and pelt them with eggs. In 1894, the AOH national delegate thundered: "True men love the people who stand up in a manly way." The Hibernians also insisted on demonstrating Irish American strength through numbers, playing a critical role in reviving and expanding St. Patrick's Day parades in cities across the country in the 1890s and early 1900s.[30]

With political nationalism, especially physical force nationalism, flagging in Ireland and America, the Hibernians and their allies had difficulty finding an outlet for their own brand of militant nationalist enthusiasm. Prompted by the Gaelic revival in Ireland, they turned to vigorous promotion of the Irish language revival in America and encouraged the organization of Irish hurling and/or Gaelic football teams in Chicago and many cities across the Northeast. They also looked for opportunities to strike at Britain, raising money for British enemies like the Boers in South Africa, and collaborating with the huge German American National Alliance to prevent an alliance between the United States and Britain. Interestingly, unlike many Catholic liberals, who celebrated the spread of American ideals through overseas colonies, the Hibernians and their allies also criticized America's own imperial adventurism in the Philippines, even favorably comparing Filipino rebels fighting American troops to "the Irish men who fought Cromwell."[31]

In 1908, however, even as Hibernian membership neared its all-time peak, AOH president Matthew Cummings warned: "Emigration from Ireland cannot much longer furnish the material for the upbuilding of this society. . . . Their sons in the future must take up this work where the fathers laid it down." The Hibernians would hold their own for another decade or more but, as Cummings suggested, their future decline seemed inevitable. Such an ethnically isolated conception of Irish America had less appeal to an Irish American Catholic population now dominated by the American-born and limited usefulness to an Irish American ethnic group needing allies as they jockeyed for power with multiple ethnic groups. As the attraction of the Hibernians and their allies plateaued, American-born Irish Americans, "the sons," were already beginning to find a new fit and define a new identity for themselves and their people in America.[32]

9. Finding Their Place

The Irish American Community, 1900–1928

Charlie Murphy did not seem cut out for politics. He rarely spoke in public and was notoriously close mouthed and terse even in conversation, given to long pauses that even friends and allies sometimes found unnerving. He was a staunch Catholic, something of a puritan, and rarely drank though he bought his first saloon by age twenty-two and soon purchased more. Yet he would be boss of Tammany Hall, its Grand Sachem, from 1902 until his death in 1924, making a small fortune for himself with scarcely a whiff of scandal. Much more important, he became the smartest, most successful, and most powerful Tammany leader in its history.

Murphy was born on New York City's East Side in 1858, the son of famine Irish immigrants. If he was quiet and prudish, he was a good athlete, at baseball and rowing, and a "tough guy." If he had little education, dropping out of school at an early age, he had a "political ear," which meant that he was usually exceptionally shrewd in discerning what the New York City electorate wanted or, at least, would tolerate: as Tammany nemesis Fiorello La Guardia acknowledged, "he had his hand on the pulse of the people." He took over the Hall after a notoriously sleazy orgy of corruption had led to its disastrous defeat at the hands of reformers in 1901; he would lose only one New York mayoral election during his tenure, backed three successful governors of the state, controlled the state legislature in the early 1910s, and by the end of his life had groomed second-generation Irish Catholic Alfred E. Smith, Tammany's own, for a run at the presidency.[1]

He had a problem, however. Italian and Jewish immigrants had been arriving in New York since the 1880s but began to come in a vast flood after Murphy

Figure 14. *Tim Sullivan's Funeral*. Tammany Hall leaders and other mourners at the funeral of "Big Tim" Sullivan, boss of the Bowery, in 1913. From left to right, Thomas McManus, "the MacManus," boss of Hell's Kitchen on New York's West Side; Judge Otto Rosalsky, a Jewish Republican but born and raised in Sullivan's district; Tom Foley, boss of the Fourth Ward near the Brooklyn Bridge; and the most important of the four, Charles F. Murphy, boss of Tammany Hall. Photo by Bain News Service, http://hdl.loc.gov/loc.pnp/ggbain.14182. Library of Congress Prints and Photographs Division.

took over Tammany. By the 1910s they were threatening to completely transform the New York City electorate and thoroughly disrupt Tammany Hall's political calculus. Murphy tried many solutions to this new problem, but one, in particular, was noteworthy: he became a backer of Progressive social and economic reform, and a key player in one of the great reform eras in New York's history.[2]

By the early twentieth century, a majority of the American-born children of the famine migrants had finally grown to maturity and begun to dominate the Irish American community, perhaps the most important generational transition in the history of Irish America. They had affection for Ireland, which they would soon prove when the island erupted in a rebellion, evolving into a war for independence in the 1910s. They were native-born Americans, however, with limited interest in the Ancient Order of Hibernians' efforts to replicate Irish culture. They were also a people with broad ambitions for power that transcended the ethnic isolation of the Hibernians' narrow ethnocentric focus of the preceding decade.

Nevertheless, they alone would not determine where Irish American Catholics fit in American society nor how they would define their own identity. Changes in their environment would shape those responses too. Yankee Protestant prejudice and their own church's conservatism, for example, had combined to prevent further Catholic liberal outreach to native-stock Protestants by the end of the nineteenth century. With that door slammed shut, they looked for other opportunities. As William Shannon suggested over a half century ago, Irish American Catholics, blocked from becoming insiders in American life but the "closest to being 'in' while still being 'out,'" would take advantage of their American savvy and achievements to make themselves the leaders of the "outs." More specifically, they would become the leader of most of the other "outs" in urban America, now more powerful than ever before because of the flood of new immigrants arriving in American cities from southern and eastern Europe.

Irish American Catholic relationships with those Italian, Polish, other Catholic newcomers and Jewish immigrants would be complicated and always fractious in the arenas the Irish had come to dominate, the labor movement, the urban Democratic Party, and the Catholic Church, especially in the first two decades of the twentieth century. Yet responding to a variety of the era's events and trends like a Democratic Party revival or the rise of Progressivism, they would adapt. By the 1920s, helped by a new explosion of anti-Catholic, anti-immigrant nativism, they would be largely successful in securing their leadership over the new immigrants in those arenas and, as important, in defining a new, pan-ethnic people, militant American Catholics, as well as a new identity for themselves as its leaders and models.[3]

By the early twentieth century the AFL's membership had increased to about 1.6 million members. Though a Jewish immigrant from England, Samuel Gompers, ruled over the federation then, fifty of the leaders of its one hundred and ten affiliated unions were Irish American Catholics. As much as the AFL had grown, however, industrial trade associations of corporation owners with an "unbending hostility to trade unions" had grown as much or more, and had found allies in the federal judiciary to cripple union power.[4]

Battered from above and suffering in important industries from changing technologies which were eroding their skill advantages, Irish American Catholic workers and labor leaders confronted the tidal wave of new immigrant workers challenging them from below. Sometimes those encounters erupted in violence such as fights between Irish and Italian laborers in New York's subway tunnels or on the city docks, where striking Irish longshoremen and even their wives, mothers, and sisters attacked Italian "scabs." The AFL's preferred solution to the problem of new immigrant competition in the workplace was to convince the federal government to restrict immigration, but they would have no success doing that until the late 1910s and early 1920s. In the meantime, some Irish American labor leaders tried to integrate Italian, Polish, or other immigrant workers into their unions, in some cases even forcing resistant Irish Americans to include the new immigrants, "like it or not." That was hard to do, but the alternative, ignoring the newcomers, simply made Irish workers more vulnerable to losing their jobs to their new rivals.[5]

An upsurge in political and labor radicalism in the early twentieth century complicated these relations between Irish American union leaders and new immigrant workers. When conservative Irish and other leaders of the AFL ignored them, Italians and other immigrants in places like Lawrence, Massachusetts, turned to socialists or the radical Industrial Workers of the World to take up their cause. There were Irish American radicals and socialists in this era, including many women like the American-born Leonora O'Reilly, and Elizabeth Gurley Flynn and the immigrant Mary Harris "Mother" Jones, but most Irish Catholic labor leaders opposed socialism. They did so in part for ideological reasons and because the Catholic Church in America was obsessed with the socialist threat in America and by the 1910s was attacking it relentlessly. They did so also simply because the radicals threatened their power and the sometimes corrupt economic niches Irish American union leaders had carved out for themselves in the American labor movement.[6]

After the outbreak of war in Europe in 1914, however, American workers flocked to unions to take advantage of tightening labor markets in America and win relief from rising prices. By 1917, trade union membership passed three million members for the first time in history. Some Irish Americans were part of this labor surge: Boston's largely second-generation Irish women telephone workers, for example, became the first national trade union controlled and officered by women in 1918. As chair of a Federal Commission on Industrial Relations from 1913 to 1915, American-born Irish lawyer Frank Walsh also led a crusade for industrial democracy, which tried to cross ideological, ethnic, and even racial boundaries in rallying the labor movement. Most Irish American union leaders, however, were still, at best, ambivalent about what to do with the sometimes radicalized new immigrants flocking to unions in the 1910s. Nevertheless, Irish American Catholics remained the single largest ethnic group in the leadership of an increasingly powerful AFL.[7]

While Irish labor leaders struggled to deal with new immigrant workers, Irish American political bosses began to receive plaudits for their dealings with the newcomers. Even reformers, like settlement house leader Jane Addams, and the muckraking journalist Lincoln Steffens, noted how the bosses distributed favors to poor immigrants in reciprocal exchanges that stipulated no moral conditions, no cultural adjustments, only the return of "friendship" with a vote. Many scholars since have celebrated how the bosses' politics of personal exchanges and cultural tolerance eased the incorporation of new immigrant Italians, Poles, and Jews into the broader processes of American political life.[8]

That happy and simple tale is too happy and too simple. Irish American Catholic bosses were not quite as generous as they were depicted. Though they were willing to dispense cheap favors to the new immigrants—coal in the winter, turkeys at Christmas, and picnics in the summer—they usually reserved the most precious favors, jobs, for their own fellow Irish American Catholics. They did so in part out of prejudice, but also because the Irish were dependable voters and party workers. Irish American machines actually often sought to restrict the size of their electorates, not expand them, to enhance the impact of those reliable Irish city employees on election day.[9]

Yet there were limits to that strategy. One was that where Democratic machines faced significant Republican opposition or even broke into competitive Democratic factions, both sides had incentives to seek new voters to break the stalemate. Naturalization rates were thus higher in Chicago, where Republicans and Democrats were about evenly matched, than in New York, where the Democrats ruled. Furthermore, because new immigrant migration kept rising, the number of eligible new immigrant voters did too, with or without politicians' help: more than doubling for Italian Americans and near tripling for Russian Jews in New England and mid-Atlantic cities between 1900 and 1910.[10]

Irish American Catholic politicians had also long used cultural issues like fighting restrictions on the sale of liquor or defending parochial schools to rally their voters, but at the beginning of the twentieth century a new political movement, Progressivism, was beginning to revolutionize both the issue agenda and the electoral tactics of American politics. Progressives pushed a broad array of new economic, political, and social reforms, including mothers' pensions, direct election of senators, the minimum wage, factory inspection, and progressive taxation, into the center of American political discourse. Party allegiances began to soften at this time and national politicians and reformers also began to employ new campaigning techniques, heavy use of speeches, and media focusing on personalities and issues to win elections, rather than simply rely on the local party bosses' old "military style" of mobilizing the party faithful. Though he lost badly in the 1896, 1900, and 1908 elections, William Jennings Bryan's aggressive public campaigning and soaring rhetoric in those contests nonetheless attracted attention and helped set a precedent for this new political style. Not just the "what" and the "how" of politics, but the "where" was changing as well. Irish and other bosses had long believed that only local politics really mattered, but now only the states or the federal government had the legal powers and resources to address the new broad range of possible political, economic, and social reforms affecting workers and the poor in the cities Irish American Catholics sought to run.[11]

The rise of Progressivism had a powerful effect on Irish American Catholic Democrats. It helped wreck their Republican opposition, for example, opening abundant new opportunities for Irish American Catholic Democratic Party candidates. In 1909, frustrated progressive Republicans "went into open revolt," as conservatives in the party refused to budge on progressive issues like tariff reform and protection of the environment. Three years later the progressive faction bolted the GOP altogether and created their own new Progressive Party led by former Republican president Teddy Roosevelt. Meanwhile, Bryan had been busily working to transform Irish American Catholics' own party, the Democrats, into the party of progressive reform. In 1906, for example, he had struck an alliance with the AFL, which helped the Democrats attract eastern urban workers and thus broaden their appeal beyond their base among southern and western farmers. The results of the Republicans' fracture and the Democrats' transformation were stunning. Between 1904 and 1912, the Democrats picked up 155 new congressional seats, 104 of them in the "Metropole," the urban industrial core stretching from southern New England west to Illinois. The Democratic percentage of seats in state legislatures outside the South also rose by one-third in just the two years from 1908 to 1910. Thus, the long hapless Democrats started to revive, a surge climaxing when the Democrat Woodrow Wilson won the presidency in 1912 but one that persisted until 1918.[12]

Irish American Catholic Democrats rode this party revival. They made up over half of the growing number of Democrats elected in both legislative chambers in Massachusetts and more than half in Rhode Island by 1912. Irish American Catholics also became speakers of the lower houses in New York, New Jersey, and Illinois in the 1910s. Five Irish Catholics were elected governors and four U.S. senators between 1906 and 1918. All the governors and two of the senators were the first Irish Catholics elected to those positions in their states. Irish American Catholic Democrats made striking gains in the U.S. House of Representatives, as well, their numbers rising from twelve in 1908 to twenty in 1910 to a stunning forty-three in 1912 (including all five of Connecticut's congressmen) as the new Progressive Party nominated its own candidates to compete with the Republicans and Democrats that year. In 1914, many Progressive Party members returned to the GOP, and the number of Irish Catholic Democrats in the House plummeted to twenty-six, but that was still more than it had ever been before 1912.[13]

Once in office, Irish American Catholic politicians backed progressive reform in almost every state in the Northeast and Midwest where they had a political presence. In Rhode Island, Connecticut, and Illinois, Republicans blocked their efforts, but they were extraordinarily successful in New Jersey, led by Joseph Tumulty and other young American-born graduates of St. Peter's College in Jersey City, in New York by Charlie Murphy and Al Smith, and in Massachusetts by second-generation Irish Boston ward boss Martin Lomasney. Among the many reforms they helped promote were factory inspection laws, widows' pensions, public housing, minimum wages and maximum working hours for women, and an income tax amendment to the national constitution. Irish American politicians rarely set this agenda. Women, usually Yankees or Jews from women's clubs and settlement houses but sometimes Irish American Catholics as well, were critical in defining and publicizing social reforms. In fighting for these reforms, however, Irish American Catholic politicians helped supply working-class, neighborhood roots for progressive reforms and significant political muscle to enact them. While this storm of reform swept state legislatures in the 1910s, Irish American Catholics also joined other Democrats in Congress backing Wilson, notably when he turned left in 1916 to position himself for reelection. They backed his child labor bill then, and eight-hour day legislation for railroad workers pushed on the president by his advisor, Irish American labor reformer Frank Walsh.[14]

The fact that Bryan had remade their party, the Democrats, into a progressive party undoubtedly helped convince Irish American Catholics to embrace progressive reform, but they also had their own motives for supporting it. Some of those motives were deeply rooted in old country anti-aristocratic feeling and communal egalitarianism, but more recent trends and events had also made them more aware of the potential usefulness of the state in helping workers: Patrick Ford's radical Irish American nationalism, the Knights of Labor, Pope Leo XIII's encyclical *Rerum Novarum,* and the havoc wreaked on families by the 1893 depression. Irish American politicians, however, also voted for progressive legislation for practical reasons. Importantly, it helped them undercut the appeal of radicals like the socialists to new immigrant voters while saving Irish bosses from having to spend any of their precious patronage capital on the newcomers. To further cultivate the support of those Italian, Jewish, and Polish immigrants, they also aggressively defended the rights of new immigrants in an age rife with anti-immigrant antagonism. Irish American Catholic Democrats in the U.S. House, for example, were virtually unanimous in voting against bills to restrict European immigration in the 1910s. The House voted three times, in 1913, 1915, and 1917, on whether to require immigrants to pass a literacy test before they would be permitted to enter the United States—a requirement explicitly designed to bar most immigrants from southern and eastern Europe. Only one Irish American Catholic voted for the test in 1913; none did in 1915 and 1917. Fifteen voted against the literacy test in 1913 (two did not vote); thirty-eight were against it in 1915 (five not voting); and twenty-four opposed it in 1917 (two not voting).[15]

Despite all these efforts and their continued distribution of favors, Democrats led by Irish American Catholics could not unite all the new immigrants in a political coalition of "outs" in most cities. In New York the Jewish commitment to the socialists persisted, and though the Democrats had more success with Italian Americans in New York, Boston, and elsewhere, that support for the Democrats was still conditional and limited.[16]

Yet even without securing that immigrant coalition, Irish American Catholic Democrats were enormously successful in the first two decades of the twentieth century. They certainly benefited from Progressivism's disruption of the Republican Party. The emergence of a Progressive third party in 1912, largely made up of Republicans, clearly helped Irish Americans win their forty-three seats in the House that year. Furthermore, both Edward Dunne in Illinois in the same year and David Walsh in Massachusetts in the next one also profited from Republican fragmentation to win their elections for governor. Dunne was not reelected but Walsh was, over a largely reunited GOP, and he would become Massachusetts' first Irish American Catholic U.S. Senator in 1918.[17]

That the maturing of the second-generation Irish peaked in 1910 at precisely this moment of opportunity was also critical to their success. The number of second-generation Irish voters, for example, doubled between 1880 and 1910. Yet American-born Irish politicians also adapted well to the new progressive political style of persuasion and media manipulation. Few were better at it than Al Smith and, perhaps surprisingly, the charismatic "rogue" James Michael Curley of Boston. Curley was elected mayor of Boston four times, congressman twice, and governor of Massachusetts once in a long political career that began in his election to Boston's Common Council in 1901 and ended with the close of his last term as mayor in 1950. Notorious for his flouting of the law, Curley had to operate in a Boston politics remade by reformers—limited patronage and at-large (not ward) nonpartisan elections for city council seats—which crimped the mobilization methods of machine politicians but rewarded the new progressive politics of publicity, personality, and issues. Curley's innate rhetorical skills, natural theatricality, and talent for media manipulation were crucial to his success. Yet his pitch to voters also worked well in this new political environment: a smart mix of new progressive rhetoric pitting the people against corporate interests, with appeals to traditional Irish antagonism to aristocrats, Catholic religious triumphalism, and contemporary Irish American resentments of Yankee privilege. If he gave jobs and peddler licenses to individuals—the divisible benefits essential to machine politics—he also talked about broader universal benefits like his fight in Congress against immigration restriction legislation. He was, then, not just a retail but a wholesale politician, debating issues, but also creating a distinctive public persona. If Curley's ethnic parochialism and corruption wore thin outside of Boston, his modern campaign style, nonetheless, worked well enough to elect him governor of Massachusetts in 1934 and win nominations for statewide offices throughout most of his career.[18]

Unlike Smith and Curley, who dropped out of school at ages fourteen and fifteen, respectively, a majority of the most successful Irish American Catholic politicians of the era had gone to college or professional school or both. They included all of the Irish American Catholics elected governor save Smith and sixteen of the twenty-six Irish American Catholics elected to the Congress in 1914. Going to college or law school and practicing as lawyers probably added to the respectability of second-generation Irish candidates, but it also meant that they were used to public speaking, debate, and the arts of persuasion, the critical tools of the Progressive-era politician. Intriguingly, some of the most success-ful new, young, American-born Irish Catholic Democrats from the East and Mid-west, Dunne, David Walsh, and Tumulty of New Jersey, for example, had thrilled to the aggressive public campaigning and electric reform rhetoric of Bryan, the populist from the faraway plains, when they first entered politics.[19]

It is important to recognize, however, that this embrace of progressive issues and tactics was an adaptation, by this generation and Irish Americans generally, not a simple imitation of Protestant and other reformers—as Curley perhaps most clearly demonstrated. There would, for example, be a Catholic Church progressivism, led by Monsignor John A. Ryan, who became the "Father of the Minimum Wage" in this era, and Catholic women social and charity work-ers, who fought for mothers' pensions and maximum working hours for women at the same time. This Catholic progressivism sought support for families and communities more than individual liberation, drawing heavily on Pope Leo XIII's encyclical *Rerum Novarum,* and traditional Catholic theology and philos-ophy to inspire and shape its activism. Furthermore, as noted, Irish American political machines did not disappear in this wave of reform; indeed, bosses like Charlie Murphy and Martin Lomasney led it in New York and Massachusetts, largely because they thought it would help them win elections. Yet even for suc-cessful college-educated politicians like Tumulty, David Walsh, and Tom Walsh, Senator from Montana, their politics was their profession as much or more as it was their cause. Having grown up in families deeply involved in local Demo-cratic Party politics, they were adept at the "mechanics" of winning elections: Tom Walsh ran Woodrow Wilson's 1916 campaign in the West; David Walsh would rebuild the Democratic Party in Massachusetts in the mid-1920s; and Tumulty would handle President Wilson's patronage as his secretary. The busi-ness of politics was still their business.[20]

Irish American Catholicism, too, was transformed in this era, and it was through the Catholic Church and Catholic organizations that Irish American Catholics began to actually forge a new identity, as leaders and models of a mil-itant American Catholic people. In the years following Leo XIII's condemna-tion of Americanism in 1899, "Catholic liberal" became an epithet in the Irish American Catholic community: defined and denounced as a "traitor to his Church and his God." Meanwhile organized anti-Catholic nativism persisted, if now most prominently in the South, and the more decorous discrimination of the Protestant establishment also endured, especially strong in the Northeast.[21]

Yet it was not just prejudice outside the group, but an increasingly conservative Vatican working hard to tighten Church authority within it, which prevented liberalism's revival. Leo's successor, Pius X, condemned "modernism," specifically cracking down on recent biblical and theological scholarship but more symbolically warning against any dissent in the Church, and he also strengthened prohibitions on religious intermarriage. More subtly, Roman experience and Roman connections became essential to clerical promotion. Irish American archbishops appointed to the major sees of New York, Boston, Philadelphia, and San Francisco in the first two decades of the twentieth century all studied in Rome and some were ordained there. Bishops in America also strengthened their authority in their own dioceses by creating central departments to control schools and charitable institutions. Meanwhile, they also made efforts to complete Catholic segregation by building more schools, in particular Catholic high schools, which would help keep the more ambitious within the fold and, by isolating them from non-Catholics, perhaps help limit marriage outside the Church.[22]

Catholic women religious were, of course, essential to the expansion of the school system. Rev. Philip McDevitt, head of the Philadelphia Catholic schools, freely acknowledged that his school system would quickly "crumble" without them. American bishops would have preferred more male teachers and complained about their absence in their schools but could do little about it. In Philadelphia, the dominance of female teachers only grew from 17 to 1 male in 1903 to 36 to 1 in 1920. Women religious teachers were simply much cheaper, and though bishops and pastors exploited them shamelessly, the number of Catholic women religious kept growing from 900 in 1840 to over 46,000 in 1900, before nearly doubling to almost 90,000 in 1920. Despite these numbers, religious orders were under constant pressure not only to supply more teachers to the expanding educational system of the early twentieth century, but also to meet new standards for teacher training set by the emerging diocesan central offices or by state governments responding to Progressive reform demands. Nuns, however, fought hard to resist those pressures from infringing on their lives and commitment as religious women as well as the rights and traditions of their religious orders.[23]

In Philadelphia, Sister Assisium McEvoy, mistress of novitiates and director of Sister Studies for the Sisters of St. Joseph in Philadelphia (SSJ), worked at the center of those conflicting pressures. Born in Leeds, England, to an Irish immigrant family, she moved at age five with her parents to Philadelphia in 1848, just a few years after the great nativist riot in the city. After being expelled from her public school for taking a day off to prepare for her St. Patrick's parish May Day procession, she transferred into a Catholic school run by the Sisters of St. Joseph. She and her sister later found their vocations in that French order, contributing to its accelerating "Irish Americanization." She worked hard along with others to improve teacher training among the sisters, writing a manual addressing "new ways" of teaching Catholic doctrine, which would be used throughout the United States and Australia. Yet she was very passionate about Catholic education's spiritual superiority over the public school and very conscious of Catholic sisters' need to balance attention to their religious vocation with their teaching. You are "religious first and religious teachers second. . . . If you are putting your secular work first, you are not living up to your vocation."[24]

If Irish American Catholics had thus now given up on getting "in" in America and were fully committed to their separate subsociety, they were not disheartened but "triumphant," confident, for the number of Catholic Church members doubled from 1890 to 1916, seemingly assuring Catholicism's bright future in America. Cardinal William O'Connell of Boston proclaimed: "We have passed the days, and passed forever, when . . . we were grateful for being ignored."[25]

New immigrant Catholics, however, made up much of that growth, so that triumph required Irish American Catholics to hold the newcomers to the Church, which was not so simple. Many poorer Italian immigrants were suspicious of the clergy, remembering them as a bulwark of the oppressive old regime in Italy. By contrast, Polish Catholic immigrants, fleeing German or Russian Poland, had experienced religious *and* national discrimination at home, fusing the two for them in a single emotional allegiance. For Irish Catholic leaders, if the Italians seemed to care too little about the institutional Church, the Poles seemed to care too much, fiercely determined to maintain their control over the hundreds of parishes and schools they had established in America.[26]

In the thirty years before 1900, Irish American priests and bishops clashed repeatedly with both groups, but in the new century, though conflicts hardly ended, Irish American Church leaders seemed more active but also more careful in trying to address tensions with recent immigrant groups. Some Irish bishops and clerics, for example, began to participate in Italian festivals, send Irish priests to Italy to learn Italian, or help finance Italian churches. Bishop Clement Kelly described the reign of James Quigley as archbishop of Chicago from 1903 to 1915 as "a long peace treaty," an ongoing, still wary, but familiar process of negotiation with the newcomers.[27]

There were many reasons for this emerging fragile peace. In part it was simply a matter of time. The two sides knew each other better and there were fewer intra-community battles among the new immigrants which had often provoked Irish American bishops to restore order by taking sides in such conflicts. In the long run, however, Irish American Catholics also needed such a "peace treaty." Before 1900, Italian and Polish immigrant populations had been small, unimportant, seemingly easy to condemn and dismiss, but they were small no more: in just the six years between 1910 and 1916, the number of both Italian and Polish parishes almost doubled to 436 and 735, respectively. Irish Americans were well entrenched in the American Church and still the best model and leaders for an American, English-speaking, Catholic Church in America, but if it was to be a "triumphant" one, they had to learn to deal with the newcomers.[28]

While Irish American bishops and priests were still working out their relationships with the new immigrants, Irish American Catholic–led organizations emerged in the early twentieth century to unite all Catholic ethnics in assertion of their common Catholic interests. Founded in 1900, the American Federation of Catholic Societies, for example, brought together representatives from Irish, German, and other Catholic ethnic organizations to counter anti-Catholic discrimination. The old liberal Archbishop John Ireland warned the leader of the new federation, the Ulster-born Bishop James McFaul, that "we are, after all, a minority," and that minority should be careful about challenging the majority. McFaul brusquely retorted: "We ought on every possible occasion enter our protests against the assumption that this is a Protestant country." Loosely organized and wracked by factions, the federation was hardly the powerful instrument McFaul envisioned, and by the time America entered World War I in 1917, it was sputtering to its demise.[29]

The Knights of Columbus would be much more powerful. Already long established by the early twentieth century, it was only then that its numbers begin to take off as it became the clearest and strongest organizational representative of the new militantly Catholic, patriotically American, pan-ethnic, American Catholicism. In 1897, the K of C had 16,651 members but by 1910 over 240,000, surpassing the AOH. The Knights, however, kept growing: between 1917 and 1923 more than 400,000 men joined the organization.[30]

As noted earlier, Irish Americans, more specifically American-born and upwardly mobile Irish, dominated the order, but the Knights welcomed Catholics of all ethnic and racial backgrounds. They were not, however, a federation of separate groups, but a single society, which they understood as representing a single people, American Catholics. Like American Catholic liberals, they wanted new immigrants and their children to become Americans, but they had no interest now in accommodating Protestants. Irish American Knights thus believed that the new immigrants should assimilate into a separate Catholic not Protestant version of America. They selected Columbus as a patron because he was the first Catholic in America, and thus the common ancestor of all the Catholic peoples who followed him to America. Yet as important, they chose him because, by their reckoning, he was also the first American—ignoring millions of Native Americans but self-consciously displacing the Pilgrims as America's founders—and thus as Columbus' descendants, the Knights argued, all American Catholics were "entitled to all the rights and privileges due to such a discovery by one of our faith."[31]

To defend those rights, the Knights created a Commission on Religious Prejudice in 1914, to investigate the causes of religious bigotry, but also to carry out Catholic counterattacks against anti-Catholic movements. Local K of C councils also organized parades of all Catholic ethnic groups on Columbus Day as "imposing celebration[s] of Catholic power." At the same time, the Knights vigorously opposed socialism, seeing it as a threat to both their religion and their nation, but also a crusade that neatly merged the Catholic and American poles of their identity.[32]

If relations between Irish American and other Catholic ethnics in the Church thus remained tentative and fragile in the first two decades of the twentieth century, the spectacular growth of the Knights of Columbus suggested a stunningly popular new solution for Irish Catholic Americans to the challenges of their early twentieth-century environment. It required neither their assimilation into a Protestant American mainstream nor retreat to an old world culture, but their creation of a new people, militantly Catholic but thoroughly American, and if open to Catholics of all ethnicities, dominated by them, Irish Americans.

This new formula for Irish American Catholic identity left little room for Irish Americans' homeland. Through the 1890s, Irish and Irish American nationalism had been moribund, but at the beginning of the new century, parliamentary moderate nationalism began to revive in Ireland. By 1910, a reunited Irish Parliamentary Party (IPP), with help from a support group in the United States, the United Irish League of America (UILA), appeared on the verge of achieving Parnell's long-sought goal of home rule for Ireland. Then it all blew up as Ulster

Unionists opposed to home rule armed themselves and resisted it, and home rule nationalists armed in turn, pushing the island to the brink of civil war in 1914. By then, World War I had broken out, the British government postponed home rule, and John Redmond, the leader of the IPP, seeking some kind of guarantee for home rule's future, pledged his party to fight for the United Kingdom in the war.[33]

Irish Americans' response to Redmond was immediate and explosive, denouncing him and his party as "traitors" for sending Irish boys to France to die for the empire. The UILA thus disintegrated in most of America, and the militantly nationalist Clan na Gael, so long marginalized by the moderate IPP's success, now moved to the forefront of a resurrected Irish American nationalism. Led by John Devoy and Judge Daniel Cohalan, the Clan would begin funding planning in Ireland for a rebellion and secretly connecting that rebel band to the German government. Meanwhile, it also ginned up its longtime campaign to prevent an American alliance with Britain, now at war with Germany. Though it seems likely that immigrants, like those who joined the Hibernians, supported the Clan, there is little evidence that many second-generation Irish American Catholics did. Indeed, American Catholic newspapers, many of them edited by Irish Americans, were largely indifferent to Irish issues, and when they did focus on Ireland, some dismissed the notion of an independent Irish republic altogether.[34]

The Irish rebels, led by language teacher Padraic Pearse, launched their uprising in Dublin on Easter Monday 1916. After its failure, British executions of its leaders outraged even the most implacable American Irish critics of the Clan but did little to boost the membership of its popular front organization, the Friends of Irish Freedom (FOIF). The second-generation Irish, extremely sensitive to questioning of their American patriotism, seemed wary of being labeled "hyphenates" not "real Americans," a distinction Woodrow Wilson had made even before the war in an attack on the Clan's alleged meddling in American foreign policy. Practical political interests also tied the American-born Irish to Wilson as they rode the Democratic Party revival to new heights of power. Thus, though the Clan worked hard to defeat Wilson's bid for reelection in 1916, most evidence suggests that few Irish American Catholic voters defected to the Republicans that year. Indeed, Wilson did significantly better in Massachusetts and Rhode Island, the most heavily Irish state electorates in America, than any Democratic candidate had since before the Civil War.[35]

When the United States entered World War I on the side of the allies on

April 2, 1917, therefore, most in the Irish American Catholic community backed the war effort wholeheartedly. The Knights of Columbus, fearful that "German Catholics and Sinn Feiners . . . will bring the patriotism of Catholics [in America] into question," pledged "the devotion of the 400,000 members of this Order" to the war. Soon after, the Knights began establishing recreational and religious facilities for Catholic servicemen in military camps in America and overseas. About the same time, American Catholic bishops created a National Catholic War Council (NCWC), administered almost exclusively by Irish American Catholics, to mobilize Catholic support for the war. The best measure of Irish Americans' commitment to the war, however, was their willingness to fight in it. According to the 1930 United States Census, over 37 percent of second-generation Irish men who had been age-eligible for the armed forces in 1918 served in the war, a higher proportion than that of native-stock Americans and second-generation Germans, Swedes, Norwegians, and even English. After the war, statistics gathered from Catholic parishes by the NCWC revealed that 2,246 men from the Irish-dominated parishes of Dorchester in Boston, 2,224 from churches next door in South Boston, and even 1,151 from Irish churches in Butte, Montana, joined the army or navy during the war. Meanwhile, the American government cracked down hard on the Clan and other Irish American nationalists, banning some Irish American newspapers from the mails and detaining seventy-seven Irish American nationalist activists.[36]

When the war ended in November 1918, however, Irish American nationalism erupted almost instantly with an energy and on a scale that dwarfed the prewar movement. In that month priests in New York, Philadelphia, Boston, and St. Louis petitioned President Wilson on Ireland's behalf, and mass meetings in Lowell, New Haven, Omaha, and Buffalo among other cities passed resolutions for Irish independence. At the end of February, 5,000 delegates, including thirty American Catholic bishops and archbishops, attended an FOIF-sponsored Irish Race Convention promoting Irish independence.[37]

Yet this was just the beginning. On June 11, 1919, Eamon de Valera, president of the Dail, or parliament of the new Irish Republic, landed in New York, and a few weeks later barnstormed across the country and back, speaking to over half a million people. At the time of the Race Convention in February 1919, the Friends of Irish Freedom had only about 6,000 members; by December they had over 70,000 and by September 1920, over 200,000. The Knights of Columbus endorsed Ireland's cause and a number of second-generation Irish, prominent in the American war effort, joined it, including Frank Walsh, recently co-chair of Wilson's War Labor board; Patrick Henry Callahan, head of the Knights of Columbus' Wartime service; and Bishop Peter Muldoon, co-chair of the NCWC. The second-generation Irish and other previously hesitant Irish Americans had now caught nationalist fever and transformed what had been a relatively limited prewar agitation into a mass movement.[38]

That was, in part, because the situation in Ireland had changed radically since America had entered the war in 1917. By December 1918, Sinn Fein, the political party of the rebellion, had become all powerful in southern Ireland, winning almost three-quarters of all Ireland's seats in the British parliament. Instead of going to London, the newly elected MPs met in Dublin, declaring themselves the parliament of an Irish Republic, the Dail, the realization of a dream dating back to the United Irishmen.[39]

Yet however much Ireland had changed, new circumstances in America were also critical to the new American-born Irish enthusiasm for Irish nationalism. Most obviously, the end of World War I had swept away the complications of support for Germany or Britain and divided Irish and American loyalties. Even more important, President Wilson had made national self-determination—"that every people has the right to choose the sovereignty under which they live"—an American war aim, one that easily harmonized Ireland's aspirations with American ideals.[40]

Yet Irish Americans read Wilson's self-determination not just as permission for them to back their homeland, but as a promise of American support for Ireland's independence. They were outraged when Wilson backed the homeland causes of even recent poor immigrants—as Bishop Muldoon sneered in a confrontation with Wilson, "Slavic" peoples—but stubbornly refused to take up Ireland's cause. By the spring of 1919, infuriated Irish American nationalists in the FOIF had joined efforts to reject the peace treaty Wilson had negotiated in Paris, claiming his pet treaty provision for a League of Nations, a kind of world parliament of nations, would entangle America in defense of Britain's empire.[41]

Even as the FOIF won its battle over the League, a diaspora fight was brewing between Irish American nationalists Cohalan and Devoy, and the Irish De Valera, over who should control an American movement committed to Ireland's liberation. Ultimately, De Valera abandoned the FOIF and formed a rival organization, the American Association for the Recognition of the Irish Republic (AARIR). By February and March 1921, the AARIR was claiming a half million or more members; meanwhile, Cohalan and Devoy's FOIF withered away, falling to only a little over twenty thousand stalwarts by the end of 1921.[42]

Thus, in this diaspora battle, most Irish Americans chose the Irish leader, De Valera, and his colleagues, not the Irish Americans, Devoy and Cohalan, though the latter claimed to represent them. It is a good question, however, given the outcome of this diaspora fight, whether Cohalan and Bishop Michael Gallagher, the president of the FOIF, both political conservatives, and the aging Devoy were representative of the many Irish Americans, especially the American-born, who poured into the nationalist movement after the war ended. Cohalan and Devoy's "aggressively masculine" Clan na Gael, for example, had long relegated women to "subsidiary" roles in their nationalist movement. Even after Irish American women became more active nationalists during and after the war, Devoy continued to complain about them. The AARIR would be ideologically diverse, but it seemed especially attractive to the nationalist left, not just the radical Irish Progressive League, but American-born Irish progressives like Patrick Callahan and Frank Walsh, and especially to Irish American women. Women became prominent in the leadership of the AARIR, most likely in Massachusetts, but also in Connecticut, Missouri, Ohio, New York, New Jersey, and California. De Valera may well have often been arrogant and clumsy in his negotiation of the complexities of American politics, as Devoy and Cohalan claimed. Nevertheless, it was he, and a host of speakers from Ireland, many of them women, traveling through the United States telling tales about their revolution, who seemed to best embody the moment of a new nation being born and a long-desired hope being realized.[43]

On December 6, 1921, Irish revolutionaries and United Kingdom representatives agreed to a treaty ending the Irish War of Independence, but the treaty's demand that Irish officials take an oath of loyalty to the king provoked De Valera and his allies to start a civil war in Ireland. Irish American Catholics did not understand this internal Irish conflict and now turned away from Ireland. There would be an Irish America after 1921, but one largely without Ireland for nearly another half century.[44]

One reason Irish American Catholics turned their back on Ireland so quickly was that they were already deeply involved in American racial, religious, and ethnic battles of their own, including a new and stormy era in their long, often troubled, relationship with African Americans. Declining immigration and booming industries during the war created a labor shortage in northern cities, prompting over 400,000 Blacks to migrate north between 1910 and 1920. In Chicago, the African American population more than doubled, and the new Black migrants had an almost immediate impact on Chicago politics, helping the florid Republican "Big Bill" Thompson become mayor in 1915. More important, the bulging Black ghetto on the city's South Side had no room for the new migrants, forcing African Americans into abutting Irish neighborhoods where Irish American Catholics and other whites frequently attacked them.[45]

In July 1919, Chicago, already seething with racial tensions, exploded in the summer heat. A white man killed seventeen-year-old African American Eugene Williams at a beach on the city's South Side, igniting a riot that left thirty-eight people, most of them African Americans, dead. Irish American Catholics, especially Irish youth gangs like the Ragen Colts, were prominent in the violence, while recent immigrant Poles and Italians largely stayed out of it, resisting Irish attempts to provoke them into joining the mayhem. Yet that was already changing. As new immigrants' second-generation numbers began to grow in the twenties and thirties, many joined pan-ethnic gangs, often led by Irish Americans. Such gangs defended the "turf" of their ethnically mixed territory against rival white ethnic gangs or pan-ethnic gangs from other neighborhoods. "Once they perceived a racial threat," however, "warring 'white' gangs embraced racial solidarity" and presented a united front against the Black "other."

Nevertheless, such Irish racial turf battles continued to combine with cautious Irish American political recognition of African Americans, as the paradox which seemed to have governed Irish American relations with African Americans in the North since Reconstruction persisted into the 1920s. Irish American Catholic Democratic politicians like David Walsh in Massachusetts and Mayor John "Red Mike" Hylan in New York drew heavy African American votes in the 1920s, and five of the nine Democrats in the House of Representatives who voted for an anti-lynching bill in 1922 were Irish American Catholics.[46]

The Chicago race riot was both a reminder of past battles and a harbinger of future racial conflict in Irish and African American life, but in the 1920s, Irish American Catholics were more worried about the rebirth of religious and ethnic nativism. Wartime anti-hyphenate xenophobia, a postwar economic depression, the shift of the longtime struggle over prohibition from a local to a national battleground, and reactions to Irish nationalism all contributed to a new surge of American ethnic and religious nativism in the "tribal twenties." Since the early 1900s, southern native-stock whites' fear of the new southern and eastern European immigration had made identification as Anglo-Saxon elastic enough that southerners ignored the region's Ulster Scot roots and insisted that "there is no purer Anglo Saxon people in the world today than the whites in the

Southern States of the Union." Thus in 1924, southern Democrats joined with Republicans to pass an immigration restriction law, which officially enshrined notions of Anglo-Saxon superiority and virtually ended further immigration from eastern and southern Europe. By that year, a second Ku Klux Klan, founded in 1915, had enrolled as many as four million members. This Klan, like the first one, was anti-Black, but, as one historian has pointed out, their "most basic and pervasive concern [now] was the Pope." The new Klan thrived in the North, taking the lead in trying to shut down parochial schools in Nebraska, Michigan, and Oregon.[47]

Though postwar disillusion with Wilson's war and peace and this mounting ethnic and religious tumult blew up the Democratic Party in the early 1920s, the Republican turn to nativism and the smothering of socialism by a postwar "red scare" had reduced political alternatives for new immigrants like Italians and Jews. In New York, Rhode Island, and Massachusetts, then, they began to turn to Irish-led Democratic parties. No one would be more important to the effort to bind recent immigrants to the Democrats in the 1920s than Al Smith, a child of New York's Lower East Side. Smith won four of five elections for governor of New York between 1918 and 1926. He was a successful reformer in a decade when there were few of them, increasing state spending for schools tenfold, extending state control over electric power production, and reorganizing New York's balkanized state administration. He was also an engaging campaigner and surrounded himself with aides like the Jewish Americans Belle Moskowitz and Joseph Proskauer, who were well attuned to the new politics of personality and issues. Smith had lost the nomination for president in the "little religious war" that broke out in the Democratic party's 1924 convention but steamrolled through the primaries to clinch the Democratic nod in 1928. If the nomination proved easy, however, the election did not. Herbert Hoover, the Republican nominee, won in a landslide, picking up nearly 60 percent of the vote.[48]

Despite the margin in the election or its seeming inevitability, it was extraordinarily, intensely fought. Smith and Hoover seemed to embody all the divisions that ran through tribal twenties America: rural versus urban; wet versus dry; and immigrant versus native stock. The religious division of Catholic versus Protestant, however, trumped them all. Smith did extraordinarily well among Catholics, even in northern cities where they had become used to voting Republican like Philadelphia or Pittsburgh. The emotional fire of the 1928 election seemed to burn hottest in southern New England, where he won the longtime Republican strongholds of Massachusetts and Rhode Island—the first Democratic majorities in either of those states since Franklin Pierce in 1852. In Worcester, thousands of Irish and Italian Catholics attacked a Republican parade held just the day before the election, provoking a gigantic brawl among over 30,000 people in the city's downtown.[49]

Some historians have talked about an Al Smith revolution among American Catholic voters. Given that Irish American Catholics had already been building multiethnic coalitions before 1928 and that the Depression, Franklin Roosevelt, and the New Deal would follow so soon after, it is difficult to tease out the singular impact of Smith's election on the Catholic vote. Nevertheless, capping the incessant religious and ethnic warfare of the 1920s, the 1928 election confirmed in a uniquely stark and public way the continuing importance of the boundary between Catholic outsiders and Protestant insiders in America.[50]

In 1921 Cardinal Gibbons died and Irish immigrant Michael Curley, who replaced him as Archbishop of Baltimore, quickly announced that he would tolerate no "spineless," "wishy-washy" Catholic pussyfooters in the one-time capital of Catholic liberalism. Yet Catholic liberalism had long been dead nearly everywhere in America and the Church only continued to bury it in the twenties by tightening links with Rome and reinforcing episcopal authority within dioceses. In the shadow of a reviving nativism, however, it seemed more sensitive to ethnic differences among American Catholic ethnic groups. During the war, the NCWC had worked to Americanize Catholic immigrants to prove Catholic patriotism. Now, however, it joined most Irish American politicians at the state as well as national level in attacking the racist 1924 immigration restriction act, hammered at coercive Americanization, and articulated a new kind of Catholic pluralism. Ironically, even the paragons of Catholic Americanism, the Knights of Columbus, led by Irish nationalist Edward McSweeney, took part in this effort, sponsoring books, including *The Gift of Black Folk: The Negroes in the Making of America* by W. E. B. Du Bois, celebrating the "contributions" of non-Anglo Saxon peoples to American life.[51]

Irish and other American Catholics also took on the nativist enemy, particularly the KKK, directly. The Knights of Columbus were active in this direct combat, but the principal opponent of the Klan was an ad hoc organization, the American Unity League (AUL). Led by Patrick O'Donnell, American-born Irish Catholic and another fierce Irish nationalist, it welcomed Poles, Italians, Jews, and Blacks and won praise from Chicago's African American newspaper, the *Defender,* but Irish Catholics dominated it (the Klan called the AUL an "Irish Catholic clique"). The AUL organized boycotts against Klan businessmen and,

Figure 15. *Holy Name Parade, September 21, 1924.* President Coolidge, flanked on the right by Cardinal William O'Connell, addressing marchers in the Holy Name parade at the Washington Monument. Photo by the National Photo Company. Library of Congress: LC-DIG-npcc-12147.

in age-old Irish and Irish American fashion, showed their numbers in 1923, by staging a parade on St. Patrick's Day in Indianapolis, the biggest city in Klan-dominated Indiana. The next year, at the height of the Klan's power, 100,000 Holy Name men did the same, marching down Pennsylvania Avenue from the Capitol to the White House before gathering in front of the Washington Monument to receive greetings from President Coolidge and hear mass. The Klan, infuriated, would respond by making the same march down Pennsylvania Avenue the next year—but with fewer people.[52]

Even as Irish American Catholics embraced pluralism to counter the nativists, however, there were signs that ethnic loyalties within American Catholicism were beginning to weaken. The number of foreign-language parishes stopped growing in major dioceses by the end of the 1920s as the new immigration restriction act reduced immigration from southern and eastern Europe to a trickle. Some of the new immigrant Italians and Poles or their children had begun to move to more mixed peripheral areas of cities and into "American," English-language churches, often run by Irish American priests. Polish and even French-Canadian American Catholics still occasionally rebelled at Irish authority, but the religious firestorm of the "tribal twenties" had helped smudge ethnic boundaries within the Catholic community even as it reinforced religious ones against non-Catholics.[53]

Trends in American culture, however, also helped reinforce differences between Catholics and non-Catholics and, at the same time, foster Catholic solidarity. By the 1920s the scholastic philosophy of Thomas Aquinas thoroughly dominated American Catholic thought. Pushed hard by Rome, Thomism's assertion of natural moral certainties and clear, fixed rules of behavior, however, also seemed useful to a people like Irish Americans and other Catholics fighting their way up the ladder into the middle class. Through some strained, if enthusiastic, proofs, Catholic intellectuals even insisted that it was their Catholic principles which actually underlay the founding fathers' vision of America. Nevertheless, such ideas set Catholics apart from "modern," educated, native-stock Protestant and Jewish Americans, who had become disillusioned by the war's carnage, and now embraced new ideas like Freudian psychology, in part to help make some sense of the war's seemingly irrational catastrophic violence. If, to this point, Irish American Catholics had seemed like cultural liberals in opposing curbs on men's drinking and recreation, when the culture war focus shifted to women's roles and sexuality in a new more daring popular culture of movies, records, and radio, Thomism would help them justify their conservatism. While it walled Catholics off from other Americans, this Catholic preservation of American "innocence" also enhanced pan-ethnic Catholic solidarity by highlighting the cultural "stuff" that all Catholic ethnic groups shared as well as their belief in a common destiny of inevitable triumph. In that 1928 election year, Theodore McManus, a Detroit businessman, proclaimed: "If [the Catholic] is alone, if he is isolated from much of the thought and culture of his time, it is a proud and glorious isolation. . . . Think kindly and charitably of your heart hungry and soul hungry fellow men . . . who have none of the conviction and the certitude which you enjoy."[54]

10. Rising Power

Irish Americans in New Deal America, 1928–1939

On May 25, in 1939 over six hundred people, including three members of the Supreme Court (Felix Frankfurter, Hugo Black, and William O. Douglas), thirty Congressmen, and two Cabinet secretaries, celebrated Monsignor John A. Ryan's seventieth birthday at Washington's prestigious Willard Hotel. Two years earlier, in 1937, Ryan had given the opening prayer at Franklin Roosevelt's second inauguration (the first clergyman to offer a prayer at an inauguration). The birthday party honored Ryan's long commitment to Catholic social justice, but also his active embrace of the New Deal. In the Progressive era, Ryan had been known as the "father of the minimum wage"; in the 1930s he became "the Right Reverend New Dealer." It was, however, also a testament to the new power of his people, Irish American Catholics, in a surging labor movement, revived urban Democratic Party, unified Catholic Church, and the popular culture of the New Deal era.[1]

Yet it was a terrible crisis, the Great Depression, that made them more powerful. The catastrophe virtually ended Irish immigration to America and wreaked havoc in Irish American Catholic families, as unemployment ran as high as 25 percent of the national work force and lingered throughout the decade. There were limits, too, to their power. Irish American Catholics were still not yet "in," even if they were more clearly leaders of a far stronger, heavily Catholic group of urban "outs." For some that outsider status, mixed with Depression agonies and ignited by the venomous, anti-Semitic speeches of Father Charles Coughlin, prompted a vicious hatred of new ethnic rivals, the Jews. Yet even Irish American Catholics who condemned Coughlin, like Ryan, also understood themselves, as a people apart, even from their New Deal liberal political

Figure 16. *Monsignor John A. Ryan's 70th Birthday Party Testimonial Dinner, May 25, 1939.* Ryan's seventieth birthday celebration with three justices of the Supreme Court: from left to right, Justice Hugo Black, Ryan, Justice Felix Frankfurter, and Justice William O. Douglas. The Catholic University of America Special Collections (ACUA), Washington, D.C.

allies. Those differences became increasingly clear by the end of the 1930s as Americans fought over how to respond to the disturbing rise of fascism and communism in Europe.

Despite gaining political autonomy in 1921, the Irish Free State remained a poor country. Its economy was still overwhelmingly agricultural, and still an agriculture of small farms: of the Free State's 380,000 farms in 1930, for example, only 80,000 or 21 percent were over fifty acres; in the western province of Connaught, two-thirds were under thirty acres. Irish people enjoyed few of the modern amenities, like automobiles, that many Americans had come to take for granted. As late as 1939, there were only 7,480 private cars in the Irish Free State, one for every 397 people—and then the number actually fell (in America the proportion was one car to every five people in 1929). One historian has suggested that "much in 1930s rural Ireland would have been recognizable to a ... Victorian traveler."[2]

As the world plunged into depression so did Ireland. After the crash the value of Irish agricultural products fell about 40 percent by 1935–1936, and savings bank deposits began to decline in 1933. After a principled abstinence from politics since the Irish Civil War had gained them nothing, Eamon de Valera and his backers formed a new Fianna Fail Party in 1926 and won control of the government in 1932. De Valera envisioned an Ireland that would be economically self-sufficient and at heart rural and simple—a "people who were satisfied with frugal comfort and devoted their leisure to the things of the spirit." Though his government was also committed to industrial self-sufficiency, building tariff walls to shield Irish companies from foreign competition, manufacturing remained negligible in the new state.[3]

So as before—as, indeed, since the seventeenth century, in the new independent Ireland as in the old Ireland of the empire—"Poor Pat" and "Biddy" must emigrate, but to where? In 1932 almost no one left the Irish Free State because none of the likely destinations, America, Britain, or Canada, seemed much better off; indeed, some 7,000 Irish emigrants returned to Ireland from those countries that year. By the late 1930s, however, 25,000 to 30,000 people were emigrating from Ireland. As had been the pattern since the late nineteenth century, the west, Connaught, Munster, and the Free State county Donegal of western Ulster, had the highest migration rates. Yet if people were leaving Ireland, they were not going to the United States. The Hoover administration, spooked by the Depression, made it hard for immigrants to enter America. Even migrants from countries like Ireland, which had high quotas for legal immigrants under the new immigration restriction laws of the twenties, were rejected on grounds that they were "liable to become a public charge" or their applications were simply tied up with red tape. The American economic collapse, however, was a far greater deterrent to Irish immigration to the United States. It virtually stopped dead with the Depression, dropping from 24,268 immigrants in 1928 to 7,305 in 1929 and but 338 in 1933. It picked up some in the late 1930s but still remained only a little over 1,000 people a year then. Such tiny numbers of Irish immigrants to America had not been seen for nearly two centuries.[4]

The emigrating Irish went to Britain now, not to the United States. Britain had suffered from the Depression, too, of course, but it began to emerge from the depths of the crash earlier than the United States, and Irish immigrants to Britain easily qualified for welfare benefits since Ireland was still part of the British Commonwealth. Yet, equally or even more important, the trip to Britain cost but a pittance in terms of money and time: the decision to go thus carried few risks since it could be undone in a day. The advent of World War II both drove up British demands for labor and released German submarines into the North Atlantic, virtually shutting down sea lanes to North America for all but the most daring or desperate. By the time the war ended, the networks of friends and family that made up a migration machine now inevitably drew the Irish to Britain, not America. The United States would never again be the principal destination of Irish immigration.[5]

With the flow of newcomers drying up, the Irish immigrant population in America not only shrank by almost a quarter to 572,031, probably the lowest number since the early 1840s, but became much older. The proportion in prime migration years, ages eighteen to thirty, fell to a mere 7 percent. In 1940, as before the Depression, Irish immigrants' occupational status remained worse than that of the shrinking numbers of German or English immigrants and much like the still large Italian- and Polish-born populations. Yet as the Depression subsided at the end of the decade, the 1940 census reported that Irish immigrant families had higher incomes than those of most other immigrant households, far more than the new immigrant Italians and Poles. This was not because Irish immigrants had higher status jobs, though many held jobs in somewhat stable industries, like utilities or the government. More likely, they were probably still following the age-old strategy of relying on children for income, and because they were so old, those "children," who had even more reason now than ever to postpone leaving their parents' household, were old, too, and, if they could find employment, in their prime earning years.[6]

Nevertheless, the immigrants' advanced years along with their declining numbers made them seem increasingly marginal within the Irish American Catholic community of the 1930s. They became an ethnic group within an ethnic group, a small subgroup, almost a little enclave. Yet even then, the decline of immigration began to eat away at their social and cultural community. Ancient Order of Hibernians divisions began to disappear at a rapid rate during the Depression, and the AOH paper, the *National Hibernian,* lost half its readers, over 50,000, in just the six years after the crash. The "golden age" of traditional Irish music and dance that America had enjoyed in the early twentieth century largely ended with the Depression too.[7]

By 1940, the second-generation Irish outnumbered the immigrants by more than three to one. Yet even the second-generation Irish had long since passed their peak in numbers in 1910. The Protestant Irish population had long been dominated by third or more generations but now the Catholic Irish population was too. The absence of reliable data makes it hard to know exactly when and by how much, but a very rough guess based on later surveys suggests that perhaps 6.6 million or 5 percent of Americans in 1940 were Irish Catholics of all generations.[8]

The Depression had a powerful impact on American-born Irish Catholics all across the country, but in New England, already suffering before the crash, it was especially harsh. The region's mill owners had begun shifting operations to the low-wage South as early as the 1890s, but that movement accelerated in the late 1920s and early 1930s. In Lowell, for example, five of the city's original textile mills closed between 1926 and 1936, and by 1940, Lowell's average manufacturing wage was 20 percent below the national mean. Mabel Delehanty Mangan had been born in the old center of Lowell's Irish life, the Acre, in 1901, and attended St. Patrick's Grammar School and then Notre Dame High School for two years, when "my father was taken sick . . . so I went into the mills to help out. . . . We had no choice." During the Depression, her husband lost his job when his company moved south and she worked in a biscuit factory, but the speedup of the assembly line overwhelmed her. She lost so much weight (down to eighty-nine pounds) that she quit. She later worked in every mill in the city as they folded one by one.[9]

Yet Irish American troubles were not just in New England mill towns. Almost half of the second-generation Irish lived in the large metropolitan areas of the Northeast and Midwest, and those areas "recovered more slowly from the slump and suffered the greatest permanent setbacks." In Chicago, 600,000 were unemployed by the early 1930s, and wages of manufacturing workers still employed in the city fell by a half. James Farrell captured the chilling panic of the Depression in Chicago in his novel *The Young Manhood of Studs Lonigan,* when he depicted the forlorn quest for a job by the main character, William "Studs" Lonigan. As Farrell wrote, Studs had lost much of his savings in the stock market crash and had just impregnated his girlfriend but was too physically weak to work for his father's house painting business, a business already staggering. Making his way from office to office in Chicago's Loop looking for work, he feels the Depression closing in: "Four straight turndowns, one right after the other. . . . Disappointment was deep and like a worm inside of him. . . . He was afraid, afraid that he was no good, useless, that he would never be able to get anywhere."[10]

For all the havoc wreaked by the Depression, however, like Irish immigrants, the American-born Irish who survived its hardships and trauma appeared to hold their own. Second-generation occupational status was about what it had been in the 1930s—a few percentage points more of the second-generation Irish were professionals in 1940 than had been in 1930, though, notably, a higher proportion, about 30 percent, were also unskilled. Second-generation-headed families, like those of the first, seemed to have higher family incomes than those of rival second-generation ethnics and paid higher rents in 1940. By now, second-generation Irish American heads of households could themselves rely on older children, especially so now in the Depression, when for their family's or their own sakes, many of them stayed home.[11]

In the 1960s and 1970s, surveys of American born Catholics of Irish ancestry, including third and later generations, found that many who had came of age during the Depression appeared to weather the economic crisis successfully. About one third, for example, revealed that they had gone to college despite the catastrophe or its lingering aftereffects. That was significantly higher than the proportion of the 1920s cohort who managed to go on to higher education.[12]

Despite their survival of the catastrophe, the Depression appeared to reinforce Irish Americans' traditional caution about marriage. A higher proportion of second-generation Irish in their late twenties and thirties remained unmarried in 1940 than 1930, and, indeed, the percentage of never married second-generation Irish (unmarried over age forty-five) rose by over one fifth. The sociologist Ellen Horgan Biddle remembered that in her neighborhood in Worcester, Massachusetts, during the 1930s, Irish American Catholic mothers and fathers believed "marriages should be delayed for as long as possible, certainly until the young people established themselves economically." There is only scattered evidence, but one scholar has also concluded that the weight of it suggests that "a significant minority of Catholics [including Irish American ones]—some of them devout—made a kind of personal peace with contraceptive practice" during the hard times as well. Between the failure to marry and this limiting of children in marriage, Monsignor Ryan, for all his economic liberalism a conservative in family matters, worried in 1934 that "the trend of our Catholic people is towards extinction."[13]

The Catholic Church also struggled to survive the hard times. Irish American–led dioceses like Boston, Philadelphia, New York, and Pittsburgh added only twenty-five, five, thirteen, and twelve new parishes, respectively, in the 1930s—half to an eighth of the number created in the 1920s. Meanwhile older parishes suffered from falling revenues while mortgages contracted by churches in headier times began to pinch.[14]

Yet if their dioceses and parishes confronted financial troubles, Irish American Catholics' commitment to their religion did not flag. The number of Catholic priests in the United States grew by almost one third. For some of these young men, economics may have tipped the scales of considering a clerical career, but their choice of the priesthood was, nonetheless, a sign of continued, even increased, Irish Catholic religious interest. Huge crowds flocked to devotional services around the country, testifying to laymen and laywomen's religious zeal as well. In Chicago, every week 30,000 and sometimes as many as 50,000 people attended weekly prayers to Our Lady of Sorrows at the church of the same name. Usually, they included people of many ethnic backgrounds, Germans, Italians, Polish, but most of them "probably claimed Irish heritage." St. Sabena's, a heavily Irish parish in South Side Chicago, scheduled seven Mother of Sorrows novenas back to back on Friday nights. One parishioner recalled that as many as 8,500 people came and that they clogged the street waiting: "some people would wait two and three hours to get into the Church."[15]

Devotionalism, of course, had flourished among Irish American Catholics since the Catholic Revival of the nineteenth century, but the Depression seemed to give it a special urgency. Some of the popular devotions were old, but others to St. Jude, St. Theresa of Lisieux, or Our Lady of Sorrows were almost brand new. The popularity of these new devotions, which had few or no traditional ethnic roots, reflected and hastened the formation of a common Catholic religious practice for Irish Americans and all other Catholics, and would thus strengthen the pan-ethnic American Catholic identity that Irish Americans had been trying to forge since the turn of the century.[16]

Meanwhile, major organizations like the Knights of Columbus, which Irish American and other Catholics had founded in the previous era, survived, if weakened, during the troubled years of the economic crisis, and some new ones appeared, which would eventually become central to Irish American Catholic life. One of the most important was the Catholic Youth Organization, a New Deal, Catholic "regular guy," and masculine (it aimed principally to save the "boys") version of save-the-children programs which had a long history in the American city. Founded in Chicago by Irish American auxiliary bishop Bernard Sheil, the CYO spread quickly through other Catholic dioceses and would ultimately become a staple of the American Catholic subculture for decades.[17]

If the Depression punished so many Irish American Catholic families and individuals, it also made them as a people enormously more powerful, most notably through the spectacular revival of the Democratic Party. After three years of

Republican failures to resolve the economic crisis, the chances of a Democratic victory in the presidential election year of 1932 seemed bright. Irish American Catholics, as longtime leaders of the party in northeastern and midwestern cities, seemed well placed to take advantage of such a victory also. The front-runner for the Democratic nomination for president, Franklin Delano Roosevelt, then governor of New York, was fully capable of winning the election. Though once snootily hostile to Irish American Catholics as a young blue blood reformer, he had later become close to Charlie Murphy, the head of Tammany Hall, and Al Smith. After brooding since his loss in 1928, however, Smith suddenly decided he wanted to be president and jumped into the race in the winter of 1932.[18]

For Irish American Catholic politicians, the choice, then, was between a likely victor, Roosevelt, and one of their and their constituencies' own but someone less certain to win, Smith. Roosevelt had understood his need for help in connecting to Irish American Catholic and other party regulars as far back as his first campaign for governor in 1928, and so he had brought James Farley, grandson of Irish immigrants and involved in politics since childhood, in to manage his reelection in 1930. Now Farley would play a key role in FDR's bid for the presidency. Most Irish American Catholic politicians in Massachusetts, Connecticut, and Rhode Island, where there really had been something of an "Al Smith revolution," backed Smith. Many Irish American Catholic Democrats— including Frank Murphy, mayor of Detroit; David Lawrence, the emerging Democratic leader in Pittsburgh; and Tom Pendergast of Kansas City—backed Roosevelt. Their reasons for choosing FDR were complicated, but they all operated in more ethnically and religiously diverse social, and/or politically competitive environments than southern New England, and recognized and needed a winner.[19]

Roosevelt, of course, won convincingly in 1932, as did the Democrats generally, gaining a majority in the House, which grew even larger in the off-year election of 1934. Irish American Catholic voters contributed to these victories. In some places, particularly southern New England, Roosevelt did not spark the same excitement among Irish American Catholic voters as Smith had. Their turnout in Boston, for example, was lower in 1932 than in 1928, but FDR did win a big majority of the Irish American Catholic vote in the city, nonetheless. He also won strong majorities among Irish Americans in Philadelphia, Chicago, Jersey City, and New York City that year.[20]

The question now was not whether Irish American Catholic politicians would back him, but whether he would accept them. After the 1932 election, the Roosevelt administration began doling out millions of dollars and creating hundreds of thousands of jobs through a variety of relief programs to defeat the Depression. Some Irish bosses were cut out of those programs, some for their failure to commit to Roosevelt before the nomination, but most because of their unreliability or political vulnerability.

Tammany Hall had backed Smith, but more important for Roosevelt, new leaders of the Hall had sought to return to the old, conservative Tammany. It had thus become mired in a notorious scandal, embarrassing FDR in his home state as he made his bid for the presidential nomination. Yet, as important, Tammany had alienated growing populations of Jews and Italians and thus lost control of the city to a reform movement led by the former Republican Fiorello La Guardia. Roosevelt eventually decided to back La Guardia, though cagily at first, inviting an Irish Catholic alternative candidate, Joseph McKee, to run for mayor against both Tammany's hapless nominee and La Guardia and then refusing to endorse him, ensuring La Guardia's victory. The New Deal would then funnel some money and patronage to New York City through a few friendly Tammany factions, and more through Ed Flynn, boss of the Bronx, already a longtime Roosevelt ally. To Flynn and Farley's chagrin, however, most of the jobs and money, including a huge part of the federal relief budget, went through La Guardia, leaving Tammany to continue its decline.[21] James Michael Curley, the mayor of Boston, had backed FDR for the Democratic nomination in 1932, but Roosevelt snubbed him as well. Curley's power was personal; he had no permanent party organization that could automatically deliver votes to anyone other than himself. Finding no suitable Irish alternative in Massachusetts, the administration used local Yankee or Jewish liberals or even brought their own men in from outside to run New Deal programs there.[22]

Yet Roosevelt was pragmatic in dealing with Irish American political machines. He detested the corrupt Frank Hague who had backed Smith, but after Hague's machine turned out a 118,000 vote majority for him in his Hudson County bastion, helping FDR squeak out a win in New Jersey, relief jobs and dollars flowed into the state through him. Elsewhere Roosevelt not only supported Irish American Catholic bosses, but in some cases he quite literally made them. A Republican machine had ruled Pittsburgh for decades, but David Lawrence, a Catholic with Ulster roots, helped FDR carry the rock-ribbed Republican city in 1932, and his organization too became a conduit for New Deal money and jobs. In Chicago, the Czech American mayor Anton Cermak had built the first dominant Democratic machine in the city's history in the late 1920s and was elected mayor in 1931, but he was killed by an assassin aiming for Roosevelt when Cermak and FDR met in 1933. The new head of the Chicago machine, Irish American Catholic Pat Nash then chose his fellow Irish, Edward Kelly, to replace Cermak as mayor. Egged on by Harold Ickes, an old Chicago Progressive Party reformer and now Secretary of Interior, Roosevelt seemed ready to ignore the new Chicago Irish machine and find a potentially popular reformer, like La Guardia in New York, and make him the New Deal's man in the city. Yet, unlike Tammany, Cermak had incorporated many ethnics into the Chicago machine already, including Jews led by Jake Arvey, and Kelly and Nash were smart enough to continue to do so. In the mayoral election of 1935, Kelly crushed his Republican opponent by over four to one, and the Roosevelt administration began pouring funds and jobs into Chicago through Kelly and Nash.[23]

Roosevelt's impact on Irish American Catholic politics and Irish American Catholics' impact on him, however, extended far beyond the city bosses. Between 1928 and 1934 the number of Irish American Catholic Democratic senators rose from two to nine and House members from 23 to 57. Once elected, their backing of the New Deal, measured by political scientists and historians, varied significantly by chamber, but also, perhaps more fundamentally, by region and state. In broad terms, the support of the new Irish American Catholic House members for the New Deal's economic liberalism was stunning. Of the 57 Irish Catholic representatives in the 74th Congress, 11 were ranked among the House's top 25 economic liberals, 12 more among the top fifty, and another 12 for a total of 35 in the top one hundred. The median Irish rank among economic liberals was 75 in a House of 435 members. By contrast, of the nine senators, one ranked in the top ten, two more in the top 40. The median rank was 48 in a Senate of 96 members.[24]

There were any number of possible influences producing these rankings, but the geographical spread is certainly noticeable. Irish Catholic House members came from seventeen states compared to eight in 1928, but most were from the Northeast, and that region had a higher proportion of economically liberal Irish House members as well. The ethnic makeup of the Northeast may have had an important impact on them, as the growing second-generation new immigrant, Italian, Polish, and Jewish Americans put pressure on politicians in the East to back the New Deal. Irish Catholic progressivism had also flourished in much of that region in the 1910s. Most of the Irish American Catholic senators came from the West, from Wisconsin to Nevada, and most of the conservative Irish Catholic members of the House came from the West and parts of the Midwest as well. Irish Catholic Democrats in most states in those regions had not been part of that earlier Irish Catholic reform movement. Some former progressive Democrats, including Al Smith, opposed the New Deal, however, so the causes of these varying patterns of votes were much more complex than simply the absence or presence of a progressive Democratic inheritance, and we can only speculate about what some of those complications might have been. House members from Pennsylvania, for example, where Irish progressivism had not taken root in the Democratic Party, ranked higher than ones from southern New England, where it had. The Democratic surge was brand new in Pennsylvania, as all but one of the state's seven representatives had been elected since Roosevelt ran in 1932. They had profited not only from his coattails, but also from his close relationship with Pennsylvania's new Democratic senator Joseph Guffey, the state's labor revolution, which was nourished by the New Deal, and looked forward to a federal bounty of patronage and relief funds. Most southern New England Irish American Catholics were Smith Democrats as much as Roosevelt ones, building their power on the long history of religious and ethnic tension in the state, climaxing in Smith's strong showing in the region in the 1928 election. As noted, Roosevelt also bypassed most of the Massachusetts Irish in distributing New Deal largesse after his election. In the West, the enduring power of Republican or third-party progressivism in states like Nebraska, Wisconsin, and Minnesota had pushed many Democrats in those states, including some of their new congressmen in the 1930s, to the right, even before the New Deal. Roosevelt had also long cultivated western Progressive Republicans, including Senator George Norris of Nebraska and the La Follettes of Wisconsin, frustrating some western Irish American Democrats like Nebraska's Senator Edward Burke, one of Roosevelt's fiercest Democratic opponents.[25]

The New Deal's impact on the labor movement was even more powerful than its effect on Democratic Party politics. The decline in union membership, begun in the 1920s, actually continued in the first four years of the Depression, but that would change, and change quickly. In 1933, when Congress passed the National Industrial Recovery Act (NIRA), it included a brief paragraph, Section 7a, which guaranteed workers the right to organize and bargain. After the Supreme Court struck down the NIRA, Congress passed the Wagner Act reinstating and broadening workers' rights. Unleashed, the children of the new immigrants, Poles, Italians, and others, poured into unions, especially industrial unions which would become part of the Committee (later Congress) of Industrial Organizations (CIO). Warned by his immigrant father about the dangers of joining a union, one young Hungarian American replied simply: "We don't want to live like Hunkies anymore." John Brophy, the British-born son of Irish Catholic parents, organizing miners in the Pennsylvania coal fields, was dumbstruck: they "moved into the union en masse. . . . They organized themselves for all practical purposes."[26]

Some Irish American labor activists were at the forefront of this labor rising. In Minneapolis, for example, the teamsters led by the communist Dunne brothers ignited a successful general strike in the city. Joe Curran, a radical and rebel, led a ship's mutiny for fair wages in 1935 that touched off a long mariners' strike and headed the Maritime Union, which emerged from it. Finally, in New York City, Irish immigrants, many of them Irish Republican Army veterans of Ireland's civil war, collaborated with communists to create a union for the city's transit workers.[27]

Many long-established Irish union leaders, however, felt threatened or seemed befuddled by the new labor insurgency's radicalism, speed, and sweep. County Clare–born Dan Tobin, national president of the Teamsters, fiercely anti-radical and anti-communist, for example, worked hard to stifle the Dunne brothers' general strike in Minneapolis, though without success. In 1934 leaders of the Textile Workers, Limerick-born Thomas McMahon and Francis Gorman, born in Britain of Irish parents, seemed to simply fumble their way through the largest strike in American history, involving as many as 350,000 to 400,000 textile workers, unable to prevent mill owners from ultimately crushing it.[28]

Nevertheless, Irish Americans remained well represented at the top of the labor hierarchy during the 1930s and poised for future domination of the labor movement. In 1937, four of the sixteen members of the American Federation of Labor's national executive council were Irish Americans, and by the late 1930s three of the five members of the board of its rival, the new CIO, were as well. Two men, Philip Murray and George Meany, also emerged in the Depression era, who would eventually establish Irish American dominance over labor in the 1940s and 1950s. Murray was United Mine Workers' president John L. Lewis's right-hand man at the onset of the Depression. In 1936, Lewis chose him to organize steelworkers and in 1940 to succeed him as president of the CIO. Though a longtime anti-communist, inspired at least in part by his devout Catholicism, Murray nevertheless worked with communists to build the Depression era's new labor movement. George Meany's rise would take a little longer, but he would eventually become president of a united AFL-CIO in 1955. Following his father into the plumbing trade and union at the age of sixteen,

Meany was an old school, AFL conservative. During the Depression, however, he became head of the New York State Federation of Labor, and there he worked successfully with liberals like Herbert Lehman, governor of New York, and Fiorello La Guardia to push important unemployment, health, and workplace safety bills through the state legislature. By 1939, Meany had become national secretary/treasurer of the AFL and was on his way to the top of the federation's hierarchy.[29]

Well aware of the prominence of Irish American Catholic leaders in the revival of the Democratic Party and labor movement, the Roosevelt administration went out of its way to recognize their Church as well. It invited scores of Catholic clergymen as well as Catholic college faculty, like Elizabeth Morrisey and Alice Leahy, to serve on government boards or on White House advisory committees or to speak at events there. Second-generation Irish Monsignor John Burke, general secretary of the National Catholic Welfare Conference (NCWC), met frequently with Roosevelt, and he and Irish immigrant Monsignor John O'Grady, head of the National Conference of Catholic Charities, were active and powerful lobbyists promoting Catholic interests and policies.[30]

Yet the Church's new public heft was not dependent on the new success of Irish American Catholic politicians and labor leaders alone. The decline of ethnic friction within the American Church and the tight solidarity strengthened by the long process of centralizing power and authority in its dioceses had made it a formidable public force, most evident in the control it began to exert over America's movies. Through the 1920s, censoring movies was still a Protestant-led crusade, and Catholics did not play a major role. In 1927, however, the Church gained a new sense of its public power, when the NCWC helped force MGM to withdraw a movie, *The Callahans and the Murphys,* laced with demeaning Irish stereotypes. Major film studios, carrying heavy debt into the Depression, were extremely vulnerable to the Catholic Church's potential influence over audiences in the industry's crucial big city markets. In 1933, the Church, led by the Mayo-born Archbishop John T. McNicholas, organized the Legion of Decency, which rated the morality of films and pledged millions of Catholics to abide by its ratings. Wielding the threat of the Legion, the bishops thus forced movie makers to adhere to a strict production code administered by Irish American Catholics Joseph Breen and Martin Quigley, which restricted movies' treatment of sexuality and other "moral" issues.[31]

Given such Catholic power over the movies, it seems no coincidence that Hollywood began to fill movie screens with Irish American Catholic priests in the 1930s. Many of the priest films, like *Angels with Dirty Faces* and *Boys Town,* however, also did very well at the box office, and several won or were nominated for Academy Awards. The popularity of Irish American Catholics' movie image in the thirties reflected their median social and political positioning between new white immigrants below and Protestant elites above. On screen, they were easily American, wise to American ways, but also recognizably and distinctly ethnic or Catholic and thus accessible to that vast market of urban ethnics, which so worried the movie studios. There was also an intriguing liminal quality to the Irish American Catholic image, a depiction of a people walking the boundary between respectable and shady. Pulp fiction reflected that liminality with accounts of tough, often violent Irish American G-men, seemingly more at home in the world of crime than outside it but vital to defending public safety. Yet it was prominent in the movies, too, most notably in the relationship between Pat O'Brien's Father Jerry Connolly and Jimmy Cagney's criminal, Rocky Sullivan, in the award-winning *Angels with Dirty Faces.* Films like the *Conquest of the City,* however, also played upon Irish American Catholics' reputation for egalitarianism and communal solidarity, taking advantage of a New Deal environment which celebrated both.[32]

As some Irish American writers of this era recognized, however, if Irish American Catholics had become leaders of the outsiders, that still meant they were not insiders and not likely to be so soon. In John O'Hara's novel *Butterfield 8,* published in 1935, the main character, Jimmy Malloy, states that bluntly: "I am a Mick. I wear Brooks clothes and I don't eat salad with a spoon, and I could probably play five goal polo in two years, but I am still a Mick." For O'Hara, a self-described social climber, the enduring Protestant establishment, and Irish Catholic exclusion from it, was an obsession, but even the great Irish American playwright Eugene O'Neill ruminated on Irish American Catholics' place in a WASP-run world in the 1930s. His play *A Touch of the Poet,* written in that decade, reenacts Irish Catholic dispossession not in Ireland but in the New England of Andrew Jackson's time, 1828. An Irish immigrant, a former officer in Wellington's Peninsular Army who thinks himself a gentleman, is humiliated by a Yankee bourgeois family and painfully forced to recognize that he must "be content to stay meself in the proper station I was born into," among the former Irish peasants, now canal diggers and Jackson men, who drink in his saloon.[33]

Yet there were deeper, broader, and more sinister resentments simmering in the Irish American community in the mid-1930s. Endowed with a uniquely powerful speaking voice, Father Charles Coughlin began his radio career in 1926,

talking about Catholic devotions and the sacraments. By 1930, he was broad-
casting nationally and with the onset of the Depression, lambasting bankers,
pushing inflationary monetary schemes, and attacking communists. His audience would grow to thirty million listeners, most of them lower middle class,
and many German and Irish, teetering on the boundary between respectability
and ruin. There was a special Irish tilt to the Canadian-born Coughlin's ravings,
as he delivered them in a faint, fake Irish brogue, focusing much of his rage on
British bankers, finding a champion in his bishop, Michael Gallagher, the old
Irish American nationalist colleague of Devoy and Cohalan, and corresponding
with an anti-Semitic fellow traveler, Father Dennis Fahey, in Ireland. Coughlin
backed Franklin Roosevelt in 1932, and after FDR's victory presumed a special
role for himself in the new administration. Roosevelt and his aides flattered him
but ignored his advice. Spurned and furious, by late 1934 he had begun to tear
into the president and joined a surging anti-Roosevelt populist uprising with
Louisiana senator Huey Long and others, aiming to bring the president down.[34]

Roosevelt and the Democratic Party, however, eventually rolled over their hap-
less Republican opponents and populist enemies in 1936, and Irish American
Catholic Democrats rolled with them. The Irish American Catholic vote for
FDR in Boston declined slightly from 1932, though defections were largely to
Father Coughlin's Social Justice Party, not the Republicans. FDR still won big
there and continued to win majorities of Irish American Catholics in Chicago,
Philadelphia, and even New York, where FDR had chosen La Guardia as his ally
over a now failing Tammany.[35]

Irish Catholics also reaped the riches of the party's—their party's—surge.
They elected governors: in Michigan, Frank Murphy; in Massachusetts, Charles F.
Hurley; and in Rhode Island, Robert Emmet Quinn, who as lieutenant gover-
nor in 1935 had led a "bloodless revolution" purging virtually the entire previ-
ous Yankee Republican administration, literally overnight. The number of Irish
American Catholics elected to the U.S. House increased to fifty-nine, making up
one-quarter of the Democrats elected outside the Old Confederacy, while Irish
American senators remained at nine.[36]

Despite Roosevelt's historic victory, however, the Democratic triumph
began to swiftly unravel. Angry that the Supreme Court had declared vital parts
of the New Deal unconstitutional, Roosevelt proposed legislation to Congress
which would add new judges to the Court, if the "old men" still on it refused to
retire. Seven Irish American Catholic Democrats in the Senate rallied with south-

ern Democratic conservatives and the chamber's few Republicans to kill the "court-packing" plan. FDR also submitted a bill reorganizing the executive branch about the same time, and it too incited a revolt within the Democratic Party. Five Irish American Catholic senators voted against that legislation.[37]

Meanwhile, the labor revolution was bogged down in its own troubles, as the New Deal's sudden vulnerability seemed to encourage conservatives to assail Roosevelt's CIO allies. Opposition to labor grew shrill when frustrated striking auto workers "sat down" and occupied their auto plants in Flint, Michigan, in 1937. Irish American Father James Gillis of the *Catholic World,* who had once backed FDR, now sniffed the "smell of socialism" in the CIO and wondered whether John L. Lewis might be "our Lenin." In 1937, some Irish American Catholic and other labor advocates founded the Association of Catholic Trade Unionists (ACTU), strongly sympathetic to the labor movement but adamantly opposed to communist influence in it.[38]

Though the principal split emerging in the Roosevelt coalition was between northern and southern Democrats, there was a growing suspicion of the New Deal among some Irish Catholics too. In opposing Roosevelt's court-packing proposal, Senator David Walsh seemed to play upon Catholics' old fears about their religion's place in America, asking, "Who may say when some majority of the moment may attempt to oppress the minority?"[39]

But who could be such a dangerous threat to Irish Catholics now? It was not evangelical nativists, of little political importance these days. For many Irish Catholics it was, in fact, their recent allies in the New Deal coalition, elite reformers, once identified as Progressives, but now calling themselves "liberals." Some Irish American Catholic archconservatives, like Father Robert Gannon, the president of Fordham, talked of liberals in fantasies of horror: "there is a swarm abroad in the land. They call themselves 'Liberals.' What they want is not so much our money as our children. They want the key positions in the civil service. They want control of relief and all the social agencies and they are getting what they want." Few Irish American Catholics were so hysterical, but many of them, who also strongly supported the New Deal, recognized the differences between liberals and themselves, especially on cultural issues concerning gender and the family. John Ryan wrote publicly about such differences even before the Depression. He believed liberals and Catholics could cooperate, largely on economic issues. He angrily resented the insistence of some liberals, like the editors of the *Nation* magazine, who contended that they could not so collaborate if they still disagreed on other issues: why "does this brand of Liberalism insist on saving men against what [they believe] are foolish loyalties [to the Church]. This seems to be the essence of Toryism."[40]

Even before the New Deal, liberals had begun to focus less on cultural or moral issues and more on economic ones and thus there seemed fewer likely sources of conflict over policy between them and Irish Catholics. Yet it was not the policies liberals promoted so much as their growing power, who they were, and their understanding of politics in the New Deal era and their role in it that became the principal sources of the growing friction between the two. As noted, Roosevelt, for example, had cultivated old Republican Progressives even before the New Deal and had brought some like Ickes into his cabinet, while giving others like La Guardia control of vast New Deal spoils. Before becoming president, he had also begun to recruit academics from elite universities, including the famous "Brain Trust," to serve as advisors. As the administration settled in after the election, some of those academics and others, like Felix Frankfurter of Harvard Law School, began to recruit hundreds of young graduates from Harvard, Columbia, the University of Chicago, and other top universities to serve in the administration. These "New Dealers" staffed the Roosevelt administration's rapidly multiplying agencies, commissions, and programs, but they were not merely bureaucrats. They were a force for creating change, drafting new legislation and advocating for it, and, therefore, became the vital base for a new "programmatic" reform movement within the executive branch.[41]

These were the people that moved Father Gannon to hysteria. They were mostly native-stock Protestants or Jews, but they included Irish Catholics James Rowe, Frank Shea, Gerard Reilly, and others, most notably Thomas Corcoran, nicknamed "Tommy the Cork." Corcoran himself recruited hundreds of them, housed some, and hosted more in his "Little Red House" in Georgetown. Yet he also wrote speeches for Roosevelt and bills for Congress, testified at committee hearings, lobbied congressmen, and—for a while—became one of the most influential men in the New Deal administration.[42]

It was not the New Dealers' legislation so much, nor their ethnicity or religion though that had some importance, but their growing political power and cocky sense of their privileged mission or role as educated "experts," "technicians in democracy," that set so many Irish Catholics against them. Though friends of the New Deal usually traced its origins back to Democrats Thomas Jefferson and Andrew Jackson, these young liberals shared something of the Federalist notion that their education bequeathed them not just the knowledge but "disinterestedness" vital to governance in a republic (though they were more modern "smart alecks" than aristocratic pretenders like the Federalists). Frank-furter, for example, would "froth at the mouth" when he talked about "the political patronage . . . [and] graft and stupidity" that afflicted American politics. Though working for a Democratic president, most of them "sneered" at the party's politicians like James Farley. They were not Democrats. They were members of Roosevelt's "party."[43]

Irish American Catholic politicians like Farley and Ed Flynn sneered back, but for them, this was a serious fight, a struggle over who had power now in the New Deal era and over fundamental beliefs about who should have it. They saw this new programmatic reform movement as an assault on the Irish American Catholic power base, the Democratic Party. It also violated their belief that the ability to win elections should determine who got power, not ideological purity, bureaucratic expertise, or educational achievement. Al Smith had little truck with Irish American Catholic voters and politicians since openly breaking with Roosevelt in 1933, but behind his raging diatribes against New Deal radicals lay an older Irish American Catholic politician's resentment of the educated elite reformer: "academic planners" who have spent their lives "in the library, writing books," ignorant of the real business of politics and out of touch with the experiences of "an earnest workingman." In New York, over Farley's and Flynn's objections, and in Boston, after all, the administration had ignored Irish American Catholic Democrats and put New Deal programs in the hands of local reformers or liberal outsiders in those cities. In Washington, Farley also battled constantly against Harold Ickes and other reformers' insistence on nonpartisan, what he called "highbrow," administration appointments.[44]

Enraged by the opposition that had wrecked his second term, FDR moved to "purge" several Democrats from the Congress in the 1938 elections by supporting their opponents in the party primaries. In the end, almost all the ones he openly attacked were from the South. He did consider targeting at least one Irish American Catholic senator, but the only northerner Roosevelt opposed in the purge was Irish American Catholic congressman John O'Connor from New York, whose voting record was liberal, but as chairman of the Rules Committee had often worked to kill New Deal bills before they reached the House floor. The defeat of O'Connor by another Irish American Catholic was the purge's only success. Farley vehemently opposed the purge, and by 1940 he had left the administration and embarked on his own unlikely effort to win the presidency. Ed Flynn stayed on with FDR and replaced Farley as national chairman of the

Democratic Party, but he too continued to grouse about "so called New Dealers," the "New Deal amateur politicians," and "Corcoran and his ilk."[45]

Left to itself, the Irish American Catholics' battle with "liberals" might not have become much more than the expected rivalry and jockeying for power between political coalition partners in a successful administration with lots of opportunities to fight over power or acclaim. Just at that moment, however, the world was sliding toward an ideological showdown pitting democracies and fascist and communist regimes against one another, and the Catholic Church was raising the religious stakes in that looming conflict for Irish and other American Catholics. The Church had long condemned socialist and communist radicalism, but in 1932, led by the Vatican Secretary of State Cardinal Eugenio Pacelli, later Pope Pius XII, Rome launched "a centralized, broad based and transnational campaign, which aimed to expose Communism as the greatest existing threat to Catholicism and the Catholic Church." Thus, in the mid-1930s, Reverend Fulton J. Sheen, grandson of famine Irish immigrants, as theatrical as Coughlin but more orthodox and palatable to the American Catholic hierarchy, began hammering at communism regularly in a radio show sponsored by the National Conference of Catholic Men.[46]

The eruption of civil war in Spain pushed the fight between fascism and communism into American politics. In 1936, General Francisco Franco led a fascist rebellion against the elected left-wing government of Spain, whose supporters, including some communists, were called the Loyalists. Surveys in new American national polls like Gallup revealed that Irish American Catholics backed the Fascists over the Loyalists by almost two to one, though all Catholic ethnics, and Italian Americans even more than the Irish, were strongly pro-Franco. When backers of the Loyalists in America sought changes in the nation's neutrality law so that the Spanish government could buy American arms, Irish American Catholics, led by John McCormack in the House, and including even Monsignor John Ryan, opposed them.[47]

Irish and other American Catholics saw the Spanish Civil War as a major front in a worldwide battle between Catholicism and communism. The Fascists were closely tied to Spain's Catholic Church, and thus to many Irish American Catholics it appeared that the war waged by the Spanish government was really a war against Catholicism. They talked of it sometimes as simply another episode in a long history of anti-Catholic persecutions that included their own sufferings, stretching back through the KKK in the 1920s, to the Know-Nothings, or even to the Penal Laws in Ireland. The fact that most liberal Protestants tilted to the other side, backing the Loyalists, helped make it easy for some Irish Catholics to mix their own and Spain's narratives of anti-Catholicism together, and, in Massachusetts, for example, marry traditional Irish Catholic resentment of Protestant elites with anti-communism, denouncing Harvard as a nest of radicals.[48]

These bitter wrangles between Catholics and liberals increasingly infected Irish Catholic relations not just with liberal Protestants but with another important component of the New Deal coalition: American Jews. The speed of Jewish upward economic mobility in America in the early twentieth century had startled and alarmed many Irish American Catholics, who feared that they were being left behind. Yet, Jews in New York, once sometime allies of Tammany, had also become potent political rivals by the 1930s as the backbone of the La Guardia coalition that overthrew the Hall in 1933. Irish American Catholic Patrick Scanlan, editor of the Brooklyn diocese's newspaper, *The Tablet*, painstakingly toted up "Jewish" and "Irish" names on civil service lists and seethed about La Guardia's alleged anti-Irish and anti-Catholic discrimination. As most Jews aligned with the Loyalists in Spain, some Irish American Catholics began to suggest that all Jews were communists or communist sympathizers. Meanwhile Coughlin increasingly shifted from assaults on big bankers to targeting left radicals and communists, whom he now explicitly identified as Jewish in openly justifying the Kristallnacht Nazi attacks on Jews in November 1938. Overt support of Coughlin seemed to narrow as he became more explicitly anti-Semitic, but it also hardened, as his most militant backers enlisted in a heavily Irish American organization called the Christian Front, which engaged in anti-Jewish boycotts and fights with Jews in the streets of New York and Boston.[49]

Cracks, then, had begun to appear in the New Deal coalition. Yet Irish Catholics' relationship with the Jews was more complicated than Coughlin's vile anti-Semitism. Upon learning of the Nazis' Kristallnacht pogrom against the Jews, for example, Irish American Father Maurice Sheehy, a professor in the Department of Religious Education at Catholic University, quickly assembled a panel of largely Irish American bishops and Al Smith for a national radio broadcast the next week, November 16, to condemn it. It was a preemptive strike against Coughlin, as the organizers correctly guessed that the "Radio Priest" would approve of the Nazis' anti-Semitic assault and did so four days later.[50] Moreover, Irish American Catholics had not abandoned the economic liberalism of the New Deal. If Irish American Catholic Democratic senators remained, at best, tepid backers of New Deal policies, most Irish American Catholic House members were still stalwart supporters of the administration. The rankings of Irish Catholics as economic liberals elected in 1936 were as good or better as those elected two years before. They were nearly unanimous in support of relief and public housing, and strong on tax issues, but two-thirds of them—including almost all from New York, Massachusetts, and Pennsylvania—also rallied behind the president's executive reorganization scheme. Furthermore, while the Senate voted overwhelmingly for investigations of the sit-down strikes—with all but one of the Irish American Catholic senators, David I. Walsh—voting with the majority, Irish American Catholics in the House rejected it nearly unanimously, 48 to 6.[51]

The House's bitter and complicated fight over the first ever federal minimum wage bill exposed clearly both the sealing of a conservative alliance between southern Democrats and Republicans and the enduring commitment of Irish Catholic Democrats in the House to the "bread and butter" economic liberalism of the New Deal. The Irish were very much involved in this fight. The minimum wage had been John Ryan's signature issue since the Progressive era. Mary Norton, the child of Longford immigrants, protégée of Frank Hague but chair of the House's Labor Committee and among the most economically liberal members of Congress, would lead the fight for it over three raucous days and nights in mid-December 1937. Corcoran and Gerard Reilly among the New Dealers played roles in developing and promoting the legislation, and John O'Connor, soon to be purged, and Farley opposed it. When the roll call was completed, Democrats from the states of the old Confederacy voted four to one to recommit or kill the bill and rebel yells echoed through the chamber; nine Irish American Catholic Democrats voted to recommit it too but forty-nine to save it, making up over one quarter of its support. A weaker bill would pass in 1938, and every Irish American Catholic House member would vote for it.[52]

Amid the great struggles over economic policy in the 1930s, race and civil rights had remained largely buried for most of the decade, but in 1937 Congress took up the anti-lynching crusade that the Republicans had led in the 1920s. Irish American Catholic J. Joseph Gavagan, a Tammany congressman, led the fight in the House for the bill where it passed overwhelmingly, 277 to 120, in an almost perfect sectional divide. The debate, however, was bitter. John Rankin of Mississippi directly challenged Gavagan, arguing "that proponents of the measure were [simply] attempting to make Harlem. . . . safe for Tammany." Efforts to break a southern filibuster in the Senate failed twice and the bill died. Four Irish American Catholic senators voted for cloture, to end the filibuster; two voted

Figure 17. *The New Chairman of House Labor Committee, Washington DC June 21 [1937], Mary T. Norton.* Congresswoman Mary Norton on the day she became chair of the House's Labor Committee: June 21, 1937. Harris and Ewing Photograph. Library of Congress: LC-DIG-hec-229007.

against it; and one did not vote. Most Republicans voted against cloture, including New England GOP senators like the young Henry Cabot Lodge.[53]

Irish American Catholic politicians had begun to reach out to African American voters warily since Reconstruction, and with similar caution for an anti-lynching law in 1922. Their new fight over lynching, as in their previous support for civil rights, reflected practical calculation as well as good conscience. When Mississippi's John Rankin chided J. Joseph Gavagan about making Harlem safe for Tammany, he was correct: Harlem was part—an ever increasingly powerful part—of Gavagan's congressional district and African Americans a critical constituency for him. Yet Gavagan was not alone among Irish American Catholics in seeking and gaining Black political support in the New Deal era.

African Americans had already been voting for some Irish Catholic Democrats long before the New Deal, but from 1932 to 1936, the African American Democratic vote rocketed up from 50 percent to over 89 percent in New York City; 41 percent to nearly three-quarters in David Lawrence's Pittsburgh; and but a fifth to nearly half in Nash and Kelly's Chicago. It was not just pursuit of Black votes that prompted Irish American Catholics to oppose lynching, however. African American newspapers praised Irish American Catholic Congressman William Connery, for example, for working hard to pass the anti-lynching bill, though the Black vote in his North Shore Massachusetts district was tiny. Surveys in the late 1930s revealed, however, that a new and increasingly powerful national Democratic interracial civil rights coalition, including a substantial percentage of Catholics, had begun to emerge as African Americans embraced the New Deal and the CIO backed their cause.[54]

Despite the work of Irish Catholic politicians on behalf of African Americans, Irish American Catholics would still be prominent in efforts to exclude Blacks from workplaces like the New York City docks, or neighborhoods, notably in Philadelphia and Chicago. If the Depression hard times stiffened the resistance of some Irish workers or homeowners to Black integration, however, the struggling economy also discouraged African American migration north, temporarily reducing the pressure for integration of Irish and other white residential areas. That would not be true in the 1940s and 1950s.[55]

In the heady days of the Second New Deal in the mid-1930s, Tommy Corcoran became one of FDR's chief political advisors; some thought that, with his special easy access to the Oval Office, he was *the* chief advisor. Then as the administration lurched from one fiasco to another in the second term, and rivals for FDR's ear edged him out, he began to fall, ultimately excluded from the president's inner circle by 1939. It was not just bureaucratic rivals or the second term's missteps that brought him down, however. Despite the Depression's resurgence, by 1938, the New Deal was fading and the administration and the country were focusing on the darkening international crisis of rising fascism and communism. Corcoran had remained true to the New Deal's bread and butter liberalism, but as his chief rival, Harry Hopkins, once told him, "Tom, you are too Catholic to trust the Russians and too Irish to trust the English." Corcoran agreed: "You're right Harry, and so I am . . . so I am." So Corcoran worked within the White House to prevent changes in the Neutrality Laws which would have permitted the United States to help arm Loyalist Spain and later worried about

American entanglement in Britain and France's war with Nazi Germany. He had not hidden his Irishness during the New Deal's heyday, but now, in this era of international crisis, his ethnicity and his religion seemed to become "increasingly important to him." Edward Flynn and James Farley hated Corcoran, at one point the ultimate New Dealer, but his rise and fall in the administration reflected in important ways both the emergence of the Irish Catholic-liberal New Deal alliance and the beginnings of its breakup.[56]

11. The Old Order at High Tide

Irish America in World War II and Postwar America, 1940–1960

On March 17, 1948, Harry Truman became the first American president to review New York City's St. Patrick's Day parade. Four years earlier, Irish American
Catholic bosses like Ed Flynn and David Lawrence had helped convince Franklin Roosevelt to drop the left-leaning sitting vice president, Henry Wallace, and
replace him with Truman. Roosevelt died less than a year later, and Truman was
president. Yet he was not in New York to thank Irish American Catholics for
their past help, but to seek their aid now in winning the presidency on his own
in November. In that quest he confronted not only the likely Republican nominee, Thomas E. Dewey, the successful governor of New York, but Wallace, the
head of a new Progressive Party dedicated to rapprochement with communist
Russia. Truman dutifully reviewed the parade on the afternoon of St. Patrick's
Day. The real reason he was in the city that day, however, was to deliver a major
address on the Cold War at the traditional evening banquet of New York City's
Friendly Sons of St. Patrick, which would be broadcast across the country on
the radio. He had chosen this day and this audience deliberately for this speech,
and that night, he hammered at the Soviet Union and alleged communist subversives in America. At the very end of his speech, he attacked Henry Wallace
personally: "I do not want and will not accept the political support of Henry
Wallace and his Communists." "A burst of cheers filled the emerald decked ballroom, and for a moment the President had to halt while the tumult continued,"
the *New York Times* reported.[1]

Despite some hesitation, Irish American Catholics in this period would
back the Second World War as they had the First, and many would then ride the

postwar economic boom that the war had prompted to college educations, new and better jobs, and homes in rapidly growing suburbs. Despite a modest revival of Irish immigration after the war, the ethnic identity and interest in Ireland of most Irish American Catholics would fade in their new prosperity. They would not, however, "assimilate." Indeed, in the early years of the Cold War, many of their values seemed to triumph in America: church membership, passionate nationalism—albeit American, conservative domestic life and large families, but, most notably, their fierce anti-communism. As Cold War zeal began to flag by the middle and late 1950s, however, there would be traces of unease and hints of future change in the Irish American Catholic community. Meanwhile, Irish American Catholic politicians confronted new challenges as Irish American Catholics' role in the Democratic Party neared a critical turning point.

On September 1, 1939, Germany invaded Poland, igniting a new World War and instantly raising questions about what role, if any, Americans should play in it. In the next two years, Franklin Roosevelt cautiously tried to enlist the United States in the cause of Britain and France, setting off a broad and intense national debate between "isolationists" who opposed such a policy and "interventionists" who backed it. Coughlin, now being paid by Hitler's government, was increasingly not only anti-Semitic but pro-Nazi and vehement in his opposition to help for Britain. Newspapers like the *Irish World* and organizations like New York's Ancient Order of Hibernians, reflecting largely Irish immigrant opinion and virulent anti-British Irish nationalism, also opposed intervention. Immigrants were only a small and rapidly declining proportion of Irish America and Irish American nationalism a tiny movement by the end of the thirties, but isolationism was also popular among later generations of Irish American Catholics. They included, among many others: Joseph P. Kennedy, ambassador to Great Britain; important Irish American members of the American Catholic hierarchy; and Martin Carmody, Supreme Knight of the Knights of Columbus, which had been prominent in Irish America's strong support for the First World War. Most of these Irish American Catholic isolationists and others had affection for Ireland and little sympathy for the British empire, but few were active Irish nationalists. Rather, like many other Americans, they had come to regret the results of World War I, feared the Soviet communists as much or more than the Nazis, or simply worried about the effects of war on their own or the nation's future. Kennedy, for example, had multiple motives for his isolationism, but his boss, President Roosevelt, shrewdly contended that he was principally worried about his own fortune and whether it could survive the chaos of another world war.[2]

Nevertheless, however popular isolationism was in the Irish American Catholic community, it was not strong enough to have much influence on Irish American Catholic congressmen. Over the three years from 1939 to 1941, the Roosevelt administration pushed the House and Senate to vote on three major interventionist bills: in 1939, to amend the neutrality laws to permit Americans to sell war material to enemy combatants; in 1940, to institute a peacetime draft; and finally in March 1941, to allow the president to provide war material to other countries "vital to the defense of the United States" without payment—the Lend-Lease program. Two Irish American Catholic senators, Patrick McCarran and David Walsh, voted against all three bills. Neither was a friend of the administration, and David Walsh was perhaps the most committed Irish nationalist in the Congress. Yet of the six other Irish American Catholics in the Senate who voted on these bills—Mead, Burke, Slattery, O'Mahony, Maloney, and Murray—only James E. Murray of Montana cast a vote against the administration, opposing the draft. Murray's uncle had been the second president of De Valera's American Association for the Recognition of the Irish Republic in 1922, but he voted both to amend the Neutrality Act and to allow Lend-Lease. Irish Americans Catholics in the House were even more emphatically pro-intervention. They voted overwhelmingly (26 to 10) for "cash and carry" in 1939 and the reinstitution of the draft (27 to 7) in the summer of 1940. Finally, Irish American Catholic John McCormack introduced the Lend-Lease legislation into the House, and Irish Catholic Democrats backed it by a margin of nearly three to one (25 for and 9 against). By contrast, almost all Scandinavian and German American congressmen and even heavy majorities of New England Yankee Republicans voted against all or many of the administration's interventionist bills.[3]

After bombs rained down on Pearl Harbor, isolationist Senator Patrick McCarran wrote to his daughter: "The Japs spit in our face and the game was off." Though Coughlin railed on until 1942, and his anti-Semitic Christian Front still festered in some New York and Boston Irish neighborhoods as late as 1944, the vast majority of Irish American Catholics embraced the war. Ireland remained neutral throughout the conflict, but most Irish Americans could not square their homeland's neutrality with their own commitment to the fight against the Axis. A Gallup poll conducted in 1942 found that 82 percent of Irish Americans interviewed were convinced that Ireland must already be an ally in the war, and over half (56 percent) of those who knew that it was not believed that it should become one. More powerful evidence of Irish Americans' commitment to the war was their willingness to fight in it. The 1980 United States Census reported that 44.3 percent of those claiming Irish ancestry, who had been age eligible to serve in the armed forces in World War II (age eighteen to forty-five during the war years), did so. The Polish American rate was nearly as high, 44.2 percent, with Italian Americans 41.65 percent, English 41 percent, and Swedish, 39.4 percent, German 39.1 percent, and Norwegian Americans 38.2 percent trailing in that order. The Irish ancestry percentages were highest where recent Irish settlement was greatest, Irish American nationalism traditionally strongest, and most Irish were Catholics: the New England and mid-Atlantic states.[4]

Whether Irish American Catholics backed the war reluctantly or not, American moviemakers could not resist the temptation to make them embodiments of the American war effort. These Irish Americans were, after all, the heirs to a century or more of fighting Irish imagery, and often depicted in the Roosevelt era as a new, urban version of the American common man, New Deal "regular guys." They thus became iconic home front patriots in films like the classic *Yankee Doodle Dandy* and the more obscure *Princess O'Rourke.* Yet they were also nearly ubiquitous cinema representatives of American fighting men in the 1940s, including films about their exploits in the First World War, *The Fighting 69th* and *The Iron Major,* as well as in the current war, most notably *The Fighting Sullivans,* based on a true story of five Iowa-bred Sullivan bothers who were all on the same ship when it went down during a naval battle off Guadalcanal. Indeed, the image of Irish Americans as combat heroes became so fixed that almost every soldier John Wayne played in his movies during the war had an Irish name, among them Wedge Donovan in *The Fighting Seabees,* Joseph Madden in *Back to Bataan,* and Rusty Ryan in *They Were Expendable.*[5]

Irish American Catholics themselves celebrated their participation in the war, emphasizing the natural harmony, indeed mutual reinforcement between their Catholic devotion and American patriotism. The best example, perhaps, was the broad public attention given a letter written by Bostonian Lieutenant John J. Shea to his young son, Jackie, in 1942 when Shea was on duty in the South Pacific. Shea told his son: "Be a good Catholic and you can't help being a good American." He later died in combat. The Catholic Commission on American Citizenship quickly published the "Letter to Jackie" in its school reader, *These Are Our Freedoms,* used in an estimated two-thirds to three-quarters of the nation's parochial schools.[6]

Yet as in World War I, if the Church encouraged and proclaimed Catholic American patriotism, it also worked hard to ensure that Catholic soldiers remained faithful to their religion. In 1941 it created a National Catholic Community Service organization to serve soldiers in training and in the field, explicitly for that purpose. It flooded service men and women with millions of rosaries and medals, tangible, visible markers of Catholic identity, a kind of "Catholic dog tag." Using stories of an invented "twentieth century GI" named "Mack," in its magazine, *Contact,* it also insisted that Catholicism was not a religion like any other, but the "only hope [for the future world]."[7]

Even before World War II ended, Irish American Catholics were engaged with the next one: the Cold War with communism abroad and at home. As the war against the Axis powers still raged, Pope Pius XII, formerly Cardinal Eugenio Pacelli, the architect of the Vatican's 1930s anti-Soviet crusade, shifted that anti-communism campaign into overdrive, no matter the Soviets' wartime alliance with the democracies. This worldwide Vatican effort would ignite a Catholic anti-communist movement in Australia, egged on by the old Irish nationalist, Cardinal Mannix, which would wreck that nation's Labor Party by 1955. Yet Pius XII was convinced that the United States was the key to the defeat of communism. As early as 1945, responding to the Vatican, the National Catholic Welfare Conference (NCWC) produced a report on American communism, written by Irish American Father John Cronin in collaboration with the FBI, detailing communist infiltration of unions, the federal government, and the armed services. Monsignor John A. Ryan died that same year, and, in a suggestive changing of the guard, Cronin succeeded him as a member of the conference's longtime pro–New Deal Social Action Department.[8]

The first big battle in the fight over domestic anti-communism erupted in the labor movement. At its 1947 convention, George Meany led the AFL's embrace of a new Republican law requiring union members to pledge that they were not communists. The Communist Party, however, had much more clout in the CIO, dominating unions that constituted about one third of the Congress' membership. CIO President Philip Murray, who took his Catholicism very seriously, opposed communism but, intent on holding his organization together, refused to take the pledge. Murray, however, had long been convinced that the labor movement needed strong presidential backing to thrive, even survive. He admired Henry Wallace but thought his cause was futile, so Murray supported Truman in the 1948 election. On orders from the Communist Party, the communist-led unions backed Wallace instead, igniting a fierce internal war in the CIO. After the two factions battled through 1948 and 1949 amid rising Cold War tension, the CIO, led by Murray and supported by most Irish American Catholic union leaders, expelled eleven communist-led unions, representing about a million members.[9]

More explosive and wrenching and much more well known, was the fight led by the notorious Senator Joseph "Joe" McCarthy of Wisconsin over alleged widespread communist infiltration of the U.S. government. McCarthy would lead his own anti-communist investigations, but throughout the early 1950s, he would also be the very visible embodiment of McCarthyism, a broad movement of federal, state, and local investigations, security boards, and pressure groups pledged to rooting out the purported dangerous menace of domestic communism. Third-generation Irish Joe McCarthy understood himself more as a Catholic than as Irish or even Irish American, but he self-consciously constructed a public image proclaiming his Irish toughness, selling himself in his political campaigns as "the fighting Irish Marine," "fighting a barroom brawl against a crowd that sure has messed things up for this country."[10]

McCarthy's Irishness mixed well with his anti-elitism, for, as the language above suggests, he also defined himself as the Irish American Catholic "regular guy," battling what he insisted were traitorous elites. Rooted in Irish Americans' longtime resentments of aristocrats, but aggravated recently in conflicts with New Dealers, there seemed to be a consensus by the early 1940s among Irish American Catholic spokesmen that communism did not find a home in America on farms or factory floors but in the federal bureaucracy and in elite universities. In the angry words of second-generation Irish John Swift, the K of C's Supreme Knight, it was the "high brow," "brain trusts so called bright young planners, self-styled intelligentsia . . . college students [and] . . . their agnostic professors, pretentious, white collared aristocratic Communists," who were responsible for the spread of communism in America. McCarthy himself hammered at this theme relentlessly, focusing, in particular, on the "striped pants boys" in the State Department, led by the prep school and Ivy League-educated Secretary of State, Dean Acheson. McCarthy mocked Acheson as the "Red Dean of Fashion," nattily attired in his English tailored suits, and in 1951, called for Acheson's impeachment: "You and your lace handkerchiefs comrades . . . betrayed us."[11]

If anti-elitism was one critical hallmark of Irish American Catholic anti-communism, religion was another. McCarthy was very strongly Catholic, and though he did not attack his opponents' religion, his movement built on the religious alignment pitting Catholics against liberal Protestants and Jews, which had emerged during the political fights over the Spanish Civil War. Polls in 1952 and 1954 found that Irish Catholics were more likely to have a favorable view of McCarthy than any other major ethnic group, though most Italian, Polish, and other American Catholics supported him as well. Some Irish American Catholic editors and writers at Catholic journals like *America* and *Commonweal* opposed McCarthy, and in the end, four of the five Irish Catholics in the Senate voted to censure him in 1954. John F. Kennedy, citing health issues, avoided the vote, however, and an observer noted that Irish American Catholic Mike Mansfield, then a young senator from Montana, seemed "very conscious of the nuns scattered throughout the gallery" as he voted for censure.[12]

If McCarthy was broken by the mid-1950s, anti-communism in America was not, and he had heirs, none perhaps more important than William F. Buckley. Buckley knew McCarthy, vigorously defended him before the senator's censure and, if somewhat more cautiously, after it, but he seemed an unlikely successor to the hard-bitten "tail gunner Joe." The son of a Texas-born oil millionaire, he had grown up in privilege, attended Yale, and spoke like an English lord. He was, however, the grandson of immigrants from Cork and Limerick and devoutly Catholic, as much or more so because of his Swiss Catholic mother. Nevertheless, despite his riches and his accent, he was not a Yankee Protestant "wannabe." His father settled in largely Protestant, posh Sharon, Connecticut, where his sons and daughters waged a child's war on the Protestant enemy: planting dirty pictures in the Episcopal priest's Bible or scrambling the letters of sermon topics spelled out in the Congregational Church's sign. Buckley combined this fierce Catholicism with an equally strong commitment to free market capitalism, inherited from his father, who bitterly resented state interference in business, especially after Mexico's revolutionary government stripped him of most of his early oil profits in Mexico.[13]

In 1951, just after graduating from Yale, William Buckley published his first book, *God and Man at Yale,* a blistering critique of the university's academic freedom, which, he believed, permitted professors to attack religion and impose their left-wing views on students with impunity. Reviews by liberals and many Protestants attacked his insistence that Yale return to religion and dismissed him as a Catholic fanatic. Some Catholic reviewers, however, questioned his rigid laissez-faire economics, suggesting that "his ignorance" of Catholic social doctrine "seems fairly complete."[14]

Buckley's combination of Catholicism, anti-communism, and feisty bat-tles with liberal elites would, however, help him create a bridge for many young middle-class Irish American Catholics to a new economically conservative pol-itics. When Kieran O'Doherty was a student at St. Bonaventure College in up-state New York in the 1950s, for example, he "devoured each issue of Buckley's magazine, the *National Review,* within twenty-four hours of its receipt." In 1961, O'Doherty and J. Daniel Mahony founded a Conservative Party in New York, dedicated to vigorous anti-communism and free-market economics. What they liked most about Buckley, however, were his clever, slashing attacks on liberals: to them, he was "the scourge of the Liberal Establishment." O'Doherty believed that this fit well with his own family's and those of other Conservative Party founders' support for Ireland's revolution and the Clan na Gael. Their politics was not a turn to a staid, old-fashioned "conservatism," but a "counterrevolution."[15]

World War II had left more fundamental legacies for Irish American Catholics than a Cold War anti-communism. The mobilization of industry for the Amer-ican war effort had finally ended the Depression, but the economy kept boom-ing in the fifteen years after Japan's surrender. The government's GI Bill paid for veterans to go to college, and federal government-backed home loans and road building also subsidized their move to the suburbs. By 1960 one-third of Amer-icans lived in suburbs; only one-fifth had lived there in 1940.[16]

Such prosperity helped prompt a small revival of immigration from Ire-land to America. The war had left Ireland untouched, but its economy contin-ued to stagnate through the postwar era. In the early 1950s Ireland's income rose at only about a fifth the rate of other Western European nations. Thus between 1946 and 1961, over 500,000 Irish left Ireland and about 70,000 of them, slightly more women than men, went to the United States. This was not a desperate flight from disaster, but an escape by the ambitious and restless from an economically torpid Ireland to an America flush from the wartime and postwar boom. During the 1950s, in particular, Irish immigrants were relatively well educated and a fifth growing to a fourth had been white-collar workers in Ireland. In the United States, they concentrated more than ever in the East and in New York City in particular. There in the big city, they remained something of a people within a people, sparking a revival in New York's Gaelic sports and carving out a social world of their own focused on the City Center Ballroom in midtown Manhattan.[17]

By the 1960s, over two-thirds of Irish American Catholics were of third, fourth, or later generations. These Irish of longtime American settlement took full advantage of the opportunities opened up by the resurgent wartime and postwar economies. Irish American Catholics' college attendance rocketed up in the 1940s to 43 percent, and to nearly half by 1964. Irish Catholic women's rates of college attendance nearly equaled those of Irish Catholic men, even without the same high degree of reliance on the GI Bill and were substantially higher than those of women from all other Catholic and most Protestant ethnic groups. Irish American Catholics went to all sorts of state and private colleges, but Catholic college student bodies grew more than all university enrollments between 1940 and 1960. In a growing economy such education paid off in better jobs. By 1968, two-thirds of Irish American Catholic men were white-collar workers, compared to only 38 percent of their fathers. Mabel Delehanty Mangan, who had worked in Lowell's declining textile mills through the Depression, almost wept with joy years later when she talked about how the world had changed for her children: "My boys got the GI bill. . . . I have a boy who is a scientist and working at the Department of the Interior in Washington. He has a PhD from Georgetown University." Moving up the economic ladder, many young Irish American Catholics also moved out of old neighborhoods to the suburbs. By 1960, about 30 percent of the children of Irish immigrants lived in the suburbs in metropolitan areas compared to 23 percent in 1940. It is harder to track the much more numerous third or later generations, but 42 percent of American Catholics lived in the suburbs by the mid-1950s. Most Irish in the 1950s and 1960s had left an old world behind and now entered a new one: by 1967, only about one-sixth of Irish American Catholic adults lived in the same neighborhood as their parents or their brothers and sisters. Such percentages were scarcely higher than those of English American Protestants and far lower than those of Italian American Catholics. In Alice McDermott's novel *After This,* when an Irish American Catholic family, the Keanes, moved to a suburban town on Long Island in the 1950s, the father, John, agreed to collect donation pledges for the town's new St. Gabriel's Church. Making his rounds through the neighborhood, he finds the families he visits to be "for the most part, strangers," though their homes looked much like his, children sprawling on the floor doing homework and dogs "pushed behind basement doors," while only the kitchen smells— garlic for Italian families, roast meat for the Irish—seemed to hint at ethnic differences. These mobile Irish American Catholics were also now more likely to marry outside the ethnic group than in it: only 43 percent of American Catholics of Irish ancestry in this era married other Irish American Catholics. Almost one-tenth of all those marrying non-Irish now wed Italian Americans.[18]

Meanwhile, Irish American Catholic ties to Ireland, attenuated before the war, continued to weaken after it. As early as 1947, the American chargé d'affaires in Dublin wrote to Secretary of State George Marshall of his "growing realization that there is no longer any burning interest in Ireland on the part of the people of Irish extraction in the United States." Over a decade later, the Irish Republic's New York consul lamented that even the St. Patrick's Day parade was really just "a demonstration of Catholic presence with some Irish overtones."[19]

It was too early, however, to say that the American-born Irish, even of third or later generations, had "assimilated." There were still limits to Irish American economic progress and geographical mobility, and they were still outsiders. That was not because of their ethnicity so much as their religion, the militant and triumphant American Catholicism that they had forged at the beginning of the twentieth century and that reached its apogee in the middle of it. If this was a broadly Catholic identity, Irish Americans' commitment to it was distinctive; even among the most successful among them—or especially the most successful among them—it was more intense than it had ever been before and more than almost all other Catholics.

One reason why Irish Catholics remained distinct and separate is that they had not yet made it in America, not entirely, and as before, the most ambitious of them knew that and resented it. Irish American Catholic sociologist Andrew Greeley marveled at Catholic, particularly Irish American Catholic, success in the postwar era, but he acknowledged: "Clearly Catholics [including Irish Catholics] are not present in the upper levels of business, professional and academic life." WASP or Yankee Protestants still dominated the core of the American economy, and the old Protestant establishment still stood in the 1950s. Irish American Catholic J. F. Powers, a novelist from the Midwest and a sharp observer of Catholic life in postwar America, confessed: "You felt it was their country, handed down to them by the Pilgrims."[20]

Even the seeming success of middle-class Irish American Catholics who never approached the top might not have been as straightforward as much of the data suggested. For many sociologists at the time, the persistent absence of successful businessmen among Catholics, including Irish Catholics, was proof of their lack of an entrepreneurial sense, failure to appreciate work as a career or a vocation, or excessive concerns about job security. In a 1961 survey of college graduates, Irish American Catholics ranked eighth of eleven groups in the proportion choosing careers in private business and had lower expectations of future income than other groups. Yet it was not just their sluggish performance in business; Irish American historian Monsignor John Tracy Ellis and Bishop John Wright wondered in 1956, why, for all Catholics' huge investment in schools and colleges, American Catholics had produced so few intellectuals of note. Ellis blamed this "failure" on discrimination by non-Catholics and the poverty of the Church's immigrant population, but he also wondered whether Catholics valued the intellectual life enough. The Church poured millions into elementary education, he pointed out, and though it created many colleges and universities, he argued that perhaps it was too many, since none of them were endowed with the proper resources to support a sufficiently rich intellectual environment.[21]

Just as their economic or scholarly triumphs might be qualified, so it is important not to exaggerate too much the extent of their geographic mobility. There was, indeed, a gigantic uprooting and movement to the suburbs in the 1950s, but Catholics were less likely to move out of America's big cities than Protestants. By the 1950s Irish Catholic neighborhoods in the city were often their second, third, or more settlements within the city but located on its peripheries, not immigrant ghettoes at its center, and many of those peripheral neighborhoods remained vibrant and modestly prosperous. At St. Sabena's on Chicago's South Side, almost half the heads of households were white-collar workers in the late 1950s, and nearly as many children, 1,000, attended the parish school in 1960 as did at its peak in 1944.[22]

Furthermore, movement to the suburbs did not mean abandoning a Catholic world. Most dioceses moved with almost stunning speed to build new churches and Catholic schools there. The Chicago archdiocese, for example, created seventy-two new parishes in the suburbs between 1940 and 1965, making up a quarter of all its churches by the latter date. It does not appear, however, that the Church imposed Catholicism on reluctant, rebellious suburbanites. Catholics moving into Levittown—the sprawling, new, iconic suburban housing development outside Philadelphia—had to prod the Diocese of Trenton to let them build a new church and parochial school.[23]

Across the nation the number of Catholic school students rose from 2.4 million to nearly 6 million between 1940 and 1965, and their proportion of the school-age population doubled from 7 percent to 14 percent. Irish American

Catholics were critical contributors to this growth. By the early 1960s, no third-generation or later members of any group were more likely to have gone to Catholic schools than the Irish. Irish Americans made up an especially high proportion of Catholic high school students compared to members of other groups. Studies from the 1950s and early 1960s of all students in Catholic high schools including Irish American ones also found that they were more ambitious and "talented" than Irish and other Catholics in public high schools and more likely to be upwardly mobile later in life.[24]

The expansion of Catholic high schools as well as colleges in this era probably also helped keep such successful Irish and other Catholics from marrying outside the Church. As late as the late 1950s and early 1960s about three-quarters to nearly nine-tenths of Catholics married other Catholics. This was as true of the ambitious, upwardly mobile as it was of their poorer co-religionists.[25]

Many Irish Catholics who grew up in the 1940s and 1950s remembered later the almost overwhelming presence of Catholicism in their lives. Her best friend may have been Protestant and she may have attended public school, but for historian Doris Kearns Goodwin, religion and baseball really were the twin poles of her world. The late political commentator Tim Russert from South Buffalo recalled that "religion was everywhere in our house." Many of these memoirs and others are full of recollections of the distinguishing markers of a Catholic identity in the 1940s and 1950s: verbatim recitals of the Baltimore catechism, altar boys' Latin mass responses, descriptions of first communion processions, or jokes about the extraordinarily exacting, scrupulous detail of Catholic moral teaching: "But sister, suppose a man who'd committed a mortal sin was on his way to confession and was hit by a car?"[26]

Perhaps the most striking evidence of the fierce commitment of Irish Catholics to their faith was the number of children they had once they married. Catholic birth rates rose higher than any other religious group—20 percent higher during these years, the height of the "baby boom." What was more striking, however, is that college-educated Catholic women, particularly those who had attended Catholic colleges, had among the nation's highest birth rates in the 1950s, and as one study reported, "such women [also] tend to be disproportionately Irish in origin." A survey in 1961 also found that both wives and husbands of Irish ethnic origin desired far more children than other Catholics, and white-collar Irish Catholics wanted the largest families among all Catholics, one child more than working-class Irish Catholics.[27]

If opposition to birth control had been a long-standing official Catholic norm, the Church had never taught it so emphatically and broadly as in the 1950s. Indeed, as Protestant opposition to contraception waned, the Catholic Church, most notably in Massachusetts, moved aggressively to uphold state restrictions on it. Yet not only was the Church more explicit on the issue, it also spoke to an American laity better educated in their faith and its rules than ever before. Importantly, the new prosperity also seemed to make it more possible now to raise many children on a single salary and thus abandon the old Irish American Catholic practice of marrying late or not marrying at all. The combination of a newly urgent old dictum, avoiding birth control, with a new tendency to early marriage (over 90 percent of Irish Catholic men and women born in the late 1920s or 1930s married before age thirty; about 60 percent and 80 percent, respectively, before age twenty-five) virtually ensured big Irish Catholic families.[28]

To an extraordinary degree, then, Irish American Catholics were more intensely Catholic in the 1940s and early 1950s than they had ever been. This was true despite their increasing economic success and a massive movement to religiously diverse suburbs. Or was it because of those changes, and the resulting disruption of old relationships and breaking of old bonds of communal solidarity? Very few Irish American Catholics in the 1950s were immigrants: most were third generation, a century now removed from the famine or earlier origins. They had been climbing the ladder of America's economic hierarchy for generations, and they had built religious and ethnic communities in diverse neighborhoods long before moving to the suburbs. The pace and breadth of upward mobility and suburbanization in the postwar era, however, were revolutionary, and a renewed commitment to the community of their faith may have helped them cope with the strains of this rapid change.

Some historians point not to their personal responses to new work or neighborhoods so much, however, as to the Catholic Church's response to the Cold War and suggest that a virulent Catholic anti-communism sparked this "religious revival." One historian contends that anti-communism "entered the marrow of Catholic identity" in America in that era, as it seemed the focus of nearly every Catholic organization's work and was written into a multiplicity of strikingly popular Catholic devotions, old and new. Catholics even had their own anti-communist, unofficial "saint," Thomas Dooley, a young charismatic Irish American Catholic doctor treating refugees from communism in Vietnam. Dooley was especially beloved by Irish Americans, and promoted widely by the Church as well as the CIA. The anti-communist crusade thus helped reinforce

Catholic identity and boundaries, not just against the enemies overseas but at home, ratcheting up the battle with liberals stretching back to the thirties or earlier to new intense levels.[29]

The pope and the American hierarchy certainly pushed anti-communism relentlessly, but the crisis of the Cold War offered the Church in the United States a uniquely rich opportunity to tie Catholic morals to American patriotism. The Vatican and American bishops argued that only the return to old norms, particularly in marriage, could prevent the destruction of the family which must inevitably lead to the fall of western democracies. It also insisted that such values were not new and had always been the cultural root of America's origins and its founding documents. Accompanying this assertion was a strong effort to fashion a popular Catholic vision of American history for this now-pan-ethnic Catholic community in the Catholic Commission on Citizenship's school textbooks and even Catholic comic books. Many of the stories in the textbooks or comics stressed Catholicism's early roots in America, depicting heroes of the Revolutionary War or the early republic, including the Irish American Bishop John Carroll, but also the French Father Gabriel Richard, elected to Congress in 1823, and the Polish Thaddeus Kosciuszko, hero of the American Revolution.[30]

More than anyone else, perhaps, Bishop Fulton J. Sheen became the voice and image of this postwar Catholic, but especially Irish Catholic, America. In 1952, Sheen, long a radio and public lecture star, moved on to the new media of television. His program, *Life Is Worth Living,* won an Emmy that year and moved to a major network by 1955. Sheen thrived on television, attracting a broad audience including people of all faiths by dispensing folksy advice to help viewers cope with everyday individual or family troubles. Yet the sources of that advice as well as his relentless attacks on communism were rooted in Catholic neo-Thomist traditional values and set firmly against modern secular thought. Dressed in the lush robes of a Catholic bishop, and offering such Catholic solutions to common problems, he did not conform his Catholicism to American culture so much as conform American culture to his Catholicism.[31]

By the middle to late 1950s, though the Cold War endured, the fiery emotion of its early years, when everything seemed at stake, had begun to subside, and the zeal in much of Irish Catholics' postwar religious practice began to flag. Many Irish and other Catholic women, for example, found the Church's emphasis on motherhood increasingly suffocating, and letters expressing their discontent began to pop up in Catholic journals. Mrs. M. L. O'D. wrote to the Catholic magazine *Ligurian* in 1955: "Does it bring a pleasant picture to your mind to

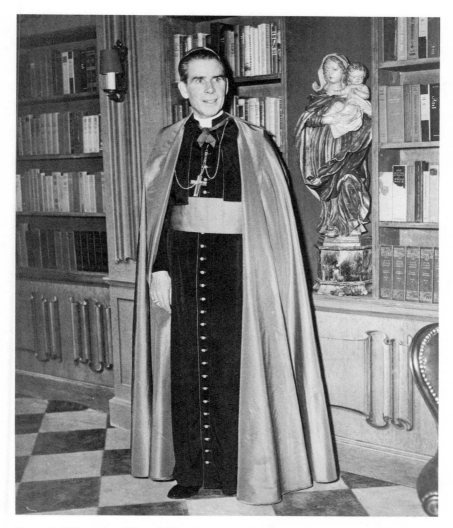

Figure 18. *Bishop Fulton J. Sheen, full-length portrait.* Bishop Sheen on the set of his television show, *Life Is Worth Living,* 1952. Photo by Fred Palumbo. Library of Congress, Prints and Photographs Division, NYWT&S Collection, LC-USZ62-123461.

think of mother of four or more feeding an infant in her arms where a year-old baby sits at her feet begging to be held." In 1956, Katherine M. Byrne confessed in the Jesuit magazine *America* that though she "chose" life as "a happy little wife and mother . . . it is nevertheless, somewhat monotonous and often very lonely." A year earlier, Mrs. Alice O'Connor made her yearning for independence clear: "Parents [not priests] have to gauge what they can bear [about having children] with the grace the Lord gives them." As early as 1955, survey data revealed that Catholic married couples in their late thirties were increasingly likely to use contraception. Since the war, more and more Irish American women had been finding alternatives to stay-at-home motherhood as well. There are no statistics revealing how many married Irish Catholic women worked outside the home during the war years, but the proportion of married second-generation Irish women of all religions who did rose from 15 percent in 1940 to 18.2 percent in 1950 and then to 27.3 percent in 1960. New England, where the Catholic Irish predominated, had the highest proportions of second-generation Irish working wives.[32]

The war also had a powerful effect on the lives of the heretofore largely hidden sexual minority of gay people. War mobilization broke millions of men and women out of their families and small-city or small-town environments, housed them in same-sex military camps, and shipped them overseas through cosmopolitan big-city ports. In the process, gay men and women found each other and gay bars began to multiply in big cities and appear for the first time in small ones. Government crackdowns in the Cold War era, sometimes led by Irish Americans like Senator Pat McCarran, helped slow the momentum of the opening of gay life but did not stop it. Even Irish American Catholic teenager James McCourt, growing up in New York in the 1950s, as well as the anti-communist icon of Catholic virtue, Tom Dooley, managed to find this active, if subterranean, gay world.

Irish American Catholic poet Frank O'Hara found it too. He grew up in a small, rural New England town, Grafton, Massachusetts, but in a recognizably Irish American Catholic family: his father was a graduate of Holy Cross; his grandfather a lonely pillar of the local Democratic Party; he attended parochial school and Catholic high school in nearby Worcester; and he profited from the attention of unmarried working aunts and grand-aunts, including a teacher and a librarian, who showered him with books, took him to the movies, and talked to him often about music and literature. After a stint in the navy and earning a college degree at Harvard and a master's at the University of Michigan, he made his way to New York. There he too flourished as a gay man. Through his "infectious excitement and love of art," and campy, witty poetic genius, he helped create a community, a lively group of talented poets and artists, many of them gay like him, working and living at the avant-garde edge of American culture.[33]

Others, far more conventional than the gay O'Hara, were also growing restless with the strictures and claustrophobia of Irish American Catholic middle-class life in the 1950s, but many of them sought not to leave the group but looked back longingly to its more "authentic" origins. Edwin O'Connor's novel *The Last Hurrah,* published in 1956, for example, sharply contrasted a charming and charismatic old political boss in his last campaign and the lingering vestiges of his richly ritualized communal life from turn-of-the-twentieth-century Irish America, with his new generation, Catholic college graduate, fifties' middle-class Irish American opponent, "a mealy mouthed, maneuverable piece of dough . . . [a] spineless clown." The Irish American director John Ford made a movie of *The Last Hurrah,* but his *The Quiet Man* (1952), about Ireland not Irish America, was much more successful. In it a troubled Irish American flees to Ireland, finds a timeless, changeless, pastoral idyll of farms and farmers, pretty villages, stunningly green fields, and quaint inefficiency, settles into his immigrant mother's old childhood cottage, engages in a day-long fist fight, deliberately burns money, and finds a new life as well as a new love in the "old" country.[34]

Beneath the polished surface of suburban prosperity and Catholic triumph there were, then, currents of disquiet, restlessness. For many Irish American Catholic women as well as gay men and lesbians, it was still just a hint of future, if imminent, dramatic changes. For searchers for another, "authentic" Irishness, it was also now but a vague, dreamy dissatisfaction. Few Irish Americans seemed interested in Ireland and even fewer went "back"—only 2 percent of all tourists visiting the Republic in the 1950s. That, too, would soon change.[35]

In 1952, Dwight Eisenhower, a war hero, became the first Republican president since Hoover, and then in 1956 he cruised to an even bigger victory. At first glance, this seemed the end of a political era for Democrats and, perhaps, for Irish American Catholic Democrats, as Eisenhower ran surprisingly well among Catholic voters. Eisenhower's success, however, obscured how well the Democrats really did below the presidential level in the 1950s, climaxing in their landslide victory in the off-year election of 1958, when eight Irish Catholic Democrats were elected to the Senate and over forty to the House. Yet if neither the Democratic Party nor the Irish American role in it were as weak as they seemed then, Irish American Catholic Democrats faced serious challenges to their political power in the postwar era, which would only grow stronger over time.[36]

One challenge was internal. In 1955, George Meany became president of a newly merged AFL-CIO. He would rule over the American labor movement for nearly a quarter century. Yet union membership had begun to decline that year, and labor, a key ally of Irish American Catholic Democrats, would never again be as powerful as it was then. Catholic union membership would eventually fall, too, as Irish and other Catholics moved out of blue-collar jobs into white-collar occupations.[37]

There were also challenges from competitors outside the group. The first was an old one, struggles with fellow Catholic ethnic rivals. Between 1940 and 1960, the number of second-generation Italian Americans in the United States grew nearly fivefold, and American-born Polish Americans about fourfold. Thus, in 1944, only nine years after Robert Emmet Quinn led his "bloodless revolution" assault on Yankee rule in Rhode Island, Italian American Democrat John O. Pastore became governor of the state. Pastore became Rhode Island's U.S. Senator in 1950 and Republican Christopher Del Sesto its governor in 1958.[38]

The second challenge to Irish American Catholic political power was even older. The paradox of Irish American Catholic relations with African Americans continued: Irish political support—if often cautious—for Black rights, combined with fierce resistance to African American integration into Irish neighborhoods and workplaces. The war, however, had restarted the massive migration of African Americans to the North, and in the process began to undermine this fragile compromise.

Irish American Catholic Democrats and their party confronted that racial challenge almost immediately after the war. At the Democratic convention in 1948, Ed Flynn and David Lawrence played critical roles in rallying other bosses, even Frank Hague, to replace the party's cautious civil rights plank with Hubert Humphrey's far more progressive one, despite the intense opposition of southern Democrats, who soon created their own "Dixiecrat "party. In 1946 Irish American Catholic Democrats led efforts in Massachusetts to establish a Fair Employment Practices Commission (FEPC) over Republican opposition. In 1950 Irish American Catholic Democrats in the U.S. House of Representatives, led by Mary Norton, voted nearly unanimously but unsuccessfully for a permanent, federal FEPC, and Irish American House Democrats from New York, Massachusetts, and Illinois voted unanimously for civil rights bills in 1957 and 1960. As before, pragmatism and practical advantage figured in Irish Democratic political leaders' advocacy for civil rights. Ed Flynn's machine, for example, had lost a congressional special election in his Bronx domain to a pro–civil rights candidate backed by Henry Wallace about six months before the 1948 convention, making him very conscious of the issue's importance to northern voters.[39]

Survey data also suggested that most Irish Americans in this era endorsed Black civil rights, but many Irish American Catholics still fiercely objected to African Americans moving into their neighborhoods, especially in Philadelphia and Chicago, or competing for jobs in their workplaces. On Chicago's South Side, some Irish Catholic pastors even helped mobilize that resistance, which erupted in a three-day anti-Black and anti-Semitic riot in Visitation parish in 1949. Similarly, while Irish American labor leaders steadfastly backed civil rights bills, Irish workers and union leaders still stubbornly opposed tinkering with seniority rules favoring whites as well as entrenched traditions of recruiting union members from families and friends.[40]

The last challenge that Irish American Catholics confronted at mid-century came from the rising power of liberal reformers in the Democratic Party. The explosion of higher education and the rapid expansion of "knowledge industries" after the war had broadened the potential base of middle-class liberals, making them even more powerful political rivals for Irish Americans now. Postwar liberal reformers had enthusiastically embraced the New Deal, but they were also heirs to an older, turn-of-the-century, middle-class urban reform politics. They were determined to transform the Democratic Party into "a committed agent of social change" but one that would also "support these goals even when it's not in its interest." They conceded that "old line leaders," their Democratic regular opponents, might back liberal policies but, they argued, that was only because it was "a politically expedient position," not because these regulars sincerely believed in such reforms. Patronage, party organizational hierarchies, ethnic ticket balancing, personal allegiances—all the mainstays of machine politics—struck the liberal reformers as selfish or impure, even if they helped racial minorities. A reform leader in New York, for example, dismissed African American political bosses' demands for power and jobs: "They are not our kind of reformers."[41]

Most of the battles between reformers and Irish and other regulars were fought locally in city and state politics, but the conflict also emerged in national presidential politics. In 1952, liberal reformers found a national political hero all their own: Adlai Stevenson. Stevenson was only a tepid backer of labor unions and expansion of the welfare state, and very cautious about civil rights. Liberal reformers, however, admired his integrity and commitment to civil liberties threatened by McCarthy and others, and loved his style: well mannered, urbane, witty, thoughtful. He was, as one biographer described him, a "patrician among the politicians."[42]

As the Truman administration unraveled amid widespread charges of corruption and cronyism, including some against prominent Irish American Catholics like J. Howard McGrath, such sentiments had a powerful appeal but not for most Catholics, including Irish American Catholics. Stevenson split the normally Democratic Catholic vote with Eisenhower in 1952, but lost it badly, 54 percent to 45 percent, in 1956. Observers have often suggested that this was an inevitable result of Catholics' upward mobility and suburbanization, which should have made them a natural fit for a moderately conservative Republicanism. Yet in the 1956 election, Stevenson lost as badly and by about the same margin both among Catholics who had not gone beyond grade school (39.5 percent of the vote) and among ones who had earned a college degree or better (38.9 percent). In Boston, a postelection survey of Irish American Catholic voters found that those in working-class *and* middle-class Irish districts doubted Stevenson's commitment to anti-communism and found him elitist and distant.[43]

In 1949, Paul Blanshard, once a La Guardia aide, published a book *American Freedom and Catholic Power,* hoping to mobilize liberal resistance to the "antidemocratic social policies of the [Catholic] hierarchy . . . and every intolerant or separatist or un-American feature of those policies." The crude anti-Catholic bigotry of the 1920s had muffled liberal intellectuals' skepticism about Catholicism, but the rise of Coughlin, American Catholic backing of the Fascists in Spain, McCarthyism, and the Church's postwar growth and ambition had since provoked widespread suspicion of Catholic power. Increasingly, many non-Catholic American intellectuals came to see democracy as a culture that celebrated dissent and individualism and had its roots in the Reformation or prophetic Jewish and Protestant traditions, but decidedly not in what they understood as authoritarian Catholicism.[44]

Blanshard made clear in a second book, published in 1953, *The Irish and Catholic Power: An American Interpretation,* that this was not a Catholic problem so much as an Irish Catholic one: "In the English speaking world, Roman Catholic power is essentially Irish Catholic power." He acknowledged that Irish Catholic congressmen were "generally progressive. . . . [their] racial policy is magnificently humane and liberal." Nevertheless, he argued that the Irish Catholics' demand for federal aid to parochial schools and its rabid anti-communism threatened basic American tenets such as the separation of Church and State and free speech.[45]

As before in their history, how Irish American Catholics responded to all these challenges varied from place to place. In New York, Irish American Catholic Democrats made a brief political comeback from their collapse in the 1930s, when Tammany was shut out of the New Deal. That revival ended, however, when County Mayo immigrant William O'Dwyer, elected mayor in 1945, resigned abruptly in his second term. Italian Americans had already seized control of Tammany Hall by then and after O'Dwyer left, an Italian American, Vincent Impellitteri, became mayor as well. Rapidly increasing numbers also helped African Americans push old Irish leaders out of Black neighborhoods too. Yet it was the liberal reformers who were the key to the decline of Irish power in the city's Democratic Party. Liberal reform flourished in New York as nowhere else, buoyed by the city's huge Jewish population and its large number of knowledge industry workers. As the Irish and other "regulars" waged, and ultimately lost, a bitter war with liberal reformers over control of the city's Democratic Party through the 1940s and 1950s, not just middle-class but working-class Irish Catholics as well began to leak out to the Republicans, the first substantial Irish movement to the GOP in what would soon become a national exodus.[46]

In Chicago, in contrast, after a rocky postwar start, the Irish machine flourished in the postwar era. Unlike New York, the New Deal had strengthened not weakened it, and neither the city's economy nor the ethnic makeup of its population made it as fertile ground for liberal reform as New York. Yet the effective strategies of the machine's unprepossessing but canny new boss, Irish American Catholic Richard J. Daley, were critical to the machine's success. Elected mayor in 1955, Daley found new allies for the machine in the city's business community through redevelopment of the downtown, ruthlessly controlled and exploited the city's rapidly growing Black vote, and managed to appease the city's largest white ethnic group, Polish Americans, by slating several of them for seats in the state legislature or Congress. Nevertheless, by the early 1960s, Daley's fragile balancing act seemed increasingly vulnerable, as city taxes ballooned, provoking many Polish American and other white ethnic homeowners to rebel against the machine, and African American numbers—and frustrations—began to grow, portending future racial conflicts.[47]

Irish American politics in Boston and Massachusetts was another variation altogether. In Boston, Irish numbers were too great for them ever to be seriously challenged by any other group, but their politics did change. James Michael Curley began his last term as mayor in 1945, but four years later, diligent, respectable, mild mannered (he was nicknamed "Whispering Johnny") Irish American Catholic John B. Hynes would end Curley's Last Hurrah. Hynes cultivated support among the younger "war generation" and like Daley in Chicago (and boss David Lawrence in Pittsburgh) struck an alliance with the city's business elite for ambitious renewal of the city's downtown. Hynes would rule the city for eleven years, but fights between "downtown" interests and the "neighborhoods" over renewal aggravated frustrations among working-class Irish which would later erupt in racial antagonism.[48]

Irish American Catholic politics in the state of Massachusetts in the postwar era was complicated. From the 1940s through the late 1950s, two Irish American Catholic Democrats were elected governor; Irish Catholics also led the Democrats' takeover of both houses of the legislature for the first time since the nineteenth century and made up most of the state's first Democratic majority congressional legation in decades. By 1959, 108 of the 169 Democrats in the Massachusetts House of Representatives (called the General Court) were Irish American Catholics. Yet after 1950 they would not elect another governor until 1978, as they suffered from Italian American competition and the new voting power of suburban middle-class Democrats emerging out of a changing Massachusetts economy. Neither the Italian challenge nor the advent of more suburban middle-class Democrats were strong enough to provoke a major Irish American Catholic exodus from the Democrats as in New York, however. Party committees and hierarchies had much less power among Democrats in Massachusetts than in Chicago or even New York City and thus were much less worth fighting over. The Irish were also too numerous and too well entrenched locally in Massachusetts to rout so easily from the Democratic Party. Finally, since many Irish American and other Catholics were as much Al Smith Democrats as New Deal ones, they might vote for Republican governors occasionally but refused to cross that bloody boundary, one that was historically both religious as well as partisan, on a permanent basis.[49]

And then there were the Kennedys. John F. Kennedy, Joseph Kennedy's second son, had emerged from the war a hero and parlayed that, his father's money and contacts, and his own youthful appeal to win a U.S. House seat in 1946. In 1952, he challenged a scion of the Massachusetts Yankee aristocracy, Henry Cabot Lodge, in a race for the Senate and won. Many political observers were stunned by how strongly Irish American Catholics in Massachusetts identified with Kennedy and his family. The young "lace-curtain Irish," in particular, they noted, seemed to appreciate Kennedy's gentility and thought that he had lifted the whole group's status—"taken them up a few steps in society." Kennedy then also helped hold the Massachusetts Irish middle class to the Democrats and a cautious liberalism.[50]

Yet he and his family had far greater ambitions than Bay State prominence. After a useful near miss for the vice-presidential nomination at the Democratic Party convention in 1956, John F. Kennedy emerged as a serious contender for the presidency in 1960.

Epilogue and Conclusion

In the summer of 1947, Congressman John F. Kennedy visited his sister Kathleen, "Kick," in Ireland. Kick and he were close. He was only two and half years older, but it was more than that. They both seemed to be finding a social acceptance that their parents and even older brother Joe never grasped and novelist John O'Hara could hardly have imagined. At Harvard, Jack was elected to one of the university's elite eating clubs, Spee, something neither his father nor older brother had achieved. Together in London in the late 1930s when their father was ambassador to the United Kingdom, Kick and he hobnobbed easily with British aristocrats and members of the political elite. Kick's embrace of the British aristocracy, however, was more personal and thorough. In May 1944, she married William "Billy" Hartington, officially William Cavendish, Marquess of Hartington, and heir apparent to the Duke of Devonshire. She wrote home to her family that "My persecuted Irish ancestors would turn over in their graves" if they heard her talk so glowingly about England, "but I don't care." "Billy," her husband, had died near the end of the war, but his family still made room for Kathleen at the family's Irish home, Lismore Castle, all towers and turrets, sitting on a hill overlooking the Blackwater River in Waterford like some Rhine River fantasy.[1]

Kathleen had little interest in Ireland or the Irish. Introduced to members of the Irish government on a trip to Dublin, she had confided later that they all looked like "gunmen" to her. She had thus invited a slew of English notables, writers and politicians, including Anthony Eden, future prime minister of the United Kingdom, to the castle to keep her company when her brother came to visit. Jack was more intrigued with Ireland than Kick, however. On a trip to Europe with a friend in 1937, he stayed up all night to see the Irish coast

as the ship passed it on the way to France. Now, at Lismore, he expressed interest in visiting Dunganstown in Wexford, where his immigrant great-grandfather,
Patrick Kennedy, came from. Kick, though dubious about such an excursion,
would, nonetheless, lend him a station wagon to drive there, and Pamela Churchill,
Winston Churchill's daughter in-law and another guest at the castle (an unlikely
companion for this trip), joined him. Jack had tea with Mary Kennedy Ryan,
descendant of his great-grandfather's brother, and her husband, and gave the
family's children rides in his car, "to their pleasure and his." "Surrounded" by
chickens and pigs, he later recalled that he loved it all and drove back to Lismore Castle in a flood of nostalgia and "sentiment." Churchill, less impressed,
muttered something on the return trip about its resemblance to the poverty of
the American South depicted in the film *Tobacco Road* (1941). Kennedy would
later claim he felt like kicking her out of the car.[2]

The next year Kathleen died in a plane crash in France's Rhone Valley. Jack
learned of it while listening to a recording of "How are Things in Glocca Morra"
from the recent Broadway hit *Finian's Rainbow*, about an Irishman in the American South, leprechauns, and a pot of gold.

John F. Kennedy would return to Ireland, including Dunganstown, as president of the United States in late June 1963. Huge, excited and jubilant crowds
gathered in Dublin, Cork, Galway, and Limerick as well as Wexford to greet him.
He was so delighted with his brief visit there that for days after he had returned
to the White House he would insist that family members and friends watch films
of it with him.

A little short of five months later he was assassinated in Dallas, Texas.[3]

John F. Kennedy's election to the presidency and subsequent assassination were critically important to Irish America. Though his victory margin in
the election was wafer thin (and disputed by some), it had broken an important
barrier for Irish American Catholics. Just as Al Smith's loss in 1928 had publicly
and emphatically confirmed their status as outsiders, Kennedy's win in 1960
clearly marked their passage inside. Moreover, despite an administration mixing
lofty hopes and youthful energy with considerable political caution, Kennedy's
death made him an instant hero, an American martyr, reinforcing the promise
of his electoral victory and Irish and Catholic acceptance. An old era had appeared to pass and a new one beckoned.[4]

Yet, of course, it was not just Kennedy alone, his victory and death, that
ended the old and opened possibilities for the new. The civil rights movement,
gaining momentum for some time in America, exploded in the 1960s in broad

protest and the passage of historic, if incomplete, legislation against racial discrimination. In this era of challenging prejudice—even the nation's most deeply
rooted one against African Americans—anti-Catholic feeling increasingly seemed
like an anachronism. More ominously, white resistance to African Americans'
search for equality also reinforced the racial boundary between Blacks and whites,
but by strengthening white solidarity, ironically, it also weakened longtime an-
tagonisms among white ethnic and religious groups. Meanwhile, the Vatican,
which had emphatically shut the door on American liberal Catholic overtures to
Protestants over sixty years before, now opened it. The Second Vatican Council
meeting in Rome from 1962 to 1965 recognized the validity of other religions
and encouraged Catholic ecumenical efforts to reach out and reconcile with all
Christians and members of all faiths.[5]

As before, changes within the community combined with these changes
outside it to remake Irish American Catholics' understanding of where they fit
and who they were. Irish American Catholics' longtime social and economic progress over the course of the late nineteenth and early twentieth centuries accelerated after 1960. In 2000–2004 election surveys, close to 14 percent of Irish
American Catholic families ranked among the top 5 percent of all Americans
in household income, and 58 percent were among the top third. In the same
surveys over 70 percent of Irish American Catholics had "some" college and 39
percent had a college or advanced degree. By contrast only about 9 percent of
the Protestant Irish were in the top 5 percent, and 29 percent in the top third
of American family income brackets. The percentages of Protestant Irish attending college or earning college or advanced degrees, 48.3 percent and 20 percent,
respectively, were lower as well.[6]

Wealthier, better educated, but, importantly, free from anti-Catholic prejudice, Irish American Catholics were no longer locked into an ethnic or religious
identity by outside forces and could now easily cross old ethnic and religious
boundaries. Some, therefore, abandoned allegiances to old institutions and organizations like the Catholic Church or the Democratic Party, which had dominated Irish Catholic America from its inception. Catholic intermarriage across
religious boundaries soared: by 1993–1994, less than half of Irish Catholics
were married to Catholics. Weekly attendance at mass fell from 44.4 percent
between 1976 and 1980 to 30 percent in 2004, and thus from highest among
the four major Catholic ethnic groups (Irish, German, Italian, and Polish) to only
higher than Italian Americans. In the 1970s, nearly 90 percent of Irish Americans born of Catholic mothers still called themselves Catholics into adulthood;

by the 2010s that proportion had fallen to two-thirds. Meanwhile, though opposition to abortion declined only very slowly among Catholics of Irish ancestry after 1970, condemnation of homosexuality began falling rapidly by the 1990s.[7]

Irish Catholic flight from the Democratic Party was about as dramatic. In 1963, nearly 70 percent of Irish Catholics identified as Democrats; by the 1990s the proportion had dropped to about a half, and by the 2010s to a little over 40 percent, slightly more than the percentage claiming to be Republicans. Though often defined by television and movies as iconic racists over much of the past sixty years, survey data suggests that Irish American Catholics have actually been slightly less racist than most other white groups in the late twentieth and early twenty-first centuries. Nevertheless, the same surveys reveal that they were more opposed to school busing for racial integration than others, and like most whites complained throughout much of the period about Blacks' aggressiveness in seeking their rights. Irish American Catholics' political dynamics have, however, continued to vary regionally since the 1960s: in New England, Irish American Catholics have been more likely to remain Democrats; in the mid-Atlantic states, more likely to have moved to the Republicans.[8]

The decline of prejudice trapping Irish American Catholics in a religious definition of their ethnicity, Irish Catholic, now also permitted them to redefine what Irish American meant. In doing so many Irish Americans tapped into a broad cultural discontent simmering in the modern America of the 1960s and after: a disenchantment with the anomic world of suburban America and a yearning for "rootedness . . . and community" and "authenticity." Many white Americans—Italian, Polish, as well as Irish—sought such "rootedness" in their ancestral home and its culture. In this the Irish and other white ethnics were helped, at least, in part, by African Americans' and other racial groups' new challenges to assimilation and conformity to a dominant Anglo-American culture.[9]

Such discontent and yearning had been hinted at by Irish Americans in the 1950s in the popularity of movies like *The Quiet Man* and books like *The Last Hurrah,* but in the 1960s and after it became more widespread and intense. The new search for authenticity and culture was reflected in the growing popularity of family genealogy among Irish Americans, the creation of university Irish Study programs and city Irish cultural and arts centers, the spectacular expansion and resilient popularity of traditional Irish music in America, and with the aid of cheaper air travel, the dramatic increase in Irish Americans—like John F. Kennedy himself—"returning" to Ireland. One historian has also argued that some Irish Americans even understood their support of the new physical force nationalists of the IRA and their American front group, NORAID, during Northern Ireland's "troubles" as proof of their authentic Irishness.[10]

Paradoxically, however, because this new authentic Irishness was rooted in Irish culture, not religion, and thus no longer tied to Catholicism, Protestant Irish were able to take it up too. Indeed, it might be said that the rural farmers of the upcountry American South had more tangible personal connections to Ireland through their music than most white-collar Irish American Catholics in the New York or Chicago suburbs. "Folk" musicians from Ireland thus began to travel to Nashville and elsewhere in the South to cultivate those bonds.[11]

The changes in Irish America following John F. Kennedy's election and assassination have been both dramatic and fundamental. Institutions and allegiances which were the very foundations of Irish American Catholic ethnicity have crumbled or withered. The search for "roots" or personal authenticity has earlier precedents, but this new freedom from outside anti-Irish or anti-Catholic constraints and from inside the discipline of Catholicism has been an important reason for its current broader appeal.

As we have seen, however, change and contingency have been a constant in Irish American history, both in Irish Americans' personal lives as individuals and families and their lives together defining their communities and identities. Irish Americans changed and changed again, invented and reinvented themselves, following paths that were not predetermined but contingent—sometimes even seemingly inexplicable—as they fell outside simple linear notions of assimilation. The decisions of second-generation Irish American Catholics at the turn of the century about whether and when to marry, for example, seemed more like their cousins' choices in Ireland than those of their own parents or even new Irish immigrants in America. A half century later, well-educated, economically successful American-born Irish, largely of the third or fourth generations, were not only more likely to have more children than their parents, but more than any other Catholic ethnic group, including the poorer, less educated members of their own. On the community level, as we have seen, Irish Americans' definitions of who they were followed a wandering course: from the Presbyterian Irish in the eighteenth century, who for years were "a people with no name"; to the invention of a religiously plural Irish America; to the slipping away of Protestants from Irish identification and the emergence of an exclusively Catholic Irish America; to Irish Catholics' establishment of themselves as leaders and models of a new pan-ethnic, militantly Catholic people. Locked into that role by the twentieth century but powerful in it, they remained such until Kennedy's election.

Yet, as argued at the very beginning of this book, it is not just *how* Irish Americans adapted or changed, but *why*—why they changed at all and why they changed in the ways that they did—that is important to understanding their history. That history reveals that the causes of such changes have been numerous and diverse and not only changed over time but also varied over space: in the colonial era, causes of adaptations were not the same for Irish Protestants in Pennsylvania, for example, as in the Carolinas, and in the nineteenth and twentieth centuries, such causes for Irish Catholics in Boston differed from those for San Francisco's Irish. Most of the causes, however, can be grouped into larger categories that have threaded throughout Irish American history from its origins in the colonial era until Kennedy's election. Broadly they have been of two kinds: causes of change emerging from within, inside the group, and those from without, in its environment.

Most notable among those from within the group were the repeated waves of immigration from the old country. Though Ireland often seemed unchanging, there were differences even between the Ireland that the famine immigrants left in the middle of the nineteenth century and the Ireland of the mass migration only a few decades later in the 1880s and 1890s. Yet it was not just the differences in the Ireland that they had left that distinguished these waves, but variations in the waves' compositions, the proportions of women and men, Protestants and Catholics, of people from different Irish regions, or from varying economic classes. The timing of these waves and thus when some of those groups left for America could be important too: Irish Protestants' migration to America began early, in the colonial era, and petered out in the nineteenth century, while most Catholics migrated later, from the 1830s through the twentieth century. The sizes of these migration waves mattered as well, like the flood fleeing the famine, or the later surge of migrants during the agricultural crisis of the 1880s.

Yet the emergence of American-born generations was as important an internal change as the succession of immigrant waves from Ireland. The second generation was particularly significant, especially when it emerged as a huge demographic echo, like the children of the famine immigrants maturing at the turn of the century. A group's future often hinged on such a second-generation "generational transition," which can be a critical bridge for any ethnic people from the immigrants to the group's American future; indeed, the experiences of members of the second generation may determine whether an ethnic group would continue to exist at all after the passing of the immigrants. For Irish American Catholics, the famine Irish immigrants' American-born children were such a bridge to an enduring Irish American ethnicity at the turn of the twentieth century; for the Protestant Irish, the American-born maturing in the early nineteenth century were not. Yet even as the famine immigrants' offspring persisted in identifying as a distinct Irish Catholic people in the early 1900s, they also fundamentally remade that group then in important ways.

It was not merely changes within the group that drove the evolution of Irish America, of course, but also trends and events outside it, in their new environment. The contingencies shaping that environment were many and varied. They included shifts in political party allegiances, which Irish Catholic Democrats rode to political power in the early 1890s but more dramatically in both the 1910s and the 1930s; or broad Protestant revivals, like the First and Second Awakenings in the eighteenth and early nineteenth centuries which scrambled Protestant evangelical, including Presbyterian, sectarian boundaries; or major events of all kinds but most notably wars, from the conflict between the empires of Britain and France in the colonial era to the overlap of America's entry into World War I and Ireland's War for Independence in the 1910s. Among the most important environmental circumstances provoking and shaping changes among Irish Americans was the transformation of the American economy from agriculture to industry and the economic opportunities it provided by its ongoing, enormous growth. Evolving configurations of power relations among racial, religious, and ethnic groups in America, however, were probably as significant. That the Irish were white, for example, made a huge difference in their personal lives, including easy entry to the United States, citizenship, and access to economic opportunities. Yet continually negotiating their relations with other whites, sorting out enemies and friends, was critical to changes in how they understood their fit in American society and defined their identity as well. Finally, the environment that shaped them extended beyond America's borders, most notably through their transnational ties to Ireland and its struggle for independence, and for Irish Catholics through the increasingly tight hierarchical structure of their worldwide church, headquartered in Rome.

To understand why Irish Americans changed and why they changed as they did, however, it is important to remember that such causes rarely worked in isolation, but as discussed throughout the book, usually in complex combinations that happened to come together at specific moments.

The history of the encounter of Irish Americans—both Catholics and Protestants—with the American economy makes that clear. Few subjects in the study of Irish Americans have been more hotly debated than the relative impact of Irish Americans' cultural inheritance and the American environment on their economic performance in the United States. Those debates have largely focused on Irish American Catholics, but the evidence of recent surveys, which permit the religious identification of Americans of Irish ancestry, offers a potentially important new perspective on it, for those surveys, as noted, reveal that contemporary Irish American Catholics are today clearly more successful than Irish American Protestants.

Yet why is that true, since Irish Protestants seemed to have had potentially much greater useful advantages for finding success when they arrived in America than Irish Catholics? As discussed earlier, Ulster Scot Presbyterians, who made up a majority of the Protestant Irish emigrating to America in the colonial era, for example, were in the vanguard of the linen industry's revolution in Ireland and were probably the most literate group on the island. They should have also profited from being both among the earliest arrivals in America and Protestants in a new, Protestant-dominated country. Catholics, in contrast, were poor, many desperately so, with few skills and little capital; they came later; and they were obviously less welcome in the United States.

The key to the difference in economic performance between Protestant and Catholic Irish Americans appears to lie in the different economic environments that the two have lived in in America. Here, the timing of the Irish Protestant migration to America was important. Irish American Protestants arrived in an agrarian early America, and sought land for farms, not just to sustain themselves, but to gain the economic independence that they had been denied in Ulster. To do so they pushed further and further south and west in the colonies or early American states to find it. The same recent surveys that measure contemporary Irish Protestant economic performance also reveal that over half of today's Irish Protestants still live in the South, where economic development stagnated until recently. When Irish Protestants came to America—an internal cause—and what regions beckoned them in America—an external one—thus combined to have a powerful effect not only on them but on their descendants. The vast majority of Irish American Catholics, however, migrated to America in the nineteenth and twentieth centuries, and settled in the Northeast, Midwest, or Pacific Coast, heartlands of an emerging, economically dynamic, urban industrial America, and their descendants have largely remained there to the present.

Though this comparison suggests the critical importance of the opportunities that economic environments provide for ethnic group mobility, that is hardly the whole story, for the adaptation of Irish American Catholics to the American economy was actually quite complicated. Famine Irish Catholic immigrants, who settled in northern cities, for example, were, indeed, poorly equipped to take advantage of that new environment, and many suffered because of it. Many of those who not only survived but even won some modest prosperity, however, did so not by embracing American individualism but by reliance on the communal ties nourished by their hardscrabble existence in the old country. The American-born children of the famine immigrants would do better than their parents, in large part because of the explosion of white-collar employment in the northern urban areas where they lived. Yet second-generation women, profiting from their community's commitment to their education and work, were more successful than their brothers, who seemed to struggle with embracing the entrepreneurial values that seemed essential to American success.

The effect of combinations of internal and external causes is also evident in how Irish Americans' understandings of where they fit in American society and who they were changed over time. The tiny but nonetheless consequential new migration of Catholic Irish merchants to America before the Revolution and the much larger wave of republican exiles flooding the new nation after it, for example, played powerful roles in creating the first, nonsectarian, Irish America. Yet changes in the environment of Irish Americans in the late eighteenth and early nineteenth century were crucial too. The fight between Presbyterians and Quakers in Pennsylvania, prompted by the French and Indian War and the Paxton Boys controversy, ignited the process of creating that identity. Then the national partisan political battles in the new United States over the rebellion of 1798 and the transnational nature of Irish American republicanism helped spread it throughout the nation. A similar process of interaction of internal and external trends helped undermine that first Irish America and create a new exclusively Catholic one. Within the group, migration of Protestant immigrants from an increasingly sectarian Ireland after 1815, the shift from Protestant to Catholic dominance of immigration from Ireland in the 1830s, and ultimately the famine flood of Catholics in the 1840s and 1850s were obviously important. The emerging dominance of American-born generations, with fading interest in Ireland among the Irish American Protestant population during that period, had an impact as well. Nevertheless, external trends, most notably the revival of anti-Catholic nativism in America during the Second Great Awakening, were also essential to breaking up the old nonsectarian Irish American identity and, combined with the transnational influence of the worldwide Catholic revival, strengthening the new Catholic one. As noted, at the turn of the twentieth century, the maturing of the Irish Catholic second generation had a powerful effect on Irish Catholics' reinvention of themselves as leaders of a new, pan-ethnic, militant American Catholic people. The revival of anti-Catholic prejudice, Vatican condemnations of Catholic liberalism, and the arrival of millions of southern and eastern European Catholic immigrants at the same time, however, were just as critical to provoking and shaping that reinvention. Persistent tension with non-Catholics and Vatican pressure through the twentieth century helped maintain that militant American Catholic community, and Irish Americans continued to be its leaders and models, even as Irish immigrants virtually disappeared and the American-born dominated the Irish American Catholic population. If Irish American Catholics remained religious outsiders, they became increasingly powerful and successful, in part, because of external events, ironically, two tragedies: an economic depression which stoked the growth of the American labor movement and made the Democrats the nation's majority party; and World War II, which ushered in a new era of prosperity for many of them. By the 1960s, that militant American Catholicism had begun to crack open, a less institutionally based and more personal Irish American identity emerged, and Irish Americans, who had seemed to ignore the land of their ancestors for much of the twentieth century, began to rediscover Ireland.

I first went to Ireland in the early 1980s and have visited it so often thereafter that I have lost track of the number of times. I also taught there twice: first at Dublin City University and more recently at University College Dublin. All eight of my great-grandparents were famine immigrants. Searching for the places they left in Ireland led my sister and me to get lost not long ago in eastern Kilkenny and ride a boat on the Blackwater River near Waterford. I understand the attraction of seeking those personal roots, and they, as well as Ireland's broader history, are very important to me. Yet, as I have written before, not a week had passed in my first trip to Ireland forty years ago before it became clear to me that I was not Irish. I realized that I had things in my head, some personal, some general, of people, games, events, organizations, heroes, places, and American contexts, in particular the presence of Yankee Protestants and Italian, Jewish, and other ethnic and racial Americans, which made up my history and that I took for granted but were critical to the making of Irish America for me. These were things that the people I was seeing on the street in Dublin then did not, could not, know except second hand, but they had their own, a very different, eclectic mix of such things, their own history, the foundation of their Ireland Irishness. I did not regret this realization, nor, clearly, did it stop me from going back to Ireland over and over again, but, indeed, if seemingly obvious, it was nonetheless a moment of clarity. Irish America was born in Ireland but has been made in "another country," America, forged in an often complicated, but richly human, history of contingency and adaptation.[12]

Notes

Introduction

1. Joann P. Kreig, *Whitman and the Irish* (Iowa City: University of Iowa Press, 2000), 12–13, quote 25, quotes 53–55, quote 70, 34–36, 53–75, 128–162, 163–175, 181–185; Walt Whitman, "Mannahatta," in *Leaves of Grass* (Minneapolis: First Avenue Editions, 2018), quote 606; Terry Golway, *Machine Made: Tammany Hall and the Creation of Modern American Politics* (New York: Norton, 2014), 107.

2. Total Ancestry Reported: Total Ancestry categories tallied for people with one or more ancestry categories reported: 2010 American Community Survey One-Year Estimates: Factfinder, census.gov; Kevin Kenny, *The American Irish: A History* (Harlow, UK: Pearson, 2000), 89–90, 181–182, 221; Kerby Miller, *Emigrants and Exiles: Ireland and the Irish Exodus to North America* (New York: Oxford University Press, 1985), 3, 137, 169, 291, 346–348.

3. Nathan Glazer and Daniel Patrick Moynihan, *Beyond the Melting Pot: The Negroes, Puerto Ricans, Jews, Italians, and Irish of New York City* (Cambridge, MA: MIT Press, 1970), 1–23, xxxvi–xliii; Michael Novak, *Unmeltable Ethnics: Politics and Culture in American Life,* 2d ed. (New Brunswick, NJ: Transaction, 1996); Richard Gambino, *Blood of My Blood: The Dilemma of the Italian Americans* (Garden City, NY: Anchor Books, 1975); Russell A. Kazal, "Revisiting Assimilation: The Rise, Fall, and Reappraisal of a Concept in American Ethnic History," *American Historical Review* 100, no. 2 (April 1995): 437–471.

4. Kathleen Neils Conzen, David A. Gerber, Ewa Morawska, George E. Pozzetta, and Rudolph J. Vecoli, "The Invention of Ethnicity: A Perspective from the U.S.A.," *Journal of American Ethnic History* 12, no. 1 (October 1, 1992): quote 5, 3–41; Donald L. Horowitz, *Ethnic Groups in Conflict* (Berkeley: University of California Press, 1985), xi–xiv, 3–140, 365–440; Yen L'Espiritu, *Asian American Pan Ethnicity: Bridging Institutions and Identities* (Philadelphia: Temple University Press, 1992), 1–111; Frederick Barth, "Ethnic Groups and Boundaries," in Werner Sollors, ed., *Theories of Ethnicity: A Classical Reader* (New York: New York University Press, 1996); Hasia Diner, *Hungering for America: Italian, Irish and Jewish Foodways in the Age of Migration* (Cambridge, MA: Harvard University Press, 2001), 53; Joan S. Wang, "Race, Gender and Laundry Work: The Roles of Chinese Laundries and American Working Women in the United States," *Journal of American Ethnic History* 24, no. 1 (2004): 58–99.

5. Conzen et al., "The Invention of Ethnicity," 5.

1. Old Ireland

1. Matthew Jacobson, *Whiteness of a Different Color: European Immigrants and the Alchemy of Race* (Cambridge, MA: Harvard University Press, 1998), quote 49–50.

2. F. H. A. Aalen, Kevin Whalen, and Matthew Stout, *Atlas of the Rural Irish Landscape* (Toronto: University of Toronto Press, 1994), 31–33; J. P. Mallory, *The Origins of the Irish* (London: Thames and Hudson, 2013), 11–159, 243–287; *New York Times,* December 22, 2021.

3. Aalen et al., *Atlas of the Rural Irish Landscape,* 44–53; Aidan O'Sullivan et al., eds., *Early Medieval Ireland, AD 400–1100: The Evidence from Archeological Excavations* (Dublin: Royal Irish Academy, 2021), 47–138, 179–214, 322–328.

4. Kenneth Nicholls, *Gaelic and Gaelicized Ireland in the Middle Ages: Gaelic History of Ireland IV* (Dublin: Gill, 1972), 10, 10–12; Donchaa O'Corrain, *Ireland before the Normans* (Dublin: Gill and Macmillan, 1972), 42, quote 48; O'Sullivan et al., *Early Medieval Ireland,* 325–326; Chris Wickham, *The Inheritance of Rome* (New York: Viking, 2009), quote 150, 164–166.

5. O'Corrain, *Ireland before the Normans,* 84–85; Kathleen Hughes, "The Church in Irish Society, 400–800," in Daibhi O'Croinin, ed., *A New History of Ireland, Volume I: Prehistoric and Early Ireland* (Oxford: Oxford University Press, 2005), 301–330; Wickham, *Inheritance,* 167–168; O'Sullivan et al., *Early Medieval Ireland,* 139–178, 320, 324–331.

6. O'Corrain, *Ireland before the Normans,* 22–23; Richard Roche, *The Norman Invasion of Ireland* (Dublin: Anvil Books, 1995), 223–224; Wickham, *Inheritance,* 495–500; O'Sullivan et al., *Early Medieval Ireland,* 328–331.

7. Marie Therese Flanagan, "Irish and Anglo-Norman Warfare in Twelfth Century Ireland," in Thomas Bartlett and Keith Jeffery, eds., *A Military History of Ireland* (Cambridge, UK: Cambridge University Press, 1996), 52–75.

8. Aalen et al., *Atlas of the Rural Irish Landscape,* 53–57; F. X. Martin, "Allies and Overlord," 67–96, and "Overlord Becomes Feudal Lord," 99–126, and James Lydon, "The Expansion and Consolidation of the Colony," 156–175, in A. M. Cosgrove, ed., *A New History of Ireland,* Volume II, *Medieval Ireland* (New York: Oxford University Press, 2008); Joep Leerson, *Mere Irish and Fior-Ghael* (Notre Dame, IN: University of Notre Dame Press for Field Day, 1997), quote 35–36; Roche, *Norman Invasion,* 224.

9. Lydon, "Years of Crisis," 156–175, Lydon, "A Land of War," 240–274, in Cosgrove, ed., *A New History of Ireland,* Volume II.

10. J. A. Watt, "Gaelic Polity and Cultural Identity," 324, and D. B. Quinn, "Aristocratic Autonomy," 591–617, in Cosgrove, ed., *A New History of Ireland,* Volume II; S. J. Connolly, *Contested Island, 1460–1635* (Oxford, UK: Oxford University Press, 2007), 50–51.

11. Connolly, *Contested Island,* 12, 22, 29, 210–272; K. W. Nicholls, "Gaelic Society and Economy," 397–435, in Cosgrove, ed., *A New History of Ireland,* Volume II; Nicholls, *Gaelic and Gaelicized Ireland,* 19, 36, 47.

12. Watt, "Gaelic Polity," in Cosgrove, ed., *A New History of Ireland,* Volume II, quote 349, 347–349.

13. Connolly, *Contested Ireland,* 58–200; Stephen Ellis, *Tudor Ireland: Crown, Community and the Conflict of Cultures, 1470–1603* (London: Longman, 1985), 19–182, 228–320.

14. Nicholas Canny, *Making Ireland British* (Oxford: Oxford University Press, 2001), 47–54, 167–178; Connolly, *Contested Island,* 333–396, 200–214; Nicholas Canny, "Identity Formation in Ireland: The Emergence of the Anglo-Irish," in Canny and Anthony Pagden, eds., *Colonial Identity in the Atlantic World* (Princeton, NJ: Princeton University Press, 1987), 159–163.

15. Canny, *Making Ireland British,* 198–248; Gillespie, *Colonial Ulster: The Settlement of East Ulster, 1600–1641* (Cork: Cork University Press, 1985) 55, 33–47; Marilyn Westerkamp, *Triumph of the Laity: The Migration of Religion from Scotland and Ireland to the Middle Colonies, 1625–1770* (New York: Oxford University Press, 1988), 15–33.

16. Louis M. Cullen, "The Irish Diaspora of the Seventeenth and Eighteenth Centuries," in Nicholas Canny, *Europeans on the Move: Studies on Emigration and Migration, 1500–1800* (Oxford: Oxford University Press, 1994), 113–121; John J. Silke, "The Irish Abroad," in Aidan Clark, Raymond Gillespie and James Maguire, eds., *A New History of Ireland,* Volume III (New York: Oxford University Press, 1993), 587–633.

17. Canny, *Making Ireland British,* 415–425; Nicholas Canny, "The Formation of the Irish Mind: Religion, Politics and Gaelic Irish Literature 1580–1750," *Past & Present* 95 (May 1, 1982): 91–116.

18. Canny, *Making Ireland British,* 390–397, quote 512, 467–512; S. J. Connolly, *Divided Kingdom: Ireland, 1630–1800* (Oxford: Oxford University Press, 2008), quote 36, 48, 8–50.

19. Michael O'Suchru, *God's Executioner: Oliver Cromwell and the Conquest of Ireland* (London: Oder and Oder, 2008), 22, 205–250; Connolly, *Divided Kingdom,* 101–138.

20. Connolly, *Divided Kingdom,* 91–93, 112–143, 165–166, quote 142.

21. Connolly, *Divided Kingdom,* 173–207.

22. S. J. Connolly, *Religion, Law and Power: The Making of Protestant Ireland, 1660–1760* (New York: Oxford University Press, 1993), 41–51; David Dickson, *Arctic Ireland: The Extraordinary Story of the Great Frost and Forgotten Famine of 1740–1741* (Belfast: White Row Press, 1997), 11–34, 50–56; Connolly, *Divided Kingdom,* 344–355.

23. Connolly, *Divided Kingdom,* 344–383; Aalen et al., *Atlas of the Rural Irish Landscape,* 159–162, 186–189, 19–203.

24. Connolly, *Divided Kingdom,* 354–368; Louis M. Cullen, *The Emergence of Modern Ireland, 1600–1900* (New York: Holmes & Meier, 1981), 23–49; Peter Connell, *The Land and People of County Meath, 1750–1850* (Dublin: Four Courts Press, 2004), 50–86.

25. Connolly, *Divided Kingdom,* 164; Joel Mokyr and Cormac Ó Gráda, "New Developments in Irish Population History, 1700–1850," *Economic History Review* 37, no. 4 (November

1984): 473–488; Cormac Ó Gráda, *Ireland: A New Economic History, 1780–1939* (New York: Oxford University Press, 1994), quote 17, 3–23; Aalen et al., *Atlas of the Rural Irish Landscape,* 106–121.

26. Connell, *Meath,* 50–80; David Dickson, *Old World Colony: Cork and South Munster, 1630–1830* (Cork: Cork University Press, 2005), quote 283, 283–288.

27. Aalen et al., *Atlas of the Rural Irish Landscape,* 70–88; Jonathan Bardon, *A History of Ulster* (Belfast: Blackstone, 2001), 179–197.

28. Bardon, *History of Ulster,* quote 183, 185, 179–205; Ian McBride, *Eighteenth Century Ireland: The Isle of Slaves* (Dublin: Gill and Macmillan, 2009), 110–111, 56–57; Neal Garnham, "How Violent Was Nineteenth Century Ireland?" *Irish Historical Studies* 30, no. 119 (May 1997): 377–392.

29. Bardon, *History of Ulster,* 184–187; Cullen, *Emergence,* 15–46, 63–84, 88–128; Dickson, *Old Colony,* 170–248, 288–320; Kevin Whelan, *Tree of Liberty: Radicalism, Catholicism and the Construction of Irish Identity, 1760–1830* (Notre Dame, IN: University of Notre Dame Press, 1996), 27–47.

30. Whelan, *Tree of Liberty,* 27–31; Connolly, *Divided Kingdom,* 266–267.

31. Connolly, *Divided Kingdom,* 197–203; McBride, *Eighteenth Century Ireland,* 194–202.

32. McBride, *Eighteenth Century Ireland,* 194–245; Emmet J. Larkin, *The Pastoral Role of the Roman Catholic Church in Pre-Famine Ireland, 1750–1859* (Dublin: Four Courts Press, 2006), 29, 144; Cullen, *Emergence,* 109–126; Connolly, *Divided Kingdom,* 198–203, 249–259; Whelan, *Tree of Liberty,* 34–38; Dickson, *Old Colony,* 166–169.

33. McBride, *Eighteenth Century Ireland,* 115; Connolly, *Religion, Law and Power,* 114–115; Connolly, *Divided Kingdom,* quote 495.

34. McBride, *Eighteenth Century Ireland,* 196, 217, 232–233, 312–313; Connolly, *Divided Kingdom,* 304–305; Bardon, *History of Ulster,* 170; Whelan, *Tree of Liberty,* 36–37, 111–112.

35. C. D. A. Leighton, *Catholicism in a Protestant Kingdom: A Study of the Irish Ancien Regime* (New York: St. Martin's Press, 1964), 45–66, 89–110; Connolly, *Divided Kingdom,* 293–297.

36. McBride, *Eighteenth Century Ireland,* 122–123, quote 191, 190–193, 376–377; Whelan, *Tree of Liberty,* quote 33, 33–34; Pauline Maier, *The Old Revolutionaries* (New York: Norton, 1976), quote 254; Connolly, *Divided Kingdom,* quote 103, 290–292, quote 292; Breandon O'Buachalla, "Irish Jacobite Poetry," *Irish Review,* no. 12 (1992): quotes 41, 43; Breandon O'Buachalla, "Irish Jacobitism and Irish Nationalism: The Literary Evidence," in Michael O'Dea and Kevin Whelan, eds., *Nations and Nationalisms: France, Britain, Ireland and the Eighteenth Century Context* (Oxford: Oxford University Press, 1995), 111.

37. Liam Chambers, "A Displaced Intelligentsia: Aspects of Irish Catholic Thought in Ancien

Regime France," 157–174, and Priscilla O'Connor, "Irish Clerics and Jacobites in Early Eighteenth Century Paris," 188, 175–190, in Thomas O'Connor, ed., *The Irish in Europe, 1580–1815* (Dublin: Four Courts Press, 2001); McBride, *Eighteenth Century Ireland,* 186–188; Cullen, "The Irish Diaspora," 113–152.

38. Connolly, *Religion, Law and Power,* 51–59; Connolly, *Divided Kingdom,* 350–351. McBride, *Eighteenth Century,* quote 125.

39. James S. Donnelly Jr., "Whiteboys Movement," *Irish Historical Studies* catalogue 21 (81) (March 1978): 22–23, 25, 29–31, 33, 40–54; James S. Donnelly Jr., "Irish Agrarian Rebellion: Whiteboys of 1769–1776," *Proceedings of the Royal Irish Academy* 83, no. 12 (1983): 293–331; McBride, *Eighteenth Century Ireland,* 312–341.

40. Toby Barnard, "The Common Name of Ireland," 230–235, and Ian McBride, "Protestantism, Ethnicity, and Irish Identities, 1660–1769," 243, 248, in Tony Claydon and Ian McBride, eds., *Protestantism and National Identity: Britain and Ireland, 1650–1850* (Cambridge, UK: Cambridge University Press, 1998); Connolly, *Divided Kingdom,* 218–245.

41. McBride, *Eighteenth Century Ireland,* 168, 286–294; Connolly, *Divided Kingdom,* 204–207, 279–285; Patrick Griffin, *The People with No Name: Ireland's Ulster Scots, America's Scots Irish, and the Creation of a British Atlantic World, 1689–1764* (Princeton, NJ: Princeton University Press, 2001), 9–25.

42. Bardon, *History of Ulster,* 171–172, 184–185, 248; Griffin, *People with No Name,* 27–31; Marilyn Cohen, "Introduction," 1–33, and Jane Gray, "The Irish and Scottish Linen Industries in the Eighteenth Century," 37–69, in Marilyn Cohen, ed., *The Warp of Ulster's Past: Interdisciplinary Perspectives on the Irish Linen Industry* (New York: St. Martin's Press, 1997), 13–62; McBride, *Eighteenth Century Ireland,* 286–294.

43. Connolly, *Divided Kingdom,* 279–285; Griffin, *People with No Name,* 37–64.

44. Bardon, *History of Ulster,* quote 208, 206–209; Eoin Magennis, "A 'Presbyterian Insurrection'? Reconsidering the Hearts of Oak Disturbances of July 1763," *Irish Historical Studies* 21, no. 122 (November 1988): 165–187; James S. Donnelly Jr., "Hearts of Oak: Hearts of Steel," *Studia Hibernica* no. 21 (1981): 7–73; McBride, *Eighteenth Century Ireland,* 323–328.

2. Irish Immigration in the Colonial Era

1. D. B. Quinn, *Set Fair for Roanoke: Voyages and Colonies, 1584–1606* (Chapel Hill: University of North Carolina Press, 1985), 42, 55, 90, 125–127.

2. O'Suchru, *God's Executioner,* 221–250; Aaron Fogleman, "From Slaves, Convicts and Servants to Free Passengers: The Transformation of Immigration in the Era of the American Revolution," *Journal of American History* 85 (1998): 43–67; Russell Menard, "British Migration to the Chesapeake Colonies in the Seventeenth Century," in Lois Carr, Philip Morgan, and Jean Burrell Risen, *Colonial Chesapeake Society* (Williamsburg, VA: Institute

of Early American History, 1988), 122–126; Aaron Schatzman, *Servants into Planters* (New York: Garland, 1989), 47, 74; Darrett Rutman, *Winthrop's Boston, Portrait of a Puritan Town, 1630–1649* (Williamsburg, VA: Omohundro, 1965), quote 109.

3. Fogleman, "From Slaves," 69. Kerby A. Miller, *Emigrants and Exiles: Ireland and the Irish Exodus to North America* (New York: Oxford University Press, 1985), 137; Thomas Truxes, *Irish American Trade, 1660–1783* (Cambridge, UK: Cambridge University Press, 1988), 129; David N. Doyle, *Ireland, Irishmen and Revolutionary America, 1760–1820* (Dublin: Mercier Press, 1981), 51–53; Marianne S. Wokeck, *Trade in Strangers: The Beginnings of Mass Migration to North America* (University Park: Pennsylvania State University Press, 1999), 183–185; R. J. Dickson, *Ulster Emigration to Colonial America, 1717–1775* (London: Routledge, Kegan and Paul, 1966), 3–5, 62–64, 238–271.

4. Miller, *Emigrants and Exiles,* 137, 152, 149, 152; Kevin Kenny, *The American Irish: A History* (New York: Longmans, 2000), 7; Doyle, *Ireland, Irishmen,* 51–61.

5. Miller, *Emigrants and Exiles,* 142–149, 152–156; Kerby Miller, Bruce Boling, and David Doyle, eds., *Irish Immigration in the Land of Canaan: Letters and Memoirs from Colonial and Revolutionary America, 1675–1815* (New York: Oxford University Press, 2003), 24–25, 31; Doyle, *Ireland, Irishmen,* 93–102.

6. Miller, *Emigrants and Exiles,* 20, 142, 152, 158, quote 160.

7. Griffin, *People with No Name,* quote 79, 67–95, 159; Miller, *Emigrants and Exiles,* 72–75, 153–159; Miller et al., *Land of Canaan,* 24, quote 29, 324, 31–37; Maurice Bric, *Ireland, Philadelphia and the Re-Invention of America, 1760–1800* (Dublin: Four Courts Press, 2009), 25–42, quote 26 quote 27.

8. Miller, *Emigrants and Exiles,* quote 142, 144; Jill Lepore, *New York Burning: Liberty, Slavery, and Conspiracy in Eighteenth-Century Manhattan* (New York: Alfred A. Knopf, 2005), 178–190; Miller et al., *Land of Canaan,* quote 54.

9. Kersten Block and Jenny Shaw, "Subjects Without an Empire: The Irish in the Early Modern Caribbean," *Past and Present,* 210, 49, 59, 33–60; Sean Cadigan, *Newfoundland and Labrador: A History* (Toronto: University of Toronto Press, 2009), 49–70; Bric, *Ireland, Philadelphia,* 21–24, quote 29, 59.

10. Doyle, *Ireland, Irishmen,* 61–70; Miller, *Emigrants and Exiles,* 147, 143–144; Miller et al., *Land of Canaan,* 270–272; Bernard Bailyn, *Voyagers to the West: A Passage in the Peopling of America on the Eve of the Revolution* (New York: Knopf, 1986), 126–203.

11. Bric, *Ireland, Philadelphia,* 29, 59; Miller, *Emigrants and Exiles,* 141–146; Thomas M. Doerflinger, *A Vigorous Spirit of Enterprise: Merchants and Economic Development in Revolutionary Philadelphia* (Chapel Hill: University of North Carolina Press, 1986), 107–114.

12. Dickson, *Ulster Emigration to Colonial America,* 200–205, 220, 235; Griffin, *People with No Name,* 94–96; Bric, *Ireland, Philadelphia,* 25–26.

13. Miller, *Emigrants and Exiles,* 147–151; Thomas L. Purvis, "The European Ancestry of the

United States Population, 1790: A Symposium," *William and Mary Quarterly* 41 (January 1984): 98.

14. Griffin, *People with No Name,* 91, 90–94; James G. Leyburn, *The Scotch Irish: A Social History* (Chapel Hill: University of North Carolina Press, 1962), 236–242; Doyle, *Ireland, Irishmen,* 39–50, 90, 80; Miller et al., *Land of Canaan,* 143–146, 234, 250; Bric, *Ireland, Philadelphia,* 34; Truxes, *Irish American Trade,* 140–142; Joyce Goodfriend, "'Upon a Bunch of Straw': The Irish in Colonial New York City," in Ronald H. Bayor and Timothy J. Meagher, eds., *The New York Irish* (Baltimore: Johns Hopkins University Press, 1996), 35–47; Purvis, "European Ancestry," 98.

15. Griffin, *People with No Name,* 89–92, 99, 115, 157–163; Bric, *Ireland, Philadelphia,* 26, 35–38, 44; Doyle, *Ireland, Irishmen,* 57, 98–101; Miller et al., *Land of Canaan,* 157; James Lemon, *The Best Poor Man's Country: A Geographical Study of Early Southeastern Pennsylvania* (New York: Norton, 1976); Warren Hofstra, *The Planting of New Virginia: Settlement and Landscape in the Shenandoah Valley* (Baltimore: Johns Hopkins University Press, 2004), 25–40, 312; Purvis, "European Ancestry," 98; Leyburn, *Scotch Irish,* 210–223; Miller, *Emigrants and Exiles,* 161.

16. David N. Doyle, "Scots Irish or Scotch Irish," in J. J. Lee and Marion Casey, eds., *The Making of Irish America* (New York: New York University Press, 2006), 151–170; Grady McWhiney, *Cracker Culture: Celtic Ways in the Old South* (University: University of Alabama Press, 1988); David Hackett Fischer, *Albion's Seed: Four British Folkways in America* (New York: Oxford University Press, 1991); Rowland Berthoff, "'Celtic Mist': Over the Old South," *Journal of Southern History* 52, no. 4 (November 1986): 523–546.

17. Doyle, "Scots Irish," quote 163; Hofstra, *The Planting,* 209–214; Adrienne Hood, "The Gender Division of Labor in the Production of Textiles in Eighteenth Century Rural Pennsylvania (Rethinking the New England Model)," *Journal of Social History* 27, no. 3 (Spring 1994): 539–542.

18. Griffin, *People with No Name,* 106–109, 115, 159; Hofstra, *The Planting,* 24–27; Timothy Silver, *A New Face on the Countryside: Indians, Colonists, and Slaves in the South Atlantic Forests, 1520–1800* (Cambridge, UK: Cambridge University Press, 1990), 96; Kevin Kenny, *Peaceable Kingdom: The Paxton Boys and the Destruction of William Penn's Holy Experiment* (New York: Oxford University Press, 2009), 76.

19. Miller, *Emigrants and Exiles,* 153, 157; Marjolene Kars, *Breaking Loose Together: The Regulation Rebellion in Pre-Revolutionary North Carolina* (Chapel Hill: University of North Carolina Press, 2007), 21, 60–62, 74; Griffin, *People with No Name,* 138–142; Seth Rohrer, *Wandering Souls: Protestant Migrations in America, 1630–1865* (Chapel Hill: University of North Carolina Press, 2010), quote 101, 98–102.

20. Warren Hofstra, "'The Extension of His Majesties' Dominions': The Virginia Backcountry and the Reconfiguration of the Imperial Frontier," *Journal of American History* 84, no. 4

(March 1999): 1284–1286; Hofstra, "American Backcountries," 453–457, in Louise Breen, ed., *Converging Worlds: Communities and Cultures in Colonial America* (New York: Routledge, 2012); Griffin, *People with No Name,* 137–141; Lemon, *Best Poor Man's Country,* 125; Miller et al., *Land of Canaan,* 135–141.

21. David Miller, "Presbyterianism and 'Modernization' in Ulster," *Past and Present* (August 1978): 80, 74–75; Warren Hofstra, "Land Ethnicity, Community at the Opequon Settlement, Virginia, 1730–1800," *Virginia Magazine of History and Biography* 98, no. 3 (July 1990): 423–448; Richard McMaster, "Searching for Community: Carlisle Pennsylvania, 1750s–1780s," in Warren A. Hofstra, ed., *Ulster to America: The Scots-Irish Migration Experience, 1680–1830* (Knoxville: University of Tennessee Press, 2011), 106–133; Rohrer, *Wandering Souls,* 93–101.

22. Griffin, *People with No Name,* 1–8.

23. Miller et al., *Land of Canaan,* 381; Rohrer, *Wandering Souls,* 105; Westerkamp, *Tradition of the Laity,* 140–148.

24. Griffin, *People with No Name,* 116–123; Miller et al., *Land of Canaan,* quote 381, 401–406; Westerkamp, *Tradition of the Laity,* 146–160.

25. Westerkamp, *Tradition of the Laity,* 14–34, 117–118; David Miller, "Searching for a New World: The Background and Baggage of the Scotch Irish Immigrant," in Hofstra, ed., *Ulster to America,* 13–16; Miller, *In the Land of Canaan,* quote, 406, quote 401.

26. Jon Butler, *Religion in a Colonial America* (New York: Oxford University Press, 1994), 96–107; Griffin, *People with No Name,* quote 149.

27. Wayland Dunaway, *The Scotch Irish of Colonial Pennsylvania* (Chapel Hill: University of North Carolina Press, 1944), 202–203; Sidney Ahlstrom, *A Religious History of the American People* (New Haven: Yale University Press, 1972), 274–279; Janet Moore Lindman, *Bodies of Belief: Baptist Community in Early America* (Philadelphia: University of Pennsylvania Press, 2011), 27–31; Ned Landsman, "Presbyterians, Evangelicals and the Educational Culture of the Middle Colonies," *Pennsylvania History* (1997): 64, 168–192; Elizabeth Nybakken, "New Light on the Old Side: Irish Influence on Colonial Presbyterianism," *Journal of American History* 68, no. 4 (1982): quote 820, 813–832.

28. Miller et al., *Land of Canaan,* 383–386, 396–399; Rohrer, *Wandering Souls,* 93–101; Lindman, *Bodies,* 32–56.

29. Kars, *Breaking Loose,* quote 87, 85–87, 97; Richard Maxwell Brown, *The South Carolina Regulation* (Cambridge, MA: Belknap Press, 1963), 15–24; Miller, "Background and Baggage," 15–17; Lacy Ford, *Origins of Southern Radicalism* (New York: Oxford University Press, 1988), 20–28.

30. Richard Beeman, *The Varieties of Political Experience in Eighteenth Century America* (Philadelphia: University of Pennsylvania Press, 2009), 162–164.

31. Griffin, *People with No Name,* 112–114, 135–136, 166; Fred Anderson, *Crucible of War: The Seven Years War and the Fates of Empire in British North America, 1754–1766* (New York: Vintage Books, 2001), 11–21; Hofstra, *The Planting,* 101, 122–125; Kenny, *Peaceable Kingdom,* quote 42, 11–61.

32. Kenny, *Peaceable Kingdom,* 41–61; Anderson, *Crucible,* 22–73; Matthew Ward, *Breaking the Backcountry: The Seven Years War in Virginia and Pennsylvania, 1754–1765* (Pittsburgh: University of Pittsburgh Press, 2003), 9–35.

33. Ward, *Breaking the Backcountry,* quote 72, 36–72; Miller et al., *Land of Canaan,* 394, 384–399; Anderson, *Crucible,* 75–123; Kenny, *The Peaceable Kingdom,* 65–75.

34. Krista Camenzid, "Violence, Race and the Paxton Boys," in William Pencak and Daniel Richter, eds., *Friends and Enemies in Penn's Woods: Indians, Colonists and the Racial Construction of Pennsylvania* (University Park: Pennsylvania State University Press, 2004), 209; Kenny, *The Peaceable Kingdom,* 76–82, quote, 80; Ward, *Breaking the Backcountry,* 76–122.

35. Anderson, *Crucible,* 22–73; Ward, *Breaking the Backcountry,* 124–184; Kenny, *Peaceable Kingdom,* 92–111.

36. Brown, *Regulation,* 4–15, quote 7; Kars, *Breaking Loose,* 6–14.

37. Patrick Griffin, *American Leviathan: Empire, Nation and the Revolutionary Frontier* (New York: Hill and Wang, 2007), 50, 90; Kenny, *Peaceable Kingdom,* 118–119.

38. Griffin, *Leviathan,* 62, 120–121.

39. Griffin, *People with No Name,* 168–172; Griffin, *Leviathan,* 46–49, 64–67; Kenny, *Peaceable Kingdom,* 123–155.

40. Kenny, *Peaceable Kingdom,* quote, 167, quote 164, 205–207; Griffin, *People with No Name,* quote 170, 168–173; Griffin, *Leviathan,* 74–78, 76; Benjamin Bankhurst, "A Looking Glass for Presbyterians: Recasting a Prejudice in Late Colonial Pennsylvania," *Pennsylvania Magazine of History and Biography* 133, no. 4 (2009): 317–348.

41. Bernard Bailyn, *The Peopling of North America: An Introduction* (New York: Vintage, 1988), quote 144; Ward, *Backcountry,* 75; Brown, *Regulation,* quote 32.

42. Beeman, *Varieties,* 177–183; Hofstra, "American Backcountries," 459; Jos. A. Waddles, *Annals of Augusta County, Virginia From 1726–1871* (Staunton, VA: C. Russell Caldwell, 1902), 122, 210, 141–142, 178.

43. Beeman, *Varieties,* 167, 173–177; Kars, *Breaking Loose,* 21–50, 36, 44–45.

44. Kars, *Breaking Loose,* quote 141, 109–146, 141, 140–146; Beeman, *Varieties,* 173, 169–177.

45. Kars, *Breaking Loose,* 169–173, 108–146.

46. Brown, *Regulation,* 37–79, 110–113; Beeman, *Varieties,* 169–177; Rachel Klein, *Unification of a Slave State: The Rise of the Planter Class in the South Carolina Backcountry, 1760–1808* (Chapel Hill: University of North Carolina Press, 2012), quote 48, 9–46, 47–51.

47. Klein, *Unification,* 109–268; Brown, *Regulation,* 147.

48. Griffin, *People with No Name,* 11, 123; Beeman, *Varieties,* 207–215, 217–218.

49. Beeman, *Varieties,* 246, 226–241; Bric, *Ireland, Philadelphia,* 46–59; James Hutson, *Pennsylvania Politics, 1746–1770* (Princeton, NJ: Princeton University Press, 1972), 101, 207–212; Doyle, *Ireland, Irishmen,* 122–124.

50. Beeman, *Varieties,* quote 246, 226–249; Hutson, *Pennsylvania Politics,* 101–103, 209–212; Kenny, *Peaceable Kingdom,* 181–202; Doyle, *Ireland, Irishmen,* 122–124; Bric, *Ireland, Philadelphia,* quote 58, 37–49.

51. Kenny, *Peaceable Kingdom,* quote 181; Wayne L. Bockelman and Owen S. Ireland, "The Internal Revolution in Pennsylvania: An Ethnic-Religious Interpretation," *Pennsylvania History* (April 1974): 41, 129, 130, 134.

52. Miller et al., *Land of Canaan,* quote 543.

53. Bric, *Ireland, Philadelphia,* 151–155; Richard Alan Ryerson, *The Revolution Is Now Begun: The Radical Committees of Philadelphia, 1765–1776* (Philadelphia: University of Pennsylvania Press, 1978), quote 65, 65–88; Catherine B. Shannon, "'With Good Will Doing Service': The Charitable Irish Society of Boston," *Historical Journal of Massachusetts* 43, no. 1 (2015): 94–123.

3. Irish America in the Age of Revolution

1. Michael Durey, *Transatlantic Radicals and the Early American Republic* (Lawrence: University Press of Kansas, 1997), quote 83.

2. Doyle, *Ireland, Irishmen,* quote 110, 109–114; Michael Stephenson, *Patriot Battles: How the War of Independence Was Fought* (New York: Harper Collins, 2007), 29–30.

3. Stephenson, *Patriot,* 29; Roger S. Warren, "Chester County," 9, 10–12; John B. Frantz and William Pencak, *Beyond Philadelphia: The American Revolution in the Pennsylvania Hinterland* (University Park: Pennsylvania State University Press, 1998); Hutson, *Pennsylvania Politics,* 210, 229, 244–245; Miller et al., *Land of Canaan,* quote, 484, 483–484; Bric, *Ireland, Philadelphia,* 61, 65, 67; Doyle, *Ireland, Irishmen,* 127–133; Robert Emmett Curran, *Papist Devils: Catholics in British America, 1574–1783* (Washington, DC: Catholic University Press, 2014), 264–267; Mary Jane Farrelly, *Papist Patriots: The Making of an American Identity* (New York: Oxford University Press, 2012), 243–245.

4. Owen S. Ireland, "The Ethnic-Religious Dimension of Pennsylvania Politics, 1778–1779," *William and Mary Quarterly* 30, no. 3 (July 1, 1973): quote 424, 423–448; Bric, *Ireland, Philadelphia,* 61–69; Ireland and Bockelman, "Internal Revolution," 132; Warren, "Chester County," 11; Beeman, *Varieties,* 178–183.

5. Beeman, *Varieties,* 177–183.

6. Beeman, *Varieties,* 177, 176; Kars, *Breaking Loose,* 13, 212–213, quote 213; Doyle, *Ireland, Irishmen,* 136, 135–136; B. G. Moss, "The Roles of the Scots and Scotch-Irishmen in the Southern Campaigns of the War of American Independence, 1780–1783" (PhD disserta-

tion, University of St. Andrews, 1979), 90–92, 201, 250–275; Robert Stansbury Lambert, *South Carolina Loyalists in the American Revolution* (Columbia: University of South Carolina Press, 1987), 27–29, 306; Miller et al., *Land of Canaan,* quote 562, quote 561, 559–566; Klein, *Unification,* 78–86, 80; Brown, *Regulation,* 122.

7. David Dickson, *New Foundations: Ireland 1660–1800* (Dublin: Helicon, 2000), 157–170; Vincent Morley, *Irish Opinion and the American Revolution, 1760–1783* (Cambridge, UK: Cambridge University Press, 2002), 99–124, 15, 47, 202; Nancy J. Curtin, *The United Irishmen: Popular Politics in Ulster and Dublin, 1791–1798* (Oxford: Clarendon, 1994), 18–21; Farrelly, *Papist Patriots,* 245–246.

8. Dickson, *New Foundations,* 157–199; Bardon, *History of Ulster,* 212–223; Curtin, *United Irishmen,* 21.

9. Dickson, *New Foundations,* 157–215; Whelan, *Tree of Liberty,* 41–59 quote 71 quote 73, 71–90, 99–129; Curtin, *United Irishmen,* 48; Marianne Elliott, *Wolfe Tone: Prophet of Irish Independence* (New Haven: Yale University Press, 1989), 115, quote 127, 122–156, 211–233; Paul Bew, *Ireland: The Politics of Enmity, 1789–1806* (Oxford: Oxford University Press, 2007), 10, 15–31.

10. Marianne Curtin, *United Irishmen,* 18–68, 74; Bardon, *History of Ulster,* 225, 223–235, quote, 229; Elliott, "Religious Polarization and Sectarianism in the Ulster Rebellion," 280–281; Daniel Gahan, "The Rebellion of 1798 in South Leinster," 109–121; Breandan Mac Suibhne, "Politicization and Paramilitarism: Northwest and Southwest Ulster, 1772–98," 243–278 and David Dickson, "Smoke Without Fire? Munster and the 1798 Rebellion," 151–153, 171, all in Thomas Bartlett, Daire Keogh, and Kevin Whelan eds., *1798: A Bicentenary Perspective* (Dublin: Four Courts Press, 2003); Jim Smyth, *The Men of No Property: Irish Radicals and Popular Politics in the Late Eighteenth Century* (New York: St. Martin's Press, 1992), 105, 104–105.

11. Bardon, *History of Ulster,* 228–235; Gahan, "South Leinster," 109–121; Dickson, "Smoke Without Fire," 147–173; Guy Beiner, *Remembering the Year of the French: Irish Folk History and Social Meaning* (Madison: University of Wisconsin Press, 2006), 6–8; James S. Donnelly Jr., "Sectarianism in 1798 and in Catholic Nationalist Memory," in Laurence M. Geary, ed., *Rebellion and Remembrance in Modern Ireland* (Dublin: Four Courts, 2001), 18–21, 32–34.

12. Charles Fanning, "Robert Emmet in Nineteenth Century America," *New Hibernia Review* 8, no. 4 (2004): 53–83.

13. Aalen et al., *Atlas of the Rural Irish Landscape,* 83; David Dickson, "Derry's Backyard: The Barony of Inishowen," 421–426; Marina O'Donnell, "Settlement and Society in the Barony of East Inishowen," 532–536, in William Nolan, Liam Ronayne, and Maired Dunlevy, eds., *Donegal: History and Society* (Dublin: Geography Publication, 1995); Norma Dawson, "Illicit Distillation and the Revenue Police in Ireland in the Eighteenth and

Nineteenth Centuries," *Irish Jurist*, 12, no. 2 (Winter 1977): 282–284; O'Grada, *New Economic History*, 6–29, 274–285; Dickson, *Old Colony*, 283–398; Kevin O'Neill, *Family and Farm in Pre-Famine Ireland: The Parish of Killishandra* (Madison: University of Wisconsin, 1989), 30–41, 78–107; Connell, *Meath*, 60, 85–89; Donald E. Jordan, *Land and Popular Politics in Ireland: County Mayo from the Plantation to the Land War* (New York: Cambridge University Press, 1994); L. M. Cullen, "Economic Development, 1750–1800," 170–187; J. H. Andrews, "Land and People c. 1780," 245, in T. W. Moody and W. E. Vaughn, eds., *A New History of Ireland: Eighteenth Century Ireland*, Volume IV (Oxford: Clarendon Press, 1998); Cormac Ó Gráda, "Industry and Communications, 1801–1845," in W. E. Vaughn, ed. *A New History of Ireland, Ireland Under the Union*, Volume V (Oxford: Oxford University Press, 1989), 139–141.

14. Miller, *Emigrants and Exiles*, 171–179; Paul W. Roberts, "Caravats and Shanavests: Whiteboyism and Faction Fights in East Munster," in Samuel Clark and James S. Donnelly Jr., eds., *Irish Peasants: Violence and Political Unrest, 1780–1914* (Madison: University of Wisconsin Press, 1983), 64–100.

15. Bric, *Ireland, Philadelphia*, 123; Fogleman, "From Slaves," 74; Hans-Jürgen Grabbe, "European Immigration to the United States in the Early National Period, 1783–1820," *Proceedings of the American Philosophical Society*, 133, no. 2 (June 1, 1989): 194–197.

16. Bric, *Ireland, Philadelphia*, 104, 123, quote 105; Miller et al., *Land of Canaan*, 94–116.

17. Cormac O'Grada, "Across the Briny Ocean: Some Thoughts on Irish Emigration to America, 1800–1850," in T. M. Devine and David Dickson, eds., *Ireland and Scotland, 1500–1850: Parallels and Contrasts in Economic and Social Development* (Edinburgh: Donald, 1983), 123–124; Fogleman, "From Slaves," 62–68; Bric, *Ireland, Philadelphia* 99, 123–124; Durey, *Transatlantic Radicals*, 87, 130, 139, 167, 199, 204; Peter Gilmore and Kerby Miller, "Searching for Irish Freedom—Settling for 'Scotch Irish' Respectability: Southwestern Pennsylvania, 1790–1810," in Warren Hofstra, ed., *Ulster to America: The Scots-Irish Migration Experience, 1680–1830* (Knoxville: University of Tennessee Press, 2011), quote 167; Miller et al., *Land of Canaan*, quote 199.

18. Edward C. Carter, "Naturalization in Philadelphia, 1789–1806: 'A Wild Irishman Under Every Federalist's Bed,'" *Proceedings of the American Philosophical Society* (June 1989): 133, 187; Edwin Burrows and Mike Wallace, *Gotham: A History of New York City to 1898* (New York: Oxford University Press, 1999), 265–289, 333–352; Anne Hartfield, "Profile of a Pluralistic Parish, Saint Peter's Roman Catholic Church, New York City: 1785–1815," *Journal of American Ethnic History* 12 (April 1993): 36; Miller et al., *Land of Canaan*, 287; Margaret McAleer, "Civil Strangers: The Irish in Philadelphia During the Early National Period" (PhD dissertation, Georgetown University, 1997), 26–27.

19. Thomas P. Slaughter, *The Whiskey Rebellion: Frontier Epilogue to the American Revolution* (New York: Oxford University Press, 1986), 6, 64–75; Donald Ratcliffe, *Party Spirit in a*

Frontier Republic: Democratic Politics in Ohio, 1793–1821 (Columbus: Ohio State University Press, 1996), 89, 119; Gilmore and Miller, "Searching for Irish Freedom," 166–178; Griffin, *Leviathan,* 187–230; McAleer, "Civil Strangers," 53–61; Miller et al., *Land of Canaan,* 201–218, 190; Purvis, "European Ancestry," 98.

20. Slaughter, *Whiskey Rebellion,* 46–60; Jackson Turner Main, *The Anti-Federalists: Critics of the Constitution, 1781–1788* (Chapel Hill: University of North Carolina Press, 2017), 190–193; Alfred Young, *The Democratic Republicans of New York: The Origins, 1763–1797* (Chapel Hill: University of North Carolina Press, 1967), 34–36, 44–54; Owen Ireland, "Partisanship and the Constitution," *Pennsylvania History* 45, no. 4 (1978): 315–322.

21. Gordon Wood, *Empire of Liberty: A History of the Early Republic* (New York: Oxford University Press, 2009), quotes 216–217, 1–52.

22. Griffin, *Leviathan,* quote 223, 225, 227, 213–246; Slaughter, *Whiskey Rebellion,* 75–204, 217–221.

23. Gilmore and Miller, "Searching for Irish Freedom," quote 184, 182–186; Griffin, *Leviathan,* quote 228, 227–228.

24. Eugene Link, *Democratic-Republican Societies, 1790–1800* (New York: Columbia University Press, 1942), 15, 13–15, 131, 133–135; Warren Hofstra and Robert D. Mitchell, "Town and Country in Backcountry Virginia: Winchester and the Shenandoah Valley, 1730–1800," *Journal of Southern History* 59, no. 4 (November 1, 1993): 644.

25. Wood, *Empire of Liberty,* quote 217, 216–218, 246–254; Hugh Brackenridge, *Modern Chivalry: Containing the Adventures of a Captain and Teague O'Regan, His Servant,* Volume I (Pittsburgh: Patterson and Lambeck, 1819), online quote 7, 16, quote 1.

26. Bric, *Ireland, Philadelphia,* 178, 185–189, 196, 241–246; Link, *Democratic-Republican Societies,* 89; Richard Miller, *Philadelphia, The Federalist City: A Study of Urban Politics, 1789–1801* (Port Washington, NY: Kennikat Press, 1976), 30, 53–71; David Wilson, *United Irishmen, United States* (Ithaca: Cornell University Press, 1998), quote 41; Jason K. Duncan, *Citizens or Papists? The Politics of Anti-Catholicism in New York, 1685–1821* (New York: Fordham University Press, 2005), 70; Young, *Democratic Republicans,* 440–443, 444–448.

27. Wood, *Empire of Liberty,* quote 253; Durey, *Transatlantic Radicals,* 224–229; Wilson, *United Irishmen,* 40, 160–164; Kim T. Phillips, "Philadelphia's Democratic-Republicans and the Origins of Modern Politics," *Pennsylvania Magazine of History and Biography* 3 (1977): quote 378.

28. Bric, *Ireland, Philadelphia,* quotes 229, 215–234, 263, quote 267, 276–279, 282; Miller, *Federalist City,* 53–54, 60, 71, 115; Wood, *Empire of Liberty,* 227–230; Durey, *Transatlantic Radicals,* 244, 253–255.

29. Burrows and Wallace, *Gotham,* 322–325; Jason K. Duncan, *Citizens or Papists? The Politics of Anti-Catholicism in New York, 1685–1821* (New York: Fordham University Press, 2005), 103–104, 121–123, 130; Durey, *Transatlantic Radicals,* 121–130, 270; Young, *Ori-*

gins, 571; Bric, *Ireland, Philadelphia,* 283–289; Edward C. Carter, "A 'Wild Irishman,'" 184; Margaret McAleer, "In Defense of Civil Society: Irish Radicals in Philadelphia during the 1790s," *Early American Studies* 4, no. 1 (2003): 189; Dale Light, *Rome in the New Republic: Conflict and Community in Philadelphia Catholicism Between the Revolution and the Civil War* (Notre Dame, IN: University of Notre Dame Press, 1996), 53; Kerby Miller, "Scotch Irish Ethnicity in Early America: Its Regional and Political Origins," in Kerby A. Miller, *Ireland and Irish America: Culture, Class and Transatlantic Migration* (Dublin: Field Day, 2008), 135–138.

30. Kenneth Keller, "Cultural Conflict in Early Nineteenth Century Pennsylvania Politics," *Pennsylvania Magazine of History and Biography* 110, no. 4 (October 1986): 509–530; Durey, *Transatlantic Radicals,* 184, 185–186, 269–274; Miller et al., *Land of Canaan,* 608–619, quote 613.

31. Burrows and Wallace, *Gotham,* quote 323, quote 324, 323–324; Young, *Democratic Republicans,* 476–478, 481–482.

32. Padraig Riley, *Slavery and the Democratic Conscience: Political Life in Jeffersonian America* (Philadelphia: University of Pennsylvania Press, 2015), 15–93, 132–159; Wilson, *United Irishmen,* 137–139; Duncan, *Citizens or Papists,* 148; Paul J. Polgar, "'Whenever They Find It Expedient': The Politics of Partisanship and Free Black Voting Rights in Early National New York," *American Nineteenth Century* 12, no. 1 (March 2011): 1–8.

33. Walter Walsh, "Religion, History and Ethnicity: Clues to the Cultural Construction of the Law," in Bayor and Meagher, *New York Irish,* 50–60.

34. Miller, *Emigrants and Exiles,* 147, 173–174; Grabbe, "European Immigration," 197; Walsh, "Religion, Ethnicity," 50–60; Jay Dolan, *Immigrant Church: New York's Irish and German Catholics* (Baltimore: Johns Hopkins University Press, 1975), 2.

35. Edward Thomas McCarron, "The World of Kavanagh and Cottrill: A Portrait of Irish Emigration, Entrepreneurship and Ethnic Diversity in Mid Maine, 1760–1820" (PhD dissertation, University of New Hampshire, 1992), 9, 254–284; Robert H. Lord, John E. Sexton, and Edward Harrington, *History of the Archdiocese of Boston in the Various Stages of Its Development,* Volume II (New York: Sheed and Ward, 1944), 697.

36. Jay Dolan, *In Search of an American Catholicism: A History of Religion and Culture in Tension* (Oxford: Oxford University Press, 2002), 16–22; Joseph Agonito, "Ecumenical Stirrings: Catholic-Protestant Relations During the Episcopacy of John Carroll," *Church History* 45, no. 3 (September 1976): 358–361, 363–373; Thomas W. Spalding, *The Premier See: A History of the Archdiocese of Baltimore, 1789–1989* (Baltimore: Johns Hopkins University Press, 1989), quote 62, 59–62.

37. Nathan Hatch, *The Democratization of American Christianity* (New Haven: Yale University Press, 1989), 60, 69, 163, 200; Christine Leigh Heyrman, *Southern Cross: The beginnings of the Bible Belt* (New York: Knopf, 1997), 253–256, 262–263.

38. Wilson, *United Irishmen,* 97, 158–159; Richard Murphy and Lawrence Mannion, *History of the Society of Friendly Sons in the City of New York, 1784–1955* (New York, 1962), 69–119; Arthur J. O'Hara, *Hibernian Society of Savannah, 1812–1912: The Story of a Century* (Savannah: Baird and Hutton, 1912); George Potter, *To the Golden Door: The Story of the Irish in Ireland and America* (Boston: Little, Brown, 1960), 202; Bric, *Ireland, Philadelphia,* 152–162; Gilmore and Miller, "Searching for Irish Freedom," 197–198; Alice Lida Cochrane, *The Saga of an Irish Immigrant Family: The Descendants of John Mullanphy* (New York: Arno Press, 1976), 57–61.

39. Wilson, *United Irishmen,* 157–160, Bric, *Ireland, Philadelphia,* 172–176, 223–239; Albrecht Koschnik, "Voluntary Associations, Political Culture and the Public Sphere of Philadelphia: 1780–1830" (PhD dissertation, University of Virginia, 2000), 1–78.

40. John D. Crimmins, *St. Patrick's Day: Its Celebration in New York and Other Places* (New York: privately published, 1902), 111.

41. Wilson, *United Irishmen,* 80, 84–85, 89; Alan Taylor, *War of 1812: American Citizens, British Subjects, Irish Rebels and Indian Allies* (New York: Random House, 2010), 323–360.

42. Robert Remini, *The Life of Andrew Jackson* (New York: Harper and Row, 1988), 86–104.

4. Irish America in Transition

1. Potter, *To the Golden Door,* 231, 295; *United States Telegraph,* April 7, 1834, May 14, 1834; Remini, *Andrew Jackson,* 165.

2. John Loughery, *Dagger John: Archbishop John Hughes and the Making of Irish America* (Ithaca, NY: Cornell University Press, 2018), 120–138, 136.

3. Joel Mokyr, *Why Ireland Starved: A Quantitative and Analytical Study of the Irish Economy, 1800 to 1850* (London: Allen and Unwin, 1985), quote 145.

4. William Forbes Adams, *Ireland and Irish Emigration to the New World: From 1815 to the Famine* (New Haven: Yale University Press, 1931), 10–54; O'Grada, "Poverty, Population and Agriculture," 108–120, and "Industry and Communications" 138–155, in Vaughn, ed., *New History of Ireland,* Volume V, *Ireland Under the Union*; James S. Donnelly, Jr. *Captain Rock: The Irish Agrarian Rebellion of 1821–1824* (Madison: University of Wisconsin Press, 2009), 52–56; O'Grada, *New Economic History,* 56–60.

5. Joel Mokyr and Cormac O'Gráda, "Poor and Getting Poorer? Living Standards in Ireland Before the Famine," *Economic History Review* 41, no. 2 (May 1998): 213, 209–235; O'Grada, "Poverty, Population" 113, 101–117.

6. O'Grada, *New Economic History,* 71–73; O'Grada, "Poverty, Population," 127–131, 138–141, 143, 145–146; Bardon, *History of Ulster,* 257–262, 266–280; Mokyr and O'Grada, "Living Standards," 229; Thomas Jordan, "Sons of St. Patrick: Quality of Life and Heights of Young Irish Males at Mid-Nineteenth Century," *Social Indicators Research* 102, no. 3

(July 2011): 396–406; Deborah Oxley, "Living Standards of Women in Prefamine Ireland," *Social Science History* 28, no. 2 (2004): 271–295; Donald Akenson, *Ireland, Sweden and the Great European Migrations, 1815–1914* (Montreal: McGill-Queens University Press, 2011), 37–39; William Williams, *Creating Irish Tourism: The First Century, 1750–1850* (London: Anthem Press, 2010), 153–182.

7.   Miller, *Emigrants and Exiles,* 60–69; Donnelly, *Captain Rock,* 5–6, 6–26; Outrage papers, Mayo, Folders 21–1 to 21–23, National Archives of Ireland, Dublin; Stephen Palmer, *Police and Protest in England and Ireland, 1780–1850* (Cambridge: Cambridge University Press, 1988), 552; James S. Donnelly Jr., "The Terry Alt Movement, 1829–31," *History Ireland* 4, no. 2 (December 1994): 34, 30–35.

8.   Donnelly, *Captain Rock,* quote 13, 68–71, 119–149, 199, 263, 268, 287, 48; Palmer, *Police,* 337, 373, 228, 258, 339–340, 374; Anne Coleman, *Riotous Roscommon: Social Unrest in the 1840s* (Dublin: Irish Academic Press, 1999), 23; Donnelly, "Terry Alt," 30–35.

9.   Mokyr, *Why Ireland Starved,* 128–134; O'Grada, *New Economic History,* 164–165; *Clare Champion,* January 15, 1858; Donnelly, "Terry Alt," 35.

10.   Fergus O'Ferrall, *Catholic Emancipation: Daniel O'Connell and the Birth of Irish Democracy, 1820–30* (Atlantic Highlands, NJ: Humanities Press International, 1985), 1–148 quote, 38, 194–240; ML 15018 ML 15018, J. H. Power to Wyse, April 18, 1826; Anonymous to Wyse, August 21, 1826; MS 15023 no. 2, John Burke to Wyse, May 30, 1826; Wyse to Galwey, September 7, 1826, Thomas Wyse papers, National Library of Ireland.

11.   Oliver MacDonagh, *The Emancipist: Daniel O'Connell, 1830–47* (New York: St. Martin's Press, 1989), 39, 80, 90–96, 187, 221–240; Gary Owens, "Nationalism Without Words: Symbolism and Ritual Behavior in the Repeal 'Monster' Meetings, 1843–1845," in Kerby A. Miller and James S. Donnelly Jr., *Irish Popular Culture: 1650–1850* (Dublin: Irish Academic Press, 1998), 243–257; Bew, *Ireland,* 115–118, 121.

12.   Andrew Boyd, *Montgomery and the Black Man: Religion and Politics in Nineteenth-century Ulster* (Blackrock: Columba Press, 2006), 9–13; Miller, *Emigrants and Exiles,* 228–235; Irene Whelan, *The Bible War in Ireland: The Second Reformation and the Polarization of Protestant-Catholic Relations, 1800–1840* (Madison: University of Wisconsin Press, 2005), 52–92, 133–138, 207; Bardon, *History of Ulster,* 257; Andrew Holmes, "Presbyterian Religion, Historiography, and Ulster Scots Identity, 1880–1914," *The Historical Journal* 52, no. 3 (2009): 615–640; Ian McBride, *Scripture Politics: Ulster Presbyterians and Irish Radicalism in the Late Eighteenth Century* (New York: Oxford University Press, 1998), 213–214, 222.

13.   Emmet J. Larkin, *The Pastoral Role of the Roman Catholic Church in Pre-Famine Ireland, 1750–1850* (Dublin: Four Courts Press, 2006), 10–37, 74–80, 174–176. S. J. (Sean J.), Connolly, *Priests and People in Pre-Famine Ireland, 1780–1845* (Dublin, Ireland: Four Courts Press, 2001), 37; David W. Miller, "Irish Catholicism and the Great Famine," *Jour-*

nal of Social History 9 (Autumn 1975): 81–99; John Quinn, *Father Mathew's Crusade: Temperance in Nineteenth Century Ireland and Irish America* (Amherst: University of Massachusetts Press, 2002), 57–85; Miller, *Emigrants and Exiles,* 74–75; Whelan, *Bible War,* 114–145, 194–206.

14. Miller, *Emigrants and Exiles,* 193; O'Grada, "Poverty and Population," 120.

15. William Forbes Adams, *Ireland and Irish Emigration to the New World from 1815 to the Famine* (New Haven: Yale University Press, 1932), 68–239.

16. David Doyle, "The Irish in North America, 1776–1845," in J. J. Lee and Marion Casey, eds., *Making the Irish American: History and Heritage of the Irish in the United States* (New York: NYU Press, 2006), 187–191; S. H. Cousens, "The Regional Variation in Emigration from Ireland Between 1821 and 1841," *Transactions of the Institute of British Geographers,* no. 37 (December 1965): 18–22, 17; Adams, *Ireland and Irish,* 191; Robert P. Gavin, William P. Kelly, and Dolores O'Reilly, *The Atlantic Gateway: The Port and City of Londonderry Since 1700* (Dublin: Four Courts Press, 2009), 38, 41; Edward J. O'Day, "The Second Colonization of New England Revisited: Irish Immigration Before the Famine," in Charles Fanning, *New Perspectives on the Irish Diaspora* (Carbondale: Southern Illinois University Press, 2000), 100, 108–109; Adams, *Ireland and Irish,* 187–190, 228–234; Edward T. McCarron, "Altered States: Tyrone Migration to Providence, Rhode Island During the Nineteenth Century," *Clogher Record* 16, no. 1 (January 1997): 151–153, 159.

17. Joseph Ferrie, "A New View of the Irish in America: Economic Performance and the Place of Origin, 1850–1920," September 1997, unpublished paper, NBER, 6–10, 7; Hiram Leroy Smith, "Emigration and the Development of the Passenger Trade" (PhD dissertation, Syracuse University, 1989), 1–11, 28–109, 210–315; Adams, *Ireland and the Irish,* 187–239; O'Neill, *Killishandra,* 12; Mathias Blum, Christopher Colvin, Laura McAtackney, and Eoin McLaughlin, "Women of an Uncertain Age: Quantifying Human Capital in Rural Ireland in the Nineteenth Century," *Economic History Review* 70, no. 1 (2017): 190–193, 215–219; Gerardine Meaney, Mary O'Dowd, and Bernadette Whelan, *Reading the Irish Woman: Studies in Cultural Encounters and Exchange, 1714–1960* (Liverpool: Liverpool University Press, 2013), 58–59.

18. George Rogers Taylor, *The Transportation Revolution, 1815–1860* (New York: Rinehart, 1951), 22–26, 32–52; Ronald Shaw, "Canals in the Early Republic: A Review of the Recent Literature," *Journal of the Early Republic* 4 no. 2 (Summer 1984): 117–142; Susan B. Carter et al., *Historical Statistics of the United States: The Millennial Edition* (New York: Cambridge University Press, 2006), online database, Tables 3300–3493, 5194–5290; Robert Gallman, "Economic Growth and Structural Change," in Stanley Engerman and Robert Gallman, eds., *The Economic History of the United States: Volume 2, The Long Nineteenth Century* (Cambridge: Cambridge University Press, 2000), 3–20, 53; Daniel Walker Howe, *What God Hath Wrought: The Transformation of America, 1815–1848* (New York:

Oxford University Press, 2007), 525–526; Bruce Laurie, *Artisans into Workers: Labor in Nineteenth Century America* (New York: Noonday Press, 1989), 15–46.

19. Gary Gerstle, *Liberty and Coercion: The Paradox of American Government from the Founding to the Present* (Princeton, NJ: Princeton University Press, 2015), quote 151, 149–172; Stephen Hahn, *A Nation Without Borders* (New York: Penguin, 2017), 48–72.

20. James J. Connolly, *An Elusive Unity* (Ithaca: Cornell University Press, 2010), 1–27, 54–86; Golway, *Machine Made,* 1–37.

21. Mathieu Billings, "Potent Legacies: The Transformation of Irish American Politics, 1815–1840" (PhD dissertation, Northern Illinois University, 2016), 1–43, 46–175, 303–476.

22. Miller, *Emigrants and Exiles,* 196–197; Doyle, *Irish North America,* 187; Adams, *Ireland and Irish Emigration,* 69–71.

23. The proportion of Irish immigrants over forty years old in 1850 in the Old Northwest—Wisconsin, Illinois, Indiana, Michigan, and Ohio—was one third; in no other region was it greater than one quarter: Steven Ruggles, Sarah Flood, Ronald Goeken, Josiah Grover, Erin Meyer, Jose Pacas, and Matthew Sobeok, IPUMS USA, U.S. Census 1850, Version 8.0 [Dataset] (Minneapolis: IPUMS, 2018). Wilma Dunaway, *The First American Frontier: Transition to Capitalism in Southern Appalachia, 1700–1760* (Chapel Hill: University of North Carolina Press, 1996), 72–97, 119, 292; McWhiney, *Cracker Culture,* 232, 233–236, 146–217; Howard Harris, "'The Eagle to Watch and the Harp to Tune the Nation': Irish Immigrants, Politics and Early Industrialization in Paterson, New Jersey 1824–1836," *Journal of Social History* 23, no. 3 (April 1990): 575–597; Christopher Clark, "The Ohio Country in the Political Economy of National Building," in Andrew R. L. Cayton and Stuart Hobbs, eds., *The Center of a Great Empire: The Ohio Country in the Early Republic* (Athens: Ohio University Press, 2005), 149–152; Donald Ratcliffe, *The Politics of Long Division: The Birth of the Second Party System in Ohio, 1818–1828* (Columbus: Ohio State University Press, 2000), 117–121, 131, 250; Miller, *In the Land of Canaan,* 218; Miller, "Searching for a New World," 16–18.

24. Potter, *To the Golden Door,* 192; Harris, "The Eagle," 478–491; Ratcliffe, *Politics of Long Division,* 109, 118–119; Remini, *Life,* 107; Robert Kelley, *The Cultural Pattern in American Politics: The First Century* (New York: Knopf, 1979), 163; Lee Benson, *The Concept of Jacksonian Democracy* (Princeton, N.J.: Princeton University Press, 1961), 167–168, 171–172.

25. William H. Williams, *T'was Only an Irishman's Dream* (Urbana: University of Illinois Press, 1996), 32–78; Doyle, "Irish in North America," 195; Jay Dolan, *The Irish Americans* (New York: Bloomsbury, 2008), 55–58.

26. Lynn Metzger and Peg Bobel, *Canal Fever: The Ohio & Erie Canal, from Waterway to Canalway* (Kent, Ohio: Kent State University Press, 2009), 45, 57; Mathieu Billings and Sean Farrell, *The Irish in Illinois* (Carbondale: Southern Illinois University Press, 2021),

43–60; Earl F. Niehaus, *The Irish in New Orleans, 1800 to 1860* (Baton Rouge: Louisiana State University Press, 1965), 23–50; Robert Howard Lord, John E. Sexton, and Edward Harrington, *History of the Archdiocese of Boston in the Various Stages of Its Development,* Vol. II (New York: Sheed and Ward, 1944), quote 124; Vincent E. Powers, "'Invisible Immigrants': The Pre Famine Irish Community in Worcester, Massachusetts, from 1826 to 1860" (PhD dissertation, Clark University, 1976), 151–222; Brian Mitchell, *Paddy Camps: The Irish of Lowell, 1821–1861* (Urbana: University of Illinois Press, 1988), 10–39.

27. Ira Rosenwaike, *Population History of New York City* (Syracuse, NY: Syracuse University Press, 1972), 53; Burrows and Wallace, *Gotham,* 478; Michael Feldberg, "The Philadelphia Riots: A Social History" (PhD dissertation, University of Rochester, 1970), 131.

28. Bruce Nelson, *Irish Nationalists and the Making of the Irish Race* (Princeton, NJ: Princeton University Press, 2012), 61; O'Ferrall, *Emancipation,* quote 50; William Carleton, *Traits and Stories of the Irish Peasantry* (New York: Garland, 1979), quotes 266, 309–310; Charles Lever, *The Works of Charles Lever: Volume I, The Confessions of Harry Lorrequer* (New York: Collier, 1882), 46.

29. Paul A. Gilje, *The Road to Mobocracy: Popular Disorder in New York City, 1763–1834* (Chapel Hill: University of North Carolina Press, 1987), 165–166; Bruce Laurie, *Working People of Philadelphia, 1800–1850* (Philadelphia: Temple University Press, 1980), 64–66, 124–126; Niehaus, *Irish in New Orleans,* 5, 27, 50–51.

30. Powers, "Invisible Immigrants," 57–262; Daniel A. Graff, "Forging an American St. Louis: Labor, Race and Citizenship" (PhD dissertation, University of Wisconsin, 2004), 155–167, 171–184; Hahn, *A Nation Without Borders,* 54–64; Potter, *To the Golden Door,* quote 375, 171–187.

31. Erik Chaput, *The People's Martyr: Thomas Wilson Dorr and His 1842 Rhode Island Rebellion* (Lawrence: University Press of Kansas, 2013), 1–72, 122, quote 166, 162–181.

32. Sean Wilentz, *Chants Democratic: New York City and the Rise of the American Working Class, 1788–1850* (New York: Oxford University Press, 2004), 61–125; Laurie, *Working People,* 3–32.

33. Laurie, *Working People,* 85–106; Wilentz, *Chants Democratic,* 145–296.

34. Laurie, *Working People,* 33–52, 107–133; Wilentz, *Chants Democratic,* 299–325.

35. Howe, *What God Hath Wrought,* 164–202; Sidney E. Ahlstrom, *A Religious History of the American People* (New Haven: Yale University Press, 1972), 555–564; Ray Allen Billington, *The Protestant Crusade, 1800–1860: A Study of the Origins of American Nativism* (New York: Macmillan, 1938), 1–220, 345–380.

36. Hidetaki Hirota, *Expelling the Poor: Atlantic Seaboard States and the Nineteenth Century Origins of American Immigration Policy* (New York: Oxford University Press, 2017), 70–81; Barnaby Faherty SJ, *St. Louis: An Unmatched Celtic Community* (St. Louis: Missouri

Historical Society, 2001), 1–22; Niehaus, *Irish in New Orleans,* 5–25; Graham Davis, *Land: Irish Pioneers in Mexican and Revolutionary Texas* (College Station: Texas A&M Press, 2002), 72–105.

37. Powers, "Invisible Immigrants," 94–285; Mitchell, *Paddy Camps,* 10–100; Margaret M. Mulrooney, *Black Powder: White Lace: The du Pont Irish and Cultural Identity in Nineteenth Century America* (Lebanon NH: University Press of New England, 2002), 1–60, 21, 44, 54, 74–76, 115–126.

38. Lord et al., *History of the Archdiocese of Boston,* Vol. II, 190–202, 260–261; Billings, "Potent Legacies," 270, 425–489; Amy Bridges, *A City in the Republic: Antebellum New York and the Origins of Machine Politics* (Ithaca, NY: Cornell University Press, 1984), quote 99.

39. Thomas O'Connor, *The Boston Irish* (Boston: Back Bay Books, 1995), 51–52; Feldberg, *The Philadelphia Riots of 1844,* 44–197; Richard Shaw, *John Hughes: the Unquiet Life and Times of Archbishop John Hughes of New York* (New York: Paulist Press, 1977), 80–82; Jerome Mushkat, *Tammany; The Evolution of a Political Machine, 1789–1865* (Syracuse, NY: Syracuse University Press, 1971), 162–164.

40. Dennis Clark, *Erin's Heirs: Irish Bonds of Community* (Lexington: University of Kentucky Press, 1991), 103–104; Walsh, "Religion, Ethnicity and History," 64–68; Paul A. Gilje, "The Development of an Irish American Community in New York City Before the Great Migration," in Bayor and Meagher, *The New York Irish,* 71–74.

41. Patrick Carey, *Priests and Prelates: Ecclesiastical Democracy and the Tensions of Trusteeism* (Notre Dame, IN: University of Notre Dame Press, 1987), quote 136, 1–137; Duncan, *Citizens or Papists,* quote 184, 185–186; Light, *Rome in the New Republic,* quote 67, quote 107; Alexis de Tocqueville, *Democracy in America* (Chicago: University of Chicago Press, 2000), quote 276.

42. Thomas Shelley, *Bicentennial History of the Archdiocese of New York* (Paris: Editions du Signe, 2007), quote 110.

43. Ronald Formisano, *The Transformation of Political Culture: Massachusetts Political Parties 1790s–1840s* (New York: Oxford University Press, 1983), 297; Patrick McGrath, "Secular Power, Sectarian Politics: The American Born Irish Elite and Catholic Political Culture in New York," *Journal of American Ethnic History* 38, no. 3 (Spring 2019): 36–75; Burrows and Wallace, *Gotham,* 523–535; Shaw, *John Hughes,* 139–175; Light, *Rome in the New Republic,* 247–302; Dolan, *Immigrant Church,* 46–53.

44. Lord et al., *History of the Archdiocese of Boston,* Vol. II, quote 301, 31, 272–273, 301–306; Light, *Rome and the New Republic,* 279–299.

45. Powers, "Invisible Immigrants," 286–322; Robert Hayman, *Catholicism and the Diocese of Providence, 1780–1886* (Providence: Diocese of Providence, 1982), 28–53; Mitchell, *Paddy Camps,* 59–77.

46. Peter Way, "Evil Humors and Ardent Spirits: The Rough Culture of Canal Construction

Laborers," *Journal of American History* 79, no. 4 (March 1993): quote 1420–1421, 1403–1424; Carl E. Prince, "The Great 'Riot Year': Jacksonian Democracy and Patterns of Violence in 1834," *Journal of the Early Republic* 5, no. 1 (April 1985): 9–10, 19–20; Billings, "Potent Legacies," 238–421.

47. Potter, *To the Golden Door,* quote 212, 207–216.

48. Ibid., 388–396, 399–402.

49. Nelson, *Nationalism and Race,* 59, quote 5, 63, quote 65, 66; John Quinn, "Expecting the Impossible? Abolitionist Appeals to the Irish in Antebellum America," *New England Quarterly,* 82, no. 4 (December 2009): 667–710; Angela Murphy, *American Slavery, Irish Freedom: Abolition, Immigrant Citizenship and the Transatlantic Movement for Irish Repeal* (Baton Rouge: LSU Press, 2010), 83, 197–198.

50. Murphy, *American Slavery,* 2, 54–99, 126–180; Hayman, *Catholicism in Rhode Island,* 40–47; Mitchell, *Paddy Camps,* 71–74.

5. The Famine and Irish Immigrants in America

1. Visit to Ballykilcline, Roscommon, by author in July 2003.

2. Alf MacLochlainn, "Gael and Peasant" in Daniel Casey and Robert Rhodes, *Views of the Irish Peasantry, 1800–1916* (Hamden, CT: Archon Books, 1977), quote 31; B. R. Mitchell, *European Historical Statistics, 1750–1975* (New York: Facts on File, 1981), 29–37; Charles E. Orser, *Unearthing Hidden Ireland: Historical Archeology at Ballykilcline, Roscommon* (Bray, Ireland: Wordwell, 2006), 1–71.

3. Robert James Scally, *The End of Hidden Ireland: Rebellion, Famine and Emigration* (New York: Oxford University Press, 1995), 1–8, 36–63; Miller, *Emigrants and Exiles,* 291.

4. Cecil Woodham-Smith, *The Great Hunger, Ireland 1845–9* (London: H. Hamilton, 1962), 91, 94–101, 196; John Crowley, William J. Smyth, and Mike Murphy, *Atlas of the Great Irish Famine* (New York: New York University Press, 2012), 34–36, 170–213; Liam Kennedy et al., *Mapping the Great Irish Famine: A Survey of the Famine Decade* (Dublin: Four Courts, 1999), Map 10, 37; Christine Kinealy, *A Death-Dealing Famine: The Great Hunger in Ireland* (London: Pluto Press, 1997), 66; James S. Donnelly Jr., *The Great Irish Potato Famine* (Thrupp, Stroud, Gloucestershire: Sutton, 2002), 177; Cathal Poirteir, *Famine Echoes* (Dublin: Gill & Macmillan, 1995), quote 34, 335–336.

5. Donnelly, *The Great Irish Potato Famine,* quote 59, 41–131; Cormac O'Grada, *Black 47 and Beyond: The Great Irish Famine in History, Economy, and Memory* (Princeton, NJ: Princeton University Press, 1999), 28–73.

6. O'Grada, *Black 47,* 206–208; James S. Donnelly Jr., *The Land and the People of Nineteenth-Century Cork: The Rural Economy and the Land Question* (London: Routledge and Kegan Paul, 1975), 87–91; Christine Kinealy, *Repeal and Revolution: 1848 in Ireland* (Manchester: Manchester University Press, 2009), 136–147.

7. Tyler Anbinder, *Five Points: The 19th-Century New York City Neighborhood That Invented Tap Dance, Stole Elections, and Became the World's Most Notorious Slum* (New York: Penguin, 2001), 44, 58–66; Cian McMahon, *The Coffin Ship: Life and Death at Sea During the Great Irish Famine* (New York: NYU Press, 2021), 26–28; Hirota, *Expelling the Poor,* quote 30; Shelley Barber, *The Prendergast Letters: Correspondence from Famine Era Ireland, 1840–1850* (Amherst: University of Massachusetts Press, 2006), quote 136.

8. Paul Connors, "America's Emerald Island: The Cultural Invention of the Irish Fishing Community of Beaver Island" (PhD dissertation, Loyola University Chicago, 1999), 47–52, 107–129; Edward M. Gill, *The Louisburgh-Clinton Connection: A Social Study* (Victoria, BC: Trafford, 2006), 5–29; Crowley et al., *Atlas of the Great Irish Famine,* 403–405.

9. Donnelly, *Cork,* 124–131, 227–228; David Doyle, "The Remaking of Irish America, 1845–1880," in Lee and Casey, *Making the Irish American,* 220–223; Tyler Anbinder and Hope McCaffrey, "Which Irish Men and Women Immigrated to the United States During the Great Famine Migration of 1846–54?" *Irish Historical Studies* 39, no. 156 (2015): 620–642; Anbinder and McCaffrey, 2015, "Replication Data for: 'Which Irish Men and Women Immigrated to the United States During the Great Famine Migration of 1846–1854?'" https://doi.org/10.7910/DVN/28757, Harvard Dataverse, V1.

10. S. H. Cousens, "Emigration and Demographic Change in Ireland, 1851–1861," *Economic History Review,* 14, no. 2 (1961): quote 276; Ciaran O'Murchadha, "Famine Clearances," *Encyclopedia of Irish History and Culture,* Volume I (Farmington, MI: Macmillan, 2004), 245–247.

11. Miller, *Emigrants and Exiles,* 353–361; Aristide R. Zolberg, *A Nation by Design: Immigration Policy in the Fashioning of America* (Cambridge, MA: Harvard University Press, 2006), 169; EPPI, *Emigration Statistics of Ireland, 1878,* Sessional Papers, Volume 75 (HMSO), 12.

12. See Chapter II and Doyle, "The Remaking," 733–740; Oxley, "Living Standards," 271–295; Seán Duffy, *Atlas of Irish History,* 2nd ed. (Dublin: Gill & Macmillan, 2000), 70–94; Crowley et al., *Atlas of the Great Irish Famine,* 13–25, 170–198, "Connacht" 281–323 and "Munster" 359–416; Aalen et al., *Atlas of the Rural Irish Landscape,* 67–69; Miller, *Emigrants and Exiles,* quote 297.

13. Anbinder and McCaffrey, *Database of Irish Immigrant Origins;* Miller, *Emigrants and Exiles,* 296; Hasia Diner, *Erin's Daughters in America* (Baltimore: Johns Hopkins University Press, 1983), 32–33; Ruggles, Flood, et al., IPUMS USA U.S. Census 1860.

14. McMahon, *The Coffin Ship,* 15–89.

15. Coleman, *Going to America,* 85–154; Henry David Thoreau, *Cape Cod* (Boston: Ticknor and Fields, 1866), quote, 4; McMahon, *The Coffin Ship,* 56–193, 154–158; O'Grada, *Black 47,* 106–107.

16. Malcolm Campbell, *Ireland's New Worlds: Immigrants, Politics, and Society in the United*

States and Australia, 1815–1922 (Madison: University of Wisconsin Press, 2008), 56–60; Donald Akenson, *The Irish Diaspora: A Primer* (Toronto: P. D. Meany, 1993), 112; Bruno Ramirez, Yves Otis, *Crossing the 49ᵗʰ Parallel: Migration from Canada to the United States, 1900–1930* (Ithaca, N.Y.: Cornell University Press, 2001), 1–2.

17. Carter et al., *Historical Statistics: Millennial, Online database,* Tables BA 814–830, DA 730–732, DA 766–767, DF 874–881, DF 883–885; Gallman, "Economic Growth and Structural Change," 20, 53.

18. Kathleen Neils Conzen, *Immigrant Milwaukee, 1836–1860: Accommodation and Community in a Frontier City* (Cambridge, MA: Harvard University Press, 1976), 41; Anbinder and McCaffrey, "Which Irish Men," 624; Joseph P. Ferrie, *Yankeys Now: Immigrants in the Antebellum United States, 1840–1860* (New York: Oxford University Press, 1999), 41–43, 51–59; Ruggles, Flood, et al., IPUMS USA U.S. Census 1880.

19. Anbinder, *Five Points,* 48–66; Ferrie, *Yankeys Now,* 59, 64.

20. Doyle, *Remaking,* 740; Diner, *Erin's Daughters,* 41–42; Ruggles, Flood, et al., IPUMS USA U.S. Census 1860; Maureen Fitzgerald, *Habits of Compassion: Irish Catholic Nuns and the Origins of New York's Welfare System, 1830–1920* (Urbana: University of Illinois Press, 2006), 55–57; U.S Bureau of the Census, *Eighth Census, 1869, Population* (Washington: GPO, 1864), 608–615.

21. Tyler Anbinder, "Irish Origins and the Shaping of Immigrant Life in Savannah on the Eve of the Civil War," *Journal of American Ethnic History* 35, no. 1 (October 2015): 7–8. Conzen, *Immigrant Milwaukee,* 26; Anbinder, *Five Points,* 48–49, 98; *Baptismal Register, Immaculate Conception Parish of Newburyport 1872 to 1877* and *Baptismal Register, St. Peter's Parish of Cambridge, 1872 to 1874,* Archives of the Archdiocese of Boston (AAB); *United States Census Manuscript Schedules 1860,* Boston, Ward One; *United States Census Manuscript Schedules 1860,* St. Louis, Ward Two; Victor Walsh, "'Across the Big Wather': Irish Community Life in Pittsburgh and Allegheny City, 1870–1890" (PhD dissertation, University of Pittsburgh, 1983), 403, 407–409; Mary Lee Dunn, *Ballykilcline Rising: From Famine Ireland to Immigrant America* (Amherst: University of Massachusetts Press, 2008), 71–72.

22. O'Grada, *Black 47,* 118; David A. Gerber, *The Making of an American Pluralism: Buffalo, New York 1825–1860* (Urbana: University of Illinois Press, 1989), 129; Census Manuscript Schedules 1860, Boston, Ward One, House numbers 267–269, Family numbers 548–557; St. Peter's of Cambridge, Register, 1872 to 1874.

23. Ferrie, *Yankeys Now,* 58–59; Campbell, *Ireland's New Worlds,* 75–79.

24. Anbinder, *Five Points,* 102; Baptismal Register, St. Peter's 1872 to 1874; Baptismal Register, Immaculate Conception, 1872 to 1877, Archives of the Archdiocese of Boston.

25. Conzen, *Immigrant Milwaukee,* 26; U.S. Immigrant Schedules 1860, Milwaukee, Ward Four, House numbers, 232–271; *Depositors, St. Patrick's Parish,* Archives Archdiocese of

San Francisco; Ann Regan, "The Irish," in June Drenning Holmquist, ed., *They Chose Minnesota: A Survey of the States Ethnic Groups* (St. Paul: Minnesota Historical Society, 1981), 130–152.

26. Stephen Birmingham, *Real Lace: America's Irish Rich* (New York: Harper and Row, 1973), 135–140.

27. Ruggles, Flood, et al., IPUMS USA U.S. Census 1860, 1880.

28. Ferrie, *Yankeys Now,* quote 79, 74–79.

29. Rebecca Fried, "No Irish Need Deny: Evidence for the Historicity of NINA Restrictions in Advertisements and Signs," *Journal of Social History* 49, no. 4 (Summer 2016): 829–852; quotes, Mark Bularik, "1854: No Irish Need Apply," *New York Times,* September 8, 2015.

30. Ferrie, "Economic Performance," Figure 16; Doyle, "Remaking," 737–738.

31. Oscar Handlin, *Boston's Immigrants: A Study in Acculturation* (Cambridge, MA: Belknap Press, 1979), 54–87; Paul Kleppner, *The Third Electoral System 1853–1892: Parties, Voters, and Political Cultures* (Chapel Hill: University of North Carolina Press, 1979), 203; Frederick Jaher, *The Urban Establishment: Upper Strata in Boston, New York, Charleston, Chicago, and Los Angeles* (Urbana: University of Illinois Press, 1982), 26.

32. R. J. Burchell, *The San Francisco Irish, 1848–1880* (Berkeley: University of California Press, 1980), 52–72; Campbell, *Ireland's New Worlds,* 85–103.

33. Walsh, "'Across the Big Wather," 316–338; "Conclusion" in Bayor and Meagher, *The New York Irish,* 534–535, 698–699; Timothy G. Conley and David W. Galenson, "Nativity and Wealth in Mid-Nineteenth-Century Cities," *Journal of Economic History* 58, no. 2 (June 1998): 469–472; Jo Ellen Vinyard, *The Irish on the Urban Frontier, 1850–1880* (New York: Arno Press, 1976), 48–64; Conzen, *Immigrant Milwaukee,* 73. Daniel Walkowitz, *Worker City, Company Town: Iron and Cotton-Worker Protest in Troy and Cohoes, New York, 1855–84* (Urbana: University of Illinois Press, 1978); Douglas Shaw, *The Making of an Immigrant City: Ethnic and Cultural Conflict in Jersey City, New Jersey, 1850–1877* (ProQuest Dissertations Publishing), 21–23; Kevin Kenny, *Making Sense of the Molly Maguires* (New York: Oxford University Press, 1998), 62–67.

34. Ruggles, Flood, et al., IPUMS USA U.S. Census 1860; Burrows and Wallace, *Gotham,* 746–748.

35. Gallman, *Receiving Erin's Children,* 103; Handlin, *Boston Immigrants,* 115; Dolan, *Immigrant Church,* quote 39, 40; Dennis Clark, *The Irish in Philadelphia: Ten Generations of Urban Experience* (Philadelphia: Temple University Press, 1981), 49; Burrows and Wallace, *Gotham,* 790; Niehaus, *Irish in New Orleans,* 51–53; Mitchell, *Paddy Camps,* 106–109, 149–150: *Sixth Annual Report of the Bureau of the Statistics of Labor: 1875* (Boston: Wright and Potter, 1875), 191–370; Alan Kraut, "Illness and Medical Care Among Immigrants in Ante Bellum New York," in Bayor and Meagher, eds., *New York Irish,* 160–161;

United States Census 1860: "Recapitulation" (Washington, DC: Government Printing Office, 1864), 644; Cormac O'Grada, *Ireland's Great Famine: Interdisciplinary Perspectives* (Dublin: UCD Press, 2006), 167–168; Robert Ernst, *Immigrant Life in New York City, 1825–1863* (New York: King's Crown Press, 1949), 204; Powers, "Invisible Immigrants," 335; Handlin, *Boston Immigrants,* Appendix Tables XXIII, XXIV; Timothy J. Guilfoyle, *City of Eros: New York City Prostitution and the Commercialization of Sex, 1790–1920* (New York: W. W. Norton, 1992), 62, 65, 61–67; Barbara Hobson, *Uneasy Virtue: The Politics of Prostitution and the American Reform Tradition* (New York: Basic Books, 1987), 35.

36. Peter Quinn, "New York's Catholic Century," *New York Times,* June 4, 2006; Ruggles, Flood, et al., IPUMS USA U.S. Census 1860.

37. Tyler Anbinder, "Moving Beyond 'Rags to Riches': New York's Irish Famine Immigrants and Their Surprising Savings Accounts," *Journal of American History* 99, no. 3 (December 2012): 741–770; O'Grada, *Ireland's Great Famine,* 167–177, 183–195.

38. Tyler Anbinder, Cormac O'Grada, and Simone Wegge, "Networks and Opportunities: A Digital History of Ireland's Great Famine Refugees in New York," *American Historical Review* 124, no. 5 (December 2019): 1591–1629, quote 1597; Tyler Anbinder, Cormac O'Grada, and Simone Wegge, "'The Best Country in the World': The Surprising Social Mobility of New York's Irish Famine Immigrants," *Journal of Interdisciplinary History* 53, no. 3 (2022): 407–438; Timothy J. Meagher, *Inventing Irish America: Generation, Class and Ethnic Identity in a New England City, 1880–1928* (Notre Dame, IN: University of Notre Dame Press, 2001), 34–36; Roy Rosenzweig, *Eight Hours for What We Will: Workers and Leisure in an Industrial City, 1870–1920* (Cambridge: Cambridge University Press, 1883), 40–46.

39. Patricia Kelleher, "Class and Catholic Irish Masculinity in Antebellum America: Young Men on the Make in Chicago," *Journal of American Ethnic History* 22, no. 4 (Summer 2009): 7–42, quote 25; Charles Tilly, "Transplanted Networks," in Virginia Yans-Mclaughlin, ed., *Immigration Reconsidered: History, Sociology, and Politics* (New York: Oxford University Press, 1990), 84, 90–94.

40. Timothy Guinnane, *The Vanishing Irish: Households, Migration, and the Rural Economy in Ireland, 1850–1914* (Princeton, NJ: Princeton University Press, 1997), 25–27; Bureau of Labor, 1875, Appendices VIII, IX; Vinyard, *Irish Detroit,* 113–114; Diner, *Erin's Daughters,* 46–59; Ruggles, Flood, et al., IPUMS USA U.S. Census 1880, 1900; David W. Galenson, "Determinants of the School Attendance of Boys in Early Chicago," *History of Education Quarterly* 35, no. 4 (December 1995): 371–400; Conzen, *Immigrant Milwaukee,* 91; Diner, *Erin's Daughters,* 54–59; Ruggles, Flood, et al., IPUMS USA U.S. Census 1880, 1900. Patricia Kelleher, "Maternal Strategies: Irish Women's Headship of Families in Gilded Age Chicago," *Journal of Women's History* 13, no. 2 (2001): 80–106.

41. Joyce Flynn, "Sites and Sights: The Iconology of the Subterranean in Late Nineteenth-

Century Irish-American Drama," *MELUS* 18, no. 1 (Spring 1993): 5–19; Williams, *T'was Only an Irishman's Dream,* quotes 99, 100, 99–102.

6. The Famine Irish American Community in an America in Crisis

1. Patrick R. Guiney and Christian G. Samito, *Commanding Boston's Irish Ninth: The Civil War Letters of Patrick R. Guiney* (New York: Fordham University Press, 1998), quote xxvii, vi–vii.

2. Michael Hogan, *The Irish Soldiers of Mexico* (Guadalajara: Fondo Editorial Universitarion, 1998), 40–81, 169–185; Potter, *To the Golden Door,* 475–485; Hahn, *A Nation Without Borders,* 115–191.

3. Tyler Anbinder, *Nativism and Slavery: The Northern Know Nothings and the Politics of the 1850s* (New York: Oxford University Press, 1992), 24–102, 115–128; Hirota, *Expelling the Poor,* 100–109; Lord et al., *History of the Archdiocese of Boston,* Vol. II, 681, 680–690; Frank Towers, *The Urban South and the Coming of the Civil War* (Charlottesville: University of Virginia Press, 2004), quote 118, 24–34, 57–168; Faherty, *The St. Louis Irish,* 64–68; Mitchell, *Paddy Camps,* 135–139; Powers, "Invisible Immigrants," 382–429.

4. Niehaus, *Irish in New Orleans,* 152; Powers, "Invisible Immigrants," 298–370; Anbinder, *Five Points,* 112, 152–172; Clark, *The Irish in Philadelphia,* 119–120; Mitchell, *Paddy Camps,* 109–110; Shaw, *Jersey City,* 52–91; Kelleher, "Young Men on the Make," 10; Dolan, *Immigrant Church,* 39–40, 57, 52–59; Light, *Rome and the New Republic,* 309–333.

5. *Seventh Census of the United States:* Appendix (Washington, DC: Armstrong, 1853), LVII; *The Eighth Census of the United States: Statistics of the United States* (Washington, DC: GPO, 1866), 500; Mitchell, *Paddy Camps,* 309–311; Timothy J. Meagher, *To Preserve the Flame: St. John's Parish and 150 Years of Catholicism in Worcester* (Worcester, MA: St. John's, 1984), 26; Dunn, *Ballykilcline Rising,* 109; Gerber, *Pluralism,* 310–311; Don Doyle, *The Social Order of a Frontier Town: Jacksonville, Illinois, 1825–1870* (Urbana: University of Illinois Press, 1978), 139–142; Ellen Skerrett, ed., *At the Crossroads: Old St. Patrick's and the Chicago Irish* (Chicago: Wild Onion Books, 1997), 4; Dolan, *Immigrant Church,* 50, 108; Lord et al., *History of the Archdiocese of Boston,* Vol. II, 520.

6. Kenneth Moss, "St. Patrick's Day Celebrations and the Formation of Irish-American Identity, 1845–1875," *Journal of Social History* 29, no. 1 (Fall: 1995)): 125–148; Skerrett, ed., *At the Crossroads,* 5–7; Mike Cronin and Daryl Adair, *The Wearing of the Green: A History of St. Patrick's Day* (London: Routledge, 2002), 34–39; Lord et al., *History of the Archdiocese of Boston,* Vol. II, quote 520.

7. Colleen McDannell, "Going to the Ladies Fair: Irish Catholics in New York City" in Bayor and Meagher, eds., *The New York Irish,* 236–237; Diner, *Erin's Daughters,* 41; Emmet Larkin, *Historical Dimensions of Irish Catholicism* (Washington, DC: Catholic University of America Press, 2012), 77; *All Hallows Annual Drumcondra, Ireland: The College, 1899,*

88–89; Timothy J. Meagher, *Guide to Irish American History* (New York: Columbia University Press, 2005), 298, 304; Elizabeth Grayson, "'Calling the Heart Home': Irish Catholic Women in America, 1845–1915" (PhD dissertation, University of Texas, 2001), 103, 116–120; Sue Ellen Hoy, "Walking Nuns: Chicago's Irish Sisters of Mercy," in Skerrett, ed., *At the Crossroads,* 41; Fitzgerald, *Habits of Compassion,* 59–100.

8. Larkin, *Historical Dimensions,* 57–90; Ann Taves, *The Household of Faith: Roman Catholic Devotions in Nineteenth-Century America* (Notre Dame, IN: University of Notre Dame Press, 1986), 6–7, 14–16, 45–128.

9. Thomas Shelley, *Greenwich Village Catholics: St. Joseph's Church and the Evolution of an Urban Faith Community, 1829–2002* (Washington, DC: Catholic University of America Press, 2003), quote 66; Light, *Rome and the New Republic,* quote 326, 327; Jay Dolan, *Catholic Revivalism: The American Experience, 1830–1900* (Notre Dame, IN: University of Notre Dame Press, 1977), 39–44, 66; Taves, *Household of Faith,* quote 107, 11–12, 118–119.

10. Dolan, *Immigrant Church,* quote 162; Powers, "Invisible Immigrants," 382–480; Mitchell, *Paddy Camps,* 121–142.

11. Eileen P. Sullivan, *Shamrock and the Cross: Irish American Novelists Shape American Catholicism* (Notre Dame, IN: University of Notre Dame Press, 2016), quote 8; James O'Toole, *Passing for White: Race, Reunion and the Healy Family, 1820–1920* (Amherst: University of Massachusetts Press, 2002), quote 110, 145, 55–81, 103–160; William Joyce, *Editors and Ethnicity: A History of the Irish American Press, 1848–1883* (ProQuest Dissertations Publishing, 1974), 56–58, 111; John McGreevy, *Catholicism and American Freedom* (New York: W. W. Norton, 2003), 20–67.

12. Graham Hodges, "'Desirable Companions and Lovers': Irish and African Americans in the Sixth Ward, 1830–1870," in Bayor and Meagher, eds., *The New York Irish,* 122–124; Anbinder, *Five Points,* 175.

13. Bryan Giemza, "Turned Inside Out: Black, White, and Irish in the South," *Southern Cultures* 18, no. 1 (Spring 2012): 34–57; *Boston Pilot,* quotes, December 31, 1853, October 16, 1852; David Roediger, *Wages of Whiteness: Race and the Making of the American Working Class* (London: Verso, 1991), 115–131.

14. Roediger, *Wages of Whiteness,* 132–163; Meagher, *Guide to Irish American History,* 217–222; *Boston Pilot,* June 2, 1855; Gordon Barker, "Anthony Burns and the North-South Dialogue, Liberty and the American Revolution" (PhD dissertation, William and Mary, 2009), 45, 54, 94, 108, 135.

15. Anbinder, *Five Points,* 306; quote *Boston Pilot* January 17, 1857, January 20, 1857; *Pittsburgh Catholic* quote, March 10, 1855; Emmons, *Beyond the Pale,* 54–55.

16. Hirota, *Expelling the Poor,* 122–126; Stephen Kantrowitz, *More than Freedom: Fighting for Black Citizenship in a White Republic* (New York: Penguin, 2012), 165–171.

17. Kelley, *Cultural Pattern,* 173, 200–221, 276–277; Anbinder, *Five Points,* 164–171; Towers, *Urban South,* 24–34, 68–93; Dale Baum, *The Civil War Party Systems: The Case of Massachusetts, 1848–1876* (Chapel Hill: University of North Carolina Press, 1984), 24–37; Harry C. Silcox, "William McMullen, Nineteenth-Century Political Boss," *Pennsylvania Magazine of History and Biography* 110, no. 3 (1986): 389–396; Mushkat, *Tammany,* 284–309; Cole, *Immigrant City,* quote 38–39; Kelleher, "Young Men on the Make," 22–23; *Boston Pilot,* January 20, 1857.

18. Baum, *Massachusetts,* 23–49; William E. Gienapp, "Nativism and the Creation of a Republican Majority in the North before the Civil War," *Journal of American History* 72, no. 3 (December 1985): 529–536, 539, 547, 552–559; *Boston Pilot,* quote January 20, 1857; Charles O'Conor, *Negro Slavery Is not Unjust* (New York: Van Evrie and Horton, 1859), 12; Arthur Quinn, *The Rivals: William Gwin, David Broderick and the Birth of California* (New York: Crown Publishers, 1994) 23–42, 247.

19. Kleppner, *The Third Electoral System,* 74; Billings and Farrell, *The Irish in Illinois,* 68–69; Susannah Ural Bruce, *The Harp and the Eagle: Irish American Volunteers and the Union Army, 1861–1865* (New York: New York University Press, 2006), 50, 53; Florence Gibson, *The Attitudes of the New York Irish Toward State and National Affairs, 1848–1892* [1st AMS ed.] (New York: AMS Press, 1968), 8, quote 114, quote 116.

20. William L. Barton, *Melting Pot Soldiers: The Union's Ethnic Regiments* (New York: Fordham University Press, 1998), 112–153; Gould, *Investigations of the Military,* 208–218; Bruce, *Harp and the Eagle,* 59–60, 199–208; W. J. Rorabaugh, "Who Fought for the North in the Civil War? Concord Massachusetts, Enlistments," *Journal of American History* 73, no. 3 (December 1986): 695–701; James Zibro, "The Life of Paddy Yank the Common Irish-American Soldier in the Union Army" (PhD dissertation, Catholic University of America, 2016), 23–122.

21. Peter Welsh, Lawrence Frederick Kohl, and Margaret Cossé Richard, *Irish Green and Union Blue: The Civil War Letters of Peter Welsh, Color Sergeant, 28th Regiment, Massachusetts Volunteers* (New York: Fordham University Press, 1986), quote 67, quote 63, 53–71.

22. Christian G. Samito, *Becoming American Under Fire: Irish Americans, African Americans and the Politics of Citizenship During the Civil War* (Ithaca NY: Cornell University Press, 2009), 1–7, 111–115; Cian McMahon, *The Global Dimensions of Irish Identity: Race, Nation, and the Popular Press, 1840–1880* (Chapel Hill: University of North Carolina Press, 2015), quote 119.

23. Bruce, *The Harp and the Eagle,* 62–63; Burton, *Melting Pot Soldiers,* 33, 135–137, Moss, "St. Patrick's Day Parades," 132; McMahon, *Global Dimensions,* 116–133, quote 124.

24. Frank A. Boyle, *A Party of Mad Fellows: The Story of the Irish Regiments in the Army of the Potomac* (Dayton: Morningside House, 1996), 391–399; Zibro, *Paddy Yank,* 185–215; William F. Fox, *Regimental Losses in the American Civil War* (Albany: Albany Publishing Co., 1889), Chapter I, 1–15, Chapter 9, 117–118, https://www.perseus.tufts.edu/hopper/text?doc=Perseus%3Atext%3A2001.05.

25. Iver Bernstein, *The New York City Draft Riots: Their Significance for American Society and Politics in the Age of the Civil War* (New York: Oxford University Press, 1990), quote, 33, 19–62; Dunn, *Ballykilcline,* 116; Kenny, *Making Sense,* 84–102; Judith Ann Giesberg, "'Lawless and Unprincipled': Women in Boston's Civil Ward Draft," in Thomas O'Connor, James O'Toole, and David Quigley, *Boston's Histories: Essays in Honor of Thomas H. O'Connor* (Boston: Northeastern University Press, 2004), 71–91; Baum, *Civil War Party System,* 95, 94–97; Vinyard, *Detroit Irish,* 258–260; Bruce, *Harp and the Eagle,* 136–232; Roediger, *Wages of Whiteness,* 171–172.

26. Ian Delehanty, "Immigrants in a Time of Civil War: The Irish, Slavery and the Union, 1845–1865" (PhD dissertation, Boston College, 2013), 205–234, quote 315, 236–286, 310–314; Tyler Anbinder, *City of Dreams: The 400-Year Epic History of Immigrant New York* (New York: Houghton Mifflin Harcourt, 2016), 209–210.

27. Guiney, *Commanding Boston's Irish Ninth,* 253–258; Phyllis Field, *The Politics of Race in New York: The Struggle for Black Suffrage in the Civil War Era* (Ithaca, NY; Cornell University Press, 1982), 150–151; Lawrence Grossman, *The Democratic Party and the Negro: Northern and National Politics, 1868–92* (Urbana: University of Illinois Press, 1976), 76; Jerome Mushkat, *The Reconstruction of the New York Democracy, 1861–1874* (London: Associated University Presses, 1981), quote 156, 154–159; Silcox, "McMullen," 410–412; Ian Kenneally, *From the Earth a Cry: The Story of John Boyle O'Reilly* (Cork: Collins Press, 2011), 151–152, 155, quote 179, 165–204; Niall Whelehan, *Changing Land: Diaspora Activism and the Irish Land War* (New York: NYU Press, 2021), quote 135; *New York Times,* April 28, 1870; July 11, 1877; August 8, 1881; November 5, 1877.

28. Randall M. Miller, "Catholic Religion, Irish Ethnicity and the Civil War," in Miller, Henry S. Stout, and Charles Reagan Wilson, eds., *Religion and the American Civil War* (New York: Oxford University Press, 1998), 276–277, 283–286; David W. Blight, *Race and Reunion: The Civil War in American Memory* (Cambridge, MA: Belknap Press, 2001), 18–30, 338–380.

29. David T. Gleeson, *The Irish in the South: 1815–1877* (Chapel Hill: University of North Carolina Press, 2001), 138–167; Grady McWhiney and Perry D. Jamieson, *Attack and Die: Civil War Military Tactics and the Southern Heritage* (University: University of Alabama Press, 1982), 172–174; John C. Inscoe, *Race, War and Remembrance in the Appalachian South* (Lexington: University Press of Kentucky, 2008), 103–123.

30. David O'Connell, *Furl the Banner: The Life of Abram Ryan, Poet Priest of the South* (Macon, GA; Mercer University Press, 2006), 83, 65–79, 99, 123, 8–14; Kieran Quinlan, *Strange Kin: Ireland and the American South* (Baton Rouge: Louisiana State University Press, 2005), 4–6, 104–112, 131, 141; Gleeson, *The Irish in the South,* 174–179.

31. Jack Morgan, *Through American and Irish Wars: The Life and Times of General Thomas Sweeny, 1820–1892* (Dublin: Academic Press, 2006), quote 125; William D'Arcy, *The*

Fenian Movement in the United States, 1858–1886 (PhD dissertation, Catholic University Press, 1947), 124, 86–89; Simon Winchester, *The Professor and the Madman: A Tale of Murder, Insanity, and the Making of the Oxford English Dictionary* (New York: HarperCollins, 1998); John Kuo Tchen, "Quimbo Appo's Fear of Fenians: Chinese-Irish-Anglo Relations in New York City," in Bayor and Meagher, eds., *The New York Irish*, 125–126; Miller, *Emigrants and Exiles*, 336; *Official Monthly Circular,* Financial Contributions: no. 6, Treasurer's Returns from May 10 to June 10, 1865, Fenian Brotherhood Collection, Series 1, subseries 4 Box 3, Folder 3, Archives of the Catholic University of America (ACUA); Patrick Steward, "Erin's Hope: Fenianism in the North Atlantic World" (PhD dissertation, University of Missouri, 2003), 159; Dunn, *Ballykilcline,* 120–123; Burchell, *San Francisco Irish,* 99–101, 279–328.

32. Burchell, *San Francisco Irish,* 101; Darcy, *Fenian Movement,* 35, 331; John O'Dea, *History of the Ancient Order of Hibernians and Ladies Auxiliary* (Notre Dame, IN: University of Notre Dame Press, 1995), vol. II, 970; *Boston Daily Advertiser,* August 27, 1866; *Irish Republic,* August 24, 1867; *New Haven Palladium,* July 13, 1865; *Milwaukee Daily Sentinel,* September 19, 1866.

33. "Roster of the Officers of the Fenian Brotherhood: New York ca. 1865," Fenian Brotherhood Collection, Series 1, Subseries 3, Box 2, Folder 6, Archives of Catholic University of America.

34. James S. Donnelly Jr., "The Construction of the Memory of the Famine in Ireland and the Irish Diaspora, 1850–1900," *Eire-Ireland* 31, no. 1 (1996): 26–61; "Roster of the Fenian Brotherhood"; William O'Brien, *When We Were Boys,* 2nd ed. (London: Longmans, Green, 1890), quote 155.

35. Owen McGee, *The IRB: The Irish Republican Brotherhood, from the Land League to Sinn Féin* (Dublin: Four Courts Press, 2005), 52–54; Niall Whelehan, *The Dynamiters: Irish Nationalism and Political Violence in a Wider World, 1867–1900* (Cambridge: Cambridge University Press, 2012), 71–83; Darcy, *Fenian Movement,* 67–93; Miller, *Emigrants and Exiles,* quote 338; Fenian Brotherhood Collection; William H. Murphy and James Stephens, *Stephens' Fenian Songster* (New York: Murphy, 1866), 54.

36. Steward, "Erin's Hope," quote 197; Lucy Salyer, *Under the Starry Flag: How a Band of Irish Americans Joined the Fenian Revolt and Sparked a Crisis Over Citizenship* (Cambridge, MA: Belknap Press, 2018), 89–175.

37. Table XVII A and B, "Statistics of Churches in the United States at the Censuses of 1870, 1860 and 1850," 520–521: *1870 Census: Vol. I. The Statistics of the Population of the United States*; Charles Morris, *American Catholic* (New York: Vintage, 2011), 16–21; Burrows and Wallace, *Gotham,* 901–924, 986–998; Bernstein, *Draft Riots,* 195–236; Alan Dawley and Paul Faler, "Working-Class Culture and Politics in the Industrial Revolution: Sources of Loyalism and Rebellion," *Journal of Social History* 9, no. 4 (July 1976): 477; Richard

Schneirov, *Labor and Urban Politics: Class Conflict and the Origins of Modern Liberalism in Chicago, 1864–1897* (Urbana: University of Illinois Press, 1998), 32, 52–57; Burchell, *San Francisco Irish,* 106–107, 139–141; Kenny, *Molly Maguires,* 113; Walkowitz, *Worker City,* 85–96, 159–160, 195; Shaw, *Jersey City,* 110–159.

38. Michael A. Gordon, *The Orange Riots: Irish Political Violence in New York City, 1870 and 1871* (Ithaca, NY: Cornell University Press, 1993), 104–106, 23–103, 115–130; Cecil Houston and William Smyth, *The Sash Canada Wore: A Historical Geography of the Orange Order in Canada* (Toronto: University of Toronto Press, 1980), vii, 3–6, 24–28. James Hennessy, *The First Council of the Vatican: The American Experience* (New York: Herder and Herder, 1963), 18–30, 84–85, 104, 178, 196, quote 229.

39. Philip Sheldon Foner, *The Great Labor Uprising of 1877* (New York: Monad Press, 1977), 20.

40. Foner, *Labor Uprising,* 32, 37–44, 63, 145, 201; Kenny, *The American Irish,* 148.

41. Alexander Saxton, *The Indispensable Enemy: Labor and the Anti-Chinese Movement in California* (Berkeley: University of California Press, 1971), 103–106, 76–77, 81–101; Andrew Gyory, *Closing the Gate: Race, Politics, and the Chinese Exclusion Act* (Chapel Hill: University of North Carolina Press, 1998), quote 97, quote 82, 76–85, 92, 125.

42. Burrows and Wallace, *Gotham,* 1008–1034, quote 1029, quote 1032.

43. Richard Hofstadter, *Social Darwinism in American Thought* (New York: G. Braziller, 1959), 3–50, 170–200; L. Perry Curtis, *Apes and Angels: The Irishman in Victorian Caricature* (Washington, DC: Smithsonian, 1997), 58–108; Golway, *Machine Made,* 119–120, 121, 119; Burrows and Wallace, *Gotham,* quote 1034.

44. Golway, *Machine Made,* 108–119, 121–125; Steven P. Erie, *Rainbow's End: Irish Americans and the Dilemmas of Urban Machine Politics, 1840–1985* (Berkeley: University of California Press, 1988), 29–62.

7. A New Generation and New Immigrants in Turn-of-the-Century America

1. Williams, *T'was Only an Irishman's Dream,* 163–169; "David Braham and Edward Harrigan, Collected Songs, Part 1: 1873–1882," in John Finson, ed., *Music of the United States of America* (Madison, WI: AR Editions, 1997), vol. 7, 83. Patrick Blessing, *The Irish in America: A Guide to the Literature and the Manuscript Collections* (Washington, DC: Catholic University of America Press, 2007), 308; Ruggles, Flood, et al., IPUMS USA U.S. Censuses 1880, 1900, 1910.

2. Daniel Cassidy, *How the Irish Invented Slang: The Secret Language of the Crossroads* (Oakland, CA: AK Press, 2007), 1–73.

3. William V. Shannon, *The American Irish* (New York: Macmillan, 1963), 142–143; Ruggles, Flood, et al., IPUMS USA U.S. Censuses 1860, 1880, 1900.

4. Andrew Greeley, "The Success and Assimilation of Irish Protestants and Catholics in the United States," *Social Science Research,* 72, no. 4 (1985): 229–235; Ruggles, Flood, et al., IPUMS USA U.S. Censuses 1860, 1880, 1900, 1930.

5. Ruggles, Flood, et al., IPUMS USA U.S. Censuses 1860, 1880, 1900, 1930.

6. Joel Perlmann, *Ethnic Differences: Schooling and Social Structure Among the Irish, Italians, Jews, and Blacks in an American City, 1880–1935* (Cambridge: Cambridge University Press, 1988), 58, 47–61; Susan Cotts Watkins, *After Ellis Island: Newcomers and Natives in the 1910 Census* (New York: Russell Sage Foundation, 1994), 243; Anthony Kuzniewski, *Thy Honored Name: A History of the College of the Holy Cross, 1843–1994* (Washington, DC: Catholic University of America Press, 1999), 197, 206–207; *Reports of the Immigration Commission, 61st Congress, 3d session, Document no. 247:* Volume 29, "Children of Immigrants in Schools," 154–164; Kathleen Sprows Cummings, *New Women of the Old Faith: Gender and Progressivism in the Progressive Era* (Chapel Hill: University of North Carolina Press, 2009), 59–99.

7. Ruggles, Flood, et al., IPUMS USA U.S. Censuses 1880, 1900, 1930.

8. Janet Nolan, *Service to the Poor: Teachers and Mobility in Ireland and Irish America* (Notre Dame, IN: University of Notre Dame Press, 2004), 58–59, 76–77, 92–93, 112–113; Ruggles, Flood, et al., IPUMS USA U.S. Censuses 1860, 1880, 1900, 1930; Geraldine J. Clifford, *Those Good Gertrudes: A Social History of Women Teachers in America* (Baltimore: Johns Hopkins University Press, 2014), 64, 110–111; Diner, *Erin's Daughters,* 70–105; William H. A. Williams, "Green Again: Irish-American Lace-Curtain Satire," *New Hibernia Review / Iris Éireannach Nua* 6, no. 2 (July 1, 2002): 9–24.

9. Julian Drachsler, *Intermarriage in New York City: A Study of the Amalgamation of European Peoples* (New York, 1923), 10; Burchell, *San Francisco Irish,* 80–81; David M. Emmons, *The Butte Irish: Class and Ethnicity in an American Town, 1875–1925* (Urbana: University of Illinois Press, 1989), 83–84; Meagher, *Inventing Irish America,* 123; Robert McCaa, "Ethnic Intermarriage and Gender in New York City," *Journal of Interdisciplinary History* 24, no. 2 (September 22, 1993): 207–231.

10. Ruggles, Flood, et al., IPUMS USA U.S. Census 1900, 1930; Howard Chudacoff and Judith E. Smith, *The Evolution of American Urban Society,* 6th ed. (Englewood Cliffs, NJ: Pearson/Prentice Hall, 2005), 67–86; Albert J. Kennedy and Robert Woods, *The Zone of Emergence* (Cambridge, MA: Harvard University Press, 1962), 2, 36, 151; Watkins, *After Ellis Island,* 196, 200–201; Ellen Skerrett, "The Catholic Dimension," in Lawrence McCaffrey, ed., *The Irish in Chicago* (Urbana: University of Illinois Press, 1987), 39–41.

11. Williams, *T'was Only an Irishman's Dream,* 119–120, 130, 147; Daniel Snyder, *The Voice of the City: Vaudeville and Popular Culture in New York* (New York: Oxford University Press, 1989), quote 23; Armond Fields, *Women Vaudeville Stars: Eighty Biographical Profiles* (Jefferson, NC: McFarland, 2006), 13–16, 155–156, 242, 66; David L. Fleitz, *The Irish in*

Baseball: An Early History (Jefferson, NC: McFarland, 2009), 28–29, 58; Jerrold Casway, *Ed Delahanty in the Emerald Age of Baseball* (Notre Dame, IN: University of Notre Dame Press, 2004); Elizabeth Titrington Craft, "Becoming American Onstage: Broadway Narratives of Immigrant Experiences in the United States" (PhD dissertation, Harvard University, 2014), 31–87; Steven A. Reiss, *City Games: The Evolution of American Urban Society and the Rise of Sports* (Urbana: University of Illinois Press, 1989), 87; *Catholic Telegraph*, July 28, November 24, 1904, May 15, 1919; *Monitor*, September 11, 1909, April 1904, January 21, October 30, 1905; Meagher, *Inventing Irish America*, 73–78.

12. Kennedy and Woods, *The Zone of Emergence*, 2, 36, 151; James K. Benson, "Social Structure and Ethnic Conflict in Frontier Towns: The Case of St. Paul, Minnesota" (PhD dissertation, University of Minnesota, 1980), quote 318.

13. William Guilfoy, "The Death-Rate of the City of New York as Affected by the Cosmopolitan Character of Its Population," *Publications of the American Statistical Association* 10, no. 80 (December 1, 1907): 515–532; Niles Carpenter, *Immigrants and Their Children: Census Monographs Volume 7* (Washington, DC: GPO, 1927), 199–203.

14. Benson, "Social Structure," 304; David C. Hammack, *Power and Society: Greater New York at the Turn of the Century* (New York: Russell Sage Foundation, 1982), 68; Meagher, *Inventing Irish America*, 99–107; Ruggles, Flood, et al., IPUMS USA U.S. Census 1900.

15. Meagher, *Inventing Irish America*, quote 105; Williams, "Green Again," 13, 9–24; James Barrett, "The Irish and the Americanization of the New Immigrant in the Streets and Churches of the Urban United States, 1900–1930," *Journal of American Ethnic History* 24, no. 4 (2005): quote 11; *Reports of the Immigration Commission*, Volume 36: Immigrants and Crime, 97.

16. Erie, *Rainbow's End*, 5, 98–105; *Reports of the Immigration Commission*, "Children in Schools," Volume I, 154, Table 111, 12; Ruggles, Flood, et al., IPUMS USA U.S. Census 1900, 1930.

17. E. Digby Baltzell, *The Protestant Establishment: Aristocracy and Caste in America* (New York: Random House, 1964), 26–142; Shannon, *The American Irish*, 86–94, 182–200; Meagher, *Inventing Irish America*, quote 102.

18. Drachsler, *Intermarriage in New York City*, 10; Burchell, *San Francisco Irish*, 80–81; Emmons, *The Butte Irish*, 83–84; Meagher, *Inventing Irish America*, 123; Michael F. Funchion, "Ties That Bind: Ethnic and Religious Factors in the Marriage Choices of Irish-American Catholics on the Dakota Frontier," *New Hibernia Review* 14, no. 3 (2010): 121–142; Barrett, "Irish and Americanization," quote 11, 3–33; Skerrett, "The Catholic Dimension," quote 39–41; ACUA: Papers of James Aloysius Geary: Series one, Personal Papers, Box 3, folder 5.

19. Guinnane, *Vanishing Irish*, 199–240; Mark C. Foley and Timothy C. Guinnane, "Did Irish Marriage Patterns Survive the Emigrant Voyage? Irish-American Nuptiality, 1880–1920,"

Irish Economic and Social History 26, no. 1 (June 1999): 22–34; Catherine Burns, "The Courtship of John Rooney and Katharine Cusack, 1887–93: Obligations and Marriage Ideals in Irish-American New England," *New Hibernia Review* 16, no. 4 (2012): 43–63; Meagher, *Inventing Irish America*, 116–123, 328–329; Nancy S. Landale and Stewart Tolnay, "Generation, Ethnicity and Marriage: Historical Patterns in the Northern United States," *Demography* 30, no. 1 (February 1993): 103–127; Ruggles, Flood, et al., IPUMS USA U.S. Census 1880, 1900.

20.   Cummings, *New Women of the Old Faith*, 65–67; James R. Barrett, *The Irish Way: Becoming American in the Multiethnic City* (New York: Penguin Press, 2012), 79; Donna Merwick, *Boston Priests, 1848–1910: A Study of Social and Intellectual Change* (Cambridge, MA: Harvard University Press, 1973), 90–91; Ellen Skerrett, Steven Avella, and Edward Kantowicz, *Catholicism, Chicago Style* (Chicago: Loyola University Press, 1993), 12.

21.   Dolan, *Catholic Revivalism*, 44–50, 124–133; Taves, *Household of Faith*, 34 note 40; Leslie Woodcock Tentler, *Seasons of Grace: A History of the Catholic Archdiocese of Detroit* (Detroit: Wayne State University Press, 1990), 174–182; Meagher, *Inventing Irish America*, quote 86; Timothy J. Meagher, "The Miracles of St. Anthony of Padua," in Colleen McDannell, ed., *Religions of America in Practice* (Princeton, NJ: Princeton University Press, 2001), Volume I, 337–344.

22.   *The Catholic Pages of American History: Our Church and Country* (New York: Catholic Historical League of America, 1905), 523–527, 657–712; Christopher Kauffman, *Faith and Fraternalism: The History of the Knights of Columbus, 1882–1982* (New York: Harper and Row, 1982), 29–228; Skerrett, "Catholic Dimension," 47; David McCowin, "'For Faith and For Freedom': American Catholic Manhood and the Holy Name Society in Boston, 1870–1960" (PhD dissertation, Boston College, 2011), 35; Jay Dolan, "The Irish Parish," *U.S. Catholic Historian* 25, no. 2 (2007): quote 18.

23.   Tentler, *Seasons of Grace*, 142, 164; Doris Kearns Goodwin, *The Fitzgeralds and the Kennedys* (New York: Simon and Schuster, 1987), quote 27; Meagher, *Inventing Irish America*, 79–97; Hugh McLeod, "Catholicism and the New York Irish," in Jim Obelkevich et al., *Disciplines of Faith* (New York: Routledge, 1987), quote 350.

24.   Meagher, *Inventing Irish America*, 162–172; Joan Bland, *"Hibernian Crusade": The Story of the Catholic Total Abstinence Union of America* (Washington, DC: Catholic University of America Press, 1951); Charles C. Alexander, *John McGraw* (New York: Penguin, 1988), 32–33, 52–53, 8; McCowin, "Faith and Freedom," 111–117.

25.   Casway, *Emerald Age*, 126–128; Alexander, *McGraw*, 32, 171; Elliott Gorn, *The Manly Art* (Ithaca, NY: Cornell University Press, 2010), quote 236, 243, 244–245; Fields, *Women Vaudeville Stars*, 14–16, 155; Williams, *T'was Only an Irishman's Dream*, 147; Richard F. Peterson, "'Slide Kelly Slide': The Irish in American Baseball," in Lawrence Baldassaro and Richard A. Johnson, eds., *The American Game: Baseball and Ethnicity* (Carbondale:

Southern Illinois University Press, 2002), 60–61; Craft, "Becoming American Onstage," 88–176; Snyder, *Vaudeville,* 110, quote 190.

26. Williams, *T'was Only an Irishman's Dream,* quote 137, 146; Williams, "Green Again," 9–24; Craft, "Becoming American Onstage," 106–140, 147–155; Judith Weisenfeld, "The Silent Social Problem Film (1915)" in Colleen McDannell, ed., *Catholics in the Movies* (Oxford: Oxford University Press, 2008), 43–58; Williams, *T'was Only an Irishman's Dream,* quote 150–151, 2–4, 153, 146–147; Shannon, *Bowery to Broadway: The American Irish in Classic Hollywood Cinema* (Scranton, PA: University of Scranton Press, 2010), 142.

27. Diane Dunnigan, *A South Roscommon Emigrant: Emigration and Return, 1890–1920* (Dublin: Four Courts, 2007), quote 26, 15–53.

28. EPPI, *Agricultural Statistics of Ireland, 1883,* HC 1884 4069 83 313, 9–11; O'Grada, *New Economic History,* 258; Akenson, *Ireland, Sweden,* 201–204; Miller, *Emigrants and Exiles,* 380–388, 391, 395–397.

29. O'Grada, *New Economic History,* 239–244; Miller, *Emigrants and Exiles,* 361.

30. Akenson, *Ireland, Sweden,* 180, 202–206; O'Grada, *New Economic History,* 289, 295, 309, 312–313; Guinnane, *Vanishing Irish,* 193–240; Diarmaid Ferriter, *The Transformation of Ireland: 1900–2000* (London: Profile, 2005), quote 47.

31. Miller, *Emigrants and Exiles,* 405–409; Janet Nolan, *Ourselves Alone: Women's Emigration from Ireland, 1885–1920* (Lexington: University of Kentucky Press, 2009), 40, 70–71; quote 54; Meaney et al., *Reading the Irish Woman,* 87–102.

32. EPPI, *Emigration Statistics of Ireland, 1880,* HC 1881 Volume 64 703, 12; *Emigration Statistics of Ireland, 1911,* Volume 60 701, 15; Guinnane, *Vanishing Irish,* 45, 183–186; Ciara Breathnach, *The Congested Districts Board of Ireland, 1891–1923; Poverty and Development in the West of Ireland* (Dublin: Four Courts, 2005), 26; EPPI, *Agricultural Statistics of Ireland, 1884–1885,* Volume 85, I, 10; O'Grada, *New Economic History,* 233–235, 240–244, 252–254; Miller, *Emigrants and Exiles,* 397–404.

33. Philip Taylor, *The Distant Magnet* (New York: Harper and Row, 1971), 161, 179, 278; Miller, *Emigrants and Exiles,* 354–356.

34. Arnold Schrier, *Ireland and the American Emigration, 1850–1900* (Minneapolis: University of Minnesota Press, 1958), 110–111; Guinnane, *Vanishing Irish,* 108–111, quote 111; Meaney et al., *Reading the Irish Woman,* 99–100; Cole Moreton, *Hungry for Home: Leaving the Blaskets; A Journey from the Edge of Ireland* (New York: Viking, 2000), 113–118; Gill, *Louisburgh-Clinton Connection,* 19–33, Appendix III, 1–22, Appendix IV, 1–5; David Fitzpatrick, "Irish Emigration in the Late Nineteenth Century," *Irish Historical Studies* 22, no. 86 (September 1980): 127–143.

35. Emmons, *The Butte Irish,* 1–34; Ruggles, Flood, et al., IPUMS USA U.S. Census 1900.

36. Anbinder, *City of Dreams,* xx; Guilfoy, "The Death-Rate," 515–531; Dublin, "The Mortality of Race Stocks," 15–22; Martin Dribe, J. David Hacker, and Francesco Scalone, "Im-

migrants and Child Mortality," *Social Science History* 44, no. 1 (2020): 57–89; Carpenter, *Immigrants and Their Children,* 199–203.

37. Diner, *Erin's Daughters,* 107–108; Schrier, *Ireland and the American Emigrations,* 34; Ruggles, Flood, et al., IPUMS USA U.S. Census 1930; Stephan Thernstrom, *Other Bostonians: Poverty and Progress in the American Metropolis, 1880–1970* (Cambridge, MA: Harvard University Press, 1973), 130–137; Miller, *Emigrants and Exiles,* 514, 519.

38. Grayson, "Calling the Heart Home," 266–267, 270, 302; Foley and Guinnane, "Irish Marriage in America," 16; Meagher, *Inventing Irish America,* 53–55; Diner, *Erin's Daughters,* quote 62, 54–69, 74–94; Andrew Urban, "Irish Domestic Servants, 'Biddy' and Rebellion in the American Home, 1850–1900," *Gender & History* 21, no. 2 (August 1, 2009): 264–280; Ruggles, Floyd, et al. IPUMS USA U.S. Census 1880, 1900, 1930; Niles Carpenter, *Immigrants and Their Children,* 185; Guinnane and Foley, "Irish Marriage Patterns," 22–34.

39. Ruggles, Flood, et al., IPUMS USA U.S. Census 1900; Watkins, *After Ellis Island,* 196, 200–201; John Ridge, "The County Societies of New York," in Bayor and Meagher, *New York Irish,* 285–289; Baptismal Register, Mission Church, 1884 to 1886, Archives of the Archdiocese of Boston.

40. *Reports of the Immigration Commission:* Volume 36, 100, 19; Diner, *Erin's Daughters,* 116–117; Suellen Hoy, "The Journey Out: The Recruitment and Emigration of Irish Religious Women to the United States, 1812–1914," *Journal of Women's History* 7, no. 1 (1995): 64–98; Mary Elizabeth Fraser Connolly, *Women of Faith* (New York: Fordham University Press, 2014), 28; Richard Gribble CSC, *An Archbishop for the People: The Life of Edward J. Hanna* (Mahwah, NJ: Paulist Press, 2006), 76–78.

41. *Reports of the Immigration Commission:* Volume 36, 97; Diner, *Erin's Daughters,* 113–114; Miller, *Emigrants and Exiles,* 417–419; Gearóid Ó hAllmhuráin, *Flowing Tides: History and Memory in an Irish Soundscape* (New York: Oxford University Press, 2016), 86–121; Mick Moloney, "Irish Ethnic Recordings and the Irish American Imagination," in *Ethnic Recordings in America: A Neglected Heritage* (Washington, DC: American Folklife Center, Library of Congress, 1982), 92.

8. Searching for Their Place at the End of the Nineteenth Century

1. Susan Levine, "Labor's True Woman: Domesticity and Equal Rights in the Knights of Labor," *Journal of American History* 70 (September 1, 1983): 331–335, quotes 332, 334.

2. Ely Janis, *A Greater Ireland: The Land League and Transatlantic Nationalism in Gilded Age America* (Madison: University of Wisconsin Press, 2015), 3–11; T. W. Moody, *Davitt and the Irish Revolution, 1846–82* (New York: Oxford University Press, 1982), 222–327, 381–416; Thomas Brown, *Irish American Nationalism, 1870–1890* (Philadelphia: Lippincott, 1966), 85–98.

3. Janis, *A Greater Ireland,* 17–67, 75–76, 137–151; Miller, *Emigrants and Exiles,* 540.

4. Brown, *Irish American Nationalism,* quote 24, 119–128; Janis, *A Greater Ireland,* 90–103; Meagher, *Inventing Irish America,* 183–184.

5. Janis, *A Greater Ireland,* quote 62, 133, 90–136; Foner, "Class, Ethnicity and Radicalism in the Gilded Age: The Land League and Irish America," in *Politics and Ideology in the Age of the Civil War* (New York: Oxford University Press, 1980), 150–200; Paul Buhle, "The Knights of Labor in Rhode Island," *Radical History Review,* 17 (1978): 39–75; Richard Schneirov, *Labor and Urban Politics: Class Conflict and the Origins of Modern Liberalism in Chicago, 1864–1897* (Urbana: University of Illinois Press, 1998), 6–10; Kim Voss, *The Making of American Exceptionalism: The Knights of Labor and Class Formation in the Nineteenth Century* (Ithaca: Cornell University Press, 1993), 1–91.

6. Moody, *Davitt,* 222–327, 381–416; Terry Golway, *Irish Rebel: John Devoy and America's Fight for Ireland's Freedom* (New York: St. Martin's Griffin, 1998), 104–112, 126–146; McGee, *The IRB,* 67–102.

7. Janis, *A Greater Ireland,* 137–160, 193; Meagher, *Inventing Irish America,* 184–192.

8. Brown, *Irish American Nationalism,* 136–178; Janis, *A Greater Ireland,* 194–197; Meagher, *Inventing Irish America,* 195–198.

9. Foner, *Politics and Ideology,* 150–200; Buhle, "The Knights Rhode Island," 72–89; Robert E. Weir, *Beyond Labor's Veil: The Culture of the Knights of Labor* (University Park: Pennsylvania State University Press, 1996), 92–93; Schneirov, *Labor and Urban Politics,* 110–138; Voss, *The Making of American Exceptionalism,* 72–91; Janis, *A Greater Ireland,* 112–136, 133.

10. Voss, *The Making of American Exceptionalism,* 1–91, 187–228; Craig Phelan, *Grand Master Workman: Terence Powderly and the Knights of Labor* (Westport, CT: Greenwood Press, 2000), 1–6, 192–256.

11. Julie Greene, *Pure and Simple Politics: The American Federation of Labor and Political Activism, 1881–1917* (Cambridge, UK: Cambridge University Press, 1998), 19–53; Laurie, *Artisans into Workers,* 176–188, 194; *Call for the Founding of the FOTLU,* "To all Trades and Labor Unions in the United States and Canada," Gompers Papers, University of Maryland. http://www.gompers.umd.edu/docfotlu.htm.

12. Meagher, *Inventing Irish America,* quote 193; Janis, *A Greater Ireland,* 100, 102.

13. Spalding, *Premier See,* quote 259; Robert D. Cross, *The Emergence of Liberal Catholicism in America* (Cambridge, MA: Harvard University Press, 1958), 106–145; Henry J. Browne, *The Catholic Church and the Knights of Labor* (New York: Arno Press, 1976), 71–274.

14. Cross, *Liberal Catholicism,* 36–54; Marvin R. O'Connell, *John Ireland and the American Catholic Church* (St. Paul: Minnesota Historical Society Press, 1988), 84–86, 342; Meagher, *Inventing Irish America,* 146–152.

15. Ruggles, Flood, et al., IPUMS USA U.S. Census 1860; Thomas T. McAvoy, *The Great Crisis in American Catholic History* (Chicago: Henry Regnery, 1957), 15–28; Kleppner, *The Third*

Electoral System, 78–85; John O. Geiger, "H. J. Desmond: Catholic Citizen, Reformer: The Quest for Justice through Educational and Social Reform" (PhD dissertation, Marquette University, 1972), quote 157, quote 190, 30–53, 92, 125, 134–137, 149–155, 171.

16. Morris, *American Catholic,* 84–98; Cross, *Liberal Catholicism,* 88–123; O'Connell, *John Ireland,* 252–262; Dolores Liptak, *Immigrants and Their Church* (New York: Macmillan, 1989), 92–103; Glen Janus, "Bishop Bernard McQuaid: On 'True' and 'False' Americanism," *U.S. Catholic Historian* 11, no. 3 (1993): 62, 53–76.

17. Morris, *American Catholic,* 84–96; O'Connell, *John Ireland,* 84–86, quote 342.

18. Irish American mayors found in Wikipedia List of Mayors for each city and traced into biographical sources for religion, either reported or deduced usually from attendance at a Catholic school or burial in a Catholic cemetery; William Bullough, *The Blind Boss and His City* (Berkeley: University of California Press, 1972); Richard C. Lindberg, *The Gambler King of Clark Street* (Carbondale: Southern Illinois University Press, 2017); Golway, *Machine Made,* 126–135; Paul Kleppner, "From Party to Faction," 113–121, and Geoffrey Blodgett, "Yankee Leadership in a Divided City," 88–98, in Constance K. Burns and Ronald Formisano, eds., *Boston, 1700–1980: The Evolution of Urban Politics* (Westport, CT: Greenwood Press, 1984); Funchion, "The Political and Nationalist Dimensions," in Lawrence McCaffery, ed., *The Irish in Chicago* (Urbana: University of Illinois Press, 1987), 64–69; Walkowitz, *Worker City*; Cole, *Immigrant City;* NJCU, "Jersey City: Past and Present," July 14, 2021, "Robert Davis, 1848–1911" NCJU.Libguides.com/Davis; Ruggles, Flood, et al., IPUMS USA U.S. Census 1880; Democratic Senator and House members with Irish names traced into biographical sources to confirm religion.

19. Kleppner, *The Third Electoral System,* 150–153; Peter McCaffery, *When Bosses Ruled Philadelphia: The Emergence of the Republican Machine, 1867–1933* (University Park: Pennsylvania State University Press, 1993).

20. Ruggles, Flood, et al., IPUMS USA U.S. Census 1880; Donald A. Debats, "German and Irish Political Engagement" 171–183, and Walter Kamphoefner, "German and Irish Big City Mayors," 221–242, in Wolfgang Helbich and Walter D. Kamphoefner, eds., *German-American Immigration and Ethnicity in Comparative Perspective* (Madison, WI: McKade Institute, 2004).

21. Martin Shefter, "The Electoral Foundations of the Political Machine, New York City, 1884–1887," in Joel Silbey and Allan Bogue, eds., *The History of American Electoral Behavior* (Princeton, NJ: Princeton University Press, 1978), 263–264, Kleppner, "From Party to Factions," 113–121 and Blodgett, "Yankee Leadership in a Divided City, 1860–1890," 88–98, quote 98, in Burns and Formisano, eds., *Boston, 1700–1980;* Erie, *Rainbow's End,* 29–50.

22. Meagher, *Inventing Irish America,* 146–156; James W. Sanders, "Catholics and the School Question," in Robert Sullivan and James O'Toole, eds., *Catholic Boston: Studies in Religion and Community* (Boston: Roman Catholic Archdiocese of Boston, 1985), 121–123.

23. Leon Fink, *Workingmen's Democracy: The Knights of Labor and American Politics* (Urbana: University of Illinois Press, 1983), 22–35, 52–111; Phelan, *Grand Master Workman,* 22–35; Connolly, *Elusive Unity,* 87–114; Erie, *Rainbow's End,* 48.

24. Hammack, *Power and Society,* 131–140, 159–162, 173–176; Shefter, "The Electoral Foundations," 281–282; Golway, *Machine Made,* 132–144, 149–153; Janis, *A Greater Ireland,* 175–176, 201–204; Cross, *Liberal Catholicism,* 120–121; Morris, *American Catholic,* 93; O'Connell, *John Ireland,* 231–233.

25. Alvin Jackson, *Ireland: 1989–1998* (Malden, MA: Blackwell, 1999), 133–147; McAvoy, *The Great Crisis,* 261–343; Greene, *Pure and Simple Politics,* 36–69; Robin Archer, *Why Is There No Labor Party in the United States?* (Princeton, NJ: Princeton University Press, 2007), 1–22, 49–72, 177–243; "An Interesting Discussion on a Political Program at the Denver Convention of the American Federation of Labor, 1894," Proquest, History Vault: AFL and CIO Pamphlets, 1889–1955, AFL Pamphlets; Folder, 1894; Golway, *Irish Rebel,* 166–168.

26. John J. Appel, "Immigrant Historical Societies in the United States, 1880–1950" (PhD dissertation: University of Pennsylvania, 1960), 48–57; David Gleeson, "Smaller Differences: 'Scotch Irish' and 'Real Irish' in the Nineteenth-Century American South," *New Hibernia Review* 10, no. 2 (2006): 87; Kleppner, *The Third Electoral System,* 78–85; "Panic of 1893," *UXL Encyclopedia of U.S. History,* 2009 Vol. 6, 1194–1198; Donald Louis Kinzer, *An Episode in Anti-Catholicism: The American Protective Association* (Seattle: University of Washington Press, 1964), 100–179.

27. Golway, *Machine Made,* 145–185; Hammack, *Power and Society,* 121, 138–139, quote 139, 140–155, 161–181, quote 168.

28. Irish American mayors found in Wikipedia List of Mayors for each city and traced into biographical sources for religion, either reported or deduced usually from attendance at a Catholic school or burial in a cemetery. John Paul Bocock, "The Irish Conquest of Our Cities," *The Forum* 17 (April 1894): 186–195. Fink, *Workingmen's Democracy*, 52–90.

29. O'Dea, *History of the Ancient Order of Hibernians,* Vol. II, 884–894, 991–1017; Volume III, 1027–1047, 1129, 1357–1358, 1380, 1381, 1452; Meagher, *Inventing Irish America,* 243; Skerrett, "The Catholic Dimension," 46–47; John Ridge, *Erin's Sons in America: The Ancient Order of Hibernians* (New York: AOH 150th Anniversary Committee, 1980).

30. O'Dea, *History of the Ancient Order of Hibernians,* Volume III, quote 1217, quote 1107, 1106–1111, 1145, 1196, 1171, 1274, 1292, 1373, 1403–1404. Cronin and Adair, *The Wearing of the Green,* 72, 73–75; *Worcester Telegram,* March 25, 27, 1898; *New York Times,* March 18, 1897, March 17, 1897; *New Orleans Picayune,* March 17, 19, 1897; *San Francisco Call,* March 18, 1905.

31. Una Ni Bhroimeil, *Building Irish Identity in America, 1879–1915* (Dublin: Four Courts Press, 2003), 16–19, 50–57, 65, 70–75, 93, 112, 127; O'Dea, *History of AOH,* Volume III,

1131–133, 1362, 1395; Paul Darby, *Gaelic Games: Nationalism and the Irish Diaspora in the United States* (Dublin: University College Dublin Press, 2009), 30–37, 47, 69–81; David Noel Doyle, *Irish Americans: Native Rights and National Empires* (New York: Arno Press, 1976), 226–227, 240, 249, 262, 277, 288; Matthew Jacobson, *Special Sorrows: The Diaspora Imagination of Irish, Polish, and Jewish Immigrants in the United States* (Cambridge, MA: Harvard University Press, 1995), quote 205.

32. O'Dea, *History of AOH,* Volume III, quote 1381.

9. Finding Their Place

1. Golway, *Machine Made,* 180–194; Nancy J. Weiss, *Charles Francis Murphy, 1858–1924: Respectability and Responsibility in Tammany Politics* (Northampton, MA: Smith College, 1968), 7–67.

2. Weiss, *Charles Francis Murphy,* 40–83, quote 87; Golway, *Machine Made,* 183–196; Chris McNickle, *To Be Mayor of New York: Ethnic Politics in the City* (New York: Columbia University Press, 1993), 20–27.

3. Barrett, *The Irish Way,* 7; Shannon, *The American Irish,* quote 132, 131–145.

4. David Montgomery, "The Irish in the American Labor Movement," in David Noel Doyle and Owen Dudley Edwards, eds., *America and Ireland, 1776–1976* (Westport, CT: Greenwood Press, 1980), 206; Greene, *Pure and Simple,* 72–73.

5. Edwin Fenton, *Immigrants and Unions: Italians and American Labor, 1870–1920* (New York: Arno Press, 1975), 223–254, quote 230; Greene, *Pure and Simple,* 83; Barrett, *The Irish Way,* 119–122; Bruce Nelson, *Divided We Stand: American Workers and the Struggle for Black Equality* (Princeton, NJ: Princeton University Press, 2001), 21–27.

6. Emmons, *The Butte Irish,* 263–286; Barrett, *The Irish Way,* 138–150; Cole, *Immigrant City,* 185–187; Elliott Gorn, *Mother Jones: The Most Dangerous Woman in America* (New York: Hill and Wang, 2001), 180; Marc Karson, "The Catholic Church and the Political Development of American Trade Unions," *Industrial and Labor Relations Review* 4 (1951): 527–542.

7. Montgomery, *House of Labor,* 281–330; Leo Wolman, "Union Membership in Great Britain and the United States," *National Bureau of Economic Research Bulletin* 68 (December 27, 1937): 1–16; Barrett, *The Irish Way,* 137–138; Sara Deutsch, *Women and the City: Gender, Space and Power in Boston, 1870–1940* (New York: Oxford University Press, 2000), 206–218; *Proceedings of the Thirty Fifth Convention of the American Federation of Labor 1915,* x–xv. Joseph A. McCartin, *Labor's Great War: The Struggle for Industrial Democracy and the Origins of Modern American Labor Relatons* (Chapel Hill: University of North Carolina Press, 1997) 71–79.

8. Connolly, *An Elusive Unity,* 54–86, 135–164, 217–223; Jane Addams, "Why the Ward Boss Rules" (1998), http://usd116.org/profdev/ahtc/activities/addams_boss.pdf; Fred I. Green-

stein, "The Changing Pattern of Urban Politics," 5, and Elmer E. Cornwell Jr., "Bosses, Machines and Ethnic Groups," 31, *Annals of the American Academy of Political and Social Sciences* 353 (May 1964); Christopher K. Ansell and Arthur L. Burris, "Bosses of the City Unite! Labor Politics and Political Consolidation, 1870–1910," *Studies in American Political Development* 11, no. 1 (Spring 1997): 1–8.

9. Erie, *Rainbow's End,* 84–105; James Connolly, "Beyond the Machine: Martin Lomasney and Ethnic Politics," in Reed Ueda and Conrad Edrick Wright, eds., *Faces of Community: Immigrant Massachusetts 1860–2000* (Boston: Massachusetts Historical Society, 2003), 189–209.

10. Erie, *Rainbow's End,* 83–103; Connolly, "Beyond the Machine," 200–209; Ruggles, Flood, et al., IPUMS USA U.S. Census 1900, 1910.

11. Daniel Klinghard, "Reading 'Plunkitt of Tammany Hall' in the Context of Late Nineteenth Century Party Nationalization," *Polity* 43, no. 4 (2011): 488–512; Michael McGerr, *The Decline of Popular Politics in the American North, 1865–1928* (New York: Oxford University Press, 1986), 158–183; Maureen Flanagan, *America Reformed: Progressives and Progressivisms, 1890s–1920s* (New York: Oxford University Press, 2007), 35–48.

12. Paul Kleppner, *Continuity and Change in Electoral Politics, 1893–1928* (New York: Greenwood Press, 1987), 125–135; Greene, *Pure and Simple Politics,* 129–188; Heather Cox Richardson, *To Make Men Free: A History of the Republican Party* (New York: Basic Books, 2014), 139–170.

13. Sixty-eight men with Irish names were elected to the Massachusetts House, over one-quarter of the House chamber, and twelve were elected to the State Senate, over a fifth of that body in 1913: *Manual of the General Court 1913,* 439–459. Over half, twenty-two, of the thirty-six Democrats in the malapportioned Rhode Island house had Irish names in 1914: *Manual with Rules and Orders for the Use of the General Assembly of the State of Rhode Island;* Democratic governors, Senators, and House members with Irish names traced into biographical sources to confirm religion. John Buenker, *Urban Liberalism and Progressive Reform* (New York: Scribners, 1973), 20–24, 35–38; John Blum, *Joe Tumulty and the Wilson Era* (Boston: Houghton Mifflin, 1951), 3–25.

14. Golway, *Machine Made,* 156, 211–214; Blum, *Joe Tumulty,* 3–19; Buenker, *Urban Liberalism,* 48–49, 52–56, 58–79, 87–90, 95–97, 103–105, 107–110; Barrett, *The Irish Way,* 210–217; David Sarasohn, *The Party of Reform: Democrats in the Progressive Era* (Jackson: University Press of Mississippi, 1989), xi–xiii, 145–212.

15. David N. Doyle, "Catholicism, Politics and Irish America since 1890: Some Critical Considerations," 206–208, in P. J. O'Drudy, *The Irish in America: Emigration, Assimilation and Impact* (Cambridge, UK: Cambridge University Press, 1985); Montgomery, *Fall of House of Labor,* 165–169, 166; Tara McCarthy, *Respectability and Reform: Irish American Women's Activism, 1880–1920* (Syracuse: Syracuse University Press, 2018), 33–48; Francis Brod-

erick, *Right Reverend New Dealer, John A. Ryan* (New York: Macmillan, 1963), 3–18, 57, 78; Greene, *Pure and Simple Politics,* 55; Yougov.com: Irish American House members: To override Presidential vetoes of the literacy test: February 9, 1913, 15 votes no, 1 vote yes, 2 not voting; February 4, 1915, 38 votes no, 1 vote yes, 4 not voting; February 1, 1917, 24 votes no, 2 not voting.

16. Thomas Henderson, "Tammany Hall and the New Immigrants, 1910–1921" (PhD dissertation, University of Virginia, 1973), 160–194; Gerald H. Gamm, *The Making of the New Deal Democrats: Voting Behavior and Realignment in Boston, 1920–1940* (Chicago: University of Chicago Press, 1989), 82–83; Evelyn Savidge Sterne, *Ballots and Bibles: Ethnic Politics and the Catholic Church in Providence* (Ithaca: Cornell University Press, 2004), 84–85; John M. Allswang, *A House for All Peoples: Ethnic Politics in Chicago, 1890–1936* (Lexington: University Press of Kentucky, 1971), 18–58.

17. *Congressional Quarterly's Guide to United States Elections* (Washington: Congressional Quarterly, 2007) 405, 413, 494, 717.

18. Jack Beatty, *The Rascal King: The Life and Times of James Michael Curley, 1874–1958* (Reading, MA: Addison-Wesley, 1992), 140–170, 225; James Connolly, *The Triumph of Ethnic Progressivism: Urban Political Culture in Boston, 1900–1925* (Cambridge, MA: Harvard University Press, 1998), 18–38, 77–132, 105–189; O'Connor, *The Boston Irish,* 142–190.

19. Dorothy Wayman, *David I. Walsh: Citizen and Patriot* (Milwaukee, WI: Bruce, 1952), 34–44; Blum, *Joe Tumulty,* 7–8, 16; Richard Allen Morton, *Justice and Humanity: Edward Dunne, Illinois Progressive* (Carbondale: Southern Illinois University Press, 1997), 4–10; Golway, *Machine Made,* 206–233.

20. J. Joseph Huthmacher, *Massachusetts People and Politics, 1919–1933* (New York: Atheneum, 1969), 117–149; Blum, *Joe Tumulty,* 5–30; J. Leonard Bates, *Senator Thomas J. Walsh of Montana: Law and Public Affairs, from TR to FDR* (Urbana: University of Illinois Press, 1999), 1–27; Broderick, *John A. Ryan,* 1–51; Timothy Michael Dolan, *Some Seed Fell on Good Ground: Life of Edward V. O'Hara* (Washington, DC: Catholic University of America Press, 1992), 1–22, 30–35.

21. John Higham, *Strangers in the Land: Patterns of American Nativism, 1860–1925* (New Brunswick, NJ: Rutgers University Press, 2004), 178–182; Baltzell, *Protestant Establishment,* 179–226; Dolan, *American Catholic Experience,* 318–320; *Pittsburgh Catholic* July 4, 1907; quote *Kentucky Irish American* May 13, 1905; *Denver Catholic Register* July 20, 1907.

22. Morris, *American Catholic,* 109–116, 117, 169–170; James O'Toole, *Militant and Triumphant: William Henry O'Connell and the Catholic Church in Boston, 1859–1944* (Notre Dame, IN: University of Notre Dame Press, 1992), 16, 17–22, 31, 38–39, 60–71, 80–92; David O'Brien, *Faith and Friendship: Catholicism in the Diocese of Syracuse, 1886–1986* (Syracuse: Diocese of Syracuse, 1987), 173–176; Tentler, *Seasons of Grace,* 249–252, 259;

Proceedings of the Twelfth Annual Meeting of the National Catholic Education Association, 1915, 379.

23. Cummings, *New Women of the Old Faith,* 101–130; Carol K. Coburn and Martha Smith, *Spirited Lives: How Nuns Shaped Catholic Culture and American Life, 1836–1920* (Chapel Hill: University of North Carolina Press, 1999), 87–180.

24. Cummings, *New Women of the Old Faith,* quote 137, 130–151.

25. *Religious Bodies: 1916,* U.S. Bureau of the Census (Washington, DC: GPO, 1919), 29, 21–29, 7,343,186 to 15,721,813; Alfred J. Ede, *The Lay Crusade for a Christian America: A Study of the American Federation of Catholic Societies, 1900–1919* (New York: Garland, 1988), quote 75.

26. Rudolph J. Vecoli, "Prelates and Peasants: Italian Immigrants and the Catholic Church," *Journal of Social History* 2, no. 3 (April 1, 1969): 217–268; John Joseph Parot, *Polish Catholics in Chicago, 1850–1920: A Religious History* (DeKalb: Northern Illinois University Press, 1981), 1–28.

27. Parot, *Polish Catholics in Chicago,* 29–52, 78, 119–124, 140–160; Anbinder, *Five Points,* 387; Liptak, *Immigrants and Their Church,* 114–154; Richard M. Linkh, *American Catholicism and European Immigrants, 1900–1924* (Staten Island, NY: Center for Migration Studies, 1975), 25–29, 69–94; Mary Elizabeth Brown, "Italian and Italian American Secular Clergy in New York, 1880–1950," *U.S. Catholic Historian,* 6, no. 4 (Fall 1987): 296–298; Edward Kantowicz, *Corporation Sole: Cardinal Mundelein and Chicago Catholicism* (Notre Dame, IN: University of Notre Dame Press, 1983), quote 73.

28. Charles Shanabruch, *Chicago's Catholics: The Evolution of an American Identity* (Notre Dame, IN: Notre Dame University Press, 1981), 51–52, 131–133; J. A. Burns, *Catholic Education: A Study of Conditions* (New York: Longmans, 1917), 109–111.

29. Mary Adele Gorman, "Federation of Catholic Societies in the United States, 1870–1920" (PhD dissertation, University of Notre Dame, 1962), 70–85, 92–101, quotes 100–101, 124–130, 158, 237–251.

30. Kauffman, *Faith and Fraternalism,* 127, 140–141, 227.

31. Kauffman, *Faith and Fraternalism,* 16–17, 69, 71, 85–90, 121–123, quote 139.

32. Kauffman, *Faith and Fraternalism,* 87–89, 169, 184–185, 187–197; Meagher, *Inventing Irish America,* quotes 353.

33. Charles Townshend, *Easter 1916: The Irish Rebellion* (Lanham, MD: Lee, 2006), 1–89; McGee, *The IRB,* 321–323; Joseph P. Finnan, *John Redmond and Irish Unity, 1912–1918* (Syracuse, NY: Syracuse University Press, 2004), 78–90, 45–179.

34. Alan Ward, *Ireland and Anglo-American Relations, 1899–1921* (London: London School of Economics and Political Science, Weidenfeld & Nicolson, 1969), 8–104, 126; Golway, *Irish Rebel,* 172–220; Townshend, *Easter 1916,* 49, 60–223; Michael Doorley, *Irish American Diaspora Nationalism: The Friends of Irish Freedom, 1916–1935* (Dublin: Four Courts,

2005), 21–42; Thomas Rowland, "From Neutrality to War: Irish-American Catholics and World War I, 1914–1917" (PhD dissertation, George Washington University, 1992), 96–223.

35. Townshend, *Easter 1916,* 123–213; Francis M. Carroll, *American Opinion and the Irish Question, 1910–1923: A Study in Opinion and Policy* (New York: St. Martin's Press, 1978), 53–99; Ward, *Ireland and Anglo-American Relations,* quote 100; Doorley, *Irish American Diaspora Nationalism,* 48; Alan Ware, *The Democratic Party Heads North, 1877–1962* (Cambridge: Cambridge University Press, 2006), 192–193; William Leary, "Woodrow Wilson, Irish Americans, and the Election of 1916," *Journal of American History* 54, no. 1 (June 1, 1967): 61–71; *Guide to U.S. Elections,* 276–285.

36. Kauffman, *Faith and Fraternalism,* 190–200, 207–215, 286, quote 190, quote 193; Elizabeth McKeown, *War and Welfare: American Catholics and World War I* (New York: Garland, 1988), 43–73, 75, 78–101, 51; Ruggles, Flood, et al., IPUMS USA U.S. Census 1880, 1900, 1910. Germans (27.8 percent), but also Swedes (31.2 percent), Norwegians (31.1 percent), Canadians (30.1 percent), new immigrant Italians (21.9 percent), Poles (23.5 percent), and even people who claimed to be only Americans (25.8 percent); Brundage, *Irish Nationalists in America,* 152–154; Golway, *Irish Rebel,* 240–246; Whelan, *U.S. Foreign Policy,* 140–157; ACUA: National Catholic War Council Records, Box 78, Folders 48–72.

37. Doorley, *Irish American Diaspora Nationalism,* 62–104; John Buckley, "The New York Irish: Their View of American Foreign Policy: 1914–1921" (PhD dissertation, New York University, 1974), 205–220; Ward, *Ireland and Anglo-American Relations,* 158–181; Carroll, *American Opinion,* 119–127; Whelan, *U.S. Foreign Policy,* 185–207.

38. Ward, *Ireland and Anglo-American Relations,* 171–173; Doorley, *Irish American Diaspora Nationalism,* 81–115, 186–193; Carroll, *American Opinion,* 123–127; Buckley, "New York Irish," 298; *New York Times,* August 16, 1920.

39. Townshend, *Easter 1916,* 337–342; Charles Townshend, *The Republic: The Fight for Irish Independence* (London: Penguin, 2013), 6–17, 58–63, 74, 78–79.

40. Ward, *Ireland and Anglo American Relations,* 141, 150, 167; Ernest R. May, *The World War and American Isolation, 1914–1917* (Chicago: Quadrangle Books, 1959), 358.

41. Buckley, "New York Irish," 201; Quote ACUA, Bishop Peter James Muldoon Collection, Microfilm Reel III, entry March 4, 1919; Ward, *Ireland and Anglo-American Relations,* 173–201; Carroll, *American Opinion,* 133–138; Doorley, *Irish American Diaspora Nationalism,* 81–103.

42. Doorley, *Irish American Diaspora Nationalism,* 107–157, 109, 130, 136; Carroll, *American Opinion,* 156–163.

43. David Brundage, "'In Time of Peace, Prepare for War': Key Themes in the Social Thought of New York's Nationalists," in Bayor and Meagher, *The New York Irish,* quote 322, 321–

336; McCarthy, *Respectability,* 144; Damien Murray, "Progressivism, Ethnic Nationalism, and the Emergence of Catholic Democratic Liberalism in Boston, 1900–1924" (PhD dissertation, Boston College, 1905), 270–276; *Irish World,* February 19, 1921; Brundage, *Irish Nationalists in America,* 156; Joe Doyle, "Striking for Ireland on the New York Docks," in Bayor and Meagher, *The New York Irish,* 357–373.

44.   Townshend, *The Republic,* 301–447; Whelan, *U.S. Foreign Policy,* 360–466; Thomas Fleming, *Mysteries of My Father* (Hoboken, NJ: John Wiley, 2005), 137.

45.   Allan H. Spear, *Black Chicago, 1900–1920: The Making of a Negro Ghetto* (New Haven: Yale University, 1964), 11–25; William M. Tuttle, *Race Riot: Chicago in the Red Summer of 1919* (Urbana: University of Illinois Press, 1996), 104–156, 159–181, 184–207, 235–238.

46.   Tuttle, *Race Riot,* 9–10, 11–31, 103; Barrett, *The Irish Way,* quote 52, 47–52; Thomas Guglielmo, *White on Arrival* (New York: Oxford University Press, 2004), 50–57, 96–104; Dominic A. Pacyga, *Polish Immigrants and Industrial Chicago* (Chicago: University of Chicago Press, 2003), 219–226, 220; J. Joseph Huthmacher, *Massachusetts People and Politics, 1919–1933* (New York: Atheneum, 1969), 100–150; *New York Times,* July 9, 1922; Yougov .com: vote January 26, 1922.

47.   Higham, *Strangers in the Land,* 230–315. Kenneth T. Jackson, *The Ku Klux Klan in the City, 1915–1930* (New York: Oxford University Press, 1967), 3–23, 89–91, quote 20, 204–207, 196–214; *Staunton Spectator,* February 4, 1910; *Peninsula Enterprise,* May 16, 1903; *The Laurens Advertiser,* August 24, 1904; quote *The Watchman and Southron,* July 17, 1909.

48.   David Burner, *The Politics of Provincialism: The Democratic Party in Transition, 1918–1932* (New York: Knopf, 1969), 11–143, quote 114; Henderson, "Tammany Hall and the New Immigrants," 167–258; Huthmacher, *Massachusetts People,* 27–150; Sterne, *Ballots and Bibles,* 217–252; Robert A. Slayton, *Empire Statesman: The Rise and Redemption of Al Smith* (New York: Free Press, 2001), 125–263.

49.   Allan J. Lichtman, *Prejudice and the Old Politics: The Presidential Election of 1928* (Chapel Hill: University of North Carolina Press, 1979), 21–188, 189–243, 266; Meagher, *Inventing Irish America,* 317–323; John L. Shover, "The Emergence of a Two-Party System in Republican Philadelphia, 1924–1936," *Journal of American History* 60, no. 4 (March 1, 1974): 985–1002; Robert Chiles, *The Revolution of '28: Al Smith, Progressivism and the Coming of the New Deal* (Ithaca, NY: Cornell University Press, 2018), 128; Huthmacher, *Massachusetts People,* 177–185; Sterne, *Ballots and Bibles,* 228–235.

50.   Samuel Lubell, *The Future of American Politics* (New York: Harper, 1952). See Lichtman, *Prejudice and the Old Politics,* 189–243, and Chiles, *Prejudice and the Old Politics,* 8–9, for contrasting views.

51.   Spalding, *Premier See,* quote 327; Cohalan, *Archdiocese of New York,* 238–239; O'Brien,

Syracuse, 182–186; Morris, *American Catholic,* 123–128; O'Toole, *Militant and Triumphant,* 154–158; Shannabruch, *Chicago's Catholics,* 217–220; Linkh, *Catholicism and Immigration,* 152, 175–179; Jeanne Petit, "Building Citizens: Women, Men and the Immigrant Restriction Debates, 1890–1929" (PhD dissertation, Notre Dame, 2000), 157, 176; Kauffman, *Faith and Fraternalism,* 261–286.

52. Meagher, *Inventing Irish America,* 310–311; Jackson, *Ku Klux Klan,* 103–106, 242; McCowin, "Faith and Freedom," 130–138.

53. Tentler, *Seasons of Grace,* 307–308, 476; O'Toole, *Militant and Triumphant,* 145–147; Kantowicz, *Corporation Sole,* 82; Meagher, *Inventing Irish America,* 340–342; Morris, *American Catholic,* 123–132; Stern, *Ballots and Bibles,* 207.

54. William Halsey, *The Survival of American Innocence: Catholicism in an Era of Disillusionment, 1920–1940* (Notre Dame, IN: University of Notre Dame Press, 1980), 51, quote 155, 1–123, 138–168.

10. Rising Power

1. Broderick, *Right Reverend New Dealer,* 230, 241, 216–217.

2. Terence Dooley, *The Land for the People: The Land Question in Independent Ireland* (Dublin: UCD Press, 2004), 28, 99–108, 235; Ferriter, *The Transformation of Ireland,* 373; PDF, Car registrations in the United States, https://www.fhwa.dot.gov/ohim/summary95/mv200.pdf; R. F. Foster, *Modern Ireland, 1600–1972* (London: Penguin, 1988), quote 537.

3. Quote, "The Ireland that We Dreamed Of," RTE Archives Exhibition: RTE.Ie/archives/exhibition/eamon-de-valera; Ferriter, *The Transformation of Modern Ireland,* 368–391; Lee, *Modern Ireland, 1912–1985,* 177–193; Foster, *Modern Ireland,* 537–551.

4. Enda Delaney, *Demography, State and Society: Irish Migration to Britain, 1921–1971* (Montreal: McGill, 2000), 42, 36–111, 299, 303–304; Blessing, *The Irish in America,* 289; Lee, *Ireland, 1912–1985,* 187.

5. Delaney, *Demography, State, and Society,* 42–48, 69–81, 113–225.

6. Ruggles, Flood, et al., IPUMS USA U.S. Census 1930, 1940.

7. Rebecca Miller, "Irish Traditional and Popular Music in New York City: Identity and Social Change, 1930–1975," in Bayor and Meagher, eds., *The New York Irish,* 480–486; Matthew O'Brien, "Irishness in Great Britain and the United States: Transatlantic and Cross Channel Networks and Irish Ethnicity, 1920–1990" (PhD dissertation, University of Wisconsin, 2001), 327–328.

8. Ruggles, Flood, et al., IPUMS USA U.S. Census 1930, 1940; General Social Survey. The General Social Survey (GSS) is a project of the independent research organization NORC at the University of Chicago, with principal funding from the National Science Foundation. Cohort: pre-1940.

9. Marc S. Miller, *The Irony of Victory: World War II and Lowell, Massachusetts* (Urbana: Uni-

versity of Illinois Press, 1988), 10–17; Mary H. Blewett, *The Last Generation: Work and Life in the Textile Mills of Lowell, Massachusetts, 1910–1960* (Amherst: University of Massachusetts Press, 1990), 55–63, quote 93, quote 97, 98.

10. Howard P. Chudacoff, *The Evolution of American Urban Society* (Englewood Cliffs, NJ: Prentice-Hall, 1975), 211–213; Jon C. Teaford, *The Twentieth-Century American City: Problem, Promise, and Reality* (Baltimore: Johns Hopkins University Press, 1986), quote 76, 76–77; James T. Farrell, *Studs Lonigan: A Trilogy: Young Lonigan; The Young Manhood of Studs Lonigan; Judgment Day* (New York: Literary Classics of the United States, 2004), quote 886.

11. Ruggles, Flood, et al., IPUMS USA U.S. Census 1930, 1940.

12. Andrew M. Greeley, *The American Catholic: A Social Portrait* (New York: Basic Books, 1977), 44.

13. Mary Doyle Curran, *The Parish and the Hill* (1948, reprint New York: Feminist Press of CUNY, 2002), 200–213; Leslie Tentler, *Catholics and Contraception: An American History* (Ithaca: Cornell University Press, 2004), quote 76, quote 77; Ruggles, Flood, et al., IPUMS USA U.S. Census 1930, 1940; Ellen Horgan Biddle, "The American Catholic Irish Family," in Charles H. Mindel and Robert W. Habenstein, eds., *Ethnic Families in America: Patterns and Variations* (New York: Elsevier, 1976), quote 100, 89–104.

14. *Official Catholic Directories* (New York: P. J. Kennedy, 1920, 1929, 1940).

15. Eileen M. McMahon, *What Parish Are You From? A Chicago Irish Community and Racial Relations* (Lexington: University Press of Kentucky, 1995), quote 60, 62; Tentler, *Seasons of Grace,* 402, 404, 411–412; James McCartin, "The Love of Things Unseen: Catholic Prayer and the Moral Imagination in the Twentieth-Century United States" (PhD dissertation, University of Notre Dame, 2003), quote 11, 8–74.

16. Robert A. Orsi, *Thank You, St. Jude: Women's Devotion to the Patron Saint of Hopeless Causes* (New Haven: Yale University Press, 1996), 1–69; James P. McCartin, "The Sacred Heart of Jesus, Thérèse of Lisieux, and the Transformation of U.S. Catholic Piety, 1865–1940," *U.S. Catholic Historian* 25, no. 2 (April 1, 2007): 53–67.

17. Kauffman, *Faith and Fraternalism,* 318–337; *Catholic Transcript,* March 14, 1935; Timothy B. Neary, *Crossing Parish Boundaries: Race, Sports, and Catholic Youth in Chicago, 1914–1954* (Chicago: University of Chicago Press, 2016), 2–15, 169–184.

18. Golway, *Machine Made,* 233–284; Slayton, *Empire Statesman,* 363–377.

19. Huthmacher, *Massachusetts People and Politics,* 219–236; Lawrence was also an ally of pro-FDR state party leader Joseph Guffey: Bruce M. Stave, *The New Deal and the Last Hurrah: Pittsburgh Machine Politics* (Pittsburgh: University of Pittsburgh Press, 1970), 31; Lyle W. Dorsett, *Franklin D. Roosevelt and the City Bosses* (Port Washington, NY: Kennikat Press, 1977), 6–9, 70–75; Beatty, *Rascal King,* 301–308; Erie, *Rainbow's End,* 107–139; Fine, *Murphy: The Detroit Years,* 433–451; Daniel Scroop, *Mr. Democrat: Jim Farley, the New*

Deal, and the Making of Modern American Politics (Ann Arbor: University of Michigan Press, 2006), 1–25.

20. Gamm, *New Deal Democrats,* 82–83, 151–158; John L. Shover, "Ethnicity and Religion in Philadelphia Politics, 1924–40," *American Quarterly* 25, no. 5 (December 1973): 505; Ronald H. Bayor, *Neighbors in Conflict: The Irish, Germans, Jews and Italians in New York City* (Baltimore: Johns Hopkins University Press, 1978), 147; Patrick Kennedy, "Chicago's Irish Americans and the Candidacies of Franklin D. Roosevelt," *Illinois Historical Journal* 88, no. 4 (1995): 263–278; Dayton McKean, *I Am the Boss: The Hague Machine in Action* (Boston: Houghton Mifflin, 1940), 95–102.

21. McNickle, *To Be Mayor,* 32–40; Ronald Bayor, *Fiorello La Guardia: Ethnicity and Reform* (Arlington, IL: Harlan Davidson, 1993), 121–127; Golway, *Machine Made,* 286–301.

22. Beatty, *Rascal King,* 341–398; Charles H. Trout, *Boston, the Great Depression, and the New Deal* (New York: Oxford University Press, 1977), 85–86.

23. Michael P. Weber, *Don't Call Me Boss: David Lawrence, Pittsburgh's Renaissance Mayor* (Pittsburgh: University of Pittsburgh Press, 1980), 1–13, 52–55; Roger Biles, *Big City Boss in Depression and War: Mayor Edward J. Kelly of Chicago* (DeKalb: Northern Illinois University Press, 1984), 6–39; Peri Arnold, "What Bonded Immigrants to Urban Machines? The Case of Jacob Arvey and Chicago's 24th Ward," *Journal of Policy History* 25, no. 4 (October 1, 2013): 463–488; McKean, *I Am the Boss,* 95–103.

24. Representatives and Senators with Irish names were traced into biographical and newspaper sources to establish religion. Congressional votes analyzed for economic liberalism and ranks by the UCLA project, "Voteview.Com": https://voteview.com/about and votes at https://voteview.com/congress/senate/; https://voteview.com/congress/house.

25. James T. Patterson, *Congressional Conservatism and the New Deal: The Growth of a Conservative Coalition in Congress, 1933–1939* (Lexington: University of Kentucky Press, 1967), 340–352; Gamm, *New Deal Democrats,* 82–83; Stefano Luconi, "Machine Politics and the Consolidation of the Roosevelt Majority: The Case of Italian Americans in Pittsburgh and Philadelphia," *Journal of American Ethnic History* 15, no. 2 (1996): 32–59; James T. Patterson, *The New Deal and the States: Federalism in Transition* (Princeton, NJ: Princeton University Press, 2015), 18, 51, 81, 132–183.

26. Bernstein, *Lean Years,* 335–336; Irving Bernstein, *Turbulent Years: A History of the American Worker, 1933–1941* (Boston: Houghton Mifflin, 1971), 35, quote 42, 41–42, 84–89; Thomas Göbel, "Becoming American: Ethnic Workers and the Rise of the CIO," *Labor History,* 29, no. 2 (March 1, 1988): 173–198, quote 181.

27. Bernstein, *Turbulent Years,* 574–576, 780–781; Joshua B. Freeman, *In Transit: The Transport Workers' Union in New York City, 1933–1966* (New York: Oxford University Press, 1989), 17–160.

28. Bryan Palmer, *Revolutionary Teamsters: Minneapolis Teamsters Strike* (Boston: Brill, 2013),

50–51, 128–149; Janet Christine Irons, *Testing the New Deal: The General Textile Strike of 1934 in the American South* (Urbana: University of Illinois Press, 2000), 72–73, 88–89.

29. Minutes of the Executive Council of the AFL: December 3, 1937; Robert H. Zieger, *The CIO, 1935–1955* (Chapel Hill: University of North Carolina Press, 1995), 92–93; Ronald W. Schatz, "Philip Murray and the Subordination of the Industrial Unions to the Federal Government," in Melvyn Dubofsky and Warren Van Tine, eds., *Labor Leaders in America* (Urbana: University of Illinois Press, 1987), 234–257; Zieger, *The CIO,* 29–65, 67, 90–93, 110; Robert H. Zieger, "George Meany: Labor's Organization Man," in Dubofsky and Van Tine, eds., *Labor Leaders,* 324–349; Archie Robinson, *George Meany and His Times: A Biography* (New York: Simon and Schuster, 1981), 28–69.

30. George Q. Flynn, *American Catholics and the Roosevelt Presidency, 1932–1936* (Lexington: University of Kentucky Press, 1968), 55–187; Brown and McKeown, *The Poor Belong to Us,* 171–186; John B. Sheerin, *Never Look Back: The Career and Concerns of John J. Burke* (New York: Paulist Press, 1975), 157–208.

31. Thomas Patrick Doherty, *Hollywood's Censor: Joseph I. Breen and the Production Code Administration* (New York: Columbia University Press, 2007), quote 62, 10–69; M. Alison Kibler, *Censoring Racial Ridicule: Irish, Jewish and African American Struggles over Racial Representation, 1890–1930* (Chapel Hill: University of North Carolina Press, 2015), 203–215.

32. Shannon, *Bowery to Broadway,* 51, 65–98, 154–268; Christopher Dowd, "The Weird Tales, Spicy Detectives and Startling Stories of Irish America: Irish Characters in Pulp Magazines," *Irish Studies Review* 23, no. 2 (2015): 176–183.

33. John O'Hara, *Butterfield 8,* in O'Hara, *Appointment in Samara, Butterfield 8, Hope of Heaven* (New York: Random House, 1934), quote 215; "A Touch of the Poet" in *Eugene O'Neill: Complete Plays, 1932–1943* (New York: Library of America, 1988), 250–281, quote 274.

34. Tentler, *Seasons of Grace,* 301–303, 315–344, 412; James Shenton, "The Coughlin Movement and the New Deal," *Political Science Quarterly* 73, no. 3 (1958): 352–373; Mary Christine Athans, *The Coughlin-Fahey Connection: Father Charles Coughlin, Father Denis Fahey CSC, and Religious Anti-Semitism in the United States* (New York: P. Lang, 1991).

35. Gamm, *New Deal Democrats,* 151–158; Shover, "Philadelphia Politics," 505; Bayor, *Neighbors in Conflict* 147; Kennedy, "Chicago's Irish Americans and Franklin D. Roosevelt," 263–278.

36. Nicholas Easton, "The Political Machine in Providence: A Case Study" (PhD dissertation, University of Connecticut, 2012), 222–228.

37. Patterson, *Congressional Conservatism,* 116–121, 214–223; Yougov.com: Votes, Court Packing, Senate, July 22, 1937; Executive Reorganization, Senate, March 29, 1938.

38. David J. O'Brien, *American Catholics and Social Reform: The New Deal Years* (New York:

Oxford University Press, 1968), quote 108, 111; Neil Betten, *Catholic Activism and the Industrial Worker* (Gainesville: University Presses of Florida, 1976), 125–149.

39. Wayman, *David Walsh,* quote 229.

40. Nelson, *Divided We Stand,* quote 66; Scroop, *Mr. Democrat,* 86; Slayton, *Empire Statesman,* quote 378, quote 379; Trout, *Boston, the Great Depression and the New Deal*; Garrison Nelson, *John William McCormack: A Political Biography* (New York: Bloomsbury Academic, 2017), 166, quote 273; Broderick, *Right Reverend New Dealer,* 150–151, quote 151.

41. Gary Gerstle, "The Protean Character of American Liberalism," *American Historical Review* 99, no. 4 (1994): 1043–1073; Jerome M. Milleur and Sidney M. Milkis, *The New Deal and the Triumph of Liberalism* (Amherst: University of Massachusetts Press, 2002), 31–134; Joseph P. Lash, *Dealers and Dreamers: A New Look at the New Deal* (New York: Doubleday, 1988), 76–232; Scroop, *Mr. Democrat,* 86; Jordan A. Schwarz, *The New Dealers: Power Politics in the Age of Roosevelt* (New York: Knopf, 1993), 138–156.

42. David McKean, *Tommy the Cork: Washington's Ultimate Insider from Roosevelt to Reagan* (South Royalton, VT: Steerforth, 2004), 9–80.

43. Schwarz, *New Dealers,* quotes 141, 142, 135, 136, 153.

44. Scroop, *Mr. Democrat,* 86; Slayton, *Empire Statesman,* quote 378, 366–389.

45. Susan Dunn, *Roosevelt's Purge: How FDR Fought to Change the Democratic Party* (Cambridge, MA: Belknap Press of Harvard University Press, 2010), 1–59, 94–157, 202–235; Edward Flynn, *You're the Boss: The Practice of American Politics* (New York: Viking, 1947), quote 129–131, quote 164–165; Lash, *New Dealers,* quote, 360.

46. Giuliana Chamedes, "The Vatican, Nazi-Fascism, and the Making of Transnational Anti-Communism in the 1930s," *Journal of Contemporary History* 51, no. 2 (April 2016), 261–290, quote 266; Thomas C. Reeves, *America's Bishop: The Life and Times of Fulton J. Sheen* (San Francisco: Encounter Books, 2001), 9–54, 64–115.

47. Wilson D. Miscamble, "The Limits of American Catholic Antifascism: The Case of John A. Ryan," *Church History* 59, no. 4 (December 1990): 523–533; George Q. Flynn, *Roosevelt and Romanism: Catholics and American Diplomacy, 1937–1945* (Westport, CT: Greenwood Press, 1976), 41–49; J. David Valaik, "Catholics, Neutrality, and the Spanish Embargo, 1937–1939," *Journal of American History* 54, no. 1 (June 1, 1967): 73–85; Donald F. Crosby, "Boston's Catholics and the Spanish Civil War: 1936–1939," *New England Quarterly* 44, no. 1 (March 1, 1971): 80–100; Bayor, *Neighbors in Conflict,* 90–91.

48. Morris, *American Catholic,* 233–236; Shawn Michael Lynch, "In Defense of True Americanism: The Civil Liberties Union of Massachusetts and Free Speech, 1915–1945" (PhD dissertation, Boston College, 2006), 103–120; John F. Stack, *International Conflict in an American City: Boston's Irish, Italians, and Jews, 1935–1944* (Westport, CT: Greenwood Press, 1979), 60–66.

49. McNickle, *To Be Mayor,* 32–40; Bayor, *Neighbors in Conflict,* 24–28, 30–55, 76–104; Trout, *Boston, the Great Depression,* 168; Stack, *International Conflict,* 65–68.

50. "American Catholics and Nazi Anti-Semitism," American Catholic History Classroom: Catholic University Archives, cuomeka.org.

51. The UCLA project "Voteview.Com": https://voteview.com/about and votes at http://vote view.com/congress/senate/115/text; YouGov.com: Votes, Executive Reorganization, March 31, 1938; Wages and Hours, May 23–24, 1938; Public Housing, August 18, 1937; Sit Down Strike, April 7, 1937.

52. Patterson, *Congressional Conservatism,* 140, 149–154, 179–198, 242–246; Bernstein, *Turbulent Years,* 134–142; Lash, *New Dealers,* 334–341; Steve Fraser, *Labor Will Rule: Sidney Hillman and the Rise of American Labor* (Ithaca, NY: Cornell University Press, 1993), 55–84; David Porter, *Mary Norton of New Jersey: Congressional Trailblazer* (Madison, NJ: Fairleigh Dickinson University Press, 2013), 54, 177; *New York Times,* December 3, 17, 18, 1937; *Washington Post,* December 18, 1937; McKean, *Tommy the Cork,* 92–93.

53. Weiss, *Farewell to the Party of Lincoln,* 46–47, 94, 119, 206, 229–248; "Reminiscences of Joseph Andrew Gavagan: Oral History, 1950," Oral History Interviews Portal, Columbia Center for Oral History, https://oralhistoryportal.library.columbia.edu/document.php?id =ldpd_4074768. Robin Bernice Balthrope, "Lawlessness and the New Deal: Congress and Antilynching, 1934–1938" (PhD dissertation, Ohio State University, 1995), 175–180; *New York Times,* quote, April 16, 1937; Yougov.com: Votes, Anti Lynching, House, April 14, 1937; Cloture, Anti Lynching, Senate, February 16, 1938.

54. Weiss, *Farewell to the Party of Lincoln,* 46–47, 94, 119, 206, 229–248; "Reminiscences of Joseph Andrew Gavagan: Oral History, 1950"; Biles, *Big City Boss,* 89–114, 95; Weber, *Don't Call Me Boss,* 48–50, 98–99; Balthrope, "Lawlessness and the New Deal," 175–180; Eric Schickler, *Racial Realignment: The Transformation of American Liberalism, 1932–1965* (Princeton, NJ: Princeton University Press, 2016), 27–215.

55. Nelson, *Divided We Stand,* 68–70; John T. McGreevy, *Parish Boundaries: The Catholic Encounter with Race in the Twentieth-Century Urban North* (Chicago: University of Chicago Press, 1996), 35–37, quote 251, 250–254; Ron Ebest, *Private Lives: The Writing of Irish Americans, 1900–1935* (Notre Dame, IN: University of Notre Dame Press, 2005), 222–234.

56. McKean, *Tommy the Cork,* 108, quote 120, quote 122.

11. The Old Order at High Tide

1. Alan Yarnell, *Democrats and Progressives: The 1948 Election as a Test of Postwar Liberalism* (Berkeley: University of California Press, 1974), 58; quote *New York Times,* 18 March 1948; Robert Ferrell, *Choosing Truman: The Democratic Convention of 1944* (Columbia: University of Missouri Press, 2001), 61–81.

2. Donald I. Warren, *Radio Priest: Charles Coughlin, the Father of Hate Radio* (New York: Free

Press, 1996), 175–185, 230; Bayor, *Neighbors in Conflict,* 110–114; Flynn, *Roosevelt and Romanism,* 63–97, 64; McKean, *Tommy the Cork,* 108–207; David Nasaw, *The Patriarch: The Remarkable Life and Turbulent Times of Joseph P. Kennedy* (New York: Penguin Press, 2012), 314–521.

3. David Porter, *The Seventy-Sixth Congress and World War II, 1939–1940* (Columbia: University of Missouri Press, 1979), 19–21, 24–25, 42–45, 76–77, 165–166, 179–180, 201; Nelson, *McCormack,* 263–264, quote 26; Yougov.com: Votes, November 1939; October 1940; September 1941; Whelan, *U.S. Foreign Policy,* 388.

4. Michael J. Ybarra, *Washington Gone Crazy: Senator Pat McCarran and the Great American Communist Hunt* (Hanover, NH: Steerforth, 2004), quote 278; Bayor, *Neighbors in Conflict,* 125, 161–162; Stack, *International Conflict,* 136–138; J. J. Lee, *Ireland, 1912–1985: Politics and Society* (New York, 1989), 245, 244–247; John Day Tully, *Ireland and Irish Americans, 1932–1945: The Search for Identity* (Portland, OR, 2010), 111–164; O'Brien, "Irishness," 351; Ruggles, Flood, et al., IPUMS USA U.S. Census 1980.

5. Lester and Barbara Keyser, *Hollywood and the Catholic Church: The Image of Roman Catholicism in American Movies* (Chicago: Loyola University Press, 1984), 157–194; Smith, *Look of Catholics,* 56–65; IMDb: *Yankee Doodle Dandy* (1942); *Princess O'Rourke* (1943); *The Fighting Seabees* (1944); *Back to Bataan* (1945); *They Were Expendable* (1946).

6. Sister Mary Charlotte RSM and Dr. Mary Synon, "The Spirit of the Navy," in *These Are Our Freedoms* (Boston: Ginn, 1944), quote, 72, 71–74.

7. John C. Seitz, "The Mass Clock and the Spy: The Catholicization of the Second World War," *Church History,* 83 no. 4 (December 2014): quote 928, quote 941, 924–956.

8. John T. Donovan, *Crusader in the Cold War: A Biography of Fr. John F. Cronin, S.S.* (New York: P. Lang, 2005), 5, 49, 77; Giuliana Chamedes, *A Twentieth-Century Crusade: The Vatican's Battle to Remake Christian Europe* (Cambridge, MA: Harvard University Press, 2019), 242–267; Robert Murray, *The Split: Australian Labor in the Fifties* (Sydney: Hale and Ironmonger, 1984), 3–49.

9. Robinson, *George Meany,* 123–153; Zieger, "George Meany," 334–335; Zieger, *CIO,* 253–293.

10. David M. Oshinsky, *A Conspiracy so Immense: The World of Joe McCarthy* (London: Collier Macmillan, 1983), 2–12, 195–196, 230, 488, quote 233.

11. Oshinsky, *Conspiracy,* quote 195–196; Kauffman, *Faith and Fraternalism,* quote 362; Reeves, *Sheen,* 143–145, 233.

12. Oshinsky, *Conspiracy,* 205, 254, 305–306, 410; Seymour Martin Lipset, "McCarthyism and the Ethnic Factor," in Allan J. Matusow, ed., *Joseph McCarthy* (Englewood Cliffs, NJ: Prentice Hall, 1970), 157–166; Seymour Martin Lipset and Earl Raab, *The Politics of Unreason: Right Wing Extremism in America, 1790–1977* (Chicago: University of Chicago Press, 1978), 209–247, 226–231; Donald F. Crosby, *God, Church, and Flag: Senator Jo-*

seph R. McCarthy and the Catholic Church, 1950–1957 (Chapel Hill: University of North Carolina Press, 1978), 32, 132, 151, 160, 194, 204, quote 208, 239.

13. John B. Judis, *William F. Buckley: Patron Saint of the Conservatives* (New York: Simon and Schuster, 1988), 18–35.

14. Judis, *Buckley,* 26–30, 43–44, 77–96, quote 94, 96, 102–110.

15. Kevin Phillips, *The Emerging Republican Majority* (Princeton, NJ: Princeton University Press, 2015), 175–176; J. Daniel Mahoney, *Actions Speak Louder* (New Rochelle, NY: Arlington House, 1968); Glazer and Moynihan, *Beyond the Melting Pot,* lvii–lxxvi; Judis, *Buckley,* 129–161, quote 138.

16. Judith Stein, *Pivotal Decade: How the United States Traded Factories for Finance in the Seventies* (New Haven, CT: Yale University Press, 2010), 1–3; James T. Patterson, *Grand Expectations: The United States, 1945–1974* (New York: Oxford University Press, 1996), 61–69.

17. Linda Dowling Almeida, *Irish Immigrants in New York City, 1945–1995* (Bloomington: Indiana University Press, 2001), 23–37, 43, 84–124; Blessing, *The Irish in America,* 289; Ruggles, Flood, et al., IPUMS USA U.S. Census 1960; Sara Brady, "Playing 'Irish' Sport on Baseball's Hallowed Ground: The 1947 All-Ireland Gaelic Football Final," 24–47, in James Silas Rogers and Matthew O'Brien, *After the Flood: Irish America, 1945–1960* (Portland, OR: Irish Academic Press, 2009); Miller, "Irish Traditional and Popular Music," 485–504.

18. Andrew M. Greeley, *The American Catholic: A Social Portrait* (New York: Basic Books, 1977), 44; Andrew M. Greeley, *The Irish Americans: The Rise to Money and Power* (New York: Harper and Row, 1981), 117–118; Philip Gleason, *Contending with Modernity: Catholic Higher Education in the Twentieth Century* (New York: Oxford University Press, 1995), 204–234; Blewett, *Last Generation,* quote 93; GSS Cumulative File: Cohort born 1928–1940; Harold J. Abramson, *Ethnic Diversity in Catholic America* (New York: Wiley, 1973), 41–44, 53, 58, 62; Andrew M. Greeley, *Why Can't They Be Like Us? America's White Ethnic Groups* (New York: Dutton, 1971), 77, 90, 92; Alice McDermott, *After This* (New York: Farrar, Straus and Giroux, 2006), quote 78.

19. Troy Davis, *Dublin's American Policy: Irish American Diplomatic Relations, 1945–1952* (Washington, DC: Catholic University Press, 1998), 58–94, 76, quote 66; Mary E. Daly, "Nationalism, Sentiment and Economics: Relations Between Ireland and Irish America in the Postwar Years," in Kevin Kenny, ed., *New Directions in Irish American History* (Madison: University of Wisconsin Press, 2003), 263–289, quote 273.

20. Greeley, *American Catholic,* 59–65, quote 65; Baltzell, *The Protestant Establishment,* 277–293; James D. Davidson and Ralph E. Pyle, *Ranking Faiths: Religious Stratification in America* (Lanham, MD: Rowman & Littlefield, 2011), 106–114; Tentler, *Catholics and Contraception,* quote 130.

21. Gerhard Lenski, *The Religious Factor: A Sociological Study of Religion's Impact on Politics, Economic and Family Life* (Garden City, NY: Doubleday, 1963), 82–133; Greeley, *Why Can't They Be Like Us,* 209; Meagher, *Guide to Irish American History,* 136; Thomas J. Shelley, "The Young John Tracy Ellis and American Catholic Intellectual Life," *U.S. Catholic Historian* 13, no. 1 (Winter 1995): 1–6. See also other essays in this volume of the journal on this topic.

22. Greeley, *American Catholic,* 93; McMahon, *What Parish,* 77, 89–85, 93–96; Gerald H. Gamm, *Urban Exodus: Why the Jews Left Boston and the Catholics Stayed* (Cambridge, MA: Harvard University Press, 1999), 13, 30–37, 222–237.

23. James W. Sanders, *The Education of an Urban Minority: Catholics in Chicago, 1833–1965* (New York: Oxford University Press, 1977), 190–203; Herbert J. Gans, *The Levittowners: Ways of Life and Politics in a New Suburban Community* (New York: Pantheon Books, 1967), 160, 72–73; McDermott, *After This,* 78–80; Steven M. Avella, *This Confident Church: Catholic Leadership and Life* (Notre Dame, IN: University of Notre Dame Press, 1992), 15–109.

24. Andrew M. Greeley and Peter H. Rossi, *The Education of Catholic Americans* (Chicago: Aldine, 1966), 2, 39, 277–279; Greeley, *American Catholic,* 127; Andrew Greeley, *The Church and the Suburbs* (New York: Sheed & Ward, 1959), 54; Paula Fass, *Outside In: Minorities and the Transformation of American Education* (New York: Oxford University Press, 1989), 190–223.

25. Greeley, *Why Can't They,* 87.

26. Timothy J. Russert, *Big Russ and Me, Father and Son: Lessons of Life* (New York: Hyperion, 2004), 55–56, quote 55; Sharon O'Brien, *The Family Silver: A Memoir of Depression and Inheritance* (Chicago: University of Chicago Press, 2004), 86, quote, 87, 88; Thomas Lynch, *Booking Passages* (New York: W. W. Norton, 2005): 87–101; Doris Kearns Goodwin, *Wait till Next Year: A Memoir* (New York: Simon & Schuster, 1997), 84–119.

27. Tentler, *Catholics and Contraception,* quote 133; Charles F. Westoff, Robert G. Potter, and Philip C. Sagi, *Third Child—A Study in the Prediction of Fertility* (Princeton, NJ: Princeton University Press, 1963), 203–204; Paula M. Kane, "Marian Devotion Since 1940: Continuity or Casualty," in James M. O'Toole, ed., *Habits of Devotion: Catholic Religious Practice in Twentieth-Century America* (Ithaca, NY: Cornell University Press, 2004), 101–107.

28. Tentler, *Catholics and Contraception,* 120–122; GSS: Cohort, born 1928–1940.

29. Joseph Chinnici, *American Catholicism Transformed: From the Cold War Through the Council* (New York: Oxford University Press, 2021), quote 16, quote 17, 4–62; Joseph Chinnici, "The Catholic Community at Prayer," in O'Toole, ed., *Habits of Devotion,* 45–75, 67; Una Cadegan, "The Queen of Peace in the Shadow of War: Fatima and U.S. Catholic Anti-Communism," *U.S. Catholic Historian* 22, no. 4 (Fall 2004): 1–16; Richard Gribble, "Anti-Communism: Patrick Peyton CSC and CIA," *Journal of Church and State* 45 (2005):

540–541; Matthew O'Brien, "Hibernians on the March: Irish America and Ethnic Patriotism," *Eire/Ireland* 40, no. 1 (2005): 170–172; Kauffman, *Knights of Columbus;* Kane, "Marian Devotion," 101–108; James T. Fisher, *Dr. America: The Lives of Thomas A. Dooley* (Amherst: University of Massachusetts Press, 1997), 1–176, 243–245.

30. Chinnici, *American Catholicism Transformed,* 17; Synon, *These Are Our Freedoms,* 111, 90–109, 272–280.

31. Reeves, *America's Bishop,* 163–269; Anthony Burke Smith, *The Look of Catholics: Portrayals in Popular Culture from the Great Depression to the Cold War* (Lawrence: University Press of Kansas, 2018), 125–152, 222–225.

32. Chinnici, "Catholic Community at Prayer," 45, 70–75; Tentler, *Catholics and Contraception,* quote 200, quote 203, 173–203; Kane, "Marian Devotion," quote 107; Ruggles, Flood, et al., IPUMS USA U. S. Census 1940, 1950, 1960.

33. John D'Emilio, *Sexual Politics, Sexual Communities: The Making of a Homosexual Minority in the United States, 1940–1970* (Chicago: University of Chicago Press, 1983), 23–53; James McCourt, *Queer Street: Rise and Fall of an American Culture, 1947–1985* (New York: Norton, 2004), 53–122; Brad Gooch, *City Poet: The Life and Times of Frank O'Hara* (New York: Knopf, 1993), 3–68, 71, 33–34, quote 203.

34. O'Connor, *Last Hurrah,* quote 257–258, 353; Edward Hagan, "From 'Peace and Freedom' to 'Peace' and 'Quiet': The Quiet Man as a Product of the 1950s," 100–113, in Rogers and O'Brien, *After the Flood;* Luke Gibbons, *The Quiet Man* (Cork, Ireland: Cork University Press, 2002).

35. Daly, "Nationalism, Sentiment," 266–269.

36. Willliam B. and Mary E. Prendergast, *The Catholic Voter in American Politics: The Passing of the Democratic Monolith* (Washington, DC: Georgetown University Press, 1999), 119–121; Ware, *The Democratic Party Heads North,* 175–237, 212.

37. Nelson Lichtenstein, *State of the Union: A Century of American Labor* (Princeton, NJ: Princeton University Press, 2002), 98–177.

38. Ruggles, Flood, et al., IPUMS USA U.S. Census 1940, 1960; Duane Lockard, *New England State Politics* (Princeton, NJ: Princeton University Press, 1959), 209–319.

39. Carl Solberg, *Hubert Humphrey: A Biography* (New York: Norton, 1984), 3–13; *Journal of the House of Representatives of the Commonwealth of Massachusetts 1946* (Boston: Wright and Patton, 1946), 38, 80, 90, 148, 998; *Boston Globe* May 1, 12, 15, 1946; August 22, 1946; Porter, *Mary Norton,* 138–153; Daniel Keniry, "Irish American Members of the US House and their Voting Records on Civil Rights" (M.A. thesis, Catholic University, 2008).

40. McGreevy, *Parish Boundaries,* 107–110; Greeley, *Why Can't They Be Like Us?* 71, 74, 204; Nelson, *Divided We Stand,* 201–205, 210–218, 232; Zieger, "George Meany," 343–344.

41. Edgar Litt, *The Political Cultures of Massachusetts* (Cambridge, MA: MIT Press, 1965), 20–25; Alan Ware, *The Breakdown of Democratic Party Organization* (New York: Oxford

University Press, 1985), 42–142; James Q. Wilson, *The Amateur Democrat: Club Politics in Three Cities* (Chicago: University of Chicago Press, 1962), quotes 129, quote 280, 211, 308, 258–288.

42. Jeff Broadwater, *Adlai Stevenson and American Politics: The Odyssey of a Cold War Liberal* (New York: Twayne, 1994), 128–165; Bert Cochran, *Adlai Stevenson: Patrician Among the Politicians* (New York: Funk & Wagnalls, 1969), 88.

43. American National Election Survey (ANES): 1952 and 1956 elections; Lawrence H. Fuchs, "Presidential Politics in Boston: The Irish Response to Stevenson," *New England Quarterly,* 30, no. 4 (December 1, 1957): 435–447, 439–440, 444–446.

44. McGreevy, *Catholicism and American Freedom,* quotes 166, 166–188. This was diametrically opposed, of course, to Catholic arguments that American democracy was rooted in Catholic values.

45. Paul Blanshard, *The Irish and Catholic Power: An American Interpretation* (Boston: Beacon Press, 1953), quote 4, quote 289, 246–327; McGreevy, *Catholicism and American Freedom,* 182–188, 182, 185.

46. McNickle, *To Be Mayor,* 32–180; Joshua Zeitz, *White Ethnic New York: Jews, Catholics and the Shaping of Postwar Politics* (Chapel Hill: University of North Carolina Press, 2007), 11–88, 144–147; Wilson, *Amateur Democrat,* 32–58, 54, 69, 302, 313–314; Phillips, *The Emerging Republican Majority,* 160–171; Joshua Freeman, *Working Class New York: Life and Labor Since World War II* (New York: New Press, 2000), 68–71, 180–189.

47. Biles, *Big City Boss in Depression,* 133–151; Roger Biles, *Richard J. Daley: Politics, Race and the Governing of Chicago* (DeKalb: Northern Illinois University Press, 1995), 4–102; Wilson, *Amateur Democrat,* 65–95; Richard E. Cohen, *Rostenkowski: The Pursuit of Power and the End of the Old Politics* (Chicago: Ivan R. Dee, 1999), 9–40.

48. Thomas H. O'Connor, *Building a New Boston: Politics and Urban Renewal, 1950–1970* (Boston: Northeastern University Press, 1993), 20–96; O'Connor, *The Boston Irish,* 209–226; Murray Levin, *The Alienated Voter: Politics in Boston* (New York: Holt, Rinehart and Winston, 1960), 1–27.

49. Litt, *Political Cultures,* 16–106, 133–135; Alec Barbrook, *God Save the Commonwealth: An Electoral History of Massachusetts* (Amherst: University of Massachusetts Press, 1973), 48–135; Lockard, *New England State Politics,* 121–133; Lily Geismer, *Don't Blame Us: Suburban Liberals and the Transformation of the Democratic Party* (Princeton, NJ: Princeton University Press, 2014); Murray Levin, *The Compleat Politician: Political Strategy in Massachusetts* (Indianapolis: Bobbs-Merrill, 1962), 18, 34, 18–51, 58–71, 29; Murray Levin, *Kennedy Campaigning: The System and the Style as Practiced by Senator Edward Kennedy* (Boston: Beacon Press, 1966), 31–33; Phillips, *The Emerging Republican Majority,* 162–177.

50. Thomas J. Whalen, *Kennedy Versus Lodge: The 1952 Massachusetts Senate Race* (Boston: Northeastern University Press, 2000); Levin, *Kennedy Campaigning,* quote 25, 25–28.

Epilogue and Conclusion

1. Thomas Maier, *The Kennedys: America's Emerald Kings* (New York: Basic Books, 2003), quote 139, 139; Frederick Logevall, *JFK: Coming of Age in the American Century: 1917–1956* (New York: Random House, 2020), 68–227.

2. Maier, *The Kennedys,* 219–224, quote 216, quote 224.

3. Maier, *The Kennedys,* 227–229, 429–443.

4. Lawrence Fuchs, *John F. Kennedy and American Catholicism* (New York: Meredith Press, 1967), 225–237; Meagher, *Guide to Irish American History,* 150.

5. Meagher, *Guide to Irish American History,* 159–160; James M. O'Toole, *The Faithful: A History of Catholics in America (*Cambridge, MA: Harvard University Press, 2008), 204–263; Morris, *American Catholic,* 255–281.

6. Meagher, *Guide to Irish American History,* 160; ANES Surveys, 2000, 2004.

7. Meagher, *Guide to Irish American History,* 160–161; GSS surveys, 1972 to 2018. The surveys asked whether they approved of abortion for any reason, whether homosexual relations were always wrong, their religious affiliation up to age sixteen, and their current affiliation; 1993–1994, religious intermarriage; 1970s to 2010s, religion to age sixteen by current religion; ANES surveys, 1976–2004, asked about weekly mass attendance.

8. Meagher, *Guide to Irish American History,* 159–165; David Paul Kuhn, *The Hardhat Riot: Nixon, New York City and the Dawn of the White Working Class Revolution* (New York: Oxford University Press, 2020), 99–106, 142–145, 264–265; Greeley, *Why Can't,* 67; ANES, 1976–2004, party identification, by gender, family income, and education; GSS, 1972–2018, questions on why African Americans have not been more successful, discrimination, lack of education, innate ability or will, and on issues, busing, open housing, affirmative action.

9. Grace Hale, *A Nation of Outsiders: How the White Middle Class Fell in Love with Rebellion in Postwar America* (New York: Oxford University Press, 2011), quote 5; Matthew Frye Jacobson, *Roots Too: White Ethnic Revival in Post–Civil Rights America* (Cambridge, MA: Harvard University Press, 2006).

10. Meagher, *Guide to Irish American History,* 166–169; Brian Hanley, "The Politics of Noraid," *Irish Political Studies* 19, no. 1 (March 1, 2004): 1–17.

11. Https://www.thechieftains.com/down-the-old-plank-road/.

12. Timothy J. Meagher, "Why Irish? Writing Irish American History," in Alan M. Kraut and David A. Gerber, eds., *Ethnic Historians and the Mainstream: Shaping America's Immigration History* (New Brunswick, NJ: Rutgers University Press, 2013), 94–110.

Index

Figures are indicated by page numbers in italics.

AARIR. *See* American Association for the Recognition of the Irish Republic
abolitionism, 80–82, 89, 110–11, 116–18, 122–24
abortion, 243
Acheson, Dean, 222
Act of Union (1800), 56, 67, 73
ACTU (Association of Catholic Trade Unionists), 208
Adams, John, 62
Addams, Jane, 174
AFL-CIO, 204, 233. *See also* American Federation of Labor; Congress of Industrial Organizations
African Americans: civil rights movement and, 234–35, 241–42; Democratic Party and, 215, 237; in interracial relationships, 116, 122; Irish American relations with, 64, 80–81, 111, 116–18, 123, 188, 214–15, 234–35; lynching of, 122, 188, 213–15; migration of, 187–88, 215, 234; minstrel shows and, 117; racism against, 81, 116–17; segregation of, 137, 152; voting rights for, 64, 81–82. *See also* slavery
agriculture: at Céide fields site, 9; in colonial America, 35, 45; commercialization of, 24; for export, 17–19, 60, 71; post-famine crisis in, 149, 153, 245; size of farms, 194; tillage, 19, 24, 56, 72–73, 147–48; workers

in, 18–19, 56, 71, 95. *See also* tenant farmers; *specific crops*
alcohol: addiction to, 140; drunken Irish stereotype, 60; Whiskey Rebellion, 60. *See also* temperance movements
Alexander, Archibald, 43
Alien Passenger Act of 1837, 83
American Association for the Recognition of the Irish Republic (AARIR), 186, 187, 219
American Federation of Catholic Societies, 182
American Federation of Labor (AFL), 157, 161, 167, 172–75, 204–5, 221. *See also* AFL-CIO
American Gaelic League, 168
American Indians. *See* Native Americans
Americanization, 4, 157, 163, 181, 190
American Protective Association (APA), 167–69
American Republican Party, 84
American Revolution: ethnic views of, 47; heroes of, 50, 230; Hessian mercenaries in, 50; Ireland as influenced by, 53, 55; Irish Catholics in, 50, 53; political battles following, 58–64; Ulster Scot Presbyterians in, 50–52. *See also specific battles*
American Society of United Irishmen, 67

American Unity League (AUL), 190–91

Ancient Order of Hibernians (AOH), 125, 153, 168–69, 172, 182, 196, 218

Angels with Dirty Faces (film), 206

Anglican Church. *See* Church of Ireland

Anglo Normans, 12–13, 21

Anne (England), 25

anti-Catholicism: decline of, 242; discrimination based on, 182, 212, 227; of Know-Nothings, 112–16; nativist, 70, 83–84, *85*, 110–13, 157, 179, 248–49; Penal Laws and, 20–22, 53, 73, 211; in Republican Party, 167; in revolutionary era, 65, 82; riots and, 84, *85*, 87, 112

anti-communism, 204, 212, 218, 221–24, 229–30, 236

Antietam, Battle of (1862), *122*, 124

anti-Semitism, 193, 207, 212, 218, 219, 235

AOH. *See* Ancient Order of Hibernians

APA (American Protective Association), 167–69

Aquinas, Thomas, 192

aristocracy: British, 240; Church of Ireland and, 10; corruption and, 55, 69; Federalists and, 59, 64, 210; in Free-Soil ideology, 119; industrial, 159, 160; Irish American resentment of, 177, 178, 222; lay trustees and, 86; native Irish on, 22–23; planter, 52; political, 238; Ulster Scot Presbyterians on, 26, 51; Whiteboy uprisings and, 24

Arvey, Jake, 202

assimilation, 3–7, 117, 168, 183, 243–44

Association of Catholic Trade Unionists (ACTU), 208

AUL (American Unity League), 190–91

Australia: anti-communist movement in, 221; Irish immigrants in, 98, 101; labor unions in, 157, 167; priests and nuns in, 153

Back to Bataan (film), 220

Ball, Ernest, 146

Bank of the United States, 69

Baptists, 37–39, 44, 52, 66, 119

Barry, John, 50

Barry, Leonora, 155, *156*, 159–61

bartering, 34, 35, 60

baseball, 137, 139, 145–46, 228

battles. *See specific names of battles*

biases. *See* discrimination; stereotypes

Bible war, 74, 84

Biddle, Ellen Horgan, 198

Binns, John, 58

birth control. *See* contraception

Black, Hugo, 193, *194*

"Black 1847," 92, 97–98

Black community. *See* African Americans; slavery

Black Death (plague), 12

Blair, Samuel, 37

Blanshard, Paul: *American Freedom and Catholic Power*, 236; *The Irish and Catholic Power: An American Interpretation*, 236

blue-collar workers, 135, 151, 159, 234

Bocock, John Paul, 168

bosses, of political machines, 77, 164, 166, 174, 179

Boston (Massachusetts): anti-Catholic nativism in, 84; draft riots in, 121; economic and social elite in, 141; ethnic societies in, 47; expansion of, 137; Irish American Catholic leadership in, 163, 165, 178, 237–38; Irish immigrants in, 79, 99, 106, 152; political machines in, 164, 165; Ulster Scot Presbyterians in, 33

Boucicault, Dion: *The Shaughran*, 109, 133

boxing, 137, 139, 145

Boys Town (film), 206

Brackenridge, Hugh Henry: *Modern Chivalry*, 60–61, 63

Braddock, Edward, 40

Brady, Terrence, 118

Brain Trust, 209

Brannigan, Felix, 122

Breen, Joseph, 205
Brennan, Margaret, 147–49
Brennan, Paddy and Anne, 146–47
Britain/United Kingdom: Act of
  Union and, 56, 67, 73; alliance with
  Confederacy, 128; emigration from,
  102–3, 107, 135; Great Famine
  response by, 93; Irish immigrants
  in, 195–96; in World War II, 218.
  See also British empire; England
British empire: Irish American Catho-
  lics on, 218; Loyalist support of, 50,
  52–53; Orange Order's allegiance to,
  129; trade and, 9, 10, 17–18, 76; in
  War of 1812, 67–68. See also Amer-
  ican Revolution; colonial America;
  England; United Kingdom
Broderick, David, 119
Brophy, John, 204
Bryan, George, 50–51
Bryan, William Jennings, 175–77, 179
Buchanan, James, 78
Buckley, Christopher, 164, 166
Buckley, William F.: God and Man at
  Yale, 223; National Review, 224
Bunker Hill, Battle of (1775), 49
Burk, Thomas, 63–64
Burke, Edmund, 22
Burke, Edward, 203
Burke, John, 205
Burns, Anthony, 117
Byrne, Katherine M., 231

Cahill, Marie, 139
Caldwell, James, 47–49
Caldwell, Johnny, 49, 53
Calhoun, John C., 78
Calhoun, Patrick, 45, 53
Callahan, Patrick Henry, 186, 187
The Callahans and the Murphys (film),
  205
Canada: Fenian invasion of, 125–28,
  127; Irish immigrants in, 76, 78,
  97–98
Carey, Mathew, 58
Carleton, William: "Poor Scholar," 80
Carmody, Martin, 218
Carroll, Charles, 22

Carroll, John, 62, 66, 85, 162, 230
Catholic Benevolent Legion, 144
Catholic Daughters of America, 144
Catholic emancipation movement, 73,
  74, 77, 80, 88, 96
Catholic Foresters, 144
Catholicism: conservative, 82, 85,
  129, 166, 172, 179–80, 192; on
  contraception, 228–29; Counter-
  Reformation and, 14–15; devotionalism and, 115, 152, 199; Enlightenment-inspired trends in, 66; French
  Revolution and, 62; hierarchical
  nature of, 79, 86, 246; lay trustees
  in, 84–87; mass attendance and,
  74, 96, 114, 242; militant, 5–6, 84,
  172, 179, 182–83, 226, 244, 249;
  nuns and, 14, 21, 114, 143–44, 153,
  180–81, 223; pan-ethnic, 6, 172,
  182, 192, 199, 230, 244, 249; parish
  missions and, 115, 144; Pastorini's
  Prophecy and, 72; progressive, 179,
  202–3; revival of, 65, 114–15,
  143–44, 199, 249; temperance
  movements and, 144, 145, 153, 162;
  Tocqueville on, 86; Vatican Councils
  and, 129, 157, 242; Whitman on, 2.
  See also anti-Catholicism; Irish
  American Catholics; Irish Catholics;
  liberal Catholicism; papacy; priests
Catholic schools: debates regarding,
  140, 162; educational materials
  used in, 220, 230; expansion of,
  135, 180, 225, 227–28; funding for,
  83, 84, 87, 236; nuns as teachers at,
  180–81; Penal Law enforcement
  against, 21; Republican Party
  opposition to, 167; for women, 136
Catholic Youth Organization (CYO),
  199
celibacy, 143, 151
Celtic languages, 9–10
Central Labor Union, 166
Cermak, Anton, 201–2
Chambers, John, 58
Charitable Irish Society, 47
Charles II (England), 15, 16
Cherokees, 41, 45

Cheverus, Jean, 65
Chicago (Illinois): African American population of, 187–88, 237; Democratic Party in, 118; expansion of, 137; Fenianism in, 125; Great Depression in, 197; Haymarket Square bombing in, 161; Irish American Catholic leadership in, 168, 237; Irish immigrants in, 79, 99, 113, 150, 152; labor unions in, 129; political machines in, 164, 201–2, 237; race riots in, 188, 235
children: birth rates, 108, 143, 228, 244; in gangs, 142, 188; illegitimate, 20; labor of, 108–9, 176; in linen industry, 19; mortality rates for, 151
Chinese immigrants, 4, 104, 122, 130
Christian Front, 212, 219
Christianity. See Catholicism; Protestantism
Churchill, Pamela, 241
Church of Ireland: on claims to British throne, 16; in colonial America, 28, 30, 33, 44; discrimination against Presbyterians, 25–26; dissenters from, 9, 14, 16, 25; hierarchical structure of, 26; political and social dominance of, 8, 25; Second Reformation and, 74; tithes in support of, 24, 72
cinema. See film industry
CIO. See Congress of Industrial Organizations
citizenship: for immigrants, 62, 63, 68, 246; naturalized, 63, 64, 68, 119, 174; second-class, 25, 30
civil rights movement, 234–35, 241–42
civil wars: English (1641–53), 15; Irish (1922–23), 187, 195, 204; Spanish (1936–39), 211–12, 215, 223; U.S. (1861–65), 99, 105–6, 110–11, 119–25, 122, 128, 162–63
Clan na Gael (clan of the Gaels), 128, 158–60, 166, 184–85, 187, 224
Clay, William Edwards: O'Connell's Call and Pat's Reply, 89
Cleveland, Grover, 164

Cline, Maggie, 138, 139, 146
Clinton, George, 63
Cohalan, Daniel, 184, 186–87
Cohan, George M., 139, 146
Cold War, 217, 218, 221, 222, 229–30, 232
Collins, Patrick, 164, 165
colonial America: agriculture in, 35, 45; backcountry in, 27, 38–45, 52, 59–61; Church of Ireland in, 28, 30, 33, 44; discrimination in, 33; economy in, 34, 35; ethnic societies in, 47–48; Great Awakening in, 37, 38, 65–66, 246; indentured servants in, 29, 32, 57; land in, 34–35, 40, 43–44; migration patterns to, 30–33, 245; political representation in, 43–48, 52; religious tolerance in, 33, 44, 47; settlement patterns in, 33–35, 247. See also American Revolution
Committees of Correspondence, 52, 60
communal solidarity, 24, 72, 108, 160–61, 206, 229
communism: Cold War and, 217, 218, 221, 222; Coughlin's attacks on, 207, 212; labor unions and, 204, 208, 221–22; rise of, 194, 215; Spanish Civil War and, 211. See also anti-communism
Comstock Lode, 101–2
Conestoga people, 42
Confederacy (U.S. Civil War), 124, 128
Congregationalists, 33, 37, 78, 119
Congress of Industrial Organizations (CIO), 203, 204, 208, 215, 221–22. See also AFL-CIO
Connery, William, 215
Conquest of the City (film), 206
conservative Catholicism, 82, 85, 129, 166, 172, 179–80, 192
Constitution, U.S., 59, 61, 67, 121, 176
construction workers, 79, 88, 98
Continental army, 50
contraception, 198, 228–29, 232
Coolidge, Calvin, 191, 191
Corcoran, Thomas, 209, 211, 213, 215–16

corruption: aristocratic, 55, 69; crony-ism, 236; democracy and, 2; land purchases and, 44; of Tammany Hall, 131, 132, 170
cotton industry, 71, 75, 98, 99
Cottrill, Matthew, 65
Coughlin, Charles, 193, 206–7, 212, 218, 219, 236
Counter-Reformation, 14–15
Covenanters, 26
Crady, Timothy, 63–64
Craig, John, 38
Croghan, George, 40
Cromwell, Oliver, 15, 29
Cronin, John, 221
Cronin, Patrick Henry, 166
crops. *See* agriculture; *specific crops*
cultural diversity. *See* immigrants; race and ethnicity
Cummings, Matthew, 169
Curley, James Michael, 178, 179, 190, 201, 237
Curran, Joe, 204
CYO (Catholic Youth Organization), 199

Daley, Richard J., 237–38
Davis, Jefferson, 122
Davis, Robert "Little Bob," 164
Davitt, Michael, 158, 159, 166
Declaration of Independence, 22
Defenders (secret society), 55
Delaware people, 39, 40
Del Sesto, Christopher, 234
democracy, 2, 60, 76, 173–74, 209, 236
Democratic Party: African American support for, 215, 237; declining support for, 79, 111, 118, 243; divisions within, 207–8, 234; Jackson as hero to, 78; liberal reformers in, 235–38; New Departure strategy of, 123; political power of, 164–65, 174, 207, 233–35, 246; progressiv-ism and, 176–79, 203, 234; racial politics in, 123; revival of, 164, 172, 175–76, 184, 193, 199–202, 205; Roosevelt's purging of, 210; on

slavery, 119; Swallowtail faction of, 165–67; on voting rights, 81; Whit-man and, 1
Democratic-Republican Party, *51*, 59–64
deportations, 62, 83, 112
depressions: of 1837 (U.S.), 75, 82; of 1873 (U.S.), 129–32; of 1893 (U.S.), 167, 177; Great Depression, 193, 195–205, 207, 215; in Ireland, 72, 73
Desmond, Humphrey, 163
De Valera, Eamon, 185–87, 195, 219
devotionalism, 115, 152, 199
Devoy, John, 158, 159, 184, 186–87
Dewey, Thomas E., 217
diaspora. *See* Irish diaspora
discrimination: anti-Catholic, 182, 212, 227; anti-Semitism, 193, 207, 212, 218, 219, 235; in colonial America, 33; in employment, 103, 141; against Ulster Scot Presbyteri-ans, 26. *See also* racism; stereotypes
disease, 12, 15, 93, 97–98, 106, 139, 151, 155
diversity. *See* immigrants; race and ethnicity
Dixiecrats, 234
domestic service, 2, 79, 96–97, 99, 106–7, 114, 147, 151–52
Dooley, Thomas, 229, 232
Douglas, William O., 193, *194*
draft riots, 121–22
Drake, Francis, 28
Duane, William, 62
Du Bois, W. E. B.: *The Gift of Black Folk: The Negroes in the Making of America*, 190
Dunne, Edward, 177–79
Dunne, Finley Peter, 140, 146
dynastic wars, 12, 13

economic liberalism, 198, 202, 212–13
economy: in colonial America, 34, 35; market-based, 6, 20, 58, 76, 96; pastoral, 10, 12, 16, 148; transfor-mations in, 9, 16–19, 74, 246;

economy (*continued*)
during wartime, 57. *See also*
depressions
Eden, Anthony, 240
education: of Catholic priests, 14, 21;
gender differences in, 135–36, 149;
of German Americans, 135; GI Bill
and, 224, 225; of Irish Americans, 6,
135–36, 140, 178, 198, 225, 228,
242; of Presbyterian clergy, 38. *See
also* literacy; parochial schools;
teachers
Eisenhower, Dwight, 233, 236
Elder, John, 42
Ellis, John Tracy, 227
emancipation, Catholic, 73, 74, 77,
80, 88, 96
Emancipation Proclamation (1863),
121
Emmet, Robert, 56
Emmet, Thomas Addis, 58, 63, 65, 69
employment: discrimination in, 103,
141; in domestic service, 2, 79,
96–97, 99, 106–7, 114, 147,
151–52; Fair Employment Practices Commission, 234; for famine
immigrants, 96, 97, 102–4; in
textile industry, 75, 97, 99, 150,
159. *See also* unemployment;
workers
England: civil war in, 15; conquest of
Ireland by, 9, 11, 13–16; dynastic
wars within, 12, 13. *See also* Britain/
United Kingdom; British empire
Enlightenment, 26, 66
entrepreneurship, 6, 107–8, 151, 227,
248
ethnic identity, 6, 36, 218, 242
ethnicity. *See* race and ethnicity
ethnic societies, 47–48, 66–67
ethnic warfare, 190
ethnocentrism, 168, 172
evangelical Protestantism, 38, 74,
82–83, 103–4, 116, 145, 246
exports, 17–19, 60, 71

Fahey, Dennis, 207
Fair, James Gordon, 101

Fair Employment Practices Commission, 234
famine: Great Famine (1845–1851),
92–98; Great Slaughter (1741), 16,
18, 30
famine immigrants: child labor,
108–9; descendants of, 92, 162,
167, 170–72, 211, 245–46, 248–49;
diseases, 106; employment, 96, 97,
102–4; entrepreneurship, 107–8;
funding of passage, 94, 95; housing,
105, *105*; marriages, 100–101, 108,
109; migration patterns, 94–98;
poverty, 105, 113; saving habits,
107, 108; settlement patterns, 92,
98–101, 135; women as, 96–97, 99,
114
Farley, James, 200, 201, 210, 213, 216
farming. *See* agriculture; *specific crops*
Farrell, James: *The Young Manhood of
Studs Lonigan*, 197
fascism, 194, 211, 215, 236
Federalist Party, 59–64, 78, 209–10
females. *See* women
Fenian Brotherhood, 110, 111,
120–23, 125–28, *127*, 158
Fenno, John Ward, 62
Fianna Fail Party, 195
The Fighting Seabees (film), 220
The Fighting 69th (film), 220
The Fighting Sullivans (film), 220
film industry, 146, 192, 205–6, 220.
See also specific films
First Great Awakening, 38, 65–66, 246
First Vatican Council (1869–70), 129
Fitzgerald, John F., 144
Fitzsimons, Thomas, 61
Flood, John C., 101
Flynn, Edward, 201, 210–11, 216, 217,
234
Flynn, Elizabeth Gurley, 173
FOIF (Friends of Irish Freedom),
184–87
Foley, Tom, *171*
Fontenoy, Battle of (1745), 23, 121
Ford, John, 233
Ford, Patrick, 123, 158–60, 166–67,
177

France: Catholic education in, 14, 21; Irish soldiers exiled in, 23; Napoleonic, 57, 68, 70, 71; Norman settlements in, 11; revolution in, 53, 55, 62; in World War II, 218
Franco, Francisco, 211
Frankfurter, Felix, 193, *194*, 209, 210
Franklin, Benjamin, 42, 46, 52
fraternal societies, 125, 139, 145
Free-Soil ideology, 119
Fremont, John C., 119
French and Indian War, 23, 40–43, 46, 248
French Revolution, 53, 55, 62
Friendly Sons of St. Patrick, 47–48, 66, 67, 217
Friends of Irish Freedom (FOIF), 184–87
Furman, Gabriel, 64

Gaelic Athletic Association, 168
Gaelic culture: British views of, 13; chieftains in, 12–14; illegitimate children in, 20; language in, 134, 153; Norman influence on, 12; revival of, 168, 169, 224
Gaelic League, 168
Gallagher, Michael, 187, 207
Gannon, Robert, 208, 209
Gavagan, J. Joseph, 213, 214
gays. *See* homosexuality
Geary, James Aloysius, 141, *142*
gender differences: in education, 135–36, 149, 225; in incarcerations, 106; insane asylums and, 106; Irish immigrants and, 32, 96–97; in literacy, 20, 74, 97, 114. *See also* men; women
generational transitions, 171–72, 245–46
George, Henry, 166, 167
German Americans: economic achievements of, 140; education of, 135; interventionist bills opposed by, 219; political power of, 164–65; as white-collar workers, 134; in World War II, 220
German immigrants: child labor, 109;

comparison with Irish immigrants, 29, 135; cultural exchange with, 34; employment, 102–3; ethnic societies, 47; housing, 105, *105*; property ownership, 107; settlement patterns, 99; in U.S. Civil War, 120
Gibbons, James, 162, 190
GI Bill, 224, 225
Gillis, James, 208
Gompers, Samuel, 172
Goodwin, Doris Kearns, 228
Gorman, Francis, 204
Grace, William R., 165
Great Awakenings, *37*, 38, 65–66, 82, 246, 248–49
Great Depression, 193, 195–205, 207, 215
Great Famine (1845–1851), 92–98
Great Slaughter (1741), 16, 18, 30
Greeley, Andrew, 226
Gregory, William, 93–94
Guffey, Joseph, 203
Guiney, Patrick, 110, 111, 122, 123
Gunpowder Mills, 83

Hague, Frank, 201, 213, 234
Hamilton, Alexander, 60
Hanging Rock, Battle of (1780), 52
Harrigan, Ned: *The Mulligan Guard Ball*, 133, 137; in popular culture, 139, 140, 146
Hart, Tony, 133, 139, 140, 146
Hartington, William "Billy," 240
Haymarket Square bombing (1886), 161
Healy, Sherwood, 116
Hearts of Oak (secret society), 27
Henry II (England), 11
Henry VIII (England), 13
Hessian mercenaries, 50
Hewitt, Abram, 166, 167
Hibernian Provident Society, 67
Hibernian Society for the Relief of Immigrants, 63, 66
Hibernian Universal Benevolent Society, 84
Hincks, William: *The Linen Industry*, *17*

Hitler, Adolf, 218
Holy Name societies, 144, 145, 191, *191*
home rule for Ireland, 158–60, 166, 168, 183–84
homosexuality, 232, 233, 243
Hoover, Herbert, 189, 195
Hopkins, Harry, 215
House of Burgesses, 43–44, 52
housing: almshouses, 167; for immigrants, 105, *105*, 152; in military camps, 232; for peasants, 18; public, 176, 213; settlement houses, 174, 176; suburban, 227; workhouses, 93, 131
Howes, Edward, 29
Hughes, John, 70, 86, 87, 106, 115
Humphrey, Hubert, 234
Hurley, Charles F., 207
Hylan, John "Red Mike," 188
Hynes, John B., 237–38

Ickes, Harold, 202, 209, 210
identity: ethnic, 6, 36, 218, 242; group, 7, 39, 45, 48; political, 45, 46; religious, 36, 115, 242. *See also* Irish American identity; Irish identity
illness. *See* disease
immigrants: anti-immigrant nativism, 112, 172; British, 102–3, 107, 135; Chinese, 4, 104, 122, 130; citizenship, 62, 63, 68, 246; deportation, 62, 83, 112; housing, 105, *105*, 152; Jewish, 139, 151, 170–72, 174, 177; legislative restrictions on, 178, 189–92, 195; literacy tests, 177; Polish, 137, 139, 151, 172–74, 177, 181–82; segregation, 104, 105, 137, 152; voting rights, 52, 81, 83, 84, 112. *See also* assimilation; German immigrants; Irish immigrants; Italian Americans
Impellitteri, Vincent, 237
incarcerated populations, 29, 32, 68, 101, 106, 151
income: of famine immigrants, 103; of Irish Americans, 6, 198, 242; from landholdings, 21; in linen industry,

19, 71; minimum wage, 175, 176, 179, 193, 213
indentured servants, 29, 32, 57
Indigenous peoples. *See* Native Americans
industrial aristocracy, 159, 160
industrial democracy, 173–74
Industrial Workers of the World, 173
insane asylums, 101, 106
interfaith marriages, 32, 65, 66, 180, 242
interracial relationships, 116, 122, 137, 226
IPP (Irish Parliamentary Party), 183, 184
IRA (Irish Republican Army), 204, 244
IRB (Irish Republican Brotherhood), 127, 128, 158
Ireland: agriculture in, 9, 11, 14–19, 56, 70–71, 149, 153, 194, 245; American Revolution's influence on, 53, 55; aristocracy in, 10, 22–24, 26; British conquest of, 9, 11, 13–16; civil war in, 187, 195, 204; cultural exchange in, 12; economic depressions in, 72, 73, 195; home rule for, 158–60, 166, 168, 183–84; as Irish Free State, 153, 194–95; Kennedy's visits to, 240–41, 243; Normans in, 8–9, 11–13, 15, 19; pastoral economy in, 10, 12, 16, 148; population growth in, 17–19, 56, 71; poverty in, 19, 23, 71–72, 96, 241; repeal movement in, 73–74, 77, 88–90, 96, 128; revolutionary movement in, 53–56; temperance movements in, 74, 153; trade and, 9, 10, 16–18, 21; Viking raids in, 10–11; War for Independence, 171, 187, 246; World War II neutrality of, 219. *See also* famine; Gaelic culture; linen industry; native Irish; peasants
Ireland, John, 162, 163, 182
Irish American Catholics: African American relations with, 80–81, 111, 116–18, 123, 214–15, 234–35;

Democratic Party and, 81, 111, 118–19, 123, 164–65, 175–79, 200–208, 233–38, 243; during depression of 1873, 130; discrimination against, 141; draft riots by, 121–22; economic liberalism of, 198, 202, 212–13; education of, 6, 135–36, 140, 178, 198, 225, 228, 242; ethnocentrism of, 168, 172; gender differences, 6–7; during Great Depression, 197, 198; growth of, 65; identity of, 183, 199, 221, 226–30; income of, 6, 242; isolationist views of, 218–19; Kennedy's election to presidency as victory for, 241; in labor unions, 129, 130, 155, 160–61, 172–74, 205, 208; mass attendance by, 242; in Mexican-American War, 111; militant, 5–6, 84, 179, 244, 249; occupational status of, 135; political power of, 157, 163–68, 175–79, 202, 207, 233–38; racism by, 81, 116–17, 119, 243; Republican Party and, 237; revivalism among, 65, 114–15; size of families, 143, 244; on slavery, 80, 116–19; during U.S. Civil War, 121–24; in World War I, 185, 220; in World War II, 220–21, 224. *See also* anti-Catholicism

Irish American identity: assimilation and, 6; Catholic, 183, 199, 221, 226–30; evolution of, 7, 128, 248–49; nonsectarian, 48, 49, 59, 67, 248–49; public embodiments of, 67

Irish American nationalism: conservative, 158; decline of, 157; Fenianism and, 126, 128; Protestant, 129; radical, 158–59, 177; repeal movement and, 88–89; revival of, 184–87; women and, 159–60, 187

Irish American Protestants: assimilation of, 5, 129; on home rule, 158; income and education level of, 6, 242; nationalism of, 129; occupational status of, 135; rediscovery of Ireland by, 244

Irish Americans: adaptations of, 5–7, 134, 145, 179, 245–46, 250; African American relations with, 64, 80–81, 111, 116–18, 123, 188, 214–15, 234–35; anti-aristocratic views of, 177, 178, 222; in Democratic-Republican Party, 63–64; economic achievements of, 139–40; education of, 6, 135–36, 140, 178, 198, 225, 228, 242; ethnic societies for, 66–67; Fenianism among, 125–28; income of, 6, 198, 242; popular culture and, 136–40, *138*, 145–46; rediscovery of Ireland by, 243–44, 249; religious plurality and, 29, 244; social life of, 66–67; third-generation, 35, 222, 229; during U.S. Civil War, 105–6, 110–11, 119–24, *122*, 128; in War of 1812, 67–68; as white-collar workers, 134–36, 225; in World War I, 185, 220; in World War II, 220–21, 224. *See also* Irish American Catholics; Irish American identity; Irish American Protestants; Irish immigrants; second-generation Irish Americans

Irish Anglicans. *See* Church of Ireland

Irish Catholics: in American Revolution, 50, 53; on aristocracy, 22–23; in colonial era politics, 48; in Continental army, 50; in Democratic Party, 78, 81, 118–19, 246; discrimination against, 33, 103; economic performance in U.S., 6, 247–48; emancipation movement, 73, 74, 77, 80, 88, 96; history and growth of, 10; identity of, 21, 157; income sources for, 21; internal conflicts of, 87–88; land holdings of, 15, 21, 22; literacy among, 74, 114; as Loyalists, 50, 53; mass attendance by, 74, 96, 114; as merchants, 21, 32–33, 47; migration patterns, 30–33, 75–76, 245; Old English, 8, 13–15, 21, 22, 30; Old Irish, 13–15, 21, 22, 30; Penal Laws and, 20–22, 53, 73, 211; political acumen of, 77; United Irishmen and, 54–56; in U.S. Civil

Irish Catholics (*continued*)
War, 120–21, 124; voting rights for, 73, 132; Whiskey Rebellion and, 60. *See also* anti-Catholicism
Irish diaspora, 14, 92, 94, 129, 149, 158, 186–87
Irish Emigrant Society, 2
Irish Free State, 153, 194–95
Irish Home Rule Party, 158, 160, 166
Irish identity: Catholic, 21, 157; in colonial America, 47; evolution of, 7, 8; Protestant, 25, 69–70; Scotch Irish, 2, 63, 167; Ulster Scot, 30, 36, 39
Irish immigrants: in American Revolution, 50–53; chains of, 32, 57, 75, 94, 97, 100–101, 147, 150; citizenship, 62, 63, 68, 246; in colonial era politics, 43–47, 52; ethnic societies, 47–48, 66–67; family units, 57; gender differences, 32, 96–97; housing, 105, *105*, 152; as indentured servants, 29, 32, 57; migration patterns, 30–33, 58, 70, 75–78, 94–98, 149, 195–96, 245; motivations, 28, 30–34, 49, 58; Native American conflicts with, 39–43; in post-independence politics, 58–64; poverty, 105, 113, 227; quota, 195; radical, 58, 61–62; religious makeup, 30, 70; settlement patterns, 33–35, 58, 78, 92, 98–101, 135, 150, 247; social status, 36; voting rights, 81, 83, 84; in War of 1812, 68; Whitman on, 1–3; women, 96–97, 99, 114, 148–51, 224. *See also* famine immigrants
Irish language, 12, 15, 19, 22, 25, 74, 168–69
Irish music, 146, 153, 196, 243–44
Irish nationalism: African American equality and, 123; anti-British, 218; conservative, 161, 165, 166; decline of, 70, 157; emancipation movement and, 96; Fenianism and, 110, 128; hostility toward, 86, 116; liberal Catholicism and, 161–62; New Departure strategy and, 158–59; physical force, 158, 159, 169, 244; radical, 166–67; repeal movement and, 96; revival of, 183; Young Ireland and, 94
Irish Northern Aid (NORAID), 244
Irish Parliamentary Party (IPP), 183, 184
Irish Progressive League, 187
Irish Protestants: aristocracy of, 23; on claims to British throne, 16; in Democratic Party, 78–79; economic performance in U.S., 6, 247–48; identity of, 25, 69–70; literacy among, 6; migration patterns, 70, 245; militant, 74; New English, 8, 13; political and social dominance of, 8; sectarian divisions among, 25; United Irishmen and, 54–56
Irish Republican Army (IRA), 204, 244
Irish Republican Brotherhood (IRB), 127, 128, 158
Irish War for Independence (1919–21), 171, 187, 246
The Iron Major (film), 220
Iroquois, 39–40
isolationism, 218–19
Italian Americans: Democratic Party support by, 177; marriages to Irish Americans, 226; mass attendance by, 242; political power of, 234, 238; pro-Franco faction, 211; Tammany Hall and, 237; in World War II, 220
Italian immigrants: adaptations of, 4; Catholicism and, 181–82; entrepreneurship of, 151; Irish American relations with, 172–74, 177; mortality rates among, 139, 150; prevalence of, 170–71; segregation of, 137

Jackson, Andrew, 68–70, 77, 78, 209
Jacksonian democracy, 76
Jacobites, 22, 53
jails. *See* incarcerated populations
James II (England), 16, 20, 23, 25
Jay's treaty (1794), 61
Jefferson, Thomas, 61, 63, 209

Jesuits, 115, 231
Jews: anti-Semitism and, 193, 207, 212, 218, 219, 235; as immigrants, 139, 151, 170–72, 174, 177; in knowledge industries, 237; Kristall-nacht pogrom against, 212; in political machines, 201, 202
Johnson, Samuel, 22
Jones, Mary Harris "Mother," 155, 173

Kansas-Nebraska Act of 1854, 111, 112
Kavanagh, James, 65
Kearny, Dennis, 130
Keating, Geoffrey: *Foras Feasa ar Eirinn*, 15
Kelly, Clement, 181
Kelly, Edward, 202, 215
Kelly, John, 132, 164–66
Kennedy, John F., 223, 238–41, 243–45
Kennedy, Joseph P., 218–19, 238
Kennedy, Kathleen "Kick," 240, 241
Kennedy, Patrick, 241
Kenrick, Francis, 87
Keteltas, William, 64
Kings Mountain, Battle of (1780), 52
Knights of Columbus, 144, 182–83, 185–86, 190, 199, 218
Knights of Labor, 155–57, 160–62, 165–66, 177
Knights of St. Crispin, 129, 130
Knights of St. John, 144
knowledge industries, 235, 237
Know-Nothings, 112–16, 118, 128, 162, 211
Kosciuszko, Thaddeus, 230
Kristallnacht pogrom, 212
Ku Klux Klan (KKK), 189–91, 211

labor force. *See* employment; workers
labor unions: communal solidarity and, 160–61; communism and, 204, 208, 221–22; decline of, 82, 130, 166, 233–34; leadership of, 129, 130, 160, 172–74, 204–5; New Deal and, 203; radicalism of, 173, 204; strikes led by, 82, 130, 204, 208,

213; women in, 155, 156, 161, 173. *See also specific unions*
Ladies' Land League, 159–61
La Guardia, Fiorello, 170, 201–2, 205, 207, 209, 212
Lancaster, Treaty of (1744), 40
land: in colonial America, 34–35, 40, 43–44; communal ownership of, 10, 13, 20; individual ownership of, 16; Irish Catholic holdings, 15, 21, 22; Native American, 40; Norman seizure of, 11, 12; Penal Laws related to, 20–22, 53; plantations, 13–15, 110, 111; reform efforts, 158–59. *See also* agriculture
Land Leagues, 158–60, 166, 168
Lane, Ralph, 28
Lawrence, David, 200, 201, 215, 217, 234, 238
lay trustees, 84–87
League of Nations, 186
Lease, Mary Elizabeth, 155
Legion of Decency, 205
Lehman, Herbert, 205
Lend-Lease program, 219
Leo XIII (pope), 162, 177, 179
lesbians. *See* homosexuality
Lever, Charles: *Harry Lorrequer*, 80
Lewis, John L., 204, 208
liberal Catholicism: Americanization and, 163, 190; condemnations of, 115, 157, 167, 179, 249; emergence of, 156–57; Irish nationalism and, 161–62; outreach to Protestants, 172, 242; political involvement of, 166
liberal Protestantism, 73, 211–12, 223
Life Is Worth Living (television program), 230, *231*
Lincoln, Abraham, 95, 119, 121, 123
linen industry: children in, 19; exports in, 17; migration machines and, 31, 75; restructuring of, 71; spinners in, 19, 20, 56, 71; Ulster Scot Presbyterians in, 26–28, 30–31, 34, 247; weavers in, 19, 20, 26, 56; women in, *17*, 19, 20, 56, 71

literacy: gender differences, 20, 74, 97, 114; of native Irish, 6, 74, 114, 148; tests for immigrants, 177; in Ulster region, 19, 20, 26, 247. *See also* education
Lodge, Henry Cabot, 214, 238
Logan, William, 43
Lomasney, Martin, 176, 179
Long, Huey, 207
Lowell, Josephine Shaw, 131
Loyalists: in American Revolution, 50, 52–53; in Spanish Civil War, 211, 212, 215
Luther, Martin, 14
Lynch, Dominick, 61
lynching, 122, 188, 213–15

Mackey, John William, 101–2
MacNeven, William James, 58, 63, 65, 69, 84, 88, 90
Maguire, Con, 15
Maguire, Patrick J., 164, 165
Mahony, J. Daniel, 224
Makemie, Francis, 36
males. *See* men
Mangan, Mabel Delehanty, 197, 225
Mansfield, Mike, 223
Maritime Union, 204
market economy, 6, 20, 58, 76, 96
marriage: of famine immigrants, 100–101, 108, 109; interfaith, 32, 65, 66, 180, 242; interracial, 116, 137, 226; timing of, 108, 136, 142–43, 145, 151–52, 198, 229
Mary II (England), 16
mass attendance, 74, 96, 114, 242
Mathew, Theobald, 74
McCarran, Patrick, 219, 232
McCarthy, Joseph and McCarthyism, 222–23, 235, 236
McClellan, George, 122
McClenachan, Blair, 61
McCormack, John, 211, 219
McCourt, James, 232
McDermott, Alice: *After This*, 225
McDevitt, Philip, 180
McDonald, Michael, 164
McEvoy, Assisium, 180–81

McFaul, James, 182
McGinnis, Neil, 63
McGrath, J. Howard, 236
McGraw, John, 145–46
McGuire, Peter, 161
McKean, Thomas, 50, *51*, 63
McKee, Joseph, 201
McKee, William, 43–44
McLaughlin, Patrick, 101
McMahon, Thomas, 204
McManus, George, 140, 146
McManus, Theodore, 192
McManus, Thomas, *171*
McNicholas, John T., 205
McQuaid, Bernard, 129
McSweeney, Edward, 190
Meagher, Thomas Francis, 120–21
Meany, George, 204–5, 221, 233
men: as construction workers, 79, 88, 98; education for, 135–36, 140, 149, 225; entrepreneurship and, 6, 151, 248; literacy of, 20, 74, 114; as white-collar workers, 102, 104, 134–35, 151, 225. *See also* gender differences; marriage; sex and sexuality
Methodists, 66
Mexican–American War (1846–48), 111
migrant workers, 24, 72, 80–81, 149
militant Catholicism, 5–6, 84, 172, 179, 182–83, 226, 244, 249
militant Protestantism, 74
minimum wage, 175, 176, 179, 193, 213
minstrel shows, 117
Mitchel, John, 121
Monster meetings, 73–74, 88
Moore, Annie, 151
Moskowitz, Belle, 189
movies. *See* film industry
Moylan, Stephen, 47
Muldoon, Peter, 186
Mulholland, St. Clair, 124
Mulligan, James, 108
multiculturalism. *See* immigrants; race and ethnicity
Murphy, Charlie, 170–71, *171*, 176, 179, 200

Murphy, Frank, 200, 207
Murray, James E., 219
Murray, Phillip, 204, 221–22
music, 35, 144, 146, 153, 196, 243–44

Napoleon Bonaparte, 57, 68, 70, 71
Nash, Pat, 202, 215
Nast, Thomas: *The Ignorant Vote: Honors Are Easy*, *131*, 132
National Catholic War Council (NCWC), 185, 186, 190
National Catholic Welfare Conference (NCWC), 205, 221
National Conference of Catholic Charities, 205
National Industrial Recovery Act of 1933 (NIRA), 203
nationalism. *See* Irish American nationalism; Irish nationalism
National Labor Relations Act of 1935 (Wagner Act), 203
Native Americans: in French and Indian War, 23, 40–43, 46, 248; hunting techniques of, 34; Irish immigrant conflicts with, 39–43; racism against, 42; raids and attacks by, 35, 38; Roanoke colony and, 28. *See also specific peoples*
native Irish: Anglo Normans and, 13, 21; on aristocracy, 22–23; in colonial America, 30, 32, 39–45, 58; cultural sharing with Normans, 12; in French and Indian War, 40–41; language of, 12, 15, 19, 22, 25, 74, 168–69; literacy of, 6, 74, 114, 148; merger with Old English Catholics, 8; stereotypes related to, 60. *See also* Gaelic culture; Irish Catholics; Irish identity; Irish Protestants
nativism: anti-Catholic, 70, 83–84, *85*, 110–13, 157, 179, 248–49; anti-immigrant, 112, 172; political parties and, 79, 84; in Republican Party, 189; revival of, 167, 168, 188, 190; riots involving, 180; slavery and, 112, 117–18
naturalization, 63, 64, 68, 119, 174
Nazi Germany, 212, 216, 218

NCWC (National Catholic War Council), 185, 186, 190
neo-Thomism, 230
New Deal: African Americans on, 215; Catholic organizations and, 199; constitutionality of, 207; Jewish coalition and, 212; labor unions and, 203; liberal allies of, 194, 208–13, 235; patronage and, 201–3; political machines and, 201; Ryan's support for, 193; social environment created by, 206
New England: Congregationalists in, 78; Great Depression in, 197; indentured servants in, 29; Irish American Catholics in, 65, 203, 243; Irish immigrants in, 79, 88, 99, 103, 150, 168; Know-Nothings in, 112
New English Protestants, 8, 13
New Light Presbyterians, 26, 46, 55
New Orleans, Battle of (1815), 68
New Side Presbyterians, 38
New York City: anti-Catholic nativism in, 84; depression of 1873 in, 130–31; draft riots in, 122; ethnic societies in, 66; Fenianism in, 125; Irish American Catholic leadership in, 163, 165; Irish immigrants in, 1–3, 58, 63, 76, 79, 98–106, *105*, 150; labor unions in, 82, 129, 204; St. Patrick's Day parades in, 114, 217, 226; United Irishmen in, 63–65, 69. *See also* Tammany Hall
NIRA (National Industrial Recovery Act of 1933), 203
NORAID (Irish Northern Aid), 244
Normans, 8–9, 11–13, 15, 19. *See also* Anglo Normans
Norris, George, 203
Northern Ireland "troubles," 244
Norton, Mary, 213, *214*, 234
nuns, 14, 21, 114, 143–44, 153, 180–81, 223

O'Brien, Andrew Leary, 88
O'Brien, Hugh, 165
O'Brien, William: *When We Were Boys*, 126

O'Brien, William S., 101
O'Connell, Daniel, 73–74, 77, 80, 88–89, 94, 128
O'Connell, William, 181, *191*
O'Connor, Alice, 231–32
O'Connor, Edwin: *The Last Hurrah*, 233, 243
O'Connor, John, 210, 213
O'Connor, Thomas, 67, 84
O'Conor, Charles, 119
O'Doherty, Kieran, 224
O'Donnell, Patrick, 190
O'Dwyer, William, 237
O'Grady, John, 205
O'Hara, Frank, 232
O'Hara, John: *Butterfield 8*, 206
Olcott, Chauncey, 146
Old English Catholics, 8, 13–15, 21, 22, 30
Old Irish Catholics, 13–15, 21, 22, 30
Old Light Presbyterians, 26, 46, 55
Old Side Presbyterians, 38
O'Leary, Art, 22
O'More, Rory, 15
O'Neill, Domnhaill, 13
O'Neill, Eugene: *A Touch of the Poet*, 206
O'Neill, Hugh, 14
O'Neill, John, 122
O'Neill, Phelim, 15
Orange Order, 129
Order of the Star Spangled Banner (OSSB). *See* Know-Nothings
O'Reilly, Gerard, 209, 213
O'Reilly, John Boyle, 1, 123, 158, 161–62, 165
O'Reilly, Leonora, 173
O'Riley, Peter, 101
Orr, Jane, 49
O'Sullivan, John, 1
Otis, Harrison Gray, 62

Pacelli, Eugenio. *See* Pius XII
Pakenham, Edward, 68
pan-ethnic groups: Catholic, 6, 172, 182, 192, 199, 230, 244, 249; gangs, 188; invention of, 4
papacy: bishops sent to Ireland by, 10;

Catholic revival teachings on, 114; infallibility of, 129; in revolutionary era, 66. *See also specific popes*
parades: Columbus Day, 183; Fenian-sponsored, 125; Holy Name, 191, *191*; to Monster meetings, 73–74; Republican Party, 190; St. Patrick's Day, 84, 113–14, 169, 191, 217, 226
parish missions, 115, 144
Parker, Theodore, 118
Parnell, Charles Stewart, 158, 160, 166, 183
Parnell, Fanny, 159
parochial schools: cultural preservation through, 163; ethnic segregation and, 141; opposition to, 189; as political issue, 174. *See also* Catholic schools
pastoral economy, 10, 12, 16, 148
Pastore, John O., 234
Pastorini's Prophecy, 72
patronage: in British government, 25; in Irish American politics, 84, 140, 179; New Deal and, 201–3; political machines and, 77, 164, 178, 235; Republican Party and, 164
Paxton Boys massacre (1763), 42–43, 46, 248
Peale, Charles Willson: *Thomas McKean, 51*
Pearl Harbor attack (1941), 219
Pearse, Padraic, 184
peasants: on aristocracy, 22; clerical skepticism of, 85; housing for, 18; illegitimacy rates among, 20; land seized from, 15; in linen industry, 71; in nationalist movements, 158; politicization of, 73–74; racial attitudes of, 80; resistance to oppression, 23–25, 72–73
Peel, Robert, 93
Penal Laws, 20–22, 53, 73, 211
Pendergast, Tom, 200
Philadelphia (Pennsylvania): anti-Catholic nativism in, 84, *85*; ethnic societies in, 47–48, 66, 67; Irish immigrants in, 58, 61–63, 76, 79, 99, 104–5; labor unions in, 82;

parish missions in, 115; political machines in, 164; religious tolerance in, 33, 47

physical force nationalism, 158, 159, 169, 244

Phytopthora infestans (potato blight), 92–93

Pius IX (pope), 162

Pius X (pope), 180

Pius XII (pope), 211, 221

plague (Black Death), 12

Polish Americans, 220, 234, 237

Polish immigrants, 137, 139, 151, 172–74, 177, 181–82

political machines: bosses of, 77, 164, 166, 174, 179; New Deal programs and, 201; patronage and, 77, 164, 178, 235. *See also* Tammany Hall

political parties: emergence of, 59; nativist, 79, 84; transformation of, 76–77. *See also specific names of parties*

Pontiac (Ottawa chief), 42

Poor Laws, 71, 93–94

Popery Bill of 1704, 25

popes. *See* papacy; *specific popes*

popular culture, 136–40, *138*, 145–46, 192, 193

populism, 42, 179, 207

potatoes, 18–20, 24, 56, 71, 90, 92–93

poverty: in Ireland, 19, 23, 71–72, 96, 241; of Irish immigrants, 105, 113, 227

Powderly, Terence, 160, 165

Powers, J. F., 226

prejudice. *See* discrimination; stereotypes

Prendergast, Maurice, 94

Presbyterians: Covenanters, 26; Great Awakening among, *37*, 38, 66; New Light, 26, 46, 55; New Side–Old Side controversy, 38; Old Light, 26, 46, 55; Seceders, 26, 37. *See also* Ulster Scot Presbyterians

Presentation Sisters, 114

priests: education of, 14, 21; factors affecting career choice, 199; film depictions of, 205–6; immigration

of, 114, 153; in nationalist movements, 158, 185; parish missions and, 115; Penal Laws and, 20, 21; rivalries among, 87; shortages of, 65, 73; on social and economic ambitions, 140

Princess O'Rourke (film), 220

prisoners. *See* incarcerated populations

Progressive Party, 175, 176, 202, 217

progressivism, 171–72, 174–80, 193, 202–3, 209, 234

Proskauer, Joseph, 189

prostitution, 106, 153

Protestantism: abolitionism and, 117; on contraception, 229; conversion efforts, 13; evangelical, 38, 74, 82–83, 103–4, 116, 145, 246; Great Awakenings and, *37*, 38, 65–66, 82, 246, 248–49; liberal, 73, 211–12, 223; militant, 74; Second Reformation and, 74, 86. *See also* Irish American Protestants; Irish Protestants; *specific denominations*

Quakers, 30, 38, 40–42, 45–48, 50–52, 248

The Quiet Man (film), 233, 243

Quigley, Hugh, 8

Quigley, James, 181

Quigley, Martin, 205

Quinn, Robert Emmet, 207, 234

race and ethnicity: Democratic Party on, 123; group adaptations over time, 4–7, 245–46; identity associated with, 6, 36, 218, 242; interracial relationships, 116, 122, 137, 226; peasant attitudes toward, 80; race riots, 124, 188, 235; tropes in discussion of, 23. *See also* immigrants; pan-ethnic groups; racism; *specific racial and ethnic groups*

racism: against African Americans, 81, 116–17; immigration restrictions and, 190; by Irish American Catholics, 81, 116–17, 119, 243; legislation against, 242; against Native

racism (*continued*)
 Americans, 42; Social Darwinism
  as justification for, 132
Radical Republicans, 110, 128, 132
Ragen Colts, 142, 188
Raleigh, Walter, 2, 28
Rankin, John, 213, 214
Redemptorists, 115
Redmond, John, 184
red scare, 161, 189
Regeneration (film), 146
Regulation movement, 44–45, 52–53
religion: identity associated with, 36,
  115, 242; tolerance of, 33, 44, 47,
  65; warfare and, 8, 74, 115, 190.
  See also specific religions
remittances, 94, 97, 148
repeal movement, 73–74, 77, 88–90,
  96, 128
Republican Party: anti-lynching
  crusade, 213; Catholic schools
  opposed by, 167; emergence of, 111,
  116, 118; Free-Soil ideology of, 119;
  incentives for new voters in, 174;
  Irish Catholic movement to, 237;
  nativism in, 189; patronage and,
  164; progressivism and, 175–77,
  203, 209; radicalism in, 110, 128,
  132; on slavery, 116, 118–19
Revolutionary War. *See* American
  Revolution
Richard, Gabriel, 230
Ridgeway, Battle of (1866), 127, *127*
riots: anti-Catholic, 84, *85*, 87, 112;
  draft, 121–22; Irish construction
  workers (1834), 88; nativist, 180;
  race, 124, 188, 235
Roach, Philip Augustine, 130
Roanoke colony, 2, 28
Rockites (secret society), 72, 88
Roddan, John, 115
Roosevelt, Franklin Delano: Brain
  Trust of, 209; court-packing plan,
  207–8; Irish American Catholics
  and, 200–203, 205; prayer at second
  inauguration of, 193; purging of
  Democrats by, 210; during World
  War II, 218, 219. *See also* New Deal

Roosevelt, Teddy, 175
Rosalsky, Otto, *171*
Rowe, James, 209
Russert, Tim, 228
Ryan, Abram, 124
Ryan, John A., 179, 193, *194*, 198,
  208, 211, 213, 221
Ryan, Mary Kennedy, 241

St. Patrick's Day parades, 84, 113–14,
  169, 191, 217, 226
salary. *See* income
same-sex relationships. *See*
  homosexuality
Sampson, William, 63, 65, 69, 84, 86, 88
San Francisco (California): Chinese
  immigrants in, 130; depression of
  1873 in, 130; economic and social
  elite in, 141; Fenianism in, 125;
  Irish immigrants in, 104; labor
  unions in, 166; nuns in, 114; political machines in, 164
Savage sisters, 139
Scanlan, Patrick, 212
schooling. *See* education
Scotch Irish identity, 2, 63, 167
Scotch Irish Society of America, 167
Scot Presbyterians. *See* Ulster Scot
  Presbyterians
Seceders, 26, 37
second-generation Irish Americans:
  education of, 135–36, 140; generational transition of, 245–46; growth
  of, 133–34, 168, 196, 234; marriage
  and, 137, 142–43, 232, 244; nationalism among, 186; occupations of,
  134–35, 139–41, 197–98; political
  influence of, 63, 84, 164, 166, 178;
  popular culture and, 137, 139,
  145–46; religion among, 143–45,
  249; women, 134–37, 142–45,
  159–60, 173, 232, 248; in World
  War I, 185
Second Great Awakening, 66, 82, 246,
  248–49
Second Reformation, 74, 86
Second Vatican Council (1962–65),
  157, 242

secret societies: Defenders, 55; Hearts of Oak, 27; Rockites, 72, 88; Shanavests, 57; Steelboys, 27; Terry Alts, 72; Whiteboys, 24–25, 73, 88, 96
segregation, 104, 105, 137, 141, 152, 180
self-determination principle, 186
Separate Baptists, 39
settlement houses, 174, 176
Seven Years War. *See* French and Indian War
sex and sexuality: celibacy, 143, 151; contraception and, 198, 228–29, 232; discipline and, 20, 145, 152; in films, 205; homosexuality, 232, 233, 243; prostitution, 106, 153
Shanavests (secret society), 57
Shannon, William, 172
Shawnees, 40
Shea, Frank, 209
Shea, John J., 220
Sheehy, Maurice, 212
Sheen, Fulton J., 211, 230, *231*
Sheil, Bernard, 199
Sheil, Richard Lalor, 80
Sinn Fein, 185, 186
Sisters of Mercy, 114
Sisters of Notre Dame, 143
Sisters of St. Joseph, 143, 180–81
slavery: Democratic Party on, 119; Emancipation Proclamation and, 121; Irish American Catholics on, 80, 116–19; Kansas-Nebraska Act on, 111, 112; nativist views of, 112, 117–18; Republican Party on, 116, 118–19; Ulster Scot Presbyterians on, 119. *See also* abolitionism
Smith, Alfred E., 170, 176, 178, 189–90, 200–203, 210, 212, 241
Social Darwinism, 132
socialism, 173, 177, 183, 189, 208, 211
Social Justice Party, 207
Spanish Civil War (1936–39), 211–12, 215, 223
spinners, 19, 20, 56, 71
sports, 137, 139, 145–46, 168–69, 224, 228
stage Irish stereotype, 61, 79, 109, 169

Steelboys (secret society), 27
Steffens, Lincoln, 174
Stephens, James, 127, 128
stereotypes: drunken Irish, 60; emotionally unstable Irish, 106; in films, 205; inversion of, 146; political, 61; stage Irish, 61, 79, 109, 169. *See also* discrimination
Stevenson, Adlai, 235–36
Stoker, Bram, 1
Stoughton, Don Juan, 61
strikes, 82, 130, 204, 208, 213
Strong, George Templeton, 132
suburbanization, 218, 224–27, 229, 236
suffrage. *See* voting rights
Sullivan, Alexander, 159
Sullivan, John L., 145
Sullivan, Tim, *171*
Swallowtails, 165–67
Sweeny, Peter, 123
Swift, John, 222
Swift, Jonathan: "A Modest Proposal," 16

Tammany Hall: corruption of, 131, 132, 170; decline of, 201, 207; elite control of, 166, 167; Italian American seizure of, 237; Jewish allies of, 212; Kelly regime, 132, 164–66; Murphy regime, 170–71, 200; origins and evolution of, 77; Tweed regime, 129–32
teachers, 7, 134, 136, 159, 180–81, 232. *See also* education
Teamsters, 204
temperance movements: Catholic, 144, 145, 153, 162; membership growth in, 74, 87; Second Great Awakening and, 82; Ulster Scot Presbyterian support of, 119
tenant farmers: economic revolution and, 16; family boundaries and, 20; during Great Famine, 94, 95; Norman conquest and, 11; potato cultivation by, 18, 56; rent for, 18–20, 23, 92; solidarity among, 72; tillage production by, 19; Ulster Scot Presbyterians as, 14, 15, 26

Tennent, Gilbert, 36–38, *37*

Terry Alts (secret society), 72

textile industry: mechanization within, 82; mills in, 75, 99, 150, 197, 204, 225; strike in, 204; women's employment in, 97, 99, 150, 159. *See also* cotton industry; linen industry

They Were Expendable (film), 220

third-generation Irish Americans, 35, 222, 229

Thomism, 192, 230

Thompson, Bill, 188

Thoreau, Henry David, 97

tillage, 19, 24, 56, 72–73, 147–48

Tobin, Dan, 204

Tocqueville, Alexis de, 86

Toleration Act of 1719, 26

Tone, Wolfe, *54*, 55

Tories, 25, 47, 50, 53, 93

Tracy, Uriah, 62

trade: bartering, 34, 35, 60; exports, 17–19, 60, 71; global, 9, 16; immigrant, 75, 97–98; Irish Catholic networks of, 21, 32–33, 47; languages spread through, 10; Viking network for, 11

trade unions. *See* labor unions

treaties. *See specific names of treaties*

Truman, Harry, 217, 221, 236

tuberculosis, 106, 139, 151

Tumulty, Joseph, 176, 179

Twain, Mark, 125

Tweed, William Marcy "Boss," 129–32

Tyler, Robert, 90

UILA (United Irish League of America), 183, 184

Ulster Scot Presbyterians: adaptability of, 34; in American Revolution, 50–52; on aristocracy, 26, 51; in colonial era politics, 43–47, 52; Constitution opposed by, 59; discrimination against, 26; as dissenters from Church of Ireland, 9, 14, 16, 25; divisions among, 26, 36–39, 46; evangelicalism among, 74; in French and Indian War, 40–41; in linen industry, 26–28, 30–31, 34,

247; literacy of, 26, 247; migration patterns, 30–31, 77–78; in Republican Party, 119; Scotch Irish identity of, 63, 167; as second-class citizens, 25, 30; settlement patterns, 33–35, 78; as tenant farmers, 14, 15, 26; Whiskey Rebellion and, 60

unemployment, 27, 129, 193, 197, 205

Union (U.S. Civil War), 110, 111, 119–21, 125, 128

unions. *See* labor unions

United Irish League of America (UILA), 183, 184

United Irishmen: American Society of, 67; British crackdown on, 55–56, 61–62; groups influenced by, 60; leaders of, 58, 63, 69, 84; in New York City, 63–65, 69; nonsectarianism of, 4, 54–55, 69; objectives of, 53, 67, 186

United Kingdom. *See* Britain/United Kingdom

United Mine Workers, 204

United States: civil rights movement in, 234–35, 241–42; Civil War in, 99, 105–6, 110–11, 119–25, *122*, 128, 162–63; Constitution of, 59, 61, 67, 121, 176; economic depressions in, 75, 82, 129–30, 167, 177, 193, 195–205, 207, 215; in Mexican–American War, 111; migration patterns to, 70, 75–78, 94–98, 149, 245; post-independence politics in, 58–64; religious tolerance in, 65; separation of church and state in, 66, 236; settlement patterns in, 58, 78, 92, 98–101, 135, 150, 247; suburbanization in, 218, 224–27, 229, 236; in War of 1812, 67–68; in World War I, 182, 184–85, 246; in World War II, 219–21, 224, 249. *See also* colonial America

Varick, Richard, 64

Vatican Councils, 129, 157, 242

vaudeville, 137–40, *138*, 145, 146

Vikings, 10–11

violence: fratricidal, 52; lynching, 122,

188, 213–15; Paxton Boys massacre (1763), 42–43, 46, 248; in political competition, 77, 80; of secret societies, 24, 27, 72–73; by youth gangs, 142, 188. *See also* riots; warfare
voting rights: for African Americans, 64, 81–82; for immigrants, 52, 81, 83, 84, 112; for Irish Catholics, 73, 132; for white males, 76, 81

Wagner Act (National Labor Relations Act of 1935), 203
Wallace, Henry, 217, 221–22, 234
Walmesley, Charles: *The General History of the Christian Church*, 72
Walsh, David, 177–79, 188, 208, 213, 219
Walsh, Frank, 173, 176, 185–87
Walsh, Tom, 179
warfare: agrarian, 27; dynastic, 12, 13; ethnic, 190; religious, 8, 74, 115, 190. *See also* civil wars; *specific wars and battles*
War of 1812, 67–68
Washington, George, 40, 60, 62
Waterloo, Battle of (1815), 68
WBA (Workingmen's Benevolent Association), 129, 130
weavers, 19, 20, 26, 56, 82
Welsh, Peter, 120, 121
Wesley, John, 19
wheat, 11, 17–19, 24, 60, 70–71, 98
Whig Party, 64, 78–79, 81, 84, 93, 111, 118
Whiskey Rebellion (1794), 60
Whiteboys (secret society), 24–25, 73, 88, 96
white-collar workers: birth rates, 228; famine immigrants as, 102–4; men as, 102, 104, 134–35, 151, 225; women as, 7, 134–36, 151, 248
Whitefield, George, 38
Whitman, Walt: "Old Ireland," 1–3
Wilde, Oscar, 1
William III of Orange (England), 16, 25
Williamite War (1689–91), 23, 26
Williams, Eugene, 188

Williamson, Hugh, 46–47
Wilson, Henry, 128
Wilson, Woodrow, 175, 176, 179, 184–86, 189
Winthrop, John, 29
women: abortion and, 243; in domestic service, 2, 79, 96–97, 99, 106–7, 114, 147, 151–52; education for, 135, 136, 149, 225; as immigrants, 96–97, 99, 114, 148–51, 224; Irish American nationalism and, 159–60, 187; in labor unions, 155, 156, 161, 173; in linen industry, *17*, 19, 20, 56, 71; literacy, 20, 74, 97, 114; on motherhood, 230–32; as nuns, 14, 21, 114, 143–44, 153, 180–81, 223; in prostitution, 106, 153; social reform efforts by, 176, 179; as teachers, 7, 134, 136, 159, 180–81, 232; in textile industry, 97, 99, 150, 159; as white-collar workers, 7, 134–36, 151, 248. *See also* gender differences; marriage; sex and sexuality
Wood, Fernando, 118
Woodmason, Charles, 39, 43
workers: agricultural, 18–19, 56, 71, 95; blue-collar, 135, 151, 159, 234; child labor, 108–9, 176; construction, 79, 88, 98; in factories, 74, 75, 102, 104, 155–56, 159; in knowledge industries, 235, 237; migrant, 24, 72, 80–81, 149. *See also* employment; income; labor unions; white-collar workers
workhouses, 93, 131
Workingmen's Benevolent Association (WBA), 129, 130
World War I (1914–18), 182, 184–85, 218, 220, 246
World War II (1941–45), 196, 217–21, 224, 249
Wright, John, 227

Yankee Doodle Dandy (film), 220
yellow fever, 106
Young, Arthur, 18, 22
Young Ireland, 94, 113, 120–21